T0298984

The significant store of knowledge about publicly regulated pensions for old age has grown even more rapidly in the past decade. This book explores current research in four critical areas of pension policy: the political design of pension institutions; the iron links between fiscal deficits, private savings, and pension reform; how macroeconomic policy should be conducted after large private pension funds have emerged; and lessons on efficient organization of the pension industry, drawn from international comparisons including Australia, Chile, Malaysia, and the United Kingdom. The collection combines original theoretical analysis with empirical evidence. Simulations, case studies, and econometric estimates provide policy makers with information about the options they face. Scholars can also draw on the book for refining their own investigations or research.

The economics of pensions

The economics of pensions

Principles, policies, and international experience

Edited by

SALVADOR VALDÉS-PRIETO
Catholic University of Chile

CAMBRIDGE
UNIVERSITY PRESS

PUBLISHED BY THE PRESS SYNDICATE OF THE UNIVERSITY OF CAMBRIDGE
The Pitt Building, Trumpington Street, Cambridge, United Kingdom

CAMBRIDGE UNIVERSITY PRESS
The Edinburgh Building, Cambridge CB2 2RU, United Kingdom
40 West 20th Street, New York, NY 10011-4211, USA
10 Stamford Road, Oakleigh, Melbourne 3166, Australia

© Cambridge University Press 1997

This book is in copyright. Subject to statutory exception
and to the provisions of relevant collective licensing agreements,
no reproduction of any part may take place without
the written permission of Cambridge University Press.

First published 1997
First paperback edition 1999

Typeset in Times Roman [BV]

Library of Congress Cataloging-in-Publication Data

The economics of pensions : principles, policies, and international
experience / edited by Salvador Valdés-Prieto.
p.   cm.
1. Old age pensions.   I. Valdés-Prieto, Salvador.
HD7105.E28   1996
331.25′2 – dc20   96-3299

A catalog record for this book is available from the British Library.

ISBN 0 521 55230 3 hardback
ISBN 0 521 66612 0 paperback

Transferred to digital printing 2003

A mi mujer, Francisca Edwards

Contents

Acknowledgments   ix

List of Contributors   xi

1. Introduction and overview   *page* 1
   Salvador Valdés-Prieto

Part I. The politics of mandatory pensions

2. Insulation of pensions from political risk   33
   Peter Diamond

3. Democracy and pensions in Chile: Experience with two systems   58
   Oscar Godoy and Salvador Valdés-Prieto

4. Public pension governance and performance   92
   Olivia S. Mitchell and Ping-Lung Hsin

Part II. Fiscal deficits and private saving in pension reform

5. Pension reform and growth   127
   Giancarlo Corsetti and Klaus Schmidt-Hebbel

6. Transitions in the presence of credit constraints   160
   Rodrigo Cifuentes and Salvador Valdés-Prieto

7. Financing a pension reform toward private funded pensions   190
   Salvador Valdés-Prieto

Part III. Macroeconomic policy and private pensions

8. Pension funds, capital controls, and macroeconomic stability   227
   Helmut Reisen and John Williamson

9. Are there (good) macroeconomic reasons for limiting external investments by pension funds? The Chilean experience   251
   Juan Andrés Fontaine

Part IV. Policy and regulation of pension systems

10. Pension choices and pensions policy in the United
    Kingdom   277
    David Blake

11. Mandatory retirement saving: Australia and Malaysia
    compared   318
    Hazel Bateman and John Piggott

12. Public pension plans in international perspective:
    Problems, reforms, and research issues   350
    Estelle James

    Index   371

Acknowledgments

This volume consists of a revised selected set of the papers presented at the conference "Pensions: Funding, Privatization and Macroeconomic Policy," held at Hotel San Francisco Kempinski in Santiago, Chile, January 26–27, 1994. This conference was generously sponsored and financed by the following donors, listed according to the sizes of their contributions:

> The World Bank
> Citibank Chile
> Central Bank of Chile
> Rectory of the Catholic University of Chile
> Ministry of Finance of the Republic of Chile
> A.F.P. Provida (Pension Fund Management Company)
> Consorcio Nacional de Seguros (a Bankers Trust company)
> CONICYT

The Ministry of Finance of the Republic of Chile financed in part the participation of Diamond and Reisen and Williamson. A.F.P. Provida supported financially the editorial work performed after the conference, especially the preparation of the editor's introduction and overview. The World Bank granted the use of the copyrighted figures in Chapter 12. Any opinions expressed in this volume are those of the respective authors and do not necessarily reflect the views of the sponsoring organizations.

The conference included, in addition to the papers selected in this collection, a panel discussion, commentators, and other papers. The participants in the panel discussion were Nicolás Eyzaguirre from the Central Bank of Chile, Rubén Ferrufino from the National Secretariat for Pensions of Bolivia and Estelle James from the World Bank. The presentations at the conference benefited from the comments provided by the authors of the other papers and by the following persons, listed in alphabetical order: Patricio Arrau, Alvaro Donoso, Felipe Larraín, Emilio Meneses, Francisco Rosende, and Gert Wagner. The conference also benefited from presentations by Juan Luis Bour and E. Philip Davis. The organization of the conference was managed by Beatriz Birrell and Ana María Contreras, who applied their talent and initiative to present an extremely well run conference.

Preparing this material for publication was a long process in which the patience of the authors of the chapters and Scott Parris and Russell Hahn of Cambridge University Press were essential. The secretarial help of Ana María Sagüez proved to be extremely professional once again.

Contributors

David Blake
Professor, Birkbeck College, Department of Economics
University of London
7-15 Gresse Street, London W1P 1PA
United Kingdom

Hazel Bateman
Research Associate, School of Economics
The University of New South Wales
Sidney
P.O. Box 1 – Kensington 2033, Australia

Rodrigo Cifuentes
Associate Researcher, Institute of Economics
P. Universidad Católica de Chile
Vicuña Mackenna 4860
Santiago, Chile

Giancarlo Corsetti
Professor, Terza Universitá degli Studi di Roma and
Columbia University
Vía G. de Vecchi Pieralice 112
00167 Roma – Italy

Peter Diamond
Professor, Department of Economics
Massachusetts Institute of Technology
Cambridge, MA 02139, U.S.A.

Juan Andrés Fontaine
Senior Partner, Fontaine y Paul Consultores
Santa Lucía 188, piso 6
Santiago, Chile

Oscar Godoy A.
Professor of Political Science
Director of the Institute of Political Science
P. Universidad Católica de Chile

xii   **Contributers**

Alameda B. O'Higgins 340
Santiago, Chile

Ping-Lung Hsin
Research Associate, Chung Hua Institute for
Economic Research,
75 Chang-Hsing St.,
Taipei, Taiwan, ROC

Estelle James
Lead Economist, The World Bank
1818 H Street N.W.
Washington DC 20433, U.S.A.

Olivia Mitchell
Professor, The Wharton School, University of Pennsylvania
3641 Locust Walk
307 Colonial Penn Center
Philadelphia, PA 19104, U.S.A.

John Piggott
Professor, School of Economics
The University of New South Wales
Sidney
P.O. Box 1 – Kensington 2033, Australia

Helmut Reisen
Senior Economist
OECD Development Centre
94, Rue Chardon Lagache 75016, Paris, France

Klaus Schmidt-Hebbel
Senior Economist, The World Bank and Gerencia Investigación Económica
Banco Central de Chile
Agustinas 1180
Santiago, Chile

Salvador Valdés-Prieto
Professor, Institute of Economics
P. Universidad Católica de Chile
Casilla 76, Correo 17
Santiago, Chile

John Williamson
Senior Fellow, Institute for International Economics
11 Dupont Circle N.W.
Washington DC 20036, U.S.A.

CHAPTER 1

Introduction and overview

Salvador Valdés-Prieto

Old-age security is an issue of universal concern, affecting richer and poorer countries across the world. Many economic, demographic, and political factors influence observed outcomes for the currently old and the level of old-age security perceived by the active generations in each country. In the past decade, the pension system in many countries has come under pressure. In the most dramatic cases, there has been an effective default on pension promises, throwing many older people into poverty. In the OECD countries and also in China, uneasiness among the working population has spread, as it has become apparent that future pensions are threatened by the demographic changes. Few believe that contribution rates will actually rise to the extremely high levels required to continue paying current pension levels as a ratio of average wages. Even in rich countries, old age does not look secure any more.[1]

Policy makers in many countries have now realized the importance of improving their pension systems. The academic community has a significant store of knowledge to offer, based on research done in the preceding 30 years. In the past few years, international comparisons between national pension systems – which differ widely across the world – have enriched considerably the stock of academic knowledge.

This collection of essays offers up-to-date treatment of a selection of the areas that have been found to be most critical for pension policy: the political design of pension policy, fiscal deficits and private savings in pension reform, macroeconomic policy and private pensions, and options for overall design of pension systems. The collection combines theoretical analysis with empirical evidence, providing case studies, econometric estimates, and simulations, all of which show the bearing of economic analysis on the actual policy

I am grateful for the comments of Dominique Hachette and an anonymous referee. They are not responsible for the contents of this chapter.

[1] According to *Time* magazine (1995), an opinion survey of 18–34 year olds conducted by Third Millennium in the United States found that 46% believe UFOs exist, but only 28% believe Social Security will still exist when they retire. I am grateful to Tim Miller for this reference.

problems and provide policy makers with the order of magnitude of the options.

1   The collection in perspective

This section provides perspective about the place of the policies discussed in this collection within wider classes of problems. This book covers public policies and institutions designed to improve old-age security *at the state or national level*. The emphasis on national policies means that the collection does not analyze other forces and institutions that have a bearing on old-age security, such as intrafamily support, village-level institutions, charitable organizations, fertility, and mortality. This does not mean that these forces are unimportant, only that they are considered exogenous and given. For example, the demographic transition is clearly critical for pension policy in the rich countries and China. Institutions like families, villages, and charities are and will continue to be the mainstay of old-age security in countries where formal sector coverage is low. For reviews of these other forces, see Ahmad, Drèze, Hills, and Sen (1991) and Entwisle and Winegarden (1984).

Within the range of government policies and institutions that relate to old-age security, this book concentrates on one specific institution: *publicly regulated pensions for old age*. This choice leaves aside important public policies such as mandatory health insurance for the old, subsidized housing for the elderly, and reduced income tax rates for the old. Insurance for disability and early death is mentioned in passing in some chapters. In some countries, such as the United States, these public policies have a large impact on the level of old-age security. However, we chose not to discuss them because pensions already provide some coverage for them as pension benefits are used by the old to purchase these goods and services as well as food, fuel, and clothing. In addition, the required analytical approach is different. For reviews of such government policies, see Hurd (1990), Warshawsky (1992), and Rivlin and Wiener (1988).

2   Occupational or mandatory pensions?

Within publicly regulated pensions for old age, the most prevalent policy is to *mandate* workers to contribute in exchange for an entitlement to old-age benefits. However, other public policies are important for the overall design of a pension system, and are touched on in the last part of this collection. The second most prevalent policy is to *subsidize* specific classes of voluntary long-term saving and insurance contracts, either by exempting the investment income of occupational pension plans from corporate income taxes, by exempting contributions from the personal income tax of the worker, by allowing occupational plans to invest in book reserves, or by offering subsidies to voluntary saving for old age, as in the Czech Republic since 1994. The third policy, which is a minimalist approach, is to provide *solvency regulation* of the firms that offer nonsubsidized voluntary savings and insurance contracts, such as annuities and whole life and disability insurance. This third policy approach is similar to that used for investor protection in securities markets. Although the analysis in this collection concentrates on mandatory pensions, empirical evidence from subsidized pensions is also presented when relevant.

In some circles it is felt that occupational pensions are a substitute for mandatory pensions. This is in part a reflection of the experience of English-speaking countries where occupational or "private" pensions operate independently from the state-mandated pension system. However, this point of view is limited by two facts. First, countries such as Australia, Chile, Malaysia, and the United Kingdom have developed a policy approach where state mandates are satisfied by purchasing pension services in the financial market, either through the employer or individually; this contradicts the apparent opposition between mandated pensions and the financial market. Second, occupational pensions are subsidized with tax exemptions and are becoming heavily regulated to protect workers from exaggerated claims by employers about the benefits granted by their occupational plans. Therefore occupational pensions have become as regulated as mandatory pensions. Indeed, when looking at international experience, it is clear that occupational pensions are an integral part of public policy, which should be coordinated with mandatory pensions.

3 The financial and employer approaches to the study of pensions

Studying pensions from the point of view of financial markets – emphasizing the costs and benefits of pension policy for financial intermediaries – is fruitful, but may induce the observer to lose sight of the purpose of pension policy. Some commentators in emerging countries go as far as suggesting that pension reform is needed to develop the domestic financial market. Likewise, a study of occupational pensions from the point of view of employers shows their costs and benefits for employers. However, from the point of view of national policy those approaches reverse means and ends, losing sight of the aim of achieving old-age security for workers.

The financial aspects of pension policy are important (see Davis, 1995, for a good exposition), but a narrow focus on the financial market and financial intermediaries can induce the policy maker to forget that pooling of many diversifiable risks such as longevity risk, early-death risk, and disability risk does not require the participation of financial intermediaries. Alternatives are legislated formulas, like those used in traditional state-run defined benefit pensions, and the pooling formulas used by the Teachers' Insurance Association of America, College Retirement Equities Fund (TIAA-CREF), the privately managed occupational pension system for college professors in the United States (see Greenough, 1990). A narrow focus on the impact of pensions on financial intermediation may also lose sight of the importance for workers of the expenses and fees charged by intermediaries. The evidence provided by David Blake in this collection suggests that this is not a minor issue easily dealt with by competition.

The development of the financial market can be achieved with policy tools unrelated to pensions. For example, an important policy determinant of financial development is regulation of voluntary financial contracts with the aim of investor protection and elimination of externalities. Only Part III of the collection emphasizes privately managed pension funds, in a discussion of their influence on monetary and exchange rate policy.

A focus on occupational pensions from the point of view of employers alone would also be incomplete. That approach is indeed fruitful. However, Lazear (1990) has shown that human resource management by large employers can be achieved with other policy tools unrelated to pensions. For example, employers could manage retirement and employer-specific investments through compensation plans that include stock options, instead of using pension promises. Still the emphasis on the employers' perspective has left the literature devoid of analyses of the issues of consumer protection raised by occupational plans. For example, if workers do not realize how much inflation will erode their occupational pensions once granted and how large is the share of employers that will go bankrupt and default on pension promises, a government intervention should be considered.

4   Part I: The politics of mandatory pensions

This collection approaches pensions from an economic policy point of view, which involves bringing together the tools of economic analysis and of political analysis. The latter is essential because pension policy is a creation of the state, not a market phenomenon. The evidence in Part I of this book suggests that the political aspects are relatively more important in pension economics than in other areas of economic policy. One reason is that pension institutions must function suitably over a time horizon that spans six or more decades, the time any given individual is expected to be a participant in the system. This period is long enough for the state itself to experience profound changes. Political change may affect the terms of pension rights and turn into a significant source of risk for the individual member.

Therefore, choice between basic options such as full funding or pay-as-you-go financing, between defined contribution or defined benefit pensions, between government-managed or privately managed pensions, and between monopoly or competitive supply of pension services should be based first and foremost on an assessment of the political capacity of the state at hand.

Part I of this book is devoted to the politics of pensions. The chapters by Diamond, Godoy and Valdés-Prieto, and Mitchell and Hsin discuss the political framework of pension policy from the theoretical and the empirical points of view. Together, they offer an important contribution to the understanding of pension policy not previously available in the literature. They suggest that the optimal pension policy is heavily dependent on the capacities of the political regime of the country.

Up to now, the approaches available to study pension policy have relied heavily on the welfare economics and political science paradigms. In the welfare economics literature, pension policy is analyzed as if it were a response to market failure or as the least costly way to pursue a noneconomic aim such as income distribution. Examples of this approach are found in Diamond (1977) and Kotlikoff (1987). In the political science literature, pension policy is considered to evolve in response to the forces that shape state formation, including the emergence of a patronage-free civil service, the democratization of the electorate, and other aspects such as constitutional constraints, as discussed in Orloff (1993). Historical episodes, such as the discrediting of poor relief in the Anglo-Saxon countries because of the adoption of an extremely harsh approach in the late 19th century, are also given prominence in political science.

In Chapter 2, entitled "Insulation of Pensions from Political Risk," Peter Diamond incorporates the risk of politics changing future policies, and how critical this is for current pension policy. He points out that pension legislation must be simple, but this implies a need for repeated legislated changes. Poorly chosen legislation is a form of risk generation, whereas well-chosen legislation is a form of risk sharing. This approach, where policy itself is recognized to be changing over time in a less than certain way, offers a significant improvement over the traditional approach in which future policies are assumed to be predictable. Going further than perfect-foresight credibility theory, Diamond brings the risk dimension to bear into the evaluation of discretionary policy.

The applications of this concept for pension policy analysis are numerous. Diamond argues that policy makers should prefer institutions that achieve differential insulation against political risk generation, without banning good political responses. In this sense, insulation from all change is a mixed benefit. For example, consider the defined benefit versus the defined contribution designs for pensions. Diamond points out that a defined contribution

system such as the Chilean privatized mandatory pension system provides
high insulation against harmful political acts of commission, whereas a
traditional defined benefit system relies to a greater degree on legislative
correction. However, a defined contribution system may suffer from the
omission of potentially beneficial political acts.

Any example must begin by assuming that initial legislation was too
simple and did not consider some shock adequately. For example, consider a
defined contribution system that induces the expectation of a given replacement rate, but then a particular generation finds out that the conversion
price of accumulations into annuities is higher than expected. In the defined
contribution setting, politicians will find it very hard to legislate a (risk-
sharing) initiative that compensates the losers, as it would require granting
lump sum subsidies to the accounts of a particular generation, financed with
taxes or public debt.

Diamond also discusses how contribution-based and benefit-based systems
can be designed to vary the degree of reliance on further legislation. The
measures discussed include constitutional rules granting the status of "property rights" to pension benefits, automatic adjustment of benefits to available
revenue in defined benefit systems, earmarking of certain revenue sources
such as a wage tax, the role of uniform tax treatment of pension income with
other forms of income, the pros and cons of higher visibility of legislated
changes in the public arena, the use of professional panels whose advice must
be explicitly overridden, and the description of the system in the eyes of the
public.

Oscar Godoy and Salvador Valdés-Prieto in Chapter 3, entitled "Democracy and Pensions in Chile: Experience with Two Systems," offer an analysis
of the politics of Chilean pensions. They consider the old pension system in
the 1950s and 1960s, which was partially replaced in 1979–1980. Currently
two pension systems coexist in Chile, which are the new privatized and
funded system and the unified, state-run, and pay-as-you-go financed system.
The reader is advised that this chapter does not include a description of the
new Chilean pension system. Diamond and Valdés-Prieto (1994) offer a
suitable description; Piñera (1991) describes the Chilean reform's politics.

Godoy and Valdés-Prieto point out that the relationship between politics
and economics in pension systems run both ways. When the overall design
of the pension system encourages certain relationships between voters and
politicians, such as patronage, these relationships gain in strength and may
affect the path of the political process. The first part of their chapter reviews
the political ideals on which the old pension system was based, which were
the ones of welfare states. The political acceptability of the significant power
of politicians and bureaucrats found in welfare states is predicated as a
necessary means to achieve an increase in equality – in this case redistributive

pensions. However, as the Chilean political regime was characterized by heavy patronage from political parties and their controlling clique, the actual pension system delivered an increase of inequality and an increase of the power of the political cliques over the ordinary citizen. As this power reduced the legitimacy of democratic decisions, this process ultimately retarded the development of democracy in Chile.

The chapter then describes how the two current pension systems were reformed with the aim of preventing patronage, and how several of the techniques discussed by Diamond were used. Privatization, the selection of a defined contribution scheme, abandonment of redistribution within the pension system, and a constitutional provision that prevents parliamentarians from initiating law in pension matters were used to insulate the new pension system from patronage. The degree of insulation between politics and pensions increased dramatically, one result being that the new system does not have an influence on the political regime.

The state-managed system was reformed as well, by merging 32 institutions into one and by unifying the benefit and contribution conditions. It continues to be defined benefit and financed by the pay-as-you-go method. To test the effects of these political reforms, Godoy and Valdés-Prieto analyzed cost-of-living adjustments to the pensions of the state-managed system over 1985–93 and found that patronage-style manipulation is much less in the new democratic political context than it was in the 1950s and 1960s. However, the state-run system continues to be used for manipulation in the political-economic cycle. This suggests that the defined-benefit design has a separate influence that generates some costs even in the best of circumstances.

Godoy and Valdés-Prieto also note that political patronage is impracticable within the new privatized and funded pension system. Negotiation with the political class, except for the pressure to maintain universal equality before the law, is not required from members. The new private system allows selection of a fund management company, granting more freedom to individual members than well-run welfare states provide to their citizens. The authors develop a case study of the new system, concerning the 1992 default by a state-owned coal company on bonds sold to the pension funds of the new pension system. The pension fund management companies confronted in the courts the ministry that managed this coal company. That confrontation, which would be unthinkable in a state-run system, was stimulated by the fact that only a few fund managers had bought those bonds and their investment ability was at stake.[2]

---

[2] The fact that most countries exempt occupational pension funds from income taxes also suggests the effectiveness of private lobbying power in defending the rate of return from political interference.

In Chapter 4, entitled "Public Pension Governance and Performance," Olivia Mitchell and Ping-Lung Hsin offer an econometric investigation of the implications of the institutional design for the funding and rate of return earned by pension plans. Their database includes 269 separate retirement plans set up by states and municipalities in the United States for their employees. These plans vary substantially in the type of persons that can fill the role of trustees, and in their independence from politicians and elections.

This allows a natural test for the propositions enunciated by Diamond and Godoy and Valdés-Prieto. In particular, Mitchell and Hsin measure the impact on the degree of funding of institutional variables like the requirement of board members to carry liability insurance, the existence of stress in the sponsoring government's fiscal condition, the degree of employee representation on the board, and the absence of balanced-budget legislation. They find that the requirement of board members to carry liability insurance increases the degree of funding. The existence of stress in the sponsoring government's fiscal condition and a larger degree of employee representation in the board has a significant negative influence on funding.

Mitchell and Hsin also study the impact of these institutional variables on the rate of return achieved by invested funds over 1986–1990. The importance of maximizing the rate of return can be seen in a standard case, where 70% of pensions paid are funded by reinvested earnings rather than by contributions.[3] They find that boards having more trustees elected by active employees earned significantly lower investment returns over five years. The same happened to pension plans that invested a higher share of their portfolio in the home state. Another important finding is that the rate of return was not increased by hiring external money managers, augmenting the body of evidence that suggests that external fund management per se does not add much value (Lakonishok, Shleifer, and Vishny, 1992).

Summing up, Part I shows why the capacity of the national political institutions must be the basis of any realistic choice between the basic design options. If one of these options is made on the basis of a rosy assessment of the political regime's capacity, the whole policy may fail, as the international experience shows. Part I also shows how institutional design may be chosen in order to obtain the most from a given political capacity. This is where privately managed systems show their greatest advantage.

5   Part II: Fiscal deficits and private saving in pension reform

When starting a pension system de novo, policy makers can choose between full funding or pay-as-you-go financing, between defined contribution or

---

[3] This calculation is based on a constant real rate of return of 4% per year, a contribution history of 40 years, an expected retirement for 20 years, and a constant age-earnings profile.

defined benefit pensions, between government-managed or privately managed pensions, and between monopoly or competitive supply of pension services. However, most policy makers start from an existing pension system and must choose whether and how to reform it. An important policy question is whether initial conditions could make a large difference when choosing an option.

In some of these choices, initial conditions are not critical. For example, if monopoly supply of pension services is to be abandoned in favor of competitive provision, the transition is short and simple. Policy makers should only be careful about using methods that reduce the transition costs related to the marketing area. As a second example, consider a change from defined benefit to defined contribution pensions. This reform must be gradual, because workers must be informed in advance and because time is needed for purchase of deferred annuities at several points in time. Still, initial conditions are not too restrictive.

Instead, a reform of the financing method raises much more complicated issues. Change in one direction is easy, but in the reverse direction it is difficult. A reform that moves from full funding toward pay-as-you-go financing is "soft," as it allows the authorities to spend the initial pension fund and it is always easy to find politically advantageous uses for newly found resources. This reform is equivalent to starting a policy that increases the public debt–GNP ratio by 2 to 4 percentage points per year. The political obstacles to such a reform depend on the political design of the pension system and on the degree of political development of the country, as discussed in Part I. If the pension funds are collectively owned and managed by politically designated authorities, and fiscal revenue is down temporarily, there will be few objections to this reform, as shown by worldwide experience with provident funds (World Bank, 1994).

The interesting reform is the reverse movement, from pay-as-you-go financing to full funding. This is hard, just as reducing the public debt–GNP ratio is hard. The economic calculus may recommend such policies for a heavily indebted country, but the political calculus is discouraging because the benefits are obtained far into the future, when the ruling politicians will no longer be in power. Part II of this collection is devoted to this problem.

There is a third type of initial condition relevant for most developing countries. In this case, the initial financing method is pay-as-you-go but the system has not matured yet. A pension system can be immature for two reasons: recent creation or growing coverage. It is immature because of recent creation when the current ratio between pension expenditure and the contribution revenue that would have been collected if contribution rates had been set at the long-term level required to balance the budget of the pension institution is less than the steady-state ratio. This ratio can be below the steady-state level only because the first generation of contributors has not reached the pension age yet. On the other hand, a system may be immature because of growing coverage – that is, when the coverage of contributions is expected to rise over the next few decades. This sort of immaturity is the politically softest, as it allows increases in revenues without increasing the contribution rate. It works by making contributions mandatory to an ever larger portion of the employed population.

In immature systems there is a cash surplus, which must be spent if a pay-as-you-go status is to be reached in the steady state. Among ways to spend this surplus, the total contribution rate may be small (e.g., it was 3.5% in 1995 in El Salvador and it was 5.5% in the United States until 1960) or full pensions may be granted to workers who have just 20 years of contributions (as in Costa Rica in 1994) or the pension system cash surplus may be used to pay for free health care (as in Argentina in the 1950s). In the United States, the surplus generated by growing coverage was used also to increase the level of pensions in real terms.

When the initial condition is immaturity of the pension system, policy makers can consider a reform that is much less demanding for the fiscal accounts than moving back to full funding. This is to stop the *growth* of the unfunded debt of the pension system, without reducing it. This reform requires using all the revenue coming from further increases in coverage, plus the revenue from a tightening of contributions and eligibility conditions for benefits to the levels required once maturity is achieved, to build a fund invested in private sector securities. The contribution rate need not be increased until when the ratio between the pension fund and accrued liabilities threatens to fall, which happens close to maturity. This reform leads to a partially funded system in the long term, if political safeguards such as those discussed in Part I succeed in preventing shortsighted politicians from spending the fund.

As a reference, the reader should recall that a reform leading to a reduction of the public debt–GNP ratio has the same economic features as a reform from pay-as-you-go to full funding: The benefit comes far away in the future. However, from a political point of view, a reduction in the public debt ratio is preferable over a reduction in the accrued pension debt when the pension system is defined benefit, because of a framing effect: Defined benefit pension systems direct public attention to benefits alone, hiding the relationship between individual contributions and benefits (Diamond, 1995). If that relationship were made explicit, as it happens in defined contribution systems, it would be hard to justify the enormous windfall transfer granted to the generations alive when the pay-as-you-go method began to be used.

It has been claimed recently that there are circumstances in which the introduction of a pay-as-you-go financing scheme may increase voluntary private savings permanently. This runs counter to the well-established notion that in a closed economy the stock of physical capital must fall in the long term when pay-as-you-go financing is introduced or public debt is issued. The argument is that if workers are credit constrained, then mandated contributions must reduce their consumption one for one. If the revenue is granted to pensioners, but they save part of the funds (maybe because they have a precautionary savings motive, justified because no markets are available to annuitize their wealth at actuarially fair prices), then private saving increases. As government savings are untouched, national saving and the stock of physical capital must rise, although lifetime welfare must fall (Boadway and Wildasin, 1993). This type of situation appears unlikely because (1) pension benefits are usually granted as an annuity, so there is no justification for precautionary saving because of longevity risk. (Therefore, when the pension annuity becomes available, total precautionary savings should be reduced); (2) it is unlikely that all workers are credit constrained; and (3) mandatory contributions force a delay of the stage of life in which precautionary savings stocks are accumulated, reducing aggregate saving.

Another important point concerns the impact of the pension system on the labor market. One of the ways in which pay-as-you-go financing distorts the labor market is its implicit tax rate. To be more precise, let me introduce the notion of an "age-adjusted marginal tax rate on contributions" associated with a pension benefit formula, which I define as follows:

$$\tau_x = 1 - [\partial \text{EPV}\{\text{Benefits}\}/\partial c_x] \tag{1}$$

where: τ_x = age-adjusted marginal tax rate on contributions made at age x. It is given by the proportion of a contribution of \$1 that is not recovered in the form of additional pension benefits. If θ is the contribution rate, expressed as a proportion of wages, the implied marginal tax rate on labor supply to the formal sector is the product $\theta \cdot \tau_x$.

In definition (1), c_x = amount of the contribution made at age x, and

$$\text{EPV}\{\text{Benefits}\} = \int_x^\infty B(a, c_0, c_1, \ldots c_R, w) S(a, x) e^{-\int_x^a r(z) dz} da$$

is the expected present value of pension benefits, taking into account the benefit rule, the mortality table, and the discount rate. This formula is valid for a single person without survivors.

B( ) = pension benefit formula, that represents the flow of benefits (pensions) per unit time as a function of the individual's age "a," his contribution history (c_0, c_1, . . . c_R), and other factors (such as real wage growth or real interest rates in the economy) included in vector w.

$S(a,x)$ =probability of surviving to age "a," measured as of age x $(x < a)$.

$r(z)$ = instantaneous discount rate at time z. This rate may be much higher than market interest rates if the worker is credit-constrained.

A simple exercise illustrates the magnitudes of this marginal tax rate in the case where the pension system is *not* redistributive and is balanced, which corresponds to a "notional accounts" system like those introduced in Sweden and Italy in 1995. Consider the case where the real annual interest rate is 4% and the rate of return of the mature balanced pay-as-you-go system is 1.5%. If pension age is 60 and the worker expects to be pensioned for 20 years, and the mortality table is such that $S(a,0) = 1$ for all a in [0,80] and $S(a,0) = 0$ otherwise, then the marginal tax rates on contributions made at ages 20 and 60 are 70% and 20%.[4] If in addition the pension system attempts to redistribute wealth from rich to poor, say, by choosing as in the United States $B = \alpha + \beta \cdot$ (average indexed monthly earnings), the age-adjusted tax rate on contributions increases substantially, both for the poor and the rich, either young or old.[5]

These estimates do not take into account other factors, such as income taxes and the unsuitability of savings held in pension accounts for meeting the precautionary savings motive. However, they do illustrate the effects in the labor markets of a pension system that pays financial returns below market interest rates. These effects are governed by the implied marginal tax rate on labor supply, namely the product $\theta \cdot \tau_x$. Of course, as long as τ_x does not go above 100%, this implied tax rate cannot surpass θ, the full contribution rate.[6] In turn, high marginal tax rates on earnings from formal and dependent employment induce an increase in independent employment and

---

[4] In the general case, if d = rate of return offered by the PAYG system and r = rate of return on safe personal savings, then

$$\tau_x = 1 - \left[\int_R^\infty S(a,x) e^{-\int_x^a r(z)dz} da \Big/ \int_R^\infty S(a,x) e^{-\int_x^a d(z)dz} da \right],$$

where R is the age of pensioning. In a funded pension system d = r for workers who are not credit-constrained and therefore $\tau_x = 0$ for *all* ages x and all R. However, for young credit-constrained workers this tax rate should be close to 100% even in a fully funded pension system invested in the financial market.

[5] Auerbach and Kotlikoff (1987, section 10D) argue that these high marginal tax rates can be eliminated by suitable redefinition of pension benefits. They propose benefits to be *negative* for zero contributions and to increase one for one as contributions increase. Namely, if $B = \alpha + \beta \cdot$ [AIME], they propose $\alpha < 0$ to obtain $\beta = 1$. But $\alpha < 0$ is a hidden lump sum tax, which fails to be such when coverage by the social security system is not guaranteed at 100%. Moreover, if coverage were 100%, the social security system could be used to levy general revenue, so that distortionary taxes such as VAT and income tax could be abolished. We disregard these nonlinear tax schedules in the text.

[6] I owe this point to an anonymous referee.

of informal or illegal employment relationships. The illustrative numbers show that this effect should be much stronger among the young, who may lose essential experience in the formal sector.

In Chapter 5, Corsetti and Schmidt-Hebbel review the evidence about the long-term economic gains that a reform from mature pay-as-you-go to full funding can offer in two settings: if a traditional growth model represents the economy; and if a growth model with externalities represents the economy. Their discussion is relevant for policy makers because it shows very clearly the trade-off they confront: If a traditional growth model represents the economy, a pension reform that moves toward funding is fiscally expensive in the first thirty years, and its long-term payoff (after 30 years) is positive but spread over centuries, so it is rather small per year. The benefit could be much larger if a large externality is present in the economy, even if it is still far away in the future.

How likely is it that this reform will yield a substantial benefit? Corsetti and Schmidt-Hebbel point out that empirical analysis becomes essential. They report that there is simply too little evidence to be sure, as most countries have been drifting away from funding and many years of data would be needed. However, the threads of evidence that are available – the authors provide the first econometric evidence on the impact of the shift to funding on the Chilean private sector saving rate – suggest that positive externalities do exist and benefits are substantial. Recent work by Feldstein (1995) suggests that the impact on national savings of movements away from funding was much larger in the United States than what traditional models suggest. The policy maker is forced to make a choice without much reliable information.

Chapter 5 is also important because it offers one of the few systematic discussions of the possibility of social gains from reducing the size of the informal sector of the labor market. Recall first that an important feature of mature pension systems that are financed with the pay-as-you-go method is that they pay an aggregate steady-state return that is below the economy's real interest rate (Tirole, 1985).[7] Under most conventional arrangements, this

---

[7] In the late 1960s social security experts argued that pay-as-you-go financing could be more or less efficient than funding, depending on whether "g," the growth rate of the economy, was larger or smaller than "r," the real rate of return on assets, which in turn was an empirical question. However, asset market equilibrium requires $r > g$. This is because the profits of firms must grow at rate g, with the economy. If r fell below g, then it would be possible for any long-term institutional investor to borrow at rate r and invest in a diversified equity portfolio whose profits grow at rate g and earn an arbitrage profit of $g - r > 0$. However, as more and more investors engage in arbitrage, the demand for credit would rise and the demand for investment would fall until r increased above g. Another way of seeing this is that the fundamental price of the equity of an infinitely lived diversified corporation is $P = $ (initial profit)/$(r - g)$ which becomes infinite if $r < g$ (Tirole 1985, p. 1507). For empirical arguments for ignoring the case where $r < g$, see van Velthoven, Verbon, and van Winden (1993).

implies a high marginal tax rate on contributions, especially on those made by the young.

A positive externality would exist if the formal sector contributed to overall technical progress. If the noncovered or informal sector does not influence technical progress, the size of this positive externality is reduced when the informal sector grows. Therefore, Corsetti and Schmidt-Hebbel conclude that because a pension reform moving away from pay-as-you-go financing toward full funding reduces tax rates, it favors the growth of the formal sector, which is the engine of growth. The result is a higher growth rate forever. However, the transition also takes a substantial time.

Rodrigo Cifuentes and Salvador Valdés-Prieto, in Chapter 6, offer the output from a simulation model that describes the transition in detail, year by year. This approach is very important for policy makers because the study described in the previous chapter only compared steady states, without providing information about the actual path of macroeconomic variables. The authors enhance the realism of their model over those available in the literature by taking into consideration one of the most basic imperfections of capital markets – that consumers cannot borrow giving their future wages in guarantee.

Cifuentes and Valdés-Prieto find that the transition is long indeed. Due to various income, substitution, and wealth effects, the impact of the pension reform on capital accumulation, private savings, and wages begins to be substantial only 15 to 20 years after the reform date. The reason is that there is a reduction in contribution rates that allows higher consumption by credit-constrained families. On the other hand, this detailed model offers more optimistic perspectives for the longer term: Even with traditional exogenous growth, the positive effects on capital accumulation and real wages are large, and this benefit is available just 30 years after the reform date.

Finally, this study's simulations allow a concrete answer to the most critical question considered by policy makers, which is how much of the transition deficit may be financed with the issue of public debt, rather than with fiscal sacrifices in the primary accounts. The answer is that in all cases there is a period when the tax rate must increase or government spending must fall. The maximum level of fiscal sacrifice is influenced slightly by this choice. The difference made by the degree of debt financing is that it affects how far that period is from the reform date. A higher degree of debt financing, such as 75%, pushes sacrifice some 20 years into the future. With 25% of debt financing, sacrifice occurs in the first 5 years of the reform.[8] The value of this information for policy makers is evident.

[8] In the Chilean reform of 1981, a budget surplus of 5% of GDP was built *before* the reform date, to assure the availability of funds. Still, a segment of the old system was not reformed in order to reduce the fiscal cost of the transition from 7% to 5% of GNP.

In the final chapter of Part II, Salvador Valdés-Prieto tackles a fundamental aspect of pension policy, which is whether the choice between full funding or pay-as-you-go financing determines other choices, such as that between defined contribution or defined benefit pensions, or between government-managed or privately managed pensions. He argues that funding is not determinant for those other choices, as it is possible to abandon pay-as-you-go in appearance and not in substance – that is, without suffering a fiscal cost during the transition to a new situation in which there is apparent funding. This type of reform can yield important economic benefits, such as avoiding the bias against the young in the effective tax rate on contributions, avoiding the negative externalities in the labor market discussed in Chapter 5, and gaining positive externalities in the domestic capital market and access to international risk diversification.

According to Valdés-Prieto, the way to move from pay-as-you-go toward apparent funding is the following: reduce the contribution rate, since the higher expected returns of market investments will obtain the same benefit with smaller contributions; introduce a new tax on covered wages to compensate the reduction in contribution rates, keeping take-home wages constant; issue new public debt to the pension institution during a transition period, in which pension debt is gradually replaced by nontradable public debt paying market interest rates.

A common mistake is to believe that issuing new public debt alone could finance the transition. This is not true because explicit public debt pays an interest rate higher than the growth rate of the economy, and this difference must be financed with new taxes that create new distortions. If it is financed with a new tax on covered wages, as proposed, then all budget constraints, markets, and tax distortions remain in the initial equilibrium. Valdés-Prieto's point is that there is no need to link the pension reform to a rearrangement of the tax distortions that exist in the initial equilibrium. The reduction in contribution rates and the associated new wage tax can be quite large. According to his simulations, if the real return is 2 percentage points above the growth rate of the economy, then a 15% contribution rate can be reduced to 9%, keeping the benefits the same, but a wage tax of 6% must be introduced for neutrality.

Valdés-Prieto goes on to argue that this reform can yield sizable welfare gains if complemented with a further reform: to make the public debt held by the pension institution tradable. He advises that granting the freedom to rebalance the portfolio of the pension institution requires a division of that institution into several competitive units, to prevent the creation of monopoly power in the government debt market and to prevent the pension institution from obtaining control of the private domestic economy, through the equity it will buy in domestic firms. The welfare gain comes when these competitive units are subject to incentives for reaching a desirable point in the risk–return frontier. The initial situation, with 100% of the portfolio invested in government debt, is almost surely inefficient as assessed by the risk preferences of a representative worker. Valdés-Prieto uses a general equilibrium simulation model that shows that this welfare gain could be 3% to 4% of GNP for a small open economy, because allowing portfolio rebalancing yields the gains of international diversification.

It should be added that a substitution of the implicit tax on contributions for an explicit wage tax has the further benefit of avoiding the bias against the young. This is because the wage tax would affect workers of all ages at the same rate, whereas the effective tax rate on contributions associated to a below-market rate of return is higher for young workers. This age-related effect can lead to distortions in investments in human capital and in the selection of the timing of entry into employment in the formal sector of the economy.

6   Part III: Macroeconomic policy and private pensions

This part of the collection attends the concerns of policy makers in charge of monetary and exchange rate policy. Some monetary authorities point out that pension reform may give rise to a very large pension fund sector, whose investment decisions could cause large price movements in the foreign exchange market and in the long-term bond market. Conceivably, their decisions could neutralize or even overturn interventions by the Central Bank in those markets, which may be needed to maintain price and output stability.

Moreover, market forces in many countries force pension fund managers to be very attentive of their relative performance. If a fund manager consistently remains in the lower quartile in the ranking of returns, it is usually punished by loss of business, and also by regulations in some countries.[9] In this setting, pension funds can be expected to choose similar portfolios, and to move their portfolios together over time. If all of them increase their purchases of foreign assets simultaneously, the local currency could depreciate substantially, rekindling domestic inflation.

Even if one thinks that international investment by pension funds generates welfare gains, this linkage across pension funds may introduce a distortion and in addition cause a loss in the effectiveness of monetary and exchange rate policy that may translate into poor macroeconomic performance. Alternatively, one may think that there are good general macroeconomic reasons for establishing some controls over the capital account of the balance of payments, as

---

[9] In Argentina, Chile, and Peru, a regulation on privately managed pension funds imposes a stiff penalty if the return of an individual pension funds falls below the average of the industry minus 200 basis points.

many developing and newly emerging countries do. In that case, the question would be whether pension funds deserve special treatment.

This section has a narrower focus because it restricts attention to funded pension systems where funds are privately managed. Still, this situation is widespread because many pension systems include an occupational pillar or free choice by members among licensed private fund management companies. Policy makers would benefit from learning about the worldwide experience on special exchange controls for pension funds.

In Chapter 8, "Pension Funds, Capital Controls, and Macroeconomic Stability," Helmut Reisen and John Williamson argue that the fear of loss of monetary sovereignty is groundless. First, they provide empirical evidence that when pension funds are free to allocate their portfolio under prudent-man rules, their internal guidelines specify a minimum allocation for foreign investment because investing only in the home country is considered to be imprudent. Moreover, the internal investment guidelines limit investments in foreign real estate and bonds the most, giving preference to equities. Evidence by Davis (1995, p. 215) shows that the pension funds from every OECD country invest over 70% of their foreign portfolio in equities, except in Japan, Germany and Switzerland, where regulations prevent it.

Second, Reisen and Williamson point out that if pension funds wish to invest abroad only through equities and avoid foreign short-term notes, then they will participate very little in the market where central banks intervene, which is the short-term debt market. International arbitrage between equity markets is not related tightly to short-term interest rate differentials, so the degree of capital mobility and the autonomy of monetary policy would not be affected. For example, if the authorities tighten monetary policy, domestic short-term rates will increase and attract foreign funds. However, few of these will be brought in by pension funds. It is true that higher short-term interest rates will increase long-term rates of return, but only marginally. Reisen and Williamson recall that the removal of exchange controls on pension funds in the United Kingdom in 1979 reduced sharply the link between short-term and long-term interest rates. In turn, the impact on equity prices of changes in prices for long-term bonds is also small. This means that a small inflow of portfolio capital will be enough to align equity prices in the domestic and foreign markets.

In Chapter 9, "Are There (Good) Macroeconomic Reasons for Limiting External Investments by Pension Funds? The Chilean Experience," Juan-Andrés Fontaine analyzes this topic from the point of view of policy makers in developing countries. He provides an extensive review of Chilean financial, macroeconomic, and capital control policy, which will be a useful reference for policy makers in developing countries that are attempting multiple structural reforms, including a pension reform.

Fontaine argues that capital controls on the private sector are desirable in a small set of circumstances, which he defines as "abnormal" or "critical" fluctuations in capital flows. Contingent to that setting, he espouses temporary capital controls to avoid major disturbances in exchange and financial markets. In "normal" times he proposes to choose some combination of costly real exchange rate volatility and costly sterilized intervention and to eschew all capital controls. Of course, the definition of what circumstances are "abnormal" is left to the authorities. Fontaine disagrees with the Reisen and Williamson approach but comes to a similar conclusion. In his view, capital controls on pension funds should be avoided always in "normal times," regardless of whether they reduce monetary sovereignty or not.

The remaining issue is whether pension funds deserve tighter or looser exchange controls on their international investments in "abnormal" contingencies. Fontaine argues that as pension funds are large in the aggregate and are easy to control, they should be subject to additional capital controls in times of crises. As the purpose of those controls would be to reduce exchange rate and interest rate volatility, not their average level, he recommends imposing restrictions on the *aggregate flow* of net foreign exchange purchases or sales by pension funds on a monthly basis. The aggregate quota would be auctioned among pension funds to minimize adverse allocative effects. A debatable aspect of his proposal is that it allows discrimination against pension funds in "abnormal" times, instead of requiring that pension funds be treated equally (bad) as other investors in those times. This exception exposes workers to implicit taxation of a part of their old-age savings, because pension funds would be subject to these flow restrictions, but other agents, such as exporters, importers, foreign direct investors, and wealthy individuals, would not. This discrimination would prevent pension funds from adjusting their portfolios to news just when news is most critical – "abnormal" times – while asset prices change in response to other investors' decisions.

This issue is of current concern in Chile, as Congress passed a law in March 1994 that allows the Central Bank to impose restrictions on the change in the net foreign position of all "institutional investors." These include pension funds, mutual funds, investment funds, insurance companies, and commercial banks. The law does not require equal treatment between these investors, so the discrimination issue is open. This decision is subject to the veto of the minister of finance, but the Central Bank Board can override it with a unanimous vote.

There are other motivations for capital controls in general and on pension funds in particular. One is that allowing pension funds to invest abroad may lead to a loss of scarce domestic savings, which will reduce financing for the domestic investment required for growth. Both Reisen and Williamson and Fontaine agree that this is a sound consideration at stages of political development in which foreign investors are subject to expropriation risks just because they are foreign. In those stages, foreign investors cannot be expected to replace the lost funds with inward investment, and domestic investors may fear capital levies as well.

Reisen and Williamson argue that, at other stages of development, inward flows are expected to replace outward flows, so this motivation is not justified. However, there may be still other stages of development during which the risk of expropriation is very small but substitution between foreign and domestic capital is still modest, maybe because of lack of knowledge of the country among international investors. Fontaine supports this position implicitly by suggesting that in pension reforms involving a transition from mature pay-as-you-go to full funding, the government should assure financing of the transition deficit by forcing the growing pension funds to invest 100% in the domestic market. In this setting the idea of allowing domestic pension funds to swap investments with foreign pension funds appears attractive because it does not affect the stock of savings but still provides portfolio diversification.

The authors do not discuss two additional considerations relevant for policy: First, if domestic savings are scarce enough, free pension funds will still choose to remain at home to earn the supernormal returns available there. This happens if the free lunch available through risk diversification is smaller than the gain from high return to scarce savings at home. For example, Chilean pension funds held less than 1% of their portfolio abroad in early 1995 even though the limit was 6%. Second, free pension funds from a country with scarce savings may choose to invest abroad a large share of the portfolio, without compensating inflows from foreign pension funds. This may be due to domestic political risk, to high domestic taxes, to underdeveloped local financial markets, or to inefficient monetary policy that creates conditions for runs against the domestic currency. In this case the policy solution is to remove the distortion or to improve the policy. However, devising a solution to these distortions may take time. In the meantime, the concern about a loss of scarce domestic savings may be reasonable, justifying a temporary restriction on foreign investment by domestic pension funds. Of course, a restriction that prohibits all investment abroad has the defect of making it too easy to hide the actual problems, threatening to make them permanent. A useful compromise may be to allow some investment abroad from the beginning, so that the requests to increase it keep pressure on the authorities to improve policies.

7   Part IV: Policy and regulation of pension systems

This part of the collection returns to a broader perspective and discusses the overall design of pension policy, with an emphasis on the regulation of privately managed portions of the pension system. The most famous example of privatization is Chile since 1981 (for details of the Chilean approach, see Diamond and Valdés-Prieto, 1994). Switzerland also followed partly this approach when it introduced the BVG system in 1985. Since 1993, Peru, Argentina, and Colombia have allowed privately managed systems. Part IV offers policy lessons from case studies of three countries: Australia, Malaysia, and the United Kingdom.

In Chapter 10, "Pension Choices and Pensions Policy in the United Kingdom," David Blake offers an outstanding overview of the British pension system, including both the well-known branches such as SERPS and the private occupational plans, and the newer privately managed branches such as personal pension plans, employer's contracted-out money purchase schemes, group personal schemes, and industry-wide portable pension schemes.

The early lead of the United Kingdom in pension policy has allowed it to become a natural laboratory for testing different approaches to pensions. As the development of the British pension system has taken place under a common political environment and legal framework, the comparisons between the systems that coexist in this country are free from the pitfalls of international comparisons. Since 1988, it has experimented with several approaches to privately managed pensions, which are of interest for the rest of the world.

When comparing the options currently open to an individual, Blake stresses that the state-managed, defined benefit, and pay-as-you-go–financed SERPS does not provide income tax relief nor a transfer value to a private-sector scheme. Still, as it just requires 20 years of contribution for full benefits, the implied real rate of return for low-income workers is estimated at 6.7% per annum, which is double the 3.3% available in the capital markets. However, recent legislation and indexation of benefits to the Consumer Price Index in a growing economy mean that SERPS pensions will fall substantially as a share of average wages and that the implied real rate of return will fall to 1.2% per annum.

Since 1988, Britons can also choose to join a personal pension scheme offered by a financial firm, either a mutual fund or a life insurance company. These schemes are defined contribution in nature even though insurance companies offer plans with guaranteed minimum returns. The United Kingdom left these schemes virtually unregulated until 1994, providing a natural experiment on the structure of these markets that is very valuable to design effective regulatory frameworks for privately managed pensions.

Blake reports that although personal schemes are portable between employers, high implicit exit fees make portability between financial firms very expensive, except in the case of a few providers that do not charge in case of exit. Consumer protection problems have also plagued personal pension schemes. High-pressure sales tactics have been used to persuade older members of occupational schemes to switch into inappropriate personal plans.

The fee structure of personal pension schemes has been shown to be a major regulatory issue by the U.K. experience. The practices that emerged in the substantially unregulated environment after 1988 have brought large total commissions and very substantial price dispersion. For example, some insurance companies that offer personal plans use "capital units" to charge implicitly 10% of asset value over the lifetime of the contract. This is in addition to annual management fees between 0.5% and 1.5% of asset value per annum, which are proof of enormous price dispersion. On top of this, surrender values for with-profits schemes were on average 27% below maturity values when cashed in just one year before maturity. Pension schemes organized by mutual funds have a different fee structure, which includes initial charges that on average are 5% and a spread between bid and offer prices that in some cases raises the effective initial charge over 8%.

The new disclosure rules that came into force at the beginning of 1995 are expected to force insurance companies to simplify their fee structures. Competition is expected to slowly favor the mutual funds that have eliminated the bid–offer spread. Still, the important lesson for policy makers in other countries is that fees must be regulated in mandatory but privately run pension systems to reduce price dispersion, to favor clear perception of fees by the worker, and to avoid uninformed consumer decisions.

The United Kingdom also offers a natural experiment in the regulation of private occupational plans, as they were largely unregulated until 1995 and subject only to common trust law. The Maxwell case showed there is a serious problem with the safe custody of pension assets. Blake reports that the usefulness of common trust law for pension funds has been questioned, and that calls for its reinforcement by a special Pensions Act administered by a pensions regulator were made by the Goode Committee. These proposals and a compensation fund paid for by occupational plans that cover fraud and theft were made into law in the 1995 Pensions Act.

Most occupational plans are defined benefit, pay very low transfer values to early leavers, and are financed with high total contributions as compared with SERPS. Tax exemptions for occupational plans were worth 15 billion pounds in 1993, which is 2.4% of GNP. British employers refuse to contribute to the personal plans of their employees the same amount they contribute to their occupational plan, even though the tax incentive is the same. The standard explanation that employers want to own the surplus of the fund over liabilities is incorrect at face value, unless the employer counts on the ability to manipulate actuarial assumptions in the event of a deficit of the fund over liabilities. This raises doubts about the quality of pension benefit promises to workers in a setting where the employer can affect dismissal rates and wage growth rates. The British experience in this area raises questions that are important for policy makers in other countries.

On the bright side, Blake reports that full administrative charges are 10% to 20% of premiums in personal pension schemes but just 5% to 7% of premiums in occupational schemes. This implies an average differential in net contributions of 9%, which translates into a reduction of pension benefits by 9% in personal schemes as compared with that in occupational plans. For a 3% real gross return per annum, this is equivalent to a reduction in the average net return of personal pension plans from 2.806% to 2.490% real per annum, including the annuity portion.[10] This significant advantage of occupational plans over personal schemes as organized in the United Kingdom may be set against the cost of reduced mobility between employers and a higher risk of loss, either through fraud, bankruptcy of the employer, or manipulation of actuarial assumptions. The risk that the provider can escape regulation is larger for occupational plans, as the number of employers with a pension plan is much larger than the number of financial intermediaries that offer personal schemes.

Hazel Bateman and John Piggott in Chapter 11, "Mandatory Retirement Saving: Australia and Malaysia Compared," take us to the antipodes and find that similar regulatory issues emerge there. In both countries there is a mandate to employers to contribute in the name of workers to a funded pension system. The most important difference between them is that the Malaysian scheme is centralized and government managed, whereas the Australian scheme is decentralized and privately managed. Malaysia introduced its scheme in 1951; Australia did so partially in 1986 and more resolutely in 1992.

The provident fund model of mandatory retirement provision, exemplified by the Malaysian system, is typical of the approach followed in over 20 former British possessions in the 1950s and 1960s. They were introduced in developing economies that lacked developed financial markets and sophisticated tax-transfer structures. Two critical features are that central provident funds are state-owned monopolies and that they are subject to a good deal of government control. In practice, the separation of pensions from general government finance is far from clean. In the language introduced in Part I of

---

[10] This calculation is based on a 3% real gross return per annum, 40 years of contributions, 20 years of pensions, and a constant age-earnings profile. It is assumed that the fee paid while contributing covers the purchase of a deferred annuity, so there are no additional costs.

this collection, the degree of political insulation is much less than in decentralized privately managed systems.

Malaysian law provides some of the trappings of an independent body for the provident fund's board of trustees. It has 20 members representing the finance profession, employees, employers, and the government. There is a 7-member investment panel designated by the board of trustees. However, actual independence is limited. The minister of finance has the right to propose 4 of the 7 members of the investment panel. The law requires that the provident fund invests at least 70% of its assets in government securities.

After examining the rates of return, Bateman and Piggott conclude that comparison with the yields available in equities, housing, and government bonds strongly suggests that the provident fund earned substandard returns. In fact, evidence collected by Fry (1992) for the 20-year period 1971–1991 finds that the average annual real return paid by the provident fund was 2.74%, but that equity returns were 5.61% real and bank deposits yields plus half of the spread between bank loans and bank deposits[11] were 4.26% real per annum. Therefore, the average loss of the provident fund as compared with an investment portfolio that had 30% equity and 70% fixed income was 1.925% per annum. This loss may be thought of as a charge imposed by the government on members. This outcome is to be expected from provident funds, as shown in World Bank (1994).

On the other hand, Valdés-Prieto (1994) reports that the administrative costs in the Malaysian provident fund are very low. With 2,350 employees and 40 branch offices it serves 6.3 million accounts of which 51% receive contributions in any given month. The average annual administration costs were U.S.$10 per contributor, which is 0.405% of funds under management. From the figures in the previous paragraph we may conclude that out of an implicit charge of 1.925% per annum, administrative cost explains 0.405% per annum and the rest is profit plus taxes.

Bateman and Piggott offer further lessons because of the novel regulations imposed by Australia on private provision. Every employer is forced either to set up a pension trust for its own employees or to join an open trust with other firms (industry trust) or join an open trust provided by a financial services firm (a master trust). Most of these trusts are defined contribution, in contrast to Switzerland's BVG trusts. Individual workers cannot choose their trust in Australia, but can vote to choose half of the board of trustees[12] that is legally responsible for operating the individual accounts and investing the

[11] The evidence in the IFS is that the average spread between bank deposits and bank loans for 1985–1989, excepting 1988 for which no data is reported, is 3.49% per year. Therefore, half of the spread is 1.75% per year. As bank deposits yielded an average of 2.51% real, the alternative fixed-income return was 4.26%.

[12] Only for pension funds with five or more members.

funds. Therefore, Australia has prohibited personal pension schemes and has avoided the consumer protection problems that have been prominent in the U.K. experience. As Australian industry trusts serve 50% of all contributors, Australia has succeeded in extending the U.K. experience with group personal schemes and industry-wide portable pension schemes.

The problems of the Australian approach are of interest to policy makers as well. Small employers still confront high administrative costs in Australia. There are over 73,000 pension trusts in Australia, of which 65,000 have 5 or fewer members and 6,800 have between 6 and 500 members. As workers rotate between jobs, they generate new accounts, so administrative costs are duplicated or a costly search procedure for consolidation of accounts must be followed. Finally, the incentive for employers to devote much effort to assure the best investment returns of defined contribution plans in which they have no direct stake is unclear.

Recent research by Bateman, Piggott, and Valdés-Prieto (1995) shows that administrative charges in Australian master trusts – the service offered by financial firms to employer trusts – are similar to those charged by Chilean pension fund managers, after correcting for purchasing power parity. Based on their data, I find that these financial firms charged amounts roughly similar to those charged by the Magellan Fund run by Fidelity, a financial firm from the United States – namely 1.7% of assets per annum.

However, Australian Industry Trusts, an open trust managed collectively by groups of employers and unions, are significantly less expensive. This ordering is confirmed by the fact that the average administrative cost of occupational plans in the United Kingdom reported by Blake, of 6% of contributions, is equivalent to an annual charge of 0.20% of assets during a full life.[13] Of course, the true charge of U.K. plans on members is larger when the worker accepts a reduction in his take-home wage in exchange for the promised pension, and this reduction is larger than warranted by this administrative cost saving. In addition, occupational plans are inexpensive to run only in large firms, so average costs for an economy with many firm sizes should be much closer to those of Australian industry funds. Thus, allowing employers to participate in the provision of pension services can reduce administrative costs significantly.

8   Policy recommendations

The final chapter in this collection, called "Public Pension Plans in International Perspective: Problems, Reforms, and Research Issues" is provided by Estelle James, leader of the World Bank team that produced the often-cited 1994 report.

---

[13] This is based on a 3% real interest rate, 40 years of contribution, 20 years of pensions, and a constant age-earnings profile.

Her recommendation is the following: Most countries should have as a long-term goal the creation of a three-pillar pension system, where each pillar is an instrument to achieve a different aim. The first pillar should be government-managed and tax-financed, with the purpose of redistributing income to the poor old. The second pillar would be a mandatory privately managed but heavily regulated and fully funded system with the purpose of assuring individual savings and insurance. The third pillar would consist of voluntary saving and insurance, which calls for government supply of services such as solvency regulation and investor protection.

As the second pillar would be the only mandatory pillar where pension benefits would be higher for those with higher wages, her proposal implies a radical reform of public pensions as they exist now in most OECD countries except Australia, Switzerland, and the United Kingdom. She justifies this proposal as follows: the second pillar must be mandatory to counteract myopia, and it must align benefits directly to contributions to discourage evasion and avoid labor market distortions.

She offers four reasons to prefer full funding over pay-as-you-go financing: to prevent governments from making pension promises now that they will not be able to keep later; to prevent large unplanned intergenerational transfers; to help build national savings; and to enable lower contributions by drawing on investment returns (which are almost always higher than GDP growth). She also offers four reasons to prefer private management: to obtain higher investment returns (for the same risk) as political interference would be reduced; to avoid encouraging deficit finance and wasteful spending in the government; to hasten development of the local financial market; and to build a lobby for international diversification of investments.

Still, James is careful to point out three preconditions that must be met for this proposal to succeed: at least a rudimentary capital market must exist (bank certificates of deposit and government treasury bills); the buildup of a reliable regulatory body must be feasible, as regulation is essential to limit fraud and conflict of interest between fund managers and members; and a first pillar for redistribution must be possible to supply a noncontributory floor for the old poor.

James points out that her proposal is not theoretical, as it is based on successful experiences of Australia, Argentina, Chile, Colombia, Peru, Switzerland, and the United Kingdom. She suggests that the middle-income countries in Latin America have shown how to implement this reform, and offer a wealth of experience about the details of implementation.

James does not discuss explicitly the alternative of a fully funded but state-managed monopoly for middle-income countries, which has been actually implemented in Malaysia. The argument in favor of such an option, based on the experience of the United Kingdom, Chile, and other countries, would be that private provision is associated with high levels of sales effort and administrative costs. Monopoly provision is more efficient insofar as it avoids churning of members between private providers. If in addition the government has advantages to collect contributions, it may be more efficient to nationalize this monopoly than to regulate the prices charged by a private monopoly.

However, the evidence presented in the previous section of this introduction suggests that the highest-return government-managed provident fund in the developing countries, the one in Malaysia, has charged members an implicit fee of 1.925% of assets, whereas the most efficiently regulated private providers charge a much lower equivalent annual fee on members, as in Australian industry funds. Thus, private management appears better for members. The advantage of efficient privately managed systems does not come from lower administrative costs; it derives from their higher insulation from political pressures, which leads to higher rates of return than in government-managed pension funds. The range of implicit charges is much larger in government-managed systems than in privately managed ones. The implicit tax on pension assets in cases of political dominance of investment decisions has been historically much larger than in Malaysia, running in the range of 5 to 20 percentage points per year (World Bank, 1994). In privately managed experiences, the charges on pension assets are explicit, taking the form of fees or commissions, and surpass the level of 2 to 3 percentage points per year only in the rare cases of fraud. These numbers confirm the policy relevance of Part I of this collection, where privatization was argued to be a potent force for insulation.

However, economic analysis also points out that government revenue from taxation of a pension fund is not a social loss, because it allows the government to reduce other taxes or to increase expenditure in valued public goods. To analyze this point, one might ask whether the expenditures financed with this tax revenue are socially valuable or wasteful. One example of wasteful expenditure in the introduction of pay-as-you-go financing occurs when the revenue of the initial decades is used to finance patronage by the dominant political party. On the other hand, if the revenue is used to reduce other tax rates, now or in the future, the social loss may be minimal.

Still, the implicit taxes that reduce the rate of return impose an efficiency loss. As suggested before, a useful way to see this is by estimating the marginal tax rate on contributions made by workers of different ages. In particular, an implicit tax on pension fund returns introduces a deadweight loss, whose size depends on the elasticity of labor supply to the formal sector, which may be large among the young, and of the elasticity of labor demand, which depends on the strength of international competition. Dynamic effects such as those studied by Corsetti and Schmidt-Hebbel would apply in addition to these.

The ideal tax rate on pension funds should be part of an overall tax strategy that minimizes overall deadweight losses, static and dynamic. The optimal rate may be high or low, depending on the menu of tax instruments available, but the actual tax rate may be far from the optimal one. In this case deadweight losses become substantial. Another assumption that must be contrasted with reality is the one of efficient public administration. In countries such as those described by Reid and Mitchell (1995), administrative costs are likely to be higher in a monopoly state-run pension fund than in competitive private providers.

Summing up, the outcome of a comparison between two types of funded systems, one privately and competitively managed and the other government managed, is heavily dependent on the way in which political competition is conducted, on how much it ends up taxing pension funds over a long horizon of six or more decades, and on whether the tax on pension funds increases or reduces inefficiency given the rest of tax policy. For countries with political systems with outcomes far removed from those suggested by an ideal benevolent dictator, and where public administration is prone to inefficiency, private management is likely to be preferable even though its explicit administrative charges seem to be higher.

It should also be kept in mind that privately managed mandatory pension systems are just beginning to evolve. Costs may fall further in the future in those systems if some inefficient regulations are avoided and new methods of organization appear. For example, the Chilean-type systems – and also the voluntary mutual fund industry in the United States, but to a lesser degree – are subject to regulations that favor churning by preventing price adjustment: The law bans commission discounts for both individuals and groups, preventing private providers from offering group plans as Australian industry funds do.

James does not discuss explicitly a third option for middle-income countries: Avoid a fund to prevent political pressures to invest it in low-yielding government debt. This would imply the use of pay-as-you-go financing. This option presumes that efficient public management is available in the country under analysis, so that the balance of administrative costs favors a government-managed approach.

This option can be evaluated using the fiscal analysis presented in Part II. If the initial condition is either no mandatory system or a funded system, a switch to pay-as-you-go financing creates a government tax on the labor earnings of future generations. This tax distorts labor supply as the below-market individual rate of return turns a large portion of the contribution into a tax with no compensating benefit. This tax is maximized if the initial pension fund is "spent" – that is, replaced by implicit government debt that yields just the growth rate of the economy. Therefore, this option is not recommended for this initial condition.

On the other hand, if the initial condition is pay-as-you-go financing, then past intergenerational redistribution is sunk and this objection does not apply. This is close to the case discussed by James under the heading of high-income OECD countries. To analyze this case, I will set aside for a moment, but mention again below, the potential contributions of a funded approach to the development of the insurance and annuity sectors, which appear to be far from well developed even in OECD countries.

James still argues for a reform toward a multipillar system in this setting. She argues that although the introduction of current systems in the past may have been understandable, current pressures to minimize work disincentives and the opportunities for diversification opened up by vastly more reliable international financial markets justify a reform toward funding and toward a tight link between individual benefits and contributions. Therefore, her three-pillar proposal is valid for this group of countries as well.

It is useful to point out that the issue of work disincentives may be secondary in high-income countries, provided the informal economy has disappeared already and pension portability is insured by the national character of the pension systems. Disincentives on labor supply and investment in human capital of the young remain, but the young are not numerous in such societies. Therefore, James's clinching argument for a move toward funding is the opportunity for international diversification of demographic and other risks.

The standard objection is that the financial cost of the transition is excessive. James draws on the experience of the United Kingdom and Australia and proposes the following transition scheme: Reduce benefits in the current pay-as-you-go system, by flattening benefits to emphasize the poverty reduction objective and by increasing the pensioning age (implicitly, she also proposes freezing benefit levels in real terms, avoiding a linkage of benefits to the average wage, implying a falling contribution rate expressed as a proportion of wages that grow with productivity); and initiate a mandatory, fully funded, and privately managed second pillar with a small contribution rate, which would rise over time (as in Australia) to fill the space left by the falling contribution rate required by the first pillar.

This proposal should be considered together with the observation in Valdés-Prieto (Chapter 7, this volume) that the contribution rate can be reduced when a shift to full funding occurs, without sacrificing benefit levels, due to the higher rate of return. This opens space to introduce an explicit wage tax, without reducing take-home wages. The revenue from the wage tax allows financing most of the fiscal cost of the transition with the issue of explicit debt, even though such debt pays market interest rates rather than the lower implicit rate of return of pay-as-you-go financing.

To sum up, the gains from international diversification of demographic and other risks, plus the externalities from developing the insurance sector, should be compared with the change in administrative cost that comes from passing from monopoly to competitive administration.

Granting that the passage from pay-as-you-go financing to full funding is achieved by the methods proposed, why not choose government-managed monopoly rather than competitive private management? This would certainly avoid the administrative costs related to churning and marketing expenses. If the high-income country is presumed to have a reliable civil service not vulnerable to corruption, then the main objection raised for middle-income countries would not apply. The experience of Sweden's AP funds, established in 1958 and discussed by Pontusson (1984), gives some guidance: Even Sweden could not manage to avoid political interference in fund management. Sweden did manage to deal with the danger of indirect nationalization of the economy through massive government-managed pension fund investment in domestic equities, by requiring that investment be in debt securities. However, investments in bonds were directed to housing and to influential local companies. Between 1960 and 1975, the AP funds held close to 75% of their portfolio in bonds, but the return of those bonds averaged 1.7% per year. This return was obtained in a setting where average consumer price inflation was 5.6% and where bank accounts, real estate, and stocks earned average yields of 5.9%, 6.9%, and 9.0%, respectively (Pontusson, 1984, p. 30). The Swedish experience shows that the tradeoff identified above remains valid.

References

Ahmad, E., J. Drèze, J. Hills, and A. Sen (1991) *Social Security in Developing Countries*. Clarendon Press, Oxford.

Auerbach, A., and L. Kotlikoff (1987) *Dynamic Fiscal Policy*. Cambridge University Press, Cambridge.

Bateman, H., J. Piggott, and S. Valdés-Prieto (1995) "Australia y Chile: Previsión Privada con Normas Diferentes: Comparación de Regulaciones y de Comisiones de Administración." Working Paper No. 176, Instituto de Economía U. Católica de Chile, February.

Boadway, R., and D. Wildasin (1993) "Long Term Debt Strategy: A Survey." In H. Verbon and F. van Winden, editors, *The Political Economy of Government Debt*, chapter 2. North Holland.

Davis, E. P. (1995) *Pension Funds: Retirement Income Security and Capital Markets. An International Perspective*. Clarendon Press, Oxford.

Diamond, P. A. (1977) "A Framework for Social Security Analysis." *Journal of Public Economics* 8, pp. 275–298.

(1996) "Government Provisions and Regulation of Economic Support for Old Age." in M. Bruno and B. Pleskovic, eds. *Annual World Bank Conference on Development Economics, 1995*, pp. 83–103. Washington, D.C.

Diamond, P. A., and S. Valdés-Prieto (1994) "Social Security Reforms." In B. Bosworth, R. Dornbusch, and R. Labán, editors, *The Chilean Economy*, chapter 6. Brookings Institution, Washington, D.C.

Entwisle, B., and C. R. Winegarden (1984) "Fertility and Pension Programs in LDCs: A Model of Mutual Reinforcement." *Economic Development and Cultural Change* 32, no. 2 (January), pp. 331–354.

Feldstein, M. (1995) "Social Security and Saving: New Time Series Evidence." Working Paper No. 5054, NBER, Cambridge, Mass., March.

Fry, M. (1992) "Factors Affecting the Saving Ratio in Malaysia." Asian Development Bank, Operational and Policy Study Series, Manila.

Greenough, W. (1990) *It's My Retirement Money, Take Good Care of It: The TIAA-CREF Story*. Pension Research Council of the Wharton School. Irwin, Homewood, Ill.

Hurd, M. (1990) "Research on the Elderly: Economic Status, Retirement and Consumption and Saving." *Journal of Economic Literature* 28 (June), pp. 565–637.

Kotlikoff, L. (1987) "Justifying Public Provision of Social Security." *Journal of Policy Analysis and Management* 6, no. 4, pp. 674–689.

Lakonishok, J., A. Shleifer, and R. Vishny (1992) "The Structure and Performance of the Money Management Industry." In *Brookings Papers on Economic Activity: Microeconomics*, pp. 339–391. Brookings Institution, Washington, D.C.

Lazear, E. (1990) "Pensions and Deferred Benefits as Strategic Compensation." In D. Mitchell and M. Zaidi, editors, *The Economics of Human Resource Management*. Basil Blackwell, Oxford.

Orloff, A. S. (1993) *The Politics of Pensions: A Comparative Analysis of Britain, Canada and the United States, 1880–1940*. University of Wisconsin Press, Madison.

Piñera, J. (1991) *El Cascabel al Gato: La Batalla por la Reforma Previsional*. Editora Zig-zag, Santiago.

Pontusson, J. (1984) *Public Pension Funds and the Politics of Capital Formation in Sweden*. Arbetslivscentrum, Box 5606, Stockholm.

Reid, G., and O. Mitchell (1995) "Social Security Administration in Latin America and the Caribbean." Public Sector Unit, Technical Department, Latin America and Caribbean Region, World Bank, Washington, D.C., March.

Rivlin, A., and J. Wiener (1988) *Caring for the Disabled Elderly*. Brookings Institution, Washington, D.C.

Time (1995), "The Case for Killing Social Security." March 20.

Tirole, J. (1985) "Asset Bubbles and Overlapping Generations." *Econometrica* 53, no. 6 (November), pp. 1499–1527.

Valdés-Prieto, S. (1994) "Administrative Charges in Pensions in Chile, Malaysia, Zambia and the United States." Policy Research Working Paper No. 1372, World Bank, Washington, D.C. (October).

van Velthoven, B., H. Verbon, and F. van Winden, (1993) "The Political Economy of Government Debt: A Survey." In H. Verbon and F. van Winden, editors, *The Political Economy of Government Debt*, chapter 1. North Holland.

Warshawsky, M. (1992) *The Uncertain Promise of Retiree Health Benefits: An Evaluation of Corporate Obligations*. American Enterprise Institute Press, Washington, D.C.

World Bank (1994) *Averting the Old Age Crisis: Policies to Protect the Old and Promote Growth*, edited by E. James. Oxford University Press, Oxford.

PART I

The politics of mandatory pensions

CHAPTER 2

Insulation of pensions from political risk

Peter Diamond

1   Introduction

There are many sources of political risk to the public provision of pensions. After setting up a funded system, the fund might be used to grant benefits to people retiring while the system is not mature, leaving inadequate funding for later generations. More generally, we can consider the making of promises to future retirees that cannot be met. Another risk is excessive responsiveness of benefits to the short-run condition of the government budget, given the ability of retirees to absorb this risk. Similarly, there might be excessive responsiveness of benefits to the long-run condition of the government budget.[1]

On the other hand, as the rules that govern a pension system must be simple, pension systems have a limited ability to spread aggregate risks without repeated legislated changes. Well-chosen repeated legislation is a form of risk sharing. Poorly chosen repeated legislation is a form of risk generation. One way to describe the problem of the design of pension provision is to seek institutions that increase the likelihood of good patterns of legislated changes and decrease the likelihood of bad ones. The methods chosen and the success achieved will vary with the political culture of a country. To the extent that institutions insulate the pension system from all change, insulation is a mixed benefit. If it were possible to differentially insulate against political risk generation, without shutting off good political responses, insulation would be of higher value.

In contrast with the common appearance of these political risks in traditional defined benefit public pension systems, the Chilean privatized manda-

I appreciate valuable comments from Salvador Valdés-Prieto. Research supported by the Ministry of Finance, Chile.

[1] Examples of government actions affecting public pension provision can be found in World Bank, 1994. This chapter will not consider the risks to the rest of the government budget from the financial condition of the retirement system.

tory pension system appears to provide high insulation against these political risks (Diamond and Valdés-Prieto, 1993; Diamond, 1994). So far, we have not seen a number of political actions that might have occurred. Under the new system, there has been no large infusion of government funds to preserve the expectations of workers.[2] There has been no adjustment of pension benefits with the state of the government budget. In 1985 when the government budget was in trouble, the COLA on the old system was frozen, but nothing was changed on the new system. In part this may reflect the fact that benefits being paid were very small; in part it was, I think, politically insulated by the fact that the money did not flow through the government.[3] Up to now, no use has been made of the mandatory savings plan to do redistribution, even though there were calls to improve pensions for coal miners. My presumption is that the need to identify a source of financing affected the political outcome. Also I see no reason to anticipate a major crisis as Chile goes through the aging transition. Perhaps, if interest rates go down, the mandatory savings rate will have to be changed by the legislature, but that is an adjustment that should happen without a crisis – not without a political struggle, but without a crisis. A central question in this chapter is the role of different parts of the Chilean design in accomplishing this insulation from political risk and what parallel developments might increase insulation in a traditional defined benefit system. With a single data point so far, it is hard to separate the role of privatization of social security from the particular economic and political climate in Chile, and, of course, from the particular political structure of the Pinochet government (up to 1989).

The Chilean system can not suffer from the common making of benefit promises that are not met since, as a defined contribution system, there are no such promises. Rather, an evaluation of the Chilean system must use the vocabulary of whether the system induces expectations that are not met. If rates of return on fund accumulation turn out to be far less than projected, or the annuity market turns out to be very expensive in converting accumulations into annuities, retirement income levels may be much less than workers had come to expect. One must consider how the system handles the risk of such outcomes, including whether the system will be changed in a way that spreads the risks (relative to expectations) suitably. In other words, one needs to be concerned with the omission of potentially beneficial political acts, as well as the harmful political acts of commission considered already. Thus

---

[2] Since the returns earned by the privatized funds have been large and there has been no known fraud, this may reflect these circumstances as well as the social security structure.

[3] The fact that the funds do not flow through the government does not guarantee that they are not particularly vulnerable. Since the earnings on pension assets are particularly easy to tax, because in the short run it is very hard to do tax evasion, they might have been subjected to special taxes.

insulation from politics needs to be evaluated in terms of the activities that are inhibited.

In a traditional defined benefit system, there is greater reliance on legislative correction than is needed in the Chilean system. A second theme of this chapter is the implication of system design on the degree of reliance on repeated legislation. While there are differences between benefit- and contribution-based systems, there are also choices within a basic design that will vary the extent of reliance on further legislation.

The approach taken in this chapter is the analysis of repeated legislation to alter the retirement income system. This approach naturally recognizes that some changes in the system are good responses to social risks, whereas others generate such risks. Thus the discussion is in terms of the effect of institutional structure on the likelihood of alternative legislative actions. The analysis begins with three simple models to illustrate patterns of risk bearing and risk creation. Then there is discussion of the roles of earmarking of funds and automatic pension adjustment and of pension professionals in providing insulation. There is also discussion of special legislative rules for public pensions.

2   Framework

The starting place for this analysis is that public pension systems exist for long times, over which economic circumstances change. Thus the repeated nature of legislation to modify such systems is an integral part of consideration of the political economy of system design. But repeated legislation, like repeated trading in a conventional model, makes analysis of efficiency issues much more difficult. In the Arrow-Debreu model of resource allocation, with the usual assumptions, if markets are complete, then the allocation of risk bearing in the market is Pareto efficient. However, if markets are not complete, then generically the allocation is not Pareto efficient; incomplete markets imply that allocations can be improved upon.[4] Thus, in considering efficiency, a critical element is whether the allocation process happens once and for all (with complete markets) or whether there are repeated times of decision making (with incomplete markets). Repeated decision making by multiple economic agents in the presence of a changing ability to choose among alternatives is a source of inefficiencies (in contrast with complete markets).

---

[4] Geanakoplos and Polemarchakis (1986); Geanakoplos, Magill, Quinzii, and Dreze (1990). The literature on insurance normally assumes that there is no social risk, and then explores the role of insurance markets in spreading individual risks (Malinvaud, 1972). Once there are social risks, then the allocation may have different properties. For a discussion of optimal taxation in a Ramsey economy with incomplete markets and social risk, see Diamond and Mirrlees (1992).

With significant social risk[5] and limited complexity in the legislation governing the pension system, a once-and-for-all allocation will not be efficient; potentially, repeated legislation could improve allocation. However, potential allocation gains need not be realized by actual legislatures. A related set of issues comes from the lack of commitment devices for government. The lack of commitment devices by government has been approached in terms of a time-consistency vocabulary, often modeled as a game between a government and its citizens.[6] Also modeled somewhat is the risk associated with political competition. In both settings, reputation effects can play a major role in mitigating the time-inconsistency problem.[7] In any event it has been much studied, so I will concentrate on social risk and the limited complexity of the rules that govern the pension system.[8]

In a retirement income system, as with other government actions, distribution issues are inevitably intertwined with other design issues. Moreover, in terms of a social welfare function, distribution issues in this setting are of the same order of magnitude as are efficiency issues. Nevertheless, this chapter will not consider distribution issues, concentrating on risk to benefit recipients in general. Although it is analytically convenient to ignore distribution issues, they should not go totally unmentioned in a theoretical discussion such as this. For a policy discussion, they would play a central role.[9]

3   A simple example of risk sharing

It is natural to examine social provision of retirement insurance in an overlapping generations model.[10] This permits consideration of some issues not present in finite horizon models. Nevertheless, I will consider two period models, for their simplicity. I begin with three examples, reflecting aggregate income risk, pure political risk, and inaccuracy of expectations.

Consider a two-period model with two types of agents. Type A receives in-

---

[5] There are large aggregate risks associated with the provision of retirement income. For example, in the United States, the annual percentage reduction in age-adjusted central death rates for males was -0.19% for 1954–1968, but 1.56% for 1968–1988 (Social Security Technical Panel, 1991).

[6] Kydland and Prescott (1977).   [7] Stokey (1989).

[8] The mention of time inconsistency in government policy reminds us of the same issue in individual choice; see Ainslie (1992), Strotz (1955), Schelling (1984), and the collection edited by Loewenstein and Elster (1992). Once individuals show time inconsistency, it is not generally clear how one wants to do welfare analysis. I think that the same issue arises in the context of repeated democratic decision making that shows time inconsistency because of shifting political outcomes and preferences. But this is an issue that I will not explore.

[9] For some discussion of income distribution and system design, see Diamond (1996).

[10] For discussions of the use of social security and public debt to share risks in an overlapping-generations model with incomplete markets, see Gordon and Varian (1988) and Gale (1990).

come y_1 in period one, before the government passes any legislation. Type B receives income y_2 in period two, which is random at the time of period-one legislation, but known before the time of period-two legislation, if any. There is no production and no storage in this economy. Thus the credit market plays a central role in the allocation of resources, representing both a way in which each type obtains consumption in the period without income and a way in which risks of second period income could be shared. Each agent seeks to maximize the expected value of the utility function $u^i(c^i_1, c^i_2)$, $i = a, b$.

Any Pareto optimal allocation has both types of agents having the same realized (ex post) intertemporal marginal rate of substitution. (We do not consider allocations where individuals of a given type have different consumption levels.) Thus the Pareto optimal allocations satisfy

$$u^a_1 (c^a_1, c^a_2) / u^a_2 (c^a_1, c^a_2) = u^b_1 (c^b_1, c^b_2) / u^b_2 (c^b_1, c^b_2),$$

$$c^a_1 + c^b_2 = y_1$$

$$c^a_2 + c^b_2 = y_2 \tag{1}$$

Different ex ante income distributions will give different allocations that satisfy these equations. As y_2 varies, second-period consumptions, c^a_2 and c^b_2 can also vary, although lack of knowledge of the outcome of y_2 at the time of the first-period consumption decisions implies that first-period consumptions c^a_1 and c^b_1 can not vary with y_2. The question at hand is how to achieve such an allocation. One way, from Arrow-Debreu theory, is to assume a complete set of markets. That is, consumption in period two, conditional on the level of income in period two, is a different good for each possible level of income in period two. We know that the economy does not have this complete set of markets; that it would be very expensive to try to have them; and that the attempt to list all states of nature would fail, since something would happen that was not anticipated.

Consider next the allocation that occurs if there is only trading in a safe (real) bond. This restriction on available markets is chosen for its simplicity, without any attempt to model the determinants of the particular incomplete market structure that exists, although markets are obviously incomplete. We assume that marginal utility goes toward infinity sufficiently quickly with low incomes that individuals never allow themselves to be in a position to go bankrupt. The different equilibrium allocations, for different lump sum (ex ante) redistributions between the two types, all satisfy the equations

$$E\{u^a_1(c^a_1, c^a_2)\} / E\{u^a_2(c^a_1, c^a_2)\} = E\{u^b_1(c^b_1, c^b_2)\} / E\{u^b_2(c^b_1, c^b_2)\},$$

$$c^a_1 + c^b_1 = y_1 ,$$

$$c^a_2 + c^b_2 = y_2 \tag{2}$$

I have assumed that everyone has the same subjective probabilities in taking expectations, E, and that these expectations are correct – that is, everyone knows the true distribution of incomes in period two. As with the allocations in (1), c_1^a and c_1^b do not vary with y_2 for information reasons. Now, because of limited trade, c_2^a also does not vary with y_2, implying that c_2^b varies one-for-one with y_2.

Trading on competitive markets results in all traders having the same marginal rates of substitution between any pair of traded goods. In this case, the two traded (composite) goods are consumption in the first period, whatever happens in the second period, and consumption in the second period, again independent of the realization of y_2. We know these allocations (in (2)) are less efficient than those described with complete markets (in (1)).

Now, let us add to this system a pay-as-you-go social insurance system. In the first period, there is a poll tax T_1 on type A consumers used to finance a benefit B_1 for type B consumers. In the second period, the poll tax, T_2, on type B consumers is used to finance a benefit, B_2, given to type A consumers. We have simplified the story by having no distortions associated with the social insurance system.

If there were no restrictions on the complexity of legislation, then T_2 and B_2 could vary with y_2, and legislation in period one could achieve the allocations in (1), with no trade at all. The presence of a bond market would not interfere with the efficiency of this allocation. Let us consider restrictions on allowable legislation in period one and the possibility of new legislation in period two. Limited ability to deal with complexity, or equal-treatment constitutional restrictions, or the determination of legislated outcomes might require that taxes or benefits or their relationship be the same for each generation. Assuming that the generations are of equal size reduces these possibilities to a single restriction, $T_1 = T_2 = B_1 = B_2$. In this case, since the pattern of payoffs matches that of a bond, social insurance accomplishes nothing in risk sharing; the allocation is simply one of the allocations in (2), with the given level of ex ante redistribution.

One method of introducing risk sharing is to assume that taxes are proportional to income. That is, we introduce proportional taxes t_1 and t_2 rather than the poll taxes. We do not expand the set of traded assets at the same time. Whereas equity markets permit the sharing of some income risks, others, such as labor income risk, are not traded in private markets on a mass scale.[11] In the first period, the break-even condition requires $B_1 = t_1 y_1$. The question is what is legislated in period one for period two. One possibility is to legislate the same tax rate, $t_1 = t_2$, with benefits determined by the pay-as-you-go break-even condition. A different possibility is to legislate the same

[11] See Merton (1983).

benefit, $B_1 = B_2$, with taxes determined by the pay-as-you-go break-even condition. One could compare the efficiencies of systems that are indexed differently in this way, assuming no further legislation.

If the government does not choose to legislate such an indexed system, or might pass new legislation even if the system is indexed to be balanced, then the story becomes more complicated. Let the government choose an income tax rate and a benefit level that break even in period one, and legislate *both* values for both periods. This is typical of defined benefit public pension systems. Then, in period two, the government will need to legislate a change in benefits or taxes (or both) almost certainly, in order to break even.[12] Provided that people can accurately predict exactly what the government will do in period two and provided that the government, ex post, will do the correct thing from an ex ante point of view, the government can produce an allocation satisfying the full efficiency conditions in (1).

However, we have two complications: What will the government actually do in period two and what will people predict in period one.

4   A simple example of risk creation

Let us continue with the same model, except that we now assume that second-period income is determinate rather than random. There is now no risk-sharing reason for social insurance. There is also no efficiency cost to having a social insurance system of the kind described here, provided that fist-period legislation is *not* reconsidered in the second period. That is, the bond market permits individuals to undo any inefficiency in the allocation between the two periods, should benefits be set such that marginal rates of substitution are not equal. However, this ability to undo legislation does not extend to second-period legislation that reconsiders benefits and taxes. Having the second-period legislated outcome seen as random during the first period introduces political risk from the perspective of individuals. Moreover, perceptions of the possible different outcomes affect the functioning of the capital market, even though there is no taxation of capital market income.[13] In order to proceed, we need a model of the determination of political outcomes; and for the purposes of the design of social insurance, a model of the relationship between political outcomes and the structure of the social insurance system.[14]

To make this issue precise, we now assume that y_2 is not random, but is not equal to y_1. (Different population sizes would be a reasonable alternative to consider.) In the first period the government legislates $t_1 = t_2$ and $B_1 = B_2$.

---

[12] Without a capital market, the government must balance its budget each period. In a more realistic setting, the government can run deficits for a while, but the issues in the model would still be present, although with a different, and endogenous, time structure.

This works fine in the first period provided $B_1 = t_1 y_1$, but results in a system with a surplus or deficit in period two, depending on the relative sizes of y_1 and y_2. Thus second-period legislation is now needed. Let L be a random variable reflecting the uncertainties that impact on the legislative process. Thus we assume that second-period legislation yields a tax rate and a benefit level that are functions of L, and that satisfy the pay-as-you-go break even condition, $B_1(L) = t_2(L)y_2$. In this setup, the outcome in the credit market in period one depends on expectations about the legislative process. In the absence of any redistribution, trading in the bond market results in the following first-order conditions for the determination of the level of lending and borrowing, s, and the rate of return, r.

$$E\{u_1^a(c_1^a, c_2^a)\} / E\{u_2^a(c_1^a, c_2^a)\} = E\{u_1^b(c_1^b, c_2^b)\} / E\{u_2^b(c_1^b, c_2^b)\},$$

$$c_1^a + S = (1 - t_1)y_1, \quad c_1^b = S + B_1,$$

$$c_2^a = S(1 + r) + B_2(L), \quad c_2^b = (1 - t_2(L))y_2 - S(1 + r) \tag{3}$$

where expectations are taken over L. The pattern of income transfers varies with L, but available market instruments can not undo this structure, since the set of instruments in the capital market is not rich enough. The assumption that the social insurance system will not be in balance in period two is not a necessary condition for there to be legislation in period two or for there to be uncertainty about period-two legislation in period one. It does seem more likely that there will be legislation if there is imbalance.

A central question is how the dependence of legislated taxes and benefits, depicted as functions of the random variable L, varies with the structure of social insurance put in place in period one. It is natural to divide the question into two pieces – a probability of new legislation and a relationship between period-two legislation and period-one legislation. Having first- and second-period benefits and taxes the same might lower the probability of legislation to change their levels. In addition, we would expect second-period taxes and benefits to be a (stochastic) function of both what happened in period one and what was voted in period one for period two. That is, the legislated tax, $t_2(L)$, is plausibly a function of t_1 and also of what t_2 would be if there were no further legislation. The inherited legislated outcomes are a default should there be no legislation; this would naturally affect outcomes with a bargaining

---

[13] If there were real investments, with random aggregate returns, then full risk sharing would depend on two sources of risky income. Similarly, if type A's received random income in period two, with a different random structure and an identifiably different character (from the perspective of political identification), we would again have two sources of income risk. For a setup of this model with real investments, see the appendix.

[14] I will treat the political process as a given random function of social security. For a model that determines voting for political parties as a function of the tax, expenditure, and debt policies the parties will follow, see Aghion and Bolton (1990).

model of legislated outcomes. This setup lends itself to consideration of legislated levels of parameters as functions of previously legislated levels. Later we will turn to the further issue of the relationship of legislation to the structure of the program.

There is a second dimension to this issue if one views the first-period legislative process as no more worthy of respect from the analyst than the second-period process. If in the second period a new political party comes to power, and attempts to fulfill its platform by changing first-period legislation, would a design of the legislative process that prevents its undoing be a good thing?

5 Differing perceptions

In the two preceding sections, we assumed that consumers knew the distributions of both (possibly) random incomes and (possibly) random legislated redistributions. Consumers do not know these distributions; no one does. Thus we need to consider the implications of possibly inaccurate forecasts. For example, consider the model of pure political risk (no aggregate income risk) where the social insurance system legislated in the first period is definitely not viable in the second period. Then, consumers planning their transactions in the capital market must forecast the political outcomes. Thus the equilibrium will satisfy

$$E^a\{u_1^a(c_1^a, c_2^a)\} \, / \, E^a\{u_2^a(c_1^a, c_2^a)\} = E^b\{u_1^b(c_1^b, c_2^b)\} \, / \, E^b\{u_2^b(c_1^b, c_2^b)\},$$

$$c_1^a + S = y_1 - T_1, \quad c_1^b = S + B_1,$$

$$c_2^a = S(1 + r) + B_2, \quad c_2^b = y_2 - S(1 + r) - T_2 \tag{4}$$

This allocation differs from the previous one in that I have added individual tags to the expectation operator, reflecting the possibility of different beliefs by different consumers (although still assumed the same for everyone of the same type) over the levels of taxes and benefits in the second period. While first-period benefits and taxes have been legislated, the second-period levels are random variables over which expectations are needed. Exploration of the allocation implications of expectation formation would be interesting. This would include the effects on expectations of information provided by the public pension system and of the nature of political debate. Different styles of debate might leave the public with different expectations about future outcomes. When different people have different expectations, trade will be based somewhat on these differences. Such trades seem worthwhile to the individuals given their differing expectations, but might not seem advantageous when viewed with a commonly held probability distribution, whether accurate or not. In addition, the legislative process may be sensitive to the expectations about outcomes held by people before the process.

6   Some hypothetical examples

It might be useful to consider some circumstances where each of the preceding models has some relevance. While it would be better to describe real cases, I will make do with hypothetical ones. Consider an economy that is undergoing economic growth, with the rate of growth a random variable. In the event that wages grow rapidly and returns to capital are high, current workers will be well-off and the social security budget will have a large short-run surplus. However, the current elderly will not be well-off, having worked and saved at times of lower wages and lower rates of return.[15] A larger fraction of the elderly may be below the poverty threshold. Politically, it may be difficult to raise the minimum pension for the elderly to pull many of them out of poverty. But increasing benefits in the pay-as-you-go social security system may be politically easy since payroll tax revenues are high.[16] Passing such legislation in the case of rapid growth, but not passing it in the case of slow growth can be viewed as an example of the model in section 3 since the level of benefits is sensitive to aggregate incomes in a way that tends to move intertemporal marginal rates of substitution toward each other.

Conversely, we can consider the political risk that the government will give away whatever short-run surplus is available for social security, whatever the relative economic conditions of current and future retirees. If high surpluses are positively correlated with currently well-off retirees, this legislative pattern increases risk in the economy. This might happen in a cyclic economy, where wages and rates of return are high or low together, moving wages and returns on lifetime accumulations together.

As an example of political risk, consider a government that has tax revenues that are more than proportionally sensitive to the business cycle (or are particularly sensitive to other variables). Assume that the government responds to fiscal difficulties by adjusting all expenditures proportionally, including retirement pensions. Then, viewing the state of the government budget as a random variable, the variation of government-provided retirement pensions with the state of the government budget (which involves more variation than in other incomes) is an example of government created risk that worsens the efficiency of risk bearing. This example is constructed to reflect my view that pensions are not a good place to locate cyclic revenue risks, that the bearing of risk by pension income should be roughly the same whether the income flows through the government or not. In other words, this

---

[15] I am also assuming that transfers from well-off children to poorly off parents do not adequately solve this problem. This assumption seems accurate to me.

[16] I do not attempt to analyze why it seems to be the case that a debt-financed increase in the minimum pension seems politically less likely to occur than increases in a pay-as-you-go defined benefit pension system.

suggests that government pensions should fluctuate relative to this risk roughly like other pension income, not like other government expenditures.

Similar to short-run fluctuations in the government budget are long-run uncertainties, possibly related to the state of the economy (e.g., oil reserves) or possibly related to other government expenditure needs (e.g., defense). Again, if the government budget is affected more than the state of the economy, treating public pensions like other expenditures may be a poor allocation of this long-run risk.

In these examples, I have identified the pattern of consumption or income per capita as the basis for judging risk-reducing and risk-increasing changes. This reflects the economic theory of risk sharing and is the basis for the proposal by Robert Merton (1983) that social security benefits be indexed to consumption per capita.

In sum, we would like to identify good reasons for varying benefits and taxes and bad reasons for varying them, and then to choose a structure for provision of retirement income that encourages the former and discourages the later. It is probably worth remembering that encouragement and discouragement are probably the right vocabularies – there are no guarantees in politics. It is also worth reiterating that good and bad redistributions within a cohort are also important, as well as the risk sharing among "representative agents" on which I have focused.

7   Legislated outcomes

We have identified a pair of needs – the need to modify social security in some circumstances and a need not to modify it in others. Moreover, there is the concern that whatever modifications are legislated serve their purpose well. That is, the details of public pension rules can be well designed or badly designed. In addition, there is a benefit from accurate perceptions about the likelihood of both types of circumstances, so that people can adapt to accurate forecasts. Thus we want to ask about mechanisms that affect the likelihood of change in the system. We want to ask about the effect of such mechanisms on changes in both circumstances. And we probably want to distinguish between circumstances of increases and circumstances of decreases in both taxes and benefits.

All of the simple models above incorporate some legislated outcomes. At this stage of our knowledge of the determination of legislated outcomes, this process remains something of a black box, with the argument relying on intuitions of the effect on legislation, rather than on derivations from a model of legislation. There are three different types of sources of effects on the legislative process. One source is elements of the constitution that affect how the legislative process works in the consideration of social security; second is the role of the social security benefit and revenue determination processes on likely legislation; third is the role of other factors and institutions on legislative behavior. These can be considered to be the development of a political culture that limits what governments choose to do, even when they could (at least temporarily) do other things. That is, we are distinguishing between changing the rules covering legislation on the one hand and changing institutions that affect political context on the other.

Of course, these issues are not unique to social security. For example, it is interesting to reflect on the recent newspaper articles on the opening up of the Japanese rice market to imports and its effect on incomes of rice farmers. The protection system was politically vulnerable, in part, from the rise of countervailing political power (exporters concerned about GATT) and the lack of an independent claim for income protection (other than the historic cultural continuity of Japanese rice). As economists, we may not like the income protection to begin with, but it is still interesting to consider what would have made it more secure. Do tariffs have more (or less) political viability than quotas?

Constitutional rules

I will refer to the rules governing the functioning of the legislature as a constitution. These rules affect how a government that continues to live by the constitution might behave, how the constitution might be amended within the constitutional process, and how (and whether) the constitution might be replaced by an extraconstitutional process.

There are many actions that governments might take. Any asset might be taken by government. Any expected receipt might be blocked by government. Conversely, an asset might be given by government, an expectation that might otherwise be unrealized might be fulfilled by government. Let us begin by considering common constitutional restrictions on asset seizure generally.

Some constitutions protect private property and private contractual arrangements by a restriction that government must compensate if it "takes" private property. Of course, the definition of a taking is unclear so the implications on behavior of such a rule depend on ongoing political and judicial processes. In addition the definition of "private property" could be manipulated. Similarly, a government contract to purchase an item is normally subject to the same damage-payment rules as a private contract. Thus, one approach to constitutional protection for social security would be to give the social security system's promises the same status as private contracts or private property rather than the status of legislated tax and spending rules, which are subject to future legislated changes.

In a defined benefit setting, such protected status would make more difficult the reduction of benefits below the promised level. This makes more difficult both politically based reductions in benefits and economically needed reductions in benefits after poor random outcomes. Only in the rare cases where the former issue is much more important than the latter would such a high level of insulation make sense.

Giving social security benefit promises the status of property is obviously insulation against benefit reductions. A critical question in evaluating such insulation is whether such a difficulty in benefit reduction would act to limit promised benefits. If it did not, as appears in some countries that do have constitutional protections, then such insulation would be a bad idea, making it hard to adapt an overextended system. Moreover, in a setting of alternating political parties, such insulation might alter the tacit agreement limiting redistributions to party supporters because of the threat of reversal of results. Alternatively, resembling the behavior of a mutual insurance company, promises could be deliberately on the low side (and well protected) while increases beyond the guaranteed amount would be dependent on circumstances. Commonly this is done by protecting nominal but not real amounts. However, this pattern may be due instead to some degree of money illusion. For example, before the U.S. system was indexed for inflation, the benefit formula and the calculation of lifetime average wages were both in nominal terms, making for periodic increases in benefits in response to inflation. This was not a satisfactory system. However, regularity in legislating increases might leave predictability on a par with that of a defined contribution system.

Similarly, one could put the rules covering social security directly into the constitution, making changes more difficult since amending a constitution is generally a process requiring greater majorities or additional steps than with ordinary legislation. This has similar difficulties, although less susceptibility of change in a time of temporary political power.

Now consider granting property status in a defined contribution setting. Such an approach is natural in this system because there is no explicit benefit promise. Presumably, a giveaway of public debt to some individual accounts in a defined contribution system would then be treated as property, whether the giveaway went to poor people or to politically connected ones.

Such property status does not protect these funds from being the basis for means testing of other programs. The greater visibility and ease of measurement of this wealth makes it particularly susceptible to such use. While integration of the funds with other programs (as in Singapore) might be part of the design, the political risk here occurs when such means testing is not part of the design, but becomes a basis for reduction of other programs, reducing net retirement income.

Thus, it appears that giving property status to accumulations in a defined contribution system is probably a good idea, but doing it for a promised benefit formula in a defined benefit system is in most cases a bad idea. This difference reflects the lower likelihood of perverse giveaways in defined contribution systems and the different location of risks in the two types of systems. In defined contribution systems, workers bear some of the risks borne by government (or through government) in defined benefit systems. Thus the needs and likelihoods of risk shifting are different. The economy generally seems to work differently with these two types of claims. In part, this may represent different patterns of liabilities with the differently structured claims, however similar or different the patterns of income for the assets.

Social security design

The full privatization and full funding of a defined contribution plan, as in the Chilean model, seems to provide a great deal of insulation. This makes it unlikely that the government will use social security funds as part of either good or bad redistributions. It seems useful to distinguish different degrees of resistance to change along a path connecting a traditional unfunded defined benefit system with the Chilean model to identify separately some of the parts that contribute to this insulation.

The minimal design element for public provision of retirement income would be a benefit plan, with no specific identification of a revenue source. Such a system would be very vulnerable to the state of the government budget. Traditionally, a payroll tax is earmarked to pay for the promised benefits. This earmarking offers some insulation from fluctuations in the rest of the budget, although it increases sensitivity to fluctuations in the earmarked source of revenue. Earmarking will generally require periodic legislation to align taxes and benefits unless there is an automatic-adjustment mechanism. Currently legislated future increases in benefits also require some proposed future tax increases as well, although there is always the opportunity to legislate incompatible future benefit and tax changes, leaving the issue of balance to be sorted out in the future. Future legislation is likely to depend on past promises, even when they were not adequately funded at the time.

Automatic-adjustment rules in a totally unfunded system may provide considerable insulation to benefit increases in that any benefit increase requires a simultaneous tax increase, although an immature system will have low tax rates and may offer little resistance to such changes. Such an automatic-adjustment mechanism may make the future rise in taxes more visible than in a nonautomatic system. The presence of earmarking lowers the likelihood that the revenue will be used for other purposes; it also lowers the likelihood that other sources of revenue will be used for this expenditure. With limited other use of this earmarked source of funds, its availability for public pensions will be increased. Thus the absence of a fund may increase insulation in a system where benefits and taxes are adjusted to each other automatically.

It is common for traditional systems to fund benefits partially so that any excess of earmarked revenue over benefits goes into a special fund. The presence of a fund does provide some insulation from vagaries in the government budget, but it probably increases the likelihood of benefit increases (possibly unsustainable) on the basis of fund availability and also of fund use for other purposes, a more difficult trick if there is no fund.

Funding can be done with public debt. That this is primarily a political act can be seen in the following quotation from Bodie and Merton (1993). In commenting on the social security trust fund buildup in the United States, they write: "In a private plan, funding is used to insure against default by the plan sponsor. Here the promise to pay benefits has the same level of full faith and credit of the government as the bonds used to fund the plan. Yet there seems to be a belief that this change may help to ensure that, when they reach retirement, workers will indeed receive benefits approximating those promised under the current benefit formula (i.e., the one in effect in 1992)" (p. 197).

There is a role for such a promise in the effect on the legislative process. There are probably decreasing degrees of likelihood in the following actions. A government might repudiate just implicit social security debt, it might repudiate explicit public debt held by the social security system, it might repudiate all government debt. Similarly, it seems more likely that the government repudiate its debt to a social security trust fund than that it seize private assets held by the social security system, which, in turn, seems more likely than that it seize all assets. Seizure of assets is not the only risk facing trust funds. Whether invested in public or private assets, rates of return below market rates may be arranged by the government. And funds can be embezzled, by private agents, public employees, and politicians.

The idea behind the reduction in likelihood of asset seizure comes from the pooling of groups of assets or income claims so that they tend to be treated the same by the legislative process. That is, there tends to be a norm of uniformity: Assets or income flows can be taxed, but not at a discriminatory rate – a rate different from other (similar) sources of income or wealth. Insofar as groups are politically accepted as equal, they tend to get treated equally. This does not underestimate the ability of the political system to identify (or create) differences in order to have targeted benefits. By placing retirement income in the same equal treatment category with other forms of income, particularly privately provided retirement income or income from assets generally, there may be more political protection. Again, there may be asymmetry in that it is easier to invoke equal treatment to guard against losses than for the general public to cite it to guard against increased benefits. This is similar to the possibility that the arguments for a comprehensive tax base affect the extent to which tax loopholes get legislated.

The role of uniform treatment as a source of insulation is also seen in different outcomes with a single, unitary social security system, rather than multiple public programs. It appears that a setting with multiple programs is much more subject to manipulation, to transfers that are perverse, and, ex ante, a source of risk. A single uniform system is more resistant to special pleading. Moreover that larger groups are affected by changes in provisions also contributes to less manipulation. This is in contrast with an income tax code, for example, where some clauses naturally apply to just a small number of taxpayers, and others can be designed to do so.

The next step beyond funding with government debt is funding with private assets. This probably increases the insulation from political risk, although it is a little unclear why – private assets may seem more "real" to voters, more of an obligation to continue promised benefits.[17]

From this perspective, a defined contribution system differs from a defined benefit system in that the promised benefits are automatically adjusted to the availability of funds. That is, no further legislative actions are required in order to carry out the "promised" benefits. This can be done with earmarking with automatic adjustment without funding. But earmarking without automatic adjustment is not the same as earmarking with automatic adjustment, just as funding a defined benefit system is different from funding a defined contribution system.

Visibility

In a complex and indirect way, a democratic political process depends on the perceptions of the public about political decisions. Sometimes, these perceptions come directly, sometimes they come indirectly, through the observations of particular groups, both general professional groups and special interest groups. The impact of these public perceptions on the political process depends on perceptions of process as well as perceptions of outcomes. For example, the use of a base closing commission in the United States to select a set of military bases for closing, with Congress agreeing to a single yes-or-no vote on the entire set of proposed closures, has led to base closings, whereas there had been none for a long time before the creation of the commission. The difference in outcomes does not depend on visibility of outcomes, since possible closure of a nearby base is of major local interest

---

[17] The use of private assets does affect the nature of political process since the rate of return may well be different – even if the aggregate return to the economy is unchanged, and returns on the funds probably affect legislated outcomes on benefits.

and followed closely. Rather the public acceptance of the commission process, as opposed to the usual legislative process, has affected the willingness of the elected officials to go along. Thus perceptions of "responsibility" as well as perceptions of outcomes seem to matter. This is not an issue of "visibility" in the sense that both process and outcomes are "visible." Yet the degree of "responsibility" of elected officials is seen differently, making this an issue of visibility of responsibility. Perhaps visibility is an inadequate word for this issue. One might say that a direct congressional vote, base by base, would be more "transparent" to voters as to where the responsibility really lies.

Full secrecy is likely to yield corruption, favoritism, and poor policies. Yet different methods of making decisions and so having different public awareness and perceptions seem to involve different potentials for good policies.

Stephen Breyer (1993) has recently reviewed the trade-off between costs and lives saved in a range of government responses to health risks in the United States. Although these regulations are not income transfers, they again reflect the public thinking about risk. Breyer feels that public perceptions of risk are inaccurate[18] and that Congress is responsive to these public perceptions, resulting in a set of policies that are not good in aggregate. In particular, the cost of the marginal life saved varies enormously over different risks. Breyer calls for an institutional change to increase the role of administrative expertise in designing public policy responses to risks. He argues that increased power for civil servants will result in a more consistent relative treatment of alternative risks. In effect, Breyer has argued for the need to prevent Congress from doing what it appears that the public wants. Viewing institution design as a problem of combining good judgment and public responsiveness has a starting place near the observation of Schattschneider (1960, p. 137): "Democracy is like nearly everything else we do; it is a form of collaboration of ignorant people and experts." The role of different political players is at the heart of the distinction between direct and representative democracy, with different types of discussion and outcomes in referenda and in legislation.

I suspect that a similar issue is present in the determination of benefits as in the determination of health risks. In order to adjust benefits to economic realities, it is probably appropriate to move part of such decisions away from the legislative process and to a professional or private arena where there is far less visibility to the general public. For example, consider a defined contribution system where the government sets the price for converting accumulations into annuities. If this conversion is set by formula (e.g., relating to interest rates and mortality tables) or if it is set by actuaries, who

---

[18] Cognitive psychology finds that stochastic outcomes are not intuitive; frequently, people do not think consistently about them.

describe their methods to other professionals, then the process of adjustment seems likely to go relatively smoothly. However, if the price for conversion had to be voted by the legislature year by year, a smooth adjustment might be far more difficult, resulting in upward stickiness of the price of an annuity despite the presence of changes in interest rates or mortality rates. I think that a legislature would have difficulty trying to change the relationship between annuities and accumulations on a year-by-year basis. Such an adjustment seems to need to be out of sight of the public.

Similarly, there is less visibility and easier adjustment when the price is set by firms rather than by the legislature. Even here there is presumably a difference depending on whether conversion prices are quoted on an individual-by-individual basis, as in Chile today, or firms have to announce a general price schedule, or firms have to report their price schedule in the context of a possible public hearing (as with file-and-use auto insurance rates in parts of the United States). These different methods are likely to generate different degrees of public awareness and so different political pressures to affect the process. The details of the process could also affect the equilibrium markup for the usual reasons in the presence of some market power.

Indeed the public has far greater willingness to interfere with prices than do economists, whether this is for redistribution to the poor (through special prices) or to the general public (through limits on price changes). The question arises here just as it does implicitly in the preceding discussion of the relationship between institutions and good public policy, of how respect for a democratic process should treat these elements of seemingly poor public attitudes toward policy. In the context of whether economists should support redistributions that interfere with price setting, Robert Solow has stated the dilemma succinctly in his American Economic Association presidential address:

Most of us are conscious of a conflict that arises in our minds and consciences because, while we think it is usually a mistake to fiddle the price system to achieve distributional goals, we realize that the public and the political process are perversely more willing to do that than to make the direct transfers we would prefer. If we oppose all distorting transfers, we end up opposing transfers altogether. Some of us seem to welcome the excuse, but most of us feel uncomfortable. I don't think there is any very good way to resolve that conflict in practice. (1980, p. 1.)

One advantage of a defined contribution system over a defined benefit system is that it is probably easier to accept a "market-caused" change in a conversion price than to legislate a change in a benefit formula. It is easier to use either the market or professional civil servants in this case. Some help can be obtained by having an automatic-adjustment mechanism in a defined benefit system, decreasing the frequency with which legislated changes are needed.

It is natural to think of an annuity market as adjusting benefits to available resources, but there is no need for the resources to be physically present. That is, the benefits could be adjusted to various accounting measures that have no backing in physical assets. This is essentially what Boskin, Kotlikoff, and Shoven (1988) propose. In their system, each year people accrue additional (real) benefits (on retirement) based on the taxes paid that year. Accrued benefits receive high protection from political forces. However the accrual rates for future benefits are not similarly protected, but are set by actuaries based on forecasts so that the system is forecasted to be in balance over the projection period. By doing these adjustments on an annual cycle affecting current contributors and not current beneficiaries, it is much easier to preserve the professional character of these calculations from political forces. Having many small decisions should make this process even less visible than a single decision affecting all of a person's benefits. Lack of visibility of civil servants to the general public is insulation for professionalism, but it can also be insulation for theft. How to strike a balance between these two factors will vary across countries with differences in their political cultures.

Contrast this approach to one that adjusts annual benefits to annual revenues by proportionally changing all benefits to be paid that year. While benefit recipients might be passive in the face of such announcements, it is more likely that there will be pressure on politicians and so pressure on the system from politicians to protect benefits from levels felt to be too low. Taking away from people what they do not realize they have is much easier. Similarly, the public seems to think largely in nominal terms, so that reductions in cost-of-living adjustments are politically easier than adjustments in benefit levels, however curious this distinction is to economists. This is the sort of political evaluation that may not have long-run viability, since the degree of understanding of the nominal–real distinction and its political acceptance by the public could change. A problem with accepting the more easily legislated decreases is a tendency to use the more politically acceptable methods of decrease, even when they make for a less effective retirement income system. For example, contrast a once-for-all benefit cut to periodic adjustments that are less than the full COLA amount. The public seems to find reductions in COLAs more acceptable than benefit cuts. Yet a policy of repeated small cuts, implicit in not giving full COLAs, concentrates the benefit cuts on the long-lived, a group that is not well suited to absorb larger cuts. Indeed, poverty among the elderly is typically concentrated in the very elderly.

More generally, the degree of money illusion (inflation illusion) in the public depends on history, particularly exposure to inflation. Thus, in inadequately indexed social security systems, protecting retirement incomes from inflation is an important part of protecting retirement incomes. The obvious institutional response is to have an indexed system. However, even an indexed system is vulnerable to sufficiently high inflation rates because of lags. There may be no direct cure for this, with avoidance of high inflation the obvious solution.

It seems to me that visibility in the public arena is a two-edged sword. Visibility prevents some kinds of bad political action: It is harder to steal in the light of day than it is at night. Forcing identification of who pays for a new benefit is a form of increased visibility. But higher visibility will also tend to limit good professional reactions in cases where public perceptions are not well grounded in professional considerations. Thus it may be useful to try to build a respected professional expertise, somewhat insulated from political (and public) pressures, that can try to guide the system into the kinds of changes that ought to happen. A key question is what role to give such expertise. One can consider a platform for advice, a requirement to request such advice by the government, or a requirement that such advice must be explicitly overridden, by standard or super majorities. Too much insulation of a "professional" group and too much decision power can move decisions toward the preferences of such a bureaucracy, which may or may not coincide with someone else's definition of good policy. One could contemplate giving a social security institution similar powers to those given to central banks.[19] While this seems problematic, it is an interesting example to contemplate. Having monetary policy set by an independent bank rather than by Congress is both a change in the locus of responsibility and a separation of the decision-making process from the type of public scrutiny and involvement that apply to legislation.

Thus the Chilean system seems to provide insulation by having added visibility as a result of individual accounts and by having decreased visibility from the absence of a stated benefit formula or of regulated or more visible pricing of annuities. Added visibility of annuity pricing might make markups smaller, or larger. And it might set political pressures in motion to alter the system.

Political context

In addition to constitutional changes and different structure of the insurance institution, there are other ways to affect the distribution of legislated outcomes, in particular by affecting public discourse about social security. For example, an institution with professional independence can affect the dialogue about social security. Having an official actuarial office that is required to report annually and/or to comment on any proposed legislation gives

---

[19] For a discussion of independent central banks, see Cukierman (1992).

higher political visibility (and presumably resistance) to changes that may be unsustainable. In the United States, the Office of the Actuary in Social Security must forecast the financial balance of the system for 75 years. Although it is easy to ignore these pronouncements, they give a little more political prominence to these long-run issues.

With privatized management of a separate trust fund, there is again a set of professionals to comment on proposed legislated changes in the private fund managers.

Another approach to affecting political outcomes is by changing the description of the system in the eyes of the public. For example, the vocabulary of individual accounts (as opposed to a benefit formula) has suggestions to the public that may affect legislated outcomes. Referring to social security as a tax-transfer mechanism in ordinary discourse may make the system more vulnerable (by making changes in response to short-run considerations more legitimate) than referring to it as an insurance system, one where benefits have been "earned" by paying earlier premiums. Such a conversational change can be done whether the system is defined benefit or defined contribution. In a defined benefit setting, the language itself results in a primarily one-sided protection – harder to cut benefits, but not harder to raise them. If the greater risk is increases that result in unsustainable benefit levels, then this does not offer much protection.

An additional area where vocabulary matters is the vocabulary of government budget balance. One example of a subtler form of pressure is the public definition of the budget balance – whether this includes or excludes the social security system. To get some insulation for the short-run fluctuations in the state of the government budget, one can move the social security receipts and expenditures "outside" the budget. This can be done in a variety of ways with differing degrees of insulation. One can simply not include social security in official definitions of the budget deficit. One role for earmarking and a trust fund is to add to the sustainability of such a vocabulary choice. An independent institution managing the fund may also add to this sustainability. And privatization tends to keep both stocks and flows outside the budget process, although forcing below-market interest rates on funds remains a possibility.

The political viability of an arrangement can also depend on the circumstances of its creation. If people do pay for the assets that go into their accounts, these accounts may be politically more insulated than if they are given such accounts. It is not clear how much more insulation is given when the system is based on taxes paid rather than wages subject to tax. The public in the United States seems to feel it paid for its benefits even though the benefit rules reflect wages subject to tax, not taxes paid. Perceived fairness has some political effects. So too does clearly perceived unfairness.

Working in an exchange economy has kept my analysis focused on risk, the central charge of this chapter.[20] Capital accumulation is a major issue in the behavior of governments. Some of the academic support for funding comes from a desire to see more capital accumulation, not from concern with insulation. A similar analysis might be done of the capital accumulation question, recognizing that changes in capital accumulation involve income redistribution as well. Consider a three-period model. One can consider the extent to which one wants more or less capital accumulation than occurs in equilibrium in each of the first two periods. One can consider how the level of capital accumulation that occurs depends on institution design in both that period and earlier periods. The government has many tools to affect capital accumulation, of which funding retirement pensions is just one. Thus one needs to consider the relative merits of funding different activities, as well as other institution designs that affect capital accumulation. For example, one might try to inculcate the idea that national defense is shaky unless future defense expenditures are funded. The politics of such an institution would probably work differently from one focused on retirement income.

8   Conclusion

Right now, established retirement income systems are subject to the risk of oversensitivity to the state of the government budget, and new systems are subject to the risk of excessive redistribution to early generations, masked in an unsustainable formula. The Chilean structure does well with both of these problems by moving retirement incomes outside the government budget and by seeming to require the identification of an explicit source of financing for benefits for any group of individuals. It is probably too soon to rule out the ability of the political system to tap these resources for government revenue needs or for redistributions. Requiring investment in government debt, particularly debt paying less than market rates, is the obvious route for the former. Redistributing part of the return on portfolios to "needier" accounts (which may have an age component) is one route for the latter. Protection against such moves probably lies in the identification of individual accounts (and the returns on them) as private property, entitled to the same protection as other assets.

Many established systems have unsustainable benefit promises and need adjustment, often while needing overhaul of the structure of the system as well. It is interesting to ask the extent to which reductions of benefits are politically more possible in the context of a major change in the structure of the benefit system, rather than without such a changeover. This seems a different question from describing political behavior when starting a new

---

[20] A model with capital is briefly presented in the appendix.

system. It will be good to observe political outcomes as various legislatures adjust retirement systems. It would be good to have a larger empirical basis for identifying the set of risks and to be less speculative about the legislative process in thinking about this important topic.

The discussion here suggest a value in the creation of an institution giving status and visibility to professional evaluation of the condition of the retirement system and possible changes in it.

APPENDIX TO CHAPTER 2: A FUNDED SYSTEM

The chapter uses a pure exchange economy to highlight the issue of risk-sharing and risk-creating behavior of legislatures in a setting where there was little else (besides redistribution) happening in the economy. The use of a fully funded system does not change the possibilities of legislative actions to create risks or share them, although it impacts on the likely pattern of outcomes of legislative action and inaction.

To make this point formally, I want to consider a two-period economy with two groups of savers who do not interact with each other in the private market. The two groups can be considered the present generation and future generations. Lumping all of the future into a single generation ignores many issues of the carryover of institution design into the future, but does bring out some issues in a simple setting.

Consider a two-period model with two types of agents. Type A receives income y^a in period one, before the government passes any legislation. Type B receives income y^b in period one, but this income is random at the time of period-one legislation, but known before the time of period-two legislation, if any. There is a stochastic linear technology for converting first-period income into second-period income. Let R^a and R^b be the quantities of period-two income received for each unit of period-one income saved by the two types. The two groups can not trade with each other, so each makes its savings decisions based on its (stochastic) options. Thus the credit market plays no role in the allocation of risks between the groups. Direct investment separately by each group is the way that each type obtains consumption in the second period and the way in which risks of second-period income are determined.

Each agent seeks to maximize the expected value of the utility function $u^i(c^i_1, c^i_2)$, $i = a,b$ subject to the budget constraint $c^i_2 = (y^i - c^i_1)R^i$, $i = a, b$. In keeping with the interpretation of the model, we assume that the government can not alter the levels of investment, but can risk share by setting up a rule transferring between the two groups in period two as a function of the realized rates of return. Using this formulation has individual savers recognize the presence of random transfers, but does not alter the rate of return on marginal investments. Thus the budget constraint of each group is altered to read $c^i_2 = (y^i - c^i_1)R^i + B^i(R^a,R^b)$, $i = a,b$; with the constraints on the government $B^a(R^a,B^b) + B^b(R^a,B^b) = 0$.

Purely risk-sharing legislation would have $E\{B^a(R^a,B^b)\} = 0$. Redistribution from the future to the present generation would have this expectation positive. Legislation with a zero expected benefit level would be risk sharing or risk creating depending on whether it tended to move the intertemporal marginal rates of substitution toward each other or away from each other (as with pure political risk as discussed earlier).

References

Aghion, Philippe, and Patrick Bolton. 1990. Government Domestic Debt and the Risk of Default: A Political-Economic Model of the Strategic Role of Debt. In R. Dornbusch and M. Draghi, eds., *Public Debt Management: Theory and History,* pp. 315–45. Cambridge: Cambridge University Press.

Ainslie, George. 1992. *Picoeconomics: The Strategic Interaction of Successive Motivational States within the Person.* Cambridge: Cambridge University Press.

Bodie, Zvi, and Robert C. Merton. 1993. Pension Benefit Guarantees in the United States: A Functional Analysis. In R. Schmitt, ed., *The Future of Pensions in the United States,* pp. 194–234. Philadelphia: University of Pennsylvania Press.

Boskin, Michael J., Laurence J. Kotlikoff, and John B. Shoven. 1988. Personal Security Accounts: A Proposal for Fundamental Social Security Reform. In Susan M. Wachter, ed., *Social Security and Private Pensions,* pp. 179–206. Lexington, Mass.: Lexington Books.

Breyer, Stephen. 1993. *Breaking the Vicious Circle: Toward Effective Risk Regulation.* Cambridge, Mass.: Harvard University Press.

Cukierman, Alex. 1992. *Central Bank Strategy, Credibility, and Independence: Theory and Evidence.* Cambridge, Mass.: MIT Press.

Diamond, Peter A. 1994. Privatization of Social Security: Lessons from Chile. *Revista de Analisis Economico,* 9 (1), 21–53.

Diamond, Peter A. 1996. Government Provision and Regulation of Economic Support in Old Age. In M. Bruno and B. Pleskovic, eds., *Annual World Bank Conference on Development Economics 1995,* pp. 83–103. Washington D.C.: The World Bank.

Diamond, Peter A., and James A. Mirrlees. 1992. Optimal Taxation of Identical Consumers When Markets Are Incomplete. In P. Dasgupta, D. Gale, O. Hart, and E. Maskin, eds., *Essays in Honor of Frank Hahn,* pp. 561–81. Cambridge, Mass.: MIT Press.

Diamond, Peter A., and Salvador Valdés-Prieto. 1993. "Social Security Reform." In B. Bosworth, R. Dornbusch, and R. Laban, eds., *The Chilean Economy: Policy Lessons and Challenges,* pp. 257–328. Washington, D.C.: Brookings Institution.

Gale, Douglas. 1990. The Efficient Design of Public Debt. In R. Dornbusch and M. Draghi, eds., *Public Debt Management: Theory and History,* pp. 14–47. Cambridge: Cambridge University Press.

Geanakoplos, John, M. Magill, M. Quinzii, and J. Dreze. 1990. Generic Inefficiency of Stock Market Equilibria. *Journal of Mathematical Economics,* 19, 113–151.

Geanakoplos, John, and Heraklis Polemarchakis. 1986. Existence, Regularity, and Constrained Suboptimality of Competitive Allocations When the Asset Market Is Incomplete. In W. Heller, R. Starr, and D. Starrett, eds., *Essays in Honor of Kenneth Arrow,* 3:65–95, Cambridge: Cambridge University Press.

Gordon, Roger H., and Hal R. Varian. 1988. Intergenerational risk sharing. *Journal of Public Economics,* 37, 185–202.

Kydland, Finn E., and Edward C. Prescott. 1977. Rules Rather Than Discretion: The Inconsistency of Optimal Plans. *Journal of Political Economy,* 85 (3), 473–492.

Loewenstein, George, and Jon Elster. 1992. *Choice over Time.* New York: Russell Sage Foundation.

Malinvaud, Edmond. 1972. The Allocation of Individual Risks in Large Markets. *Journal of Economic Theory,* 4 (2), 312–328.

Merton, Robert C. 1983. On Consumption-Indexed Public Pension Plans. In Z. Bodie and J. Shoven, eds., *Financial Aspects of the U.S. Pension System,* chap. 10. Chicago: University of Chicago Press.

Schattschneider, E. E. 1960. *The Semi-sovereign People.* New York: Holt, Rinehart and Winston.

Schelling, Thomas. 1984. Self Command in Practice, in Policy and in a Theory of Rational Thought. *American Economic Review,* 74 (2), 1–11.

Social Security Technical Panel. 1991. *Report to the 1991 Advisory Council on Social Security.* Washington, D.C. Advisory Council on Social Security.

Solow, Robert M. 1980. On Theories of Unemployment. *American Economic Review,* 70 (1), 1–11.

Stokey, Nancy. 1989. Reputation and Time Consistency. *American Economic Review,* 79 (2), 134–139.

Strotz, Robert H. 1955. Myopia and Inconsistency in Dynamic Utility Maximization. *Review of Economic Studies,* 23, 165–180.

World Bank. 1994. *Averting the Old Age Crisis.* Oxford: Oxford University Press.

CHAPTER 3

Democracy and pensions in Chile: Experience with two systems

Oscar Godoy and Salvador Valdés-Prieto

Abstract

This chapter analyzes the two social security systems currently in operation in Chile and the democratic models that underpin them. The public pay-as-you-go system has been in force since 1952 and is based on a social democratic political model, whose economic expression is the welfare state. The new pension system, built around property rights on individual accounts and full funding, was established in 1981 and is linked to a liberal democratic model. The two systems are compared from the perspective of democratic development.

The chapter also provides two political case studies, one for each of the systems that coexist today. Both episodes occurred under the current constitutional regime. The first one analyzes the evolution of the legal mechanisms for automatic CPI indexation of pensions in the old system over 1979–1993. The second studies a financial conflict in 1992 in the new system, between a state agency and private pension fund management companies, who represented the interests of members. These case studies show that the old system continues to expose its members to some political manipulation, although less than before, whereas the new system has increased the independence of citizens from the state and the political class. Therefore, the Chilean reform appears to have made a contribution to the political value of freedom. The constitution of 1980 and the return of democracy in 1990 also appear to have made additional contributions.

1   Introduction

That the design of a publicly mandated pension system is heavily constrained by political factors is a well-known fact to public finance economists. Causation may also go in the opposite direction, as the pension system has an

We thank ex-Minister René Cortázar and an anonymous referee for their comments.

influence on the political system. When the overall design of the pension system encourages certain relationships between voters and politicians, these relationships will gain in strength and may affect the path of the political process itself. This chapter approaches these topics from the political science and political economy points of view. It does not describe in detail the contracts and regulations that define the new Chilean pension system nor its economic consequences. A suitable source for such an assessment of the recent experience in Chile is Diamond and Valdés-Prieto (1994).

We attempt a comparative study of the democratic underpinnings and implications of the two social security systems that currently exist in Chile. The two systems were established in two different moments: the first in 1952 (reforming the original system established in 1924) and the second one in 1981. They are qualitatively different because they are based on different conceptual premises, and represent two different ways of approaching the issue of mandatory earnings-related pensions. This chapter does not offer a comparison of the economic implications of these two systems. Rather, it focuses on the underlying political model for each system. For reasons not discussed here, the creation of the new system in 1981 did not imply the elimination of the old one. Those currently working were given the option to switch to the new system and many did not take it. Therefore, two pension systems coexist in Chile. Although their designs follow different democratic paradigms, they operate within the same political regime. The first part of this chapter analyzes the relationship between the two systems and the democratic models that provide their political support and backing. The first section reviews the history of the old Chilean social security system and reports about the political currents that influenced the development of pension policy. The following section evaluates the public defined benefit pay-as-you-go system, whose central political feature was its reliance on a social democratic point of view and the associated welfare state policy. In that framework, the old system was expected to deliver more equality, even at the cost of a reduction in individual freedoms and an increase in the power of bureaucrats. However, in Chile the social democratic political model was characterized by heavy patronage from political parties and their controlling cliques, which influenced strongly the actual development of the old pension system. The third section describes the current democratic model, which gives more preeminence to individual autonomy, independence, political rights, and a market economy, with less weight given to equality. The new system is characterized as a projection of this political model into the social security sphere, which turns the individual contributor into the main actor. Trying to achieve this, the new system endows the individual contributor with explicit property rights over accumulated funds and several freedoms of choice which might protect him from inefficient administration.

In the second part of the chapter, we consider two empirical case studies that control for differences in the overall political setting. The first case describes how the political system has managed an essential aspect of the economic value of pension rights in the old system, which are cost-of-living adjustments, from 1985 to 1993. Apart from the direct lessons offered by this section, which are of independent interest, it documents how inflation adjustments have been used also to further the political interests of the governing groups from 1985 to 1993. This shows that the old system continues to be vulnerable to indirect manipulation of the individual voter under the current political model. This suggests that the old system exhibits an inherent bias toward patronage, even though it has been smaller after the return of democracy in 1990. The second case study describes how the new system fared in a recent (1992) clash between the financial interest of a powerful state agency and the financial interests of workers, represented by private pension fund management companies. This episode shows that members of the new pension system have achieved more independence from political and electoral pressures than pensioners in the old system, even though the state continues to be the backbone of the new system, as contributions are mandatory and pension fund management companies are subject to strict regulation.

2   The two pension systems and their democratic models

2.1   The political basis of the old system

2.1.1   Political history of the old Chilean social security system
The ideas on social security derived from European social democracy exerted great influence on the Chilean pension reform of 1952 and afterward. For example, the proposals of William Beveridge (1942) were broadly seen as postulates for a modern and democratic social security system. The central idea of these proposals consisted in establishing a system of universal attendance to the *states of need* of the population, in which basic egalitarian solutions would be guaranteed, on the basis of mandatory contributions, of equal value for everyone. Beveridge proposes, as the central instrument of the system, the creation of a single fund that must be fed from the contributions of the workers, the contributions of employers, and the state.

The idea of this single fund made up of equal mandatory contributions was the prevalent formula for democratic societies after World War II. In Chile, in contrast to this model, there was a great variety of pensions systems, institutionalized under the form of several "Cajas" (funds) for the *white-*

collar workers, on the one hand, and the Servicio de Seguridad Social (SSS), for the *blue-collar workers,* on the other. There were substantial differences between the various Cajas, both in terms of the contribution rates and in the granting of benefits. These differences were politically important because the Cajas and the SSS served workers of disparate socioeconomic levels. The first included 450,000 members who received 59% of covered wage income, while the SSS concentrated 1.2 million members who received 33% of covered wage income.[1] The resulting segmentation of benefits and contributions was in direct conflict with the principle of equality associated with the prevalent social democratic model.

The juridical and institutional foundation of this diversity of pension systems was a large number of laws. The Prat Report indicates that there were 515 legal texts, including laws, decrees, and regulations that controlled the existence, nature, and attributions of this complex system.[2] This legal overabundance reflected the action of groups with economic capacity and political power to obtain pension legislation that would protect them in a privileged manner. Thus, each group acquired a level of benefits proportional to its social and political power (some of the benefits obtained by the members of the more privileged Cajas were premature retirement and heavily subsidized housing loans). Thus, during the decade of the fifties, the Chilean system was, in reality, an aggregation of diverse pension systems negotiated between those in political power and various groups with electoral influence. The number of social security institutions accumulated in this process reached 18 during the decade of the sixties, which administered almost 60 different regimes, not counting those of the armed forces and of the police.[3] By 1979, these institutions had increased to 32,[4] and were in charge of over 100 different social security regimes.[5] The legal and institutional profusion also increased the administrative costs of pensions.

In 1957, the Klein-Saks mission (government of Carlos Ibáñez, 1952–1958) issued the first critical report on the old pension system. According to this report, the Chilean social security system suffered from the following ailments: As contribution rates reached the 40–49% range,[6] it was an extremely onerous burden on wages and salaries and on the capital of companies; it inhibited savings; and the proliferation of Cajas increased the expense of their administration and reduced the quality of service. In reference to the accumulated funds, it added that only small investments had been made on development projects; and that, on the contrary, loans had been granted and

---

[1] Prat (1962) p. 60. [2] Ibid., p. 41.
[3] Thayer and Fernández (1981) p. 31. [4] Cheyre (1991) p. 36.
[5] Ibid., p. 170. [6] Ffrench-Davis (1973) p. 342.

homes built that benefited only a minority, not safeguarding the maintenance of the real value of the capital invested or loaned.[7]

In 1958, President Jorge Alessandri responded by creating a Commission for Studies on Chilean Social Security, presided over by Mr. Jorge Prat, to review the pension system. The Prat Report indicates that one of the most urgent problems was the chronic devaluation of pensions destined to cover old age or disability, due to inflation: "Pensioners from public administration without the *perseguidora* clause [periodic adjustment according to the active salary of the last position held by the beneficiary], entering an inactive state between the years 1940 and 1950, have suffered an 82% devaluation of their pensions."[8] In addition, Prat points to the fact that 75% of social security was not financed by the beneficiaries. The state, he tells us, contributed 31% and the employers, 44%. The first percentage comes from taxes, and the second is charged to the cost of production of goods and services that the companies provide to the market, so part of it was financed by demand. If the largest contribution to social security is that of the community, Prat maintains, the legislation should ensure that the redistribution of those funds "doesn't benefit groups or oligarchies, but rather is distributed under that healthy concept of redistribution in favor of the weakest and more numerous sectors of society."[9] A third idea developed by Prat refers to the *states of discrimination* that made the system vulnerable. These states are related to the plurality and arbitrariness of the concept of disability (10 different criteria); to the differentiation of services rendered; to discrimination on matters of pension amounts and cost of living adjustments; and to exemptions from the obligation to contribute.

Prat covers in his analysis a topic not often debated at that time: social security as an instrument of capitalization. At its inception in 1924 and until 1952, the old system had attempted to finance old-age benefits by capitalization through individual accounts. However, pension benefits had been defined in nominal terms, so inflation left the system with a huge cash surplus. The vacuum was filled by large increases in legislated benefits (health, family allowances). Investment was discredited as an alternative use of funds because of the deterioration of domestic capital markets and the huge losses experienced in financial investments. This scheme for the use of funds was translated into law in the reform of 1952.

By 1962 investment income financed only 3% of expenditures. Prat provides impressive data about the rate of return: 35% of the surplus suitable for capitalization had been invested in loans and bonds in nominal terms, and

---

[7] *Informe de la Comisión Klein-Saks,* p. 25.   [8] Prat (1962) p. 52.
[9] Ibid., p. 53.

this meant that, between 1940 and 1954, the said instruments suffered the effects of an accumulated inflation of 322.4% – that is, they lost around 80% of their real value.[10] The rest earned very low real returns.

The Prat Report's negative evaluation of the old system was very influential. During the period 1952–1973, all the presidents of the republic referred to the topic of social security in terms of crisis. President Eduardo Frei (1964–1970)[11] expanded upon the evaluation made by his predecessor Alessandri. However, neither of them obtained legislative solutions to the perceived problems. According to Prat the solution to the problem of social security was to have "a single and egalitarian system of social security, but our system is differentiated by groups and is discriminatory."[12] This policy, which succeeded in many OECD countries, proved unable to overcome the opposition of the pressure groups engendered during the first phase of development (1924–1952) and strengthened ever since. At the end of his mandate, Frei practically repeated the criticism of the social security system that he made at the beginning.

In the meantime, the mechanics of pension system maturity and the unfavorable effects of the demographic transition were beginning to reduce pensions. Pension system maturity was the strongest of the two forces, as seen from the fact that during the decade of the 1970s, the number of pensioners almost doubled, going from 581,000 in 1970 to over 1 million in 1979. However, the number of contributors grew only from 2.2 million to 2.4 million. Thus, each active worker now had to finance two inactive pensioners.[13] The maturation of the old system increased the pressures for radical reform.

During the three years that President Salvador Allende (1970–1973) was able to govern, reform was attempted again, but in a different direction from that proposed by Prat. The policy on social security of the Allende government had a hard socialist orientation. The objective was not insurance, as it wanted to achieve "solidarity of the system . . . including population groups that urgently need coverage due to the states of need" (i.e., the poor in general, regardless of contribution record). The means were radical, as the cause of this poverty was "the socioeconomic structure of a capitalist nature that existed when the current government took over."[14] In his last message to the nation, before the collapse of his government, President Allende says that his policy in this area was oriented toward the replacement of social security "for the purpose of correcting its deficiencies, products of a scheme of typical capitalist nature."[15] Although these reform initiatives continued in the

---

[10] Ibid., p. 61. [11] Frei (1966) pp. 74–75 and (1969) pp. 334–335, respectively.
[12] Prat (1962) p. 54. [13] Thayer and Fernández (1981) p. 51.
[14] Allende (1972) p. 871. [15] Allende (1973) p. 800.

legislative process when the military intervention of 1973 occurred,[16] they were directed toward a *socialist* welfare state, avoiding the previous social democrat approach. This means that the Allende government attempted a centralization in the state of politics and the economy, beyond the framework of liberal democracy and capitalism to which social democracy was committed.

Thus, from the beginnings of Chilean legislation on social security (1924) until its reform in 1980, a great tension can be observed between social security approaches that are sustained by different political and democratic models (liberalism vs. social democracy vs. socialism). The emergence of social security in the country corresponds to a crisis period of liberal democracy, in its classical form. Social security, as other social policies, constituted an answer to social problems generated by industrial capitalism during the 19th century, which were perceived as impossible to solve through voluntary exchange and thus required an extension of the state's agenda. The social democratic state expanded its activities to include social welfare and insurance of the states of need of the population.

In the first half of the 20th century, the formulas offered by the capitalist approach to prevent future contingencies, such as voluntary savings and insurance plans, appeared grossly insufficient to face the problem, and to respond to the challenges put forth by those critical of capitalism. On the other hand, a prompt development of welfare policies, founded on a strong principle of equality, offered a credible promise of achieving goals such as *universalization* of those protected (all members of a society) and of the protection granted (all contingencies); *integrality* of social security (to cover the full financial impact of each contingency); *uniformity* (each contingency must be attended to with the same quality of benefits and services rendered). Most important, this approach offered these results in a context of strong *solidarity*, by which everyone contributes to the system according to their capacity and receives its benefits according to their needs,[17] thereby robbing socialism of its appeal.

These goals, anchored in an egalitarian democratic model, could not become a reality if not through the state. There was no viable capitalist alternative, and private production subject to regulation was not considered as an alternative. For this reason, already since the application by Bismark of the *Polizeistaat*, it was assumed that social security not only should be carried out with the concurrence of the state, but was rather a function of the state, and had to have at its disposal the state's coercive power to provide for its mandatory nature, and be basically financed by the entire community, through taxes.

---

[16] Ibid., p. 800.   [17] Thayer and Fernández (1981) pp. 31, 32.

Given these characteristics the juridical statute of the services rendered had to constitute a *duty of the state toward the inhabitants of the national territory,* which has been consecrated in some modern constitutions as the *right to social security.* In the context described, the application and exercise of the right to social security is the expression of the principle of the solidarity of the entire community toward its members in a state of need.

2.1.2   Political-democratic evaluation of the old social security system
The evidence just outlined exposes the importance of the underlying political model. In the first place, we assess the social democratic approach from the political point of view. This requires some conceptual background concerning equality and freedom.

The goal or principle of equality, in a pluralist democratic system, is not an isolated and independent value. It is related to the goal or principle of freedom, on which it depends in the final instance. In this sense, the literature establishes a lexicographic order, by which freedom comes first and is a necessary condition for equality. The social democratic approach to social security, previously enunciated, may be applied in different ways, and may or may not meet this relationship between freedom and equality. Thus, neither the universality, nor the integrality, nor the uniformity of a social security system is of itself incompatible with freedom; what can make each one incompatible is the manner in which it is applied. Freedom does not exclude solidarity, voluntary or coercively supported by the state, even when in the latter case the citizens must approve it through laws. In the final analysis, compatibility between solidarity and freedom will depend on the procedures adopted to configure the social security system.

From this political perspective, the old Chilean social security system failed to achieve both goals. It not only violated the democratic principle of equality, which was documented already, but also failed to meet the political goals related to freedom. The Prat Report provides overwhelming evidence that the various social security regimes already described emerged as the effects of political patronage phenomena, or clientelism. The successive appearance of groups protected by various social security regimes can be explained, in political terms, as the result of negotiations and transactions of social security benefits for political favors, which were considered social conquests of the group. In this manner, the beneficiaries, segmented in groups, became the clients of political leaders whom they supported, and with whom exchanges of mutual favors were established. In practice, the various special interest groups competed with each other to increase the benefits granted by those in political power, by means of parliamentary action or the action of the executive power. By this route, some groups managed to obtain premature retirement, subsidized credit, or pensions with privileged inflation adjustment. The patronage phenomenon was so evident that the higher management positions of many social security institutions were political parcels, which were distributed among members of the governing party or coalition of parties. In this manner, at the start of each presidential mandate those administrative positions and functions were distributed according to the political needs of the new government and its allies, seriously affecting the continuity of the institutions and the cost of their administration.

The participation of the state in the financing of social security had two effects on political goals (freedom and equality): On the one hand, the groups with social security, through political mediation, appropriated public resources in a nonegalitarian manner (each group obtained resources in proportion to its unequal political influence); and, on the other, the political intermediaries manipulated the freedom of the said groups, under standard patronage formulas. Patronage or clientelism was more serious in the case of public sector workers, because there the government currently in power fortified this relationship of favors exchanged between the governing party or parties and public employees. Clientelism, then, had effects on the freedom of its beneficiaries in general, who could be manipulated by the political class.

In addition, patronage also had effects on the *degrees of freedom* of those covered by the social security system. We are now dealing with a phenomenon related to the previous one, but more specific. In this clientelistic setting, the groups with the greater power and influence did so to the *disadvantage* of lesser groups. Thus, the democratic goal of equal freedom for all was affected by the reduced availability of resources for the great majority of the people who fell into states of need (they were concentrated in the SSS, which covered 64.8% of the total members of the system in 1979). In addition, lower-income groups depended to a greater extent upon public financing for their social security benefits. Thus, the majority only had available a minimal social security, which was extraordinarily dependent on the state and therefore, was even more manipulable by the governing coalition leadership than the social security of the average covered worker. The system, from the point of view of the dependency of people on the will of others, was configured in such a way that the largest group of members was subject to the greatest number of political control mechanisms, which prevented it from developing a strong negotiating power.

Among the instruments of control on the most unfavored pensioners were the periodic legislative discussions to revaluate pensions, which will be discussed in the first case study. An automatic inflation adjustment mechanism did not exist. Starting in 1952 (Law 10,343) there were regulations that prescribed periodic legislation to revaluate pensions, but these revaluations were fixed at between 25% and 90% of the increase in the cost of living during the previous year, depending on the size of the pension. In fact, the majority of the compensations that pensioners periodically received did not reflect the real increase in the cost of living and remained below the level of increase of the consumer price index.[18] As was previously mentioned, at the same time and in a parallel manner, there were certain privileged pensions that benefited the higher echelons of the public administration pensioners. Even they were subject to considerable uncertainty, as real adjustments fluctuated widely between individuals.[19] The legislative approval of revaluations, privileged pensions, or the extension of access to them constituted an instrument of periodic and systematic political manipulation.

There is enough empirical evidence to maintain that, during election periods, the governments and the political class intervened in the economic cycle. Recently, drawing upon the existing international literature on this topic,[20] Assael and Larraín have explored the past 50 years of the political economic cycle (PEC) in Chile (1939–1989). This cycle consists of the manipulation of economic variables that are instrumental in obtaining a political effect.[21] These authors consider that in order to achieve favorable electoral results for those in the government, the political authorities in charge of the economic sector could control, in a total or partial manner, the monetary, fiscal, and exchange rate variables.[22] The authors conclude, regarding this period, that the governments of Aguirre Cerda, Ríos, González Videla, Alessandri, and Frei manipulated the monetary and fiscal variables during the electoral cycles. A manipulation of the currency exchange policy is also observed during the governments of Ríos, Ibáñez, Alessandri, and Frei.[23]

Apart from the first case study here, there are no specific studies that document how and to what degree the political intervention in the economic cycle affected the social security system. But it can be maintained that it was globally affected because, in general, during the electoral cycle the patronage negotiations were intensified, and this translated into revaluations, readjustments, and benefits that, at times, disappeared during the next economic cycle. That is, at least it can be maintained that social security policy was dependant on the PEC.

Another important issue is the freedom of the privileged groups. The minority groups with the greatest capacity to negotiate with the political class

---

[18] The facts for 1924–1959 are available in *"Deterioro de las Pensiones,"* Report no. 8 of the Comisión de Estudios de la Seguridad Social (Prat Report), pp. 1153–1169, May 1961.

[19] Ibid.

[20] The dominant political business-cycle model was created by William Nordhaus and Edward Juffe. See also Weatherford (1988).

[21] Assael and Larraín (1993).   [22] Ibid., p. 23.

[23] Ibid., p. 26.

for the attainment of benefits were situated at the highest echelons of the system. These sectors, in the final analysis, had more freedom than the first. However, their degree of freedom was subject to agreements with the political class, so they had little freedom to question the overall social security system and to work out alternatives.

Finally, it is useful to mention that in the old system, the pensions that were paid to pensioners were financed by the current contributions of active workers, their employers, and the state. This distribution regime, supplemented with state financing, generated contradictory incentives. In legal terms, the pension base amount was related to the individual social security record of each beneficiary. But economically, this was a fiction since the system was *pay as you go,* that is, immediate financing by the active workers of the pensions for the inactive population. The incentive was not "save today to protect your future" but rather "pay today to finance the current inactive population and thus gain access to the right of having others, in future, do the same for you." The current interests of each active worker ceased to be compatible with his own future expectations when pensioners insisted that their benefits were unsatisfactory. In this uncertain setting, the current contribution became an expensive access fee to a risky and apparently meager future solidarity. This supported a trend toward a lack of social solidarity. The phenomenon just described had larger social implications, because solidarity is a basic asset of democracy from a practical political point of view.

2.2   The political basis of the new pension system

During the 1980s, a worldwide process of review of state intervention in civilian society took place. However, none of these processes emerged in a sudden manner. The crisis of egalitarian ideologies had begun already during the sixties, as well as criticism of the size of the state and welfare policies. On the other hand, reform processes favoring capitalism had begun in various countries around the world.

These modernizations were related to the dissemination of capitalism and its effects. Where capitalist institutions and practices were established, societies became more complex: more social heterogeneity, greater concentration of populations in urban zones, more extensive and accelerated educational development, and a strengthening of social fluidity.

The emergence of literate middle classes also translated into a demand for greater political participation. Paul Drake indicates that "in almost all of Latin America, the economic growth during the decade of the 70's increased the desire for consumption in the western style, for well-being, for progress and for democracy in the 80's."[24] During the Chilean military regime, the

---

[24] Drake (1993) p. 9.

demand for a type of economy capable of generating growth in consumption and economic well-being was very strong. There were also strong underlying forces supporting a return to democracy. For this reason the reforms carried out in Chile during that period had two characteristics: They were functional to a market economy and to capitalist institutions and, also, they were tacitly functional to liberal democracy, under its constitutional and representative form, as they relied heavily on the Rule of Law. Examples were liberalization of international trade, liberalization of most domestic prices, liberalization of financial contracts including interest rates, and privatization of many state-owned enterprises.

Regarding political reforms, the Chilean process of transition from authoritarianism to democracy over 1988–1990 resulted in a type of democratic system different from the old democratic regime that ended in 1973. One of the main differences lies in the greater degree of autonomy of the individual and civilian society as a whole from the state, the government, and the political class.

One of the reforms carried out in Chile during the authoritarian regime was the creation of a new pension system alongside the old one.[25] The old system has continued to function with some corrections. Starting from the basis that social security rights are nonextinguishable, the state allowed the workers that had contributed to the old system to choose between the old and the new pension systems. The new Chilean pension system is ideologically consistent with the economic and political reforms of the authoritarian regime.

In this period, the hesitation between ideological trends that had blocked pension reform disappeared, not only because the authoritarian regime did not allow other expressions and dislodged established pressure groups, but also for other reasons that in the long run have been shown to be important. The first is that by the 1970s the development of the capital markets allowed them to offer more acceptable saving and insurance vehicles than during the 1930s. This allowed private solutions, within the framework of a constitutional democratic regime, to several of the problems that originated with social security. The second is that a technically qualified elite had emerged in the country, which was able to put into practice public politics in the area of social security that were less state-oriented and relied more on capital market development.

2.2.1 Social security and property rights

The basis of the new pension system is the accumulation, in individual accounts, of the mandatory contributions periodically deposited in them, plus interest, for the purpose of constituting a personal capital to allow for the financing of the old-age pensions. Social security contributions for old age are 10% of earnings. Contributions to finance the system of disability and

---

[25] *El Ladrillo* (1992) pp. 129–136.

survivorship pensions are paid to insurance companies (around 0.80% of earnings).[26] The old-age pension funds, owned by the holders of the individual accounts, are administered by private firms called administradoras de fondos de pensiones, AFP (pension funds administrators). Administrative charges averaging 2.20% of earnings are paid to the AFP. This is a defined contribution regime, in contrast with the standard defined benefit system. The full return is allocated to individual returns, so diversification across investments and over time is relied upon to provide stability. The defined benefit approach exposes workers to the risk of a low final wage, on which benefits are based, and must pay an implicit fee to the agents that provide the guarantee on investment returns.

Individuals entering the system have several *degrees of freedom*. The first is to choose and change AFP. Individuals may also choose to make voluntary contributions in excess of the mandatory 10% to increase their capitalization fund, which allows them to finance an early retirement. In addition, once the accumulation cycle is completed, individuals are allowed to choose between assuming the financial risk of their own longevity, or insuring against the financial cost of longevity by acquiring a life annuity pension from an insurance company chosen by the individuals themselves. These annuities must be indexed to the CPI, and offer additional options such as bequests.

The Chilean system is based on the *individual ownership* of the accumulated resources and on the *maximization of profits*, which in this case means the maximization of the return on investment. The state acts in a supplementary manner, regulating the private firms that manage the pension funds to prevent fraud and more generally to assure that they fulfill their role. These topics are discussed in more detail now.

Individual ownership: An important feature of the new pension system is private ownership of contributions and the return earned. This allows accumulation to be strongly protected by the laws governing property rights. In Chile property rights had been weakened during the 1960s, as a result of the reforms made to the constitution with the purpose of allowing uncompensated nationalization of the large copper-mining establishments and medium-sized and large agricultural estates. In addition, during the regime of President Allende, previously unused law decrees inherited from a brief socialist period in 1932 were used by the executive power to allow a move toward socialism, weakening property rights even further. A new constitution passed in 1980 restored the protections to property rights and the juridical certainty they had lost. In this new setting, the owners of individual accounts have full juridical protection for the decisions related to their utilization.

---

[26] Valdés-Prieto and Navarro (1992).

Although the individual also has rights regarding the pension benefits promised by public defined benefit pension systems, which can be defended in court, those rights have substantially less protection than private ownership, as shown by the history of legislative changes to the present value of pension benefits that have been adopted in many democratic countries.

Maximization of returns: The ownership of the accounts of the new Chilean pension system is related to the strong incentive offered by the expectation of accumulation. A fundamental role is played by the perception that a sacrifice is made today to obtain an asset that is juridically certain in the future. Each member of the system knows that the level of his pension is directly proportional to the balance accumulated in his account. He also knows that his resources are protected by the right of ownership (which allows him to change to whichever AFP better manages his resources), and by the regulatory powers of the state, which oversees the efficient and transparent investment of his resources. Finally, he knows that his resources are administered by private firms that are pushed by competition to maximize their financial yields. Each AFP competes to interpret better the dynamism of maximization of profits that spontaneously motivates the owner of each account.

2.2.2 State, mandatory contributions, and regulation

The new system is mandatory. The state forces the working population to make contributions to individual accounts. Starting from this basis of coercion, the individuals exercise rights of ownership, with limitations, in the use of their accumulated resources. Each person chooses the AFP where he wishes to open his account and, in addition, is free to change to another (after a minimum stay of four months). However, he cannot dispose freely of the accumulated contributions. We saw that retirement savings have the status of an asset on which the right of ownership is exercised. It is, then, a *private asset*. However, its use is limited, as the law says it can only be destined to finance certain states of need when these occur, that is, in the future. We now offer some thoughts on the relationship between this institution and the democratic system.

The fact that the state establishes that the contributions to the social security system are mandatory means that the existence of the pension system is guaranteed by law (by the exercise of coercion). The state has committed itself to safeguard or ensure, as a collective duty, the provision of material means to satisfy the vital needs in cases of misfortune, illness, disability, and old age of the inhabitants of the country. This approach is consistent with some of the legal trends that emerged during the 19th century and has become broadly widespread during our century. The assumption of those trends is that the attendance to the *states of need* is a solidary task of society as a whole; and that the state is in charge of institutionalizing it and making it a reality.

The constitutions of the modern democratic states have included, throughout this century, prescriptive norms in this regard. There are nations that assign to the state the obligation of establishing social security.[27] Others, like Denmark, establish the "right to assistance from the authorities" for all those "who are not in conditions to provide for their subsistence and that of their dependents."[28] The Chilean constitution includes the "right to social security" in the chapter on constitutional duties and rights. There, after establishing that social security is a *right*, it reads that "the action of the state shall be directed to guarantee the access of all the inhabitants to the enjoyment of basic uniform services, be it that these are granted through public or private institutions. The Law may establish mandatory contributions."[29] The compulsory nature of the contributions and the limitations in the use of the accumulated resources express the idea that the state safeguards the obligation of the community: the social solidarity with the *states of need* of its members.

This approach may be contrasted with the radical libertarian thesis of a minimum state, where the obligation to face the states of need is individual. In this perspective, private ownership of the social security accounts is appropriate, but not the compulsory nature of the contributions or the limitations on their use. Said in a different way, for this thesis, the individuals have the right not to anticipate their eventual *states of need.* Through a social learning process of trial and error, for example, the individuals might come to realize that lack of anticipated planning might mean loss of freedom for themselves, for reasons of indigence and dependency on others, benefactors or not. According to this position, the state would have no other function than to guarantee the inviolability of the ownership of the social security savings and the intangibility of contracts. Each person would be free to choose whether he saves for his social security or not; and if he chooses to do so, he would also be free to dispose of the accumulated resources at any moment, or as allowed by a savings contract freely entered into.

We submit that this radical thesis should not be accepted. It appears that the community has some right to anticipate that the incontinence in current spending, and the lack of anticipated planning of individuals, may have adverse effects on society, considered as a whole. In case of a decision of not planning ahead for the states of need, the individual that falls into one of them would have no other option but to resort to the aid of others. And there would always be humanitarian persons or groups that would try to fulfill the

---

[27] Daranas (1979); Federal Austrian Constitution, art. 10, no. 11, p. 243; and Spanish Constitution, art. 41, p. 747.

[28] Daranas (1979); Constitution of the Kingdom of Denmark, art. 75, p. 697.

[29] Political Constitution of the Republic of Chile (1993) art. 18.

duties of aid, for whom inanition of others is morally and humanely intolerable. On these persons and groups would fall, in a random manner, a burden that could be distributed in a more suitable manner if society as a whole assumes these duties. This form of cooperation, on the other hand, prevents the people that receive the aid from falling into potential servitude, losing their autonomy and independence. For these reasons, social cooperation to face these situations seems to be required.

This reasoning should not be confused with the concept of the *welfare state*, because it does not rely on the principle of equality and does not impose administration by the state. It is also different from anthropological considerations (pessimistic concepts of human nature, the evil tendencies of which must be corrected by the state), and from cultural arguments (negligence of individuals to take charge of their own destiny, due to low cultural, social, and educational levels, and consequent inability to plan ahead for and face the situations of need). In this manner, we justify some intervention by the state, as an instrument of social cooperation. This reasoning does not justify the manner in which this intervention has occurred in regimes of socialist and social democrat type.

An intermediate position, in the sense of increasing the autonomy of people, has been expounded by one of us (Valdés-Prieto, 1994). His argument maintains that the law falsely assumes that *all* workers are unable to plan ahead and that, under that assumption, *all* are forced to surrender the administration of their social security savings to the AFPs. However, as AFPs are subject to strong regulatory action of the state, such dependence has dangers: The regulations could be increased; governing party pressure might induce regulators to influence the voting decisions of AFPs in shareholder meetings, in order to orient the board of private companies to favor their political supporters and to help party financing; individual responsibility may be weakened by this transfer of the decision-making process on savings for old age to the statutes and the political process; and finally, compulsory social security savings may be less valuable than voluntary retirement savings because they cannot be used as precautionary saving. This author proposes specific rules for individual exemption from the compulsory nature of contributions.[30]

[30] Valdés-Prieto (1994). He proposes to allow provident workers to claim an exemption from mandatory contributions, based on a self-selection principle. The requirement for exemption is that the workers must have made voluntary contributions – in excess of the mandatory 10% of earnings – to the old-age individual account, according to a savings program with the following features: (1) there is a maximum monthly voluntary contribution valid for exemption requirements. This maximum could be set at, say, 10% of monthly earnings. (2) Cumulative voluntary contributions must exceed the equivalent of, say, 4 months of the average monthly earnings over the last 10 years. Only an individual that plans ahead could meet these requirements, and they are tight enough so that no consumer credit company can arbitrage around it.

Regulation: From the perspective of democratic development, the most innovative aspect of the new Chilean social security system is the relationship between the ownership of social security savings and the activity of the state.

The state makes it mandatory to belong to a social security regime, but together with that obligation, it assumes duties. The first, as we have seen, is to protect the individual property rights over the accumulated resources. But, in addition, the state acts as a supervisor so that the funds be duly administered by the AFPs, and their utilization in the capital markets be transparent and subjected to the least possible risk for given return. The regulatory activity of the State is *increased* as compared with standard public systems where the functions of supervision and operation have not been separated explicitly.

This regulatory activity could be interpreted under two different lights: as protection of the ownership of individual capitalization accounts, or as a result of delegation by the community of its aspiration to share the responsibility in the face of states of need of its own members.

This last interpretation is a complex one. The solidarity of the standard pay-as-you-go financed social security system seems obvious: The resources contributed by the active population, at every moment, finance the states of need of those currently affected by them. And the mechanism can be redistributive (when it works properly, which was not the Chilean case). Thus, the standard system may achieve egalitarian goals. In the individual capitalization system, the solidarity is of a different nature: The state sustains and guarantees the existence of a system that produces old-age, disability, and survivorship pensions for all. It takes care of the egalitarian demands by using subsidies to guarantee minimum pensions financed with general taxation, so that if the accumulated balance in the capitalization account is not sufficient for an old-age pension, taxpayers finance the remainder. Also, in certain cases of disability and premature death of workers with a short record of contributions, the insurance premium is financed by contributors and the owners of AFPs.[31]

The capitalization system emphasizes individual responsibility and provides incentives and instruments with which to maximize individual interests. In it, the individual does not consider himself to be protected by the state from birth to death. Instead, he demands from the state the juridical instruments and the freedoms necessary to preserve his property, understood as an extension of himself and a product of his work.

3   Social security and autonomy: Two case studies

This section offers two cases on the politics of Chilean pensions, to compare the old and the new pension systems that currently function in the new

---

[31] Cheyre (1991) p. 152.

democratic environment established in Chile since 1988, its main difference with the old democratic system being the greater degree of autonomy from the state. This exercise is superior to international comparisons because it controls for the overall political environment. In this sense, the period 1988–1993 provides a natural experiment in the politics of pensions. To stress the common environment, we offer first a short summary of the constitutional provisions under which both systems coexist.

3.1   Protection of pension rights: The political setting after 1985

Past experience and the need to provide autonomy for the people led the 1980 constituents to establish special constitutional norms to protect the social security system from the opportunistic conduct of the political class. In the final analysis, efforts were made to make the social and economic existence of the system independent from the PEC.

The constitution of 1980 establishes the basis of social security in an article that is protected by a quorum of two-thirds.[32] Elsewhere, the same document indicates that "the laws that regulate" the exercise of the right to social security "shall require qualified quorum" to be approved – that is, an absolute majority of all members.[33] Another constitutional disposition ensures equality before the law, in the sense that "there are no privileged persons or groups; neither the Law nor any authority whatsoever may establish arbitrary differences."[34] In addition, the constitutional system limits the initiative on laws concerning social security to the executive power (presidency), so that parliamentarians may not initiate legislation by themselves in the old public social security system or in the new pension system. Finally, the Congress does not have the power to initiate law on matters that involve public spending, which include the pension benefits of the old pension system, minimum pensions (partially noncontributory), and assistance pensions (noncontributory).

Other aspects of the political environment of this period include relatively independent courts, political movements, and parties that routinely expose abuses to public opinion, a Constitutional Tribunal that can strike down laws deemed unconstitutional, and a General Accounting Office that controls the legality of laws and regulations.

In 1988 there was a referendum that refused Mr. Augusto Pinochet's offer to continue as president for eight more years. In 1980–1989 there was no elected Parliament and the legislative function was performed by the military junta. In late 1989 an open presidential election took place, in which Mr. Patricio Aylwin was elected and an elected Parliament was put in place. In

---

[32] Political Constitution of the Republic of Chile (1993) art. 116, pp. 78–79.
[33] Ibid., art. 17, p. 24.   [34] Ibid., art. 19, no. 2, p. 16.

1992 there were municipal elections throughout the country. In late 1993 there was another open presidential and parliamentary election, won by Mr. Eduardo Frei Ruiz-Tagle.

3.2   Case study 1: Cost of living adjustments to pension benefits in the old pension system, 1979–1993.[35]

Cost of living adjustments (COLAs) to pensions are interesting to study because they are one of the aspects of property rights to pension benefits in the old system that are not protected by the constitution. Following international traditions, a law of 1981 interpreted the constitution that only the nominal pension is protected, not its purchasing power.[36]

3.2.1   Pension revaluation in Chile

The two Chilean pension systems have different inflation indexation mechanisms.[37] In the new pension system, pensions are adjusted every month for the CPI change during the previous month. In the case of annuities, a monthly revaluation must be included in the insurance policy contracts. In the case of programmed withdrawals, an automatic monthly revaluation is established in the pension law, apart from the fact that the amount of the pension is recalculated every 12 months.

In the old pension system, the revaluations of the four main groups – blue-collar workers, white-collar workers, public employees, and armed forces – were governed by different laws and mechanisms. Diversity was widespread within these groups (Report No. 8 Prat Commission). In 1974, a decree law unified the first three revaluation systems.[38] In 1979, another decree law unified the fourth group and eliminated the *perseguidora* revaluation system.[39] Since 1979 to the present, revaluations in the old system have been uniform, except in the instances to be discussed. The full list of uniform revaluations is provided in Table 3.A.2 of the appendix.

---

[35] We are grateful to Mr. Carlos Salineros, consultant to the Budget Office, for the information he has provided. He is not responsible for any of the interpretations contained here, which are entirely ours. Professors G. Wagner and F. Coloma contributed useful observations to this section.

[36] Law 18,252 of Chile. This is also the case in the United States. In that country, the Supreme Court held in 1960 (*Flemming v. Nestor*, 363 US 610) that retirees have no contractual right to their promised social security benefits despite their past payments into the system, and that Congress has the power to reduce or cut off the program's benefits to any or all the elderly at any time (Ferrera, 1985, p. 193).

[37] Minimum pensions and assistance pensions are adjusted to inflation according to discretionary annual legislation. We do not consider those pensions.

[38] Decree Law 670, Diario Oficial, October 2, 1974.

[39] Decree Law 2448, Diario Oficial, February 9, 1979.

In the old pension system indexation is governed by both legislated rules and legislated discretionary revaluations. From 1924 to 1951 there were no laws regarding revaluation, but inflation was always below 10% except in 1932. In 1952 the first revaluation law set the timing and magnitude of revaluations, but the magnitude was set below the change in the CPI so it lost relevance. Thereafter, political bargaining centered on legislated discretionary revaluations. Starting in December 1974, the government legislated full adjustment to past CPI inflation.[40] However, the timing was fixed for specific months of 1975, without establishing a permanent timing formula.

It was only in 1979 that both the timing and the magnitude of revaluations were fixed in a permanent law.[41] This legislation, which applied up to September 1986, established a cost of living adjustment (revaluation) for the full change in the CPI since the previous revaluation. Its timing was fixed in either June 30 of each year, or when the cumulative CPI change since the previous revaluation surpassed 15%. This was interpreted by the Contraloría (General Accounting Office) and later ratified by a law,[42] as saying that either mechanism could be used in each calendar year. If a revaluation occurred in June, then no other revaluation could be granted until January 1 of the next year, even if cumulative inflation since June was above 15%.

We discuss now the politics of revaluations for pensions in the old system, starting in 1985.

3.2.2   The 10.6% revaluation freeze
In May 1985, the government issued a law that declared that it would skip a part of the revaluation that was coming due in the old system according to the automatic legislation. The amount to be skipped was 10.6% of pensions. This created a political storm that concluded only in 1992.

Finance Minister Büchi argued that the freeze was equitable because real wages had suffered a fall of 20% during the recession of 1982–1985, while pensions had maintained their full purchasing power. However, the opposition pointed out that given the very low level of pensions paid by the old system, this policy was inhumane. The freeze covered minimum and assistance pensions, buttressing the argument that this policy was inequitable and an abuse of power. In addition, those workers who had chosen to stay in the old system argued they had been betrayed by a change in the rules. The issue grew into an important political banner against Pinochet and Büchi in the elections of 1988 and 1989.

Diamond and Valdés-Prieto (1993) discuss the hypothesis that a pension reform leaves those that remain in the old system in a weak political position,

---

[40] See Decree Law 670.   [41] See Decree Law 2448.
[42] See Law 18,549 of 1986.

because their pensions become a visible prime target for deficit reduction. They argue that this hypothesis was not borne out by the Chilean experience, because in the early 1980s the government did not follow the traditional practice of reducing real pensions when the budget worsens. Fiscal policy changes were timed early into the recession of 1982–1985: General taxes were raised in April 1982 and public investment was slashed during 1982, but the purchasing power of pensions was preserved. Only in 1985, after severe recession had reduced real wages substantially, were the pensions of the old system cut.

A more convincing hypothesis may be that the 10.6% freeze was a political mistake, not part of a political equilibrium. This was shown in the 1986 revaluation, to be discussed, and in the 1987 and 1988 revaluations, where the government attempted to regain lost political ground even though the budget cost was significant.

In January 1986 the military junta approved a discretionary early revaluation. In September the government approved a law[43] that declared that a revaluation worth 8.8% was due in July 1986, which would compensate for the CPI inflation of the first semester; and that the timing of automatic revaluations was reformed so that they would occur only in the event that cumulative past inflation since the last revaluation surpassed 15%. The second part was designed in anticipation of a reduction in average inflation rates.

In 1990, full restoration of the lost 10.6% became one of the top political priorities of the newly elected Aylwin government. Minimum pensions and assistance pensions had the 10.6% restored first, in July 1990. Parliament restored the 10.6% in full to all pensions in the old system,[44] according to a schedule based on the pension's value: starting in July 1991 for pensions below Ch.$80,000/month; starting in July 1992 for pensions between Ch.$80,001 and Ch.$120,000; and starting in December 1992 for pensions above Ch.$120,000.

This differential timing of restoration followed the tradition of discretionary redistributions in the old pension system. This has an electoral motivation and suggests that these tendencies of the old pension system continue to exist even in the new political order. Of course the fact that this happened under a military regime facilitated the arbitrary use of power over the old system.

3.2.3 Differential revaluations in 1987 and 1988

In 1987 and 1988, special laws imposed "differential revaluations." These revaluations followed a scheme that increased the real value of low pensions, but reduced the real value of high pensions and disability and survivor pensions, as shown in Table 3.A.1 of the appendix.

---

[43] Law 18,549 of September 1986.   [44] Law 19,073 of July 31, 1991.

At first sight, the reason for these two revaluations may appear to be electoral manipulation, in the tradition of the PEC. This is an especially attractive hypothesis for the second one, which was given five months before the referendum in which President Pinochet's continuation in power was rejected.

However, close scrutiny of the figures suggests that this is incorrect. The slightly higher revaluation for low pensions is not significant in total expenditure. Moreover, the text of Law 18,549 is explicit in that the purpose of the differential revaluations was to reduce government expenditure on pensions of the old system, because of fiscal and macroeconomic reasons.

Nevertheless, the higher revaluation for lower pensions provided a convenient presentation as a progressive measure. The authorities also argued that the higher revaluations for lower pensions was an important step to give back the purchasing power of the 10.6% skipped in 1985.

These attempts to distort the perceptions of the public opinion were successful. They allowed the remarkable feat of a substantial reduction in government expenditure in a setting with a slight budget surplus, with no opposition from the leftist political opposition. In the right-wing parties, the favorable electoral implications of the higher revaluations for low pensions swamped any quibbles about the higher pensions.[45]

Although manipulation of the public opinion's perception was not the primary aim of differential revaluations, it certainly was a requirement imposed by politicians to allow a reduction in pension expenditure. This suggests that the old system continues to exhibit tendencies contrary to democratic development.

3.2.4 The Special of 1989

As the presidential and parliamentary election of December 1989 drew closer, it became clear that skipping the 10.6% revaluation of 1985 had been very costly to the military government in political terms. Few voters had bought the notion that the higher revaluations for low pensions of 1987 and 1988 were a meaningful recovery of the lost 10.6%

The political damage prompted the military junta to approve a law that established a special real increase in pensions (see Table 3.1). The law established that this increase would not produce a delay of the next revaluation.

This increase benefited most pensioners of the old pension system, because over 60% of them received the minimum pension or less. Starting in July 1989 the minimum pension was Ch.$15,015.35 for those under age 70 and Ch.$16,045.10 for those over 70.

[45] These laws were approved by the military junta, not by an elected Parliament. Contrary to what might be supposed, this made the policy harder to approve, not easier, because a large share of the higher pensions in the old system are held by retired colonels and generals.

Table 3.1
The special real increase in pensions of June 1989

Type of Pension (Ch.$/month)	Real Increase
All men aged 65 and over, with pensions smaller than $21,000:	5%
All women aged 60 and over, with pensions smaller than $21,000:	5%
Those that met age requirement, with pensions between $21,000 and $21,000x(1.05):	Increase to $21,000x(1.05)
All others:	0%

Source: Law 18,806.

Because of the timing, this was a clear attempt to influence the electorate, in the tradition of the PEC. This suggests that manipulative increases to pensions continue to be a feature of the old pension system, with the associated delay of democratic development.

3.2.5   New legislation for timing of revaluations in 1992–1993

The legislated timing for revaluations established that when cumulative CPI inflation reaches 15%, a COLA would be due. As inflation is stochastic, the formula implies a stochastic timing of revaluations. In 1992–1993, the political system reformed this timing formula again.

In three recent years, 1988, 1992, and 1993, CPI inflation was only 12% to 13%. The result was that more months than normal had to pass until the next revaluation came due. In 1988 apparently no politician proposed that a minimum annual frequency be legislated, even though inflation was low in that year. The lack of interest in such a reform by government authorities is puzzling, given that a referendum was fought in August of that year. In 1992 things were different. Politicians argued that, if the country was being successful in reducing inflation, it was unfair that pensioners should "suffer through a delayed revaluation" (*La Cuarta,* October 20, 1993).[46]

In November 1992 Parliament approved the law that ordered a special revaluation for December 1992, anticipating the programmed revaluation. However, as inflation in November 1992 turned out to be higher than ex-

---

[46] Economic analysis shows that a timing rule such as "a revaluation is due when cumulative inflation reaches 15%" yields an average real pension that is independent of the level of inflation, for the case where inflation is not discontinuous. This is because the delay in getting a revaluation is compensated by the delay in the reduction of the real pension just after the revaluation. Therefore, it is not true that pensioners are worse off when inflation stabilizes at a lower level.

pected, in December cumulative inflation reached 15.05% and the provisions of this special law coincided with the general timing formula.

The notable point here is that the government proposed a discretionary special revaluation, rather than a reform to the permanent timing formula, even though the existence of a permanent problem was clearly recognized and offered as the reason for reform. Instead, the government took advantage of its exclusivity to initiate pension legislation by presenting Parliament with only a special revaluation, making sure that the same problem would arise again in 1993. Presidential and parliamentary elections were to be held in December 1993 – evidence of sophisticated electoral timing of this reform to the timing of revaluations.

The impact of this reform for pensioners goes beyond manipulation of public opinion because it also raises average real pensions. This can be seen in that the reform brought forward the next revaluation from March or April of 1994 to the first days of December 1993, eliminating the months with lower real pensions in the revaluation cycle. The purposeful avoidance of permanent reform in 1992 suggests that a real increase of pensions of the old system just before the election had been under preparation since 1992.

The reform to the permanent timing formula was finally enacted in November.[47] According to this law a revaluation will be due when either 12 months have passed since the previous adjustment, or the cumulative CPI change since the previous revaluation surpasses 15%. Note that this formula avoids the interpretation problems associated with the 1979 law.

Summing up, this case study shows that political and electoral manipulation of pension revaluations for the old pension system is still possible in Chile. Therefore, there is evidence for the hypothesis that the global design of the old pension system induces behavior that is contrary to democratic development. The behavior of the 1950s and 1960s cannot be assigned to the political regime of the time only, but appears linked to the intrinsic design of the old system also. The more intensive degree of manipulation on the one hand and the abuse of power on the other observed in 1985–1989 may be explained by the concentration of power in the military government.

3.3   Case study 2: The default on ENACAR bonds

In the new pension system, other forms of conflictive tensions with the state have arisen. These tensions reveal the type of relations that are beginning to be established between the state and the new social security system. The following case study is extraordinarily revealing.[48] Through it we can under-

---

[47] Law 19,262 of November 11, 1993.

[48] We thank Mr. Santiago Edwards, Mr. Sergio Henríquez, and Mr. José Ramón Valente for their cooperation in providing the information needed for this case study. They are not responsible for any interpretation given to the facts.

stand the high degree of autonomy that the new social security institutions (AFPs) enjoy and how they safeguard the interests of their members.

This episode occurred in 1992, after Chile returned to constitutional democracy. ENACAR is a state-owned coal company located in Lota, near the city of Concepción. It has been operating at a loss since the 1950s. It has been kept in operation because it is the only source of employment in Lota, and coal miners are poor and politically well organized. ENACAR employed close to 5,000 people in 1990. The corporate bond market in Chile includes all tradable debt securities with maturity above 1 year that are not issued by commercial banks or the government. The modern corporate bond market is relatively new, as borrowers came to use it strongly only since 1987.

3.3.1   The Origins of ENACAR's bond issue

When the Aylwin government took power in 1990, it replaced the board and management in ENACAR with persons closer to the new ruling coalition. At the beginning of 1991, ENACAR's new management convinced CORFO, the state holding company and its legal owner, that ENACAR had a chance to earn some profits if an investment program was undertaken. This required reorganization of its debts, most of which were short term, owed to banks, and guaranteed by CORFO. CORFO accepted the plan, in part because of the political clout of the new board of ENACAR.

In addition, some managers at CORFO saw this as an opportunity to bind ENACAR through the covenants included in bond contracts, so they insisted that the financial reorganization had to occur by issuing bonds rather than long-term debt to commercial banks. The bond covenants on which CORFO insisted were in the end just five, and one of them required that the ratio of obligations to equity be kept below 1.5. The penalty was acceleration of the full principal amount.

3.3.2   Conditions imposed by AFPs, the private managers
of pension funds

Private investors, specifically pension fund managers, conditioned purchase of the bonds to the existence of a CORFO guarantee. It was obvious that ENACAR could not provide reasonable security. Their lawyers concentrated on CORFO and, as they were wary of it, went to the extreme of requiring that CORFO's legal representative sign each individual coupon of the bond, acknowledging the guarantee. As is usual in these cases, the face value of the bonds was set above the selling price to limit the likelihood of prepayment by ENACAR. In this case the face value was set at 108.7% of the selling price.

The ENACAR bonds were sold in mid 1991. Only 50% of the issue was sold to pension funds, and only a few of them purchased the bond. Three of the four largest fund managers did not purchase. The other buyers were a large life insurance company and several mutual funds controlled by commercial banks.

3.3.3   Violation of bond covenants

ENACAR continued generating losses, which reduced its equity. By December 1991, 6 months after the issue, the ratio of obligations to equity reached 1.54. ENACAR failed to report the event as covenants forced it to, and CORFO did not notice – nor did the external auditor (it was fined later because of this), the representative of bondholders (a local bank), or any investors. In the next quarter the ratio rose to 1.7 and when the accounting data were reported in May 1992, the breach was noticed by one of the pension fund managers.

When this was realized, the board and management of ENACAR were fired amid a scandal. This helped those who were pushing for a restructuring of ENACAR. However, this turned out to be an inefficient method to control ENACAR, as shown by the legal battles that followed.

In the ensuing political storm, the Ministry of Finance, including the Superintendency of Securities and Insurance, the Superintendency of Pension Funds, and the rest of the government refused to take sides overtly, leaving the authorities in CORFO to fight alone. The Superintendency of Pension Funds declared that pension fund managers were required by law to act in the best interests of account holders and refused to participate further. The Superintendency of Securities suspended transaction of ENACAR bonds in the stock exchange, hurting bondholders to some extent and weakening the legal position of CORFO.

3.3.4   The legal fight

An acceleration of the bond and immediate payment would allow investors to earn an unexpected profit, because the obligation that came due was the face value of the bond. The difference with the placement value was close to US$2.5 million.

Several creditors requested an immediate payment of the bonds guaranteed by CORFO. The notable point is that most of the aggressive creditors were pension fund managers. They requested from the courts an immediate payment and argued in the press that their fiduciary obligation was to extract this profit. The life insurance company was also aggressive.

CORFO contested the required payment in the courts, arguing that the "executive procedure" to force payment by a debtor should apply only in instances of nonpayment of interest and principal, not when the obligations originated in a failure to meet a covenant. CORFO's main short-term objective was to avoid the "executive procedure" and obtain instead the ordinary procedure, which can take three or more years and make the covenants much less enforceable.

CORFO used every argument it could find to convince judges not to grant the executive procedure. Even though creditors petitioned three different judges, CORFO was successful in having two of them rule that the executive procedure did not apply. This happened in part because of the inexperience of Chilean judges in the securities laws. However, some arm twisting of judges seems to have existed. CORFO is an influential state organism that controls many companies, and its political friends and economic dependents have some power to influence the promotion of judges and the promotion of the relatives of judges.

There was one pension fund manager, AFP Protección, that obtained the approval of the executive procedure. However, CORFO appealed and the appeal was granted. After a couple of months of litigation, pension fund managers became convinced that the legal battle with CORFO could easily take 3 years. CORFO had won.

3.3.5   Renegotiation of covenants
CORFO argued that, in ENACAR's case, a relaxation of bond covenants was the standard commercial procedure. Pension fund managers countered that their risk was much higher now, because CORFO's guarantee was being proved untrustworthy and covenants unenforceable. As pension fund managers refused to accept a renegotiation of covenants, CORFO offered all investors to purchase back the bond at the issue price minus interest already paid. Simultaneously, it pursued the strategy of legal obstruction just explained.

One explanation for the unwillingness of pension fund managers to relax bond covenants is that their relative financial performance was to be decided by the outcome of this case. According to this explanation, the fact that most large pension funds did not hold ENACAR bonds was a major incentive to behave aggressively for those pension funds that did hold these bonds.

In the bondholders meeting, several pension fund managers proposed that they sue CORFO collectively, in addition to the individual suits. However, the mutual fund managers controlled by banks blocked this proposal. They also seemed more pliable to renegotiation demands. A widespread interpretation is that commercial banks were unwilling to compromise their relationships with CORFO and the state-owned companies it controls. In addition, the alternative was for banks to lend on their own account to ENACAR, with a fat spread. Both explanations imply that banks, acting as mutual fund managers, failed to meet their fiduciary obligations to their investors. However, there was no investigation or penalty from the Superintendency of Securities in this connection.

AFP Protección, the only pension fund manager that had been successful in obtaining an executive court order that forced CORFO to pay, was the first pension fund manager to back down and accept the deal CORFO was offering. One explanation for this is that the management of this firm – owned by a French group – did not wish to have a dispute with an official body like CORFO, with a view to its other investments in Chile. Another explanation is that AFP Protección acknowledged that CORFO's legal position was solid. The first hypothesis would imply that this pension fund manager failed to meet its fiduciary obligations to members, but there was no investigation in this connection.

3.3.6 Risk ratings

The ENACAR bonds were subject to three continuous risk ratings, by the semipublic Pension Fund Risk Classification Commission (RCC) and by two private risk-rating agencies. In mid-1991, when the ENACAR bonds were issued, ENACAR debts were given a rating of D by the RCC, which was raised to B due to the CORFO guarantee. The rating was not A because the law that governs the RCC establishes that guarantees can improve ratings by at most two grades.

Three out of five members of the semipublic RCC are elected by the pension fund managers, but recall that only a few had invested in ENACAR bonds. The two public sector members are the superintendent of pension fund managers and the superintendent of securities and insurance. In addition, as required by law, two private risk-rating companies were classifying this bond continuously. Both were hired by ENACAR.

The RCC and the risk-rating companies had the opportunity to reclassify the ENACAR bonds in May, June, July, August, and September of 1992. None of them did so, even though the risk of lending to ENACAR had increased and the quality of CORFO's guarantee appeared to be less than originally estimated.

The main reason, at least for the private risk-rating firms,[49] was the opinion of prominent lawyers that CORFO's ability to obtain court delays was limited to obligations coming due because of the acceleration of covenants, and did not extend to obligations of interest and amortizations coming due because of the normal schedule of payments. As the purpose of risk classification is to assess the probability of timely payment of interest and amortizations, the rating should not depend on the probability of meeting the additional obligations that come due in case a covenant is violated. This makes sense, because normally the acceleration clause is meant to force the debtor to renegotiate, not to obtain full payment.

[49] Another issue, which we discard, is that a downgrading of ENACAR bonds affects the portfolio limits that pension funds must meet by law, forcing them to sell. This is erroneous because the law allows a 12-month period to sell after portfolio limits are violated.

Of course, this justification presumes a belief in CORFO's position that it wanted to pay the bond coupons as promised, but it did not want to pay a fat profit of 8.7% to bondholders just because ENACAR had failed to meet a covenant.

3.3.7   The outcome for CORFO and ENACAR

In the end, the other pension funds and the insurance company decided to accept CORFO's offer, especially since its value had increased because of a rise in market interest rates. The mutual funds also sold. CORFO paid with the proceeds of a long-term loan given by a consortium of commercial banks, which charged a spread higher than the original one.

3.3.8   Longer-term outcomes

After this episode, the government diagnosed that the bond market was not functioning properly, as many of the actors had failed to act as expected. The authorities proposed legislation to regulate in much more detail the obligations and functions of issuers, underwriters, the representative of bondholders, the custodial bank, and external auditors. This proposal has been discussed in Congress and was approved in January 1994.

A specific proposal related to the case of ENACAR bonds is that the individual bondholder's right to sue the issuer would be restricted to events of nonpayment of capital and interests, including penal interest. However, the execution of acceleration clauses originated in violation of covenants or any other cause[50] are proposed to require collective suits endorsed by a majority (50%) agreement of the bondholders' meeting. In the proposal, at least 50% of the bonds must be represented in the first call for this meeting, but there is no minimum quorum for the meeting in a second call.

The reasoning behind this proposal is the same used by risk-rating agencies and CORFO: Acceleration clauses are meant to force the debtor to negotiate with the community of bondholders, not with each of them individually. However, as the pressure to renegotiate may be too weak if a very slow ordinary judicial procedure, as in Chile, is applied, the covenants may be rendered useless. The jury is out to evaluate this legal reform.

3.3.9   Conclusions

This case study raises an important issue: What is the political role of private pension fund managers? Observers agree that, as shown by this case study,

---

[50] A controversial change is that the right to request the bankruptcy of an issuer, and to propose an agreement with all creditors, would not be available any more to an individual bondholder, if a valid bondholder's meeting orders the representative of bondholders to bargain with the debtor with a majority of at least two-thirds. Some observers think that in cases of bankruptcy, this will weaken bondholders as compared with other creditors.

AFPs behaved independently and pushed for the rights of their members, without fear of a fight with the political establishment. This case study shows that Chilean AFPs are not controlled by their regulators. This role is positive for democratic development because individual members are protected from state interference on their pensions. It is very unlikely that a state-controlled pension fund manager could fulfill this role.

A second conclusion is that the strong defense by pension fund managers of the rights of members is feasible because the new pension system grants property rights to members and life insurance companies, allowing them or their fiduciaries (AFPs) to request protection from the courts, limiting the power of the executive branch. This defense was encouraged by the democratic environment available since 1990. In fact, a fight with CORFO would have been unlikely in 1984 or 1985, when the military government held more influence over the judiciary and exercised direct control over several of the AFPs and life insurance companies because they were subject to bankruptcy proceedings.

In addition, this conflict encouraged the benevolent forces within the political establishment to react constructively by improving the legal infrastructure for the bond market. This suggests that active support of members' rights is helpful for economic development, in addition to democratic development.

A third conclusion is that the new pension system has begun to solve one of the main obstacles for efficient political representation of the long-term interest of workers in good management of the pension system. AFPs acted as powerful intermediaries, willing to represent the collective interest of millions of dispersed members in the legal battles that are regularly needed to defend their interests.

General conclusions

This chapter discusses the relative vulnerability of individuals confronted with the decisions of government agencies regarding their pension system, in different settings. Empirical evidence from Chile is used to provide comparisons.

The issue is analyzed first in the context of a welfare state. The political acceptability of the significant power of politicians and bureaucrats found in such a welfare state is put in the context of the social democratic political model, whose key feature is centralization of political decision making in exchange for an increase in equality. The old Chilean pension system was based on this political model. It is found that the public defined benefit pay-as-you-go system was heavily affected by the failures of the Chilean democratic institutions that were associated with it. In theory, the restrictions on individual freedoms imposed by the social democratic welfare state was justified by the increase in equality. In practice, because of the limited development of democracy in Chile, the welfare policies were used as means for political patronage, in which political resources were traded for special legislated pension benefits. The political cliques managed this trade, increasing their power over the ordinary citizen. The pension system was manipulated to the benefit of political cliques, and the push for equality produced a system plagued by inequities. Apart from the negative consequences for the pension system, this also retarded the development of democracy in Chile. This is because patronage is a form of subjection, contrary to freedom, and its manipulation of legitimate interests reduces the legitimacy of democratic decisions.

In the first case study, regarding cost-of-living adjustments in the old system, it is shown how the old system, even when acting in the new democratic political context, continues to be vulnerable to manipulation in the political-economic cycle. However, patronage-style manipulation is much less than in the 1950s and 1960s. It is also less than what was observed in 1985–1989 under the military regime, even though the same constitutional rules applied, suggesting a separate influence of the political regime.

In other countries with a stronger democratic tradition and a wiser design of the pension system that leaves fewer spaces to patronage, the experience has been better. However, those countries that avoided the excess of patronage observed in Chile, but still experienced excessive dependency of the individual on the state bureaucracy, have also seen a renewed interest in the liberal democratic model. The new Chilean pension system fits this model, as it emphasizes basic freedoms. The underlying liberal democratic model is based on a democratic principle: The individual, because of his or her intrinsic value, is an end and never a means. This is the basis of the concept of a citizen, a holder of inalienable rights.

This study finds that political patronage, in its traditional form, is impracticable within the new Chilean pension system. Its beneficiaries enjoy property rights to their savings and are free to make some regulated choices. Negotiation with the political class, except for the pressure to maintain universal equality before the law, is not required from members. Since the system is administered by private fund management institutions (AFPs), and these compete among themselves in the market, there is a spontaneous regulation of administrative charges and of the profitability of investments. There is open access to the activity of pension fund management. No AFP is legally privileged to the detriment of the other AFPs, or of the system as a whole, by means of some special law. The real value of the capitalization accounts and of retirement pensions is not directly related to political decisions. Therefore, the new Chilean social security system disallows patronage and has a potential to increase the autonomy of its members. In this second aspect it also grants more freedom to members than well-run welfare states provide to their citizens.

It would be a mistake to minimize the importance of the new constitution of 1980 in achieving this result. The constituents of 1980 established norms that protect the social security system from the opportunistic conduct of the political class. It is possible that the new Chilean social security system could not operate free of patronage under the old constitutional regime. This is an important warning for countries intending to learn from the Chilean social security reform.

The second case study, concerning the default of ENACAR bonds in the new system, demonstrates the high degree of autonomy of pension fund management companies (AFPs), and their substantial capacity to defend the interests of their members when confronting the discretionary powers of the state. This case study shows empirically that the new system is effective in the defense of the pension rights of Chilean workers and pensioners, provided the rule of law is established and a democratic environment limits the powers of the executive.

The contrast between the situation of dependence and manipulation in the old system and the situation of autonomy and drive toward maximization of the rate of return in the new system is remarkable. Much can be learned from the political aspects of the Chilean experience with two pension systems.

APPENDIX TO CHAPTER 3

Table 3.A.1
Differential revaluations in 1987 and 1988
(P stands for pension level)

Group	Year 1987 Revaluation
P in (0 -$17,500) and age > 65	18.05%
P in (0 -$17,500) and age < 65	16.41%
P in ($17,501 - $43,500)	16.41%
P in ($43,501 - $100,000)	9.85%
P over $100,000	8.21%
Cumulative Inflation Since Previous Revaluation:	16.41%

continued

Table 3A.1 (cont.)

Group	Year 1988 Revaluation
P in (0 - $19,250) and age > 65	17.49%
P in (0 - $19,250) and age < 65	15.90%
P in($19,251 - $47,850)	15.90%
P in ($47,851-$109,850) and age > 65	15.90%
P in ($47,851-$109,850) and age < 65	9.90%
P over $109,851	8.40%
Cumulative Inflation Since Previous Revaluation:	15.90%

urces: Revaluation of May 1987: Law 18,549 of September 13, 1986; Revaluation of May 1988: Law 18,669 of November 28, 1987.

Table 3.A.2
Uniform revaluations in the old pension system, 1979 - 1993

Year	Month	% Revaluation	Months Since Previous Revaluation
1979	March	6.00	–
	July	11.00	4
	December	19.00	5
1980	April	8.00	4
	October	14.00	6
1981	June	13.48	8
1982	October	14.56	16
1983	May	17.09	7
1984	January	15.15	8
	November	20.00	10
1985	May	2.54(*)	6
1986	January	14.26	7
	July	8.80	6
1987	May	16.41	10
1988	April	15.90	11
1989	January	9.40	9
	June	5.00	SPECIAL of 1989
	November	16.90	10
1990	July	15.50	8
1991	February	15.02	7
	November	15.65	9
1992	December	15.05	13
1993	December	12.09	12

Source: Dirección de Presupuestos, Ministry of Finance.

(*) This is the only month in this series where the revaluation is not equal to the change in the CPI since the previous revaluation. In that month a revaluation of 10.6% was skipped.

References

Allende, Salvador (1972). *Presidential Message, 1972.* Santiago.

(1973). *Presidential Message, 1973.* Santiago.

Assael, P., and F. Larraín (1995). "Cincuenta Años de Ciclo Económico en Chile." *Cuadernos de Economía* (Santiago), no. 96, August, pp. 129–50.

Beveridge, W. (1942). *Social Insurance and Allied Services.* Reprint 1984. HMSO, London.

Cheyre, Hernán (1991). *La Previsión en Chile. Ayer y Hoy.* Centro de Estudios Públicos, Santiago, Chile.

Comisión de Estudios de la Seguridad Social (Prat Report) (1959–1964). *Informe sobre la Reforma de la Seguridad Social Chilena.* Editorial Jurídica de Chile, Santiago, 1964.

La Cuarta (Santiago), October 20, 1993.

Daranas, Mariano (1979). *Las Constituciones Europeas.* Editora Nacional, Madrid.

Diamond, P., and S. Valdés-Prieto (1994). "Social Security Reforms." In B. Bosworth, R. Dornbusch, and R. Labán, editors, *The Chilean Economy,* Chap. 6. Brookings Institution, Washington, D.C.

Drake, Paul (1993). *Los Factores Internacionales en la Coyuntura Democrática.* Document of the Seminar "Chilean Democratization in a Comparative Perspective," FLACSO, Santiago.

El Ladrillo (1992). Centro de Estudios Públicos, Santiago.

Ferrara, P., ed. (1985). *Social Security: Prospects for Real Reform.* Cato Institute, Washington, D.C.

Ffrench-Davis, Ricardo (1973). *Políticas Económicas en Chile 1952–1970.* Ediciones Nueva Universidad, Universidad Católica de Chile, Santiago.

Frei, Eduardo (1966). *Presidential Message, 1966.* Santiago.

(1969). *Presidential Message, 1969.* Santiago.

Informe de la Comisión Klein-Saks. (1957). Santiago.

Political Constitution of the Republic of Chile. (1993). Editorial Jurídica de Chile, Santiago.

Prat, Jorge (1962). *La Legislación Previsional. Comentarios y Proyectos de Reforma.* Universidad Católica de Chile, Santiago.

Thayer, William, and Fernández, Eduardo (1981). *El Nuevo Régimen Previsional y de Cotizaciones.* Editorial Jurídica de Chile, Santiago, p. 31.

Valdés-Prieto, Salvador, and Eduardo Navarro (1992). "Subsidios Cruzados en el Seguro de Invalidez y Sobrevivencia del Nuevo Sistema Previsional Chileno," *Cuadernos de Economía* 29, no. 88, December pp. 409–442.

Valdés-Prieto, Salvador. (1993). "Liberty, Responsibility and the Obligation to Contribute." *El Mercurio* (Santiago), June 30, p. B2.

Valdés-Prieto, Salvador (1994). "The Mandate to Contribute: A Solvable Mistake." *Administración y Economía U.C.,* no. 16, Summer, pp. 10–13.

Weatherford, S. (1988). "Political Business Cycle and the Process of Policymaking." *American Politics Quarterly* 16, January, pp. 99–136.

CHAPTER 4

Public pension governance
and performance

Olivia S. Mitchell and Ping-Lung Hsin

Abstract

The cost of supporting retirees has risen quickly in both developed and developing nations, and promises to become ever greater in decades to come. Policy makers seek to prepare for these costs by designing better functioning pension plan structures. An item at the top of the policy agenda is to improve public pension plan investment and funding performance. This chapter examines public sector pension plans in the United States, asking why some plans appear to have been well managed and what structural design features are associated with good pension management outcomes.

The two pension plan performance outcome measures of central interest in this chapter are the yields on public pension system assets, and the public pension plans' funding status. Investment performance is important since higher yields reduce the need for additional taxes to support current and future retirees. Pension funding is important since better funded plans stand a better chance of having assets on hand to pay promised benefits. This study relates these two pension plan outcomes to a variety of features characterizing each pension system's governance structure and authority, reporting requirements, and other factors affecting the environment in which the pension funds operate. A new dataset on more than 200 state and local public sector plans in the United States is used to examine the relationship between public sector plan performance and management practices, seeking to draw lessons

The authors acknowledge research support from the Public Sector Management and Private Sector Development Division, Country Economics Department of the World Bank; the Wharton School; and Cornell University. Useful comments were offered by Gary Fields, Edwin Hustead, Estelle James, Robert Palacios, and Don Snyder, as well as from colleagues at the National Bureau of Economic Research Summer Institute meetings and the Department of Economics at the University of Pennsylvania. Conclusions and interpretations are those of the authors and do not reflect official bank or university policy.

that might improve the design and governance of public pensions here and in other countries.

Section 1 of the chapter develops several hypotheses regarding public pension plans' investment performance and pension governance, while section 2 examines determinants of funding patterns. Empirical analysis in section 3 suggests that public plan investment performance and funding outcomes are linked to characteristics of the pension board itself, and also to public sector mandates regarding investment and asset allocation. Section 4 tests the sensitivity of the results to alternative empirical specifications. Finally, section 5 draws lessons from this research for policy makers in other countries, in the expectation that they may benefit from the experience of public pension plans in the United States.

1 The determinants of public pension investment performance

Often referred to as "public employee retirement systems" (PERS), retirement systems established for individuals employed by state and local governments have become large and powerful institutions in the past three decades. Typically these are defined benefit pension plans, which provide workers an annual benefit accrual (usually a function of pay and years of service). This accrual converts into a retirement annuity payment when the employee attains a specified age and term of service under the plan. Recent surveys show that there are approximately 2,400 public pension systems in the United States, covering about 10 million full-time public-sector employees and about 3 million pension beneficiaries – mainly employees of state and local governments, and often teachers and other school employees, police and firefighters, judges, correctional officers, and other public servants (see Table 4.1).[1] These plans pay relatively generous benefit levels amounting to 40% of preretirement pay at relatively young retirement ages; usually PERS retirement benefits are at least partially indexed to inflation.

Benefit promises that accrue under PERS plans are liabilities the sponsor is expected to pay retirees at some future date. Most public employers back up these promises by making payments to a segregated pension trust fund, which are then invested to generate eventual benefit payments. Many PERS plans have succeeded in amassing substantial funds: In the United States, public pensions held about $730 billion at the end of the 1980s, accounting for 5% of the country's total financial assets, 13% of all domestic bonds, and almost 8% of all domestic equities (Hoffman and Mondejar, 1992).

---

[1] Excluded from the PERS designation are national military and federal government employee plans, as well as federal Social Security old-age pensions. These plans are, for the most part, unfunded systems.

Table 4.1
Public pension system characteristics:
U.S. state and local pension plans

I.   U.S. Public Pension Plan Characteristics Over Time

	1980	Year 1985	1989
Number of Plans	NA	2,589	2,387
Total Participants (000)	NA	15,234	16,684
Active Participants (000)	NA	10,364	11,357
Total Assets ($B current)	$162	374	629
Annual Contributions ($B current)	$21	37	44
Annual Benefits ($B current)	$11	22	33

NA: Not available.
Source: Piacentini and Foley (1992).

II.   Survey of U.S. Public Pension Plan Participants in 1989

	Pension Characteristic
Mean Retirement Benefit[1]	$9,318
Median Retirement Benefit[1]	$7,200
Median Public Pension as % of Pre-retirement Earnings (total)[2]	42%
Median Public Pension as % of Pre-retirement Earnings for those not receiving Social Security[3]	50%
Fraction Receiving Any Post Retirement Benefit Increases[4]	34%
Fraction of Participants Covered by Defined Benefit Plan[5]	70%

Sources:
[1]Phillips (1992), Table 14.9: 367.
[2]Phillips (1992), Table 14.13: 371.
[3]Phillips (1992), Table 14.7: 375.
[4]Phillips (1992), Table 14.20: 379.
[5]Phillips (1992), Table 14.25: 384. Fraction excludes 10% of respondents unable to identify plan type.

A major responsibility of those charged with managing public-sector pensions is to direct the investment of these assets. Research suggests that PERS funds have been managed somewhat differently from those in private-sector pensions. Thus until 1960, corporate equities constituted only a negligible fraction of state and local plan assets, whereas government securities and corporate bonds were much more heavily favored than in private plans (see

Table 4.2
Pension plan portfolios in the United States:
Size and allocation 1950 - 1989

	Total Assets ($B Current)	Corporate Equities (%)	Fraction of Assets in: Corporate Bonds (%)	U.S. Govt Securities (%)	Other (%)
I. State and local government pension plans					
1950	$4.9	0.0	12.2	51.0	36.7
1955	10.8	1.9	25.0	43.5	29.6
1960	19.7	3.0	36.0	29.9	31.0
1965	34.1	7.3	50.4	22.3	19.9
1970	60.3	16.7	58.2	10.9	14.1
1975	104.8	23.2	59.0	7.4	10.4
1980	198.1	22.4	47.7	20.2	9.7
1985	404.7	29.7	31.9	30.5	7.9
1989	727.4	39.9	27.3	27.2	5.5
II. Private pension plans					
Noninsured:					
1950	$7.1	15.5	39.4	32.4	12.7
1955	18.3	33.3	43.2	16.4	7.1
1960	38.1	43.3	41.2	7.1	8.4
1965	74.4	54.8	30.5	4.0	10.6
1970	112.0	59.9	26.2	2.7	11.2
1975	225.0	48.0	18.6	8.0	25.4
1980	469.6	47.6	16.5	10.8	25.1
1985	848.4	46.4	14.3	12.3	27.0
1989	1,163.5	57.3	12.4	12.3	18.0
Insured:					
1950	4.8	4.2	41.7	22.9	31.2
1955	10.1	4.0	43.6	9.9	42.6
1960	16.8	4.8	43.5	6.0	45.8
1965	25.5	6.3	41.6	3.5	48.6
1970	37.5	13.6	37.6	2.4	46.4
1975	64.6	18.6	37.5	2.2	41.8
1980	152.2	16.0	39.9	3.7	40.3
1985	337.9	13.0	35.7	12.9	38.4
1989	525.8	12.3	39.8	11.6	36.3

Note: Insured plans are pension plans whose assets are held by insurance companies.
Source: Hoffman and Mondejar (1992), T. 16.9 and 10: 438-441.

Table 4.2). This pattern of asset holdings was in part motivated by state and local government rules prohibiting pension managers from investing in what were perceived to be "risky" assets, including equity, venture capital, and foreign holdings.

Although these strictures have diminished in the past decade, yields on public pension fund assets have frequently been low, with public plans earning rates of return substantially below those of other pooled funds and

Table 4.3
Pension plan investment yields:
Historical patterns 1968-1986

	U.S. State & Local Pension Plan Inflation Investment Return[1] (%)	U.S. Large Private Pension Plan Investment Return		Canadian Large Private Pension Plan Investment Return[4] (%)	U.S. Market Indices		U.S. Rate[5] (%)
		SEI data[2] (%)	5500 data[3] (%)		Stocks[5] (%)	Bonds[5] (%)	
1968	7.75	8.4	--	9.4	11.1	2.6	4.7
1969	-7.94	-5.2	--	-3.2	-8.5	-8.1	6.1
1970	5.63	1.3	--	1.3	4.0	18.4	5.5
1971	14.76	17.5	--	12.5	14.3	11.0	3.4
1972	12.58	15.3	--	18.4	19.0	7.3	3.4
1973	-9.32	-15.1	--	-2.1	-14.7	1.1	8.8
1974	-13.03	-20.3	--	-12.7	-26.5	-3.1	12.2
1975	19.14	23.1	--	13.2	37.2	14.6	7.0
1976	18.03	17.2	--	12.4	23.8	18.6	4.8
1977	0.31	-2.2	1.6	8.7	-7.2	1.7	6.8
1978	3.16	5.8	6.0	13.5	6.6	-0.1	9.0
1979	6.36	13.7	10.1	15.0	18.4	-4.2	13.3
1980	11.58	20.2	21.9	18.3	32.4	-2.6	12.4
1981	3.00	2.7	5.4	1.5	-4.9	-1.0	8.9
1982	27.22	23.0	18.2	21.1	21.4	43.8	3.9
1983	12.89	15.9	9.4	20.0	22.5	4.7	3.8
1984	--	--	9.9	8.8	6.3	16.4	4.0
1985	--	--	20.0	23.5	32.2	30.9	3.8
1986	--	--	14.1	12.8	18.5	19.8	1.1

Notes:
[1]Public pension plan data from SEI Financial Services reported by Berkowitz and Logue (1986), T. AIII-3.
[2]Large U.S. private plan data from SEI Financial Services reported by McCarthy and Turner (1992) T. 12.1: 253.
[3]Large U.S. private plan data from 5500 Reports reported by McCarthy and Turner (1992) T. 12.1: 253.
[4]Large Canadian private pension plan data, SEI Financial Services reported by Pesando and Hyatt (1992) T. 1: 21.
[5]McCarthy and Turner (1992), Table 12.1: 253.

often below leading market indices.[2] Tables 4.3 and 4.4 demonstrate this for the period 1968–1986 as well as more recently, when state and local pension plans reported annual returns averaging 11.1% while bonds rose by 15.5% and securities by 13.9%.

One explanation for why public plan investment yields are often low is that they are operated according to principles different from those adopted in the private sector. Specifically, many public pensions are managed by staff which must respond to political as well as economic incentives and pressures. A typical public system is governed by a board of directors composed of eight members, on average, with three elected members, three appointed members (often by the governor), and two serving ex officio (e.g., the state treasurer, the superintendent of schools). Those elected to public pension boards are frequently active employees, which is quite uncommon in the private sector; in addition, in many cases retired workers are also included as board members (Zorn, 1991).

[2] For a discussion of studies on this topic, see Beebower and Bergstrom (1977); Berkowitz, Logue & Associates (1986); Brinson, Hood, and Beebower (1986); Grinblatt and Titman (1989); Ippolito (1989); and McCarthy and Turner (1992).

Table 4.4
U.S. public sector pension plan yields:
Annual Averages 1984 - 1990

	State & Local Pension Plan Investment Return	Market Indices Bonds[7]	Securities[7]	Inflation Rate[7]
Average 1984-1990:	11.13%	15.51%	13.91%	4.11%
1990	6.85[1]	-3.17	6.78	6.11
1988	3.95[2]	16.81	10.70	4.42
Average 1988-1990	9.55[3]	15.04	11.24	5.06
Average 1986-1990	11.98[4]	13.77	10.66	4.14
Average 1986-1988	13.88[5]	13.50	10.09	3.32
Average 1984-1988	12.07[6]	15.79	15.51	3.54

Notes:
[1]Zorn (1991), T. VII-7: 34; 129 plans.
[2]Zorn (1990), T. 34: B34; 108 plans.
[3]Zorn (1991), T. VII-8: 35; 85 plans.
[4]Zorn (1991), T. VII-9: 36; 85 plans.
[5]Zorn (1990), T. 35: B35; 113 plans.
[6]Zorn (1990), T. 36: B36; 85 plans.
[7]Ibbotson Associates (1992), T. 13: 34.

Because public pension boards are often managed by political appointees and covered pension members, it is possible that the boards select invest- ments different from those chosen by nonpension money managers compet- ing in the capital market. There is little direct evidence on this point in the public sector, but pension participants in the private sector appear to invest more conservatively than do professional pension managers (EBRI, 1993). Hence, it is hypothesized that better performance from public pensions could be observed when public systems manage their funds professionally, instead of relying on former or current employees.

Another way that pension governance structures might alter PERS invest- ment yields is that board authority varies a great deal across public pension plans, depending on laws, which vary from state to state, and also depending on custom and tradition. For example, some PERS boards have a great deal of responsibility for investment decisions, control actuarial inflation and interest rate assumptions, and direct the system's reporting practices. In other cases, external professional money managers and actuaries manage investments and reporting, leaving day-to-day benefit payments and record- keeping functions to the board. The latter tasks are substantial: Public-sector pension plans reported an average of 42,000 active members per plan and $2.8 billion in assets, with annual administrative costs totaling about 1% to

4% of assets.[3] Large plans can service many of these needs in-house, employing on the average one staff member per 1,000 plan participants. Smaller plans are more likely to use external actuarial, legal, and accounting firms, and frequently employ professional money managers and/or investment consultants (Zorn, 1991).

When private-sector pension systems manage their benefits administration and investment in-house, researchers have found substantial evidence of economies of scale in larger plans (Mitchell and Andrews 1981). It is therefore possible that larger public pension plans might also experience higher yields than would smaller plans, though these scale economies could be captured in smaller plans by hiring external professional money managers and consultants. In addition to size, investment style could lead to performance differences: For example, top-10 performance group money managers apparently earn higher yields, although Lakonishok and his colleagues (1991, 1992) suggest that net returns are equalized after commissions. Our analysis controls for plan size and whether plans use investment managers in the top-10 performance group.

In addition to management style, the literature suggests that other factors can affect pension asset performance. For example, recent studies indicate that net investment returns in the private sector are sometimes reduced when investment managers are subjected to frequent performance reviews. This is because of a principal–agent problem: Money managers sometimes structure their portfolios to meet short-run objectives at the cost of long-run goals.[4] In the public sector context, PERS boards using external money managers subject to frequent valuations might face lower net rates of return than systems using only in-house managers, particularly if they are evaluated relatively infrequently (ceteris paribus). Thus the empirical analysis of pension asset yields must control not only on who is managing the portfolio, but also on how often they report how they are doing.

Pension plan asset performance clearly depends on other factors in addition to the ones just described, with perhaps the most important one being the fund's portfolio mix. As noted earlier, public plans tend to hold fewer stocks than do private pensions, in part because the federal government requires private pension fiduciaries to invest in a well-diversified portfolio of assets chosen for traditional financial reasons. Furthermore, federal regulations gov-

---

[3] See Mitchell, Sunden, Hsin, and Reid (1993) for a discussion of administrative costs in U.S. public pension plans, and Sunden and Mitchell (1994) for costs in the U.S. Social Security system. Valdés-Prieto (1994) compares private and public plans' administrative costs in four nations.

[4] This has been called "window dressing" at year end so that money managers are not seen holding "losers" (Benartzi and Thaler, 1992; Laknonishok, Shleifer, Thaler, and Vishny, 1991; Laknonishok, Shleifer, and Vishny, 1992).

erning private plans specifically require pension fiduciaries to behave according to generally accepted financial principles, a philosophy summarized as the "prudent man rule." In the public pension arena, no federal legislation controls PERS investment patterns. As a result, there are no legal constraints on those who wish to deploy public pension assets for nontraditional investment purposes, and several groups have become increasingly vocal.[5] For example, the governor of New York argued that public pension assets be loaned advantageously to firms "conducting business" within his state. Other states have asked their pension fund managers to only invest in "economically targeted" or "socially responsible" companies (defined variously as firms that do not pollute, companies headquartered in-state, etc.). Although these unconventional investment practices have their appeal, retirees and active workers have expressed concern that their pension assets may earn low returns, and perhaps be insufficiently diversified.[6]

These differences in PERS investment practices imply that public pension plan returns may vary because of strictures placed on the plans by the political process, strictures that may not be in evidence in privately run pension plans. As a result, empirical analysis of PERS performance must take into account the risk characteristics of the pension portfolio, whether investors operate under constraints such as ceilings on bond or stock holding, rules requiring fiduciaries to diversify their portfolios in a manner that might be deemed "prudent" by impartial financial experts, or requirements that money must be directed to "socially acceptable" ventures. If these strictures are effective, they may lower returns and/or increase risk.

2   The determinants of public-sector pension funding practices

Federal law in the United States requires *private-sector* pension plan sponsors to explicitly recognize their accumulating pension liabilities, and then to set aside contributions in an orderly fashion so as to build up assets sufficient to meet benefit promises when workers retire. The rationale for full pension funding in the private sector is that sponsoring companies may go bankrupt, and unless the pension plan has received assets sufficient to cover

---

[5] In the United States, the Employee Retirement Income Security Act of 1974 (ERISA) requires private-sector pension plan assets to be managed according to prudent and conservative investment practice, and furthermore holds plan trustees personally responsible for the plan's investment practices. However ERISA does not cover PERS plans, and efforts to extend national regulation to state and local pensions have been challenged by those who believe that this would undermine states' taxing authority; see Munnell (1983).

[6] See for instance Goldman, Sachs (1993), New York State Industrial Cooperation Council (1989, 1990), New York Retired Public Employees Association (1989), and Snell and Wolfe (1990).

benefit promises, retirees could face curtailed or terminated benefit payments.[7]

In the *public sector,* pension funding practice has been much more variable, both in the United States and elsewhere. This is partly because many deem the risk of government bankruptcy to be low, and thus less persuasive as a rationale for prefunding. As a result, partially funded or completely unfunded (pay-as-you-go) plans have been the norm for most developed and many developing nations around the world (James, 1993). At the state level in the United States, funding practices also vary: In some cases state constitutions explicitly require that pension liabilities be funded, but in other cases funding is less explicitly mandated. (For constitutional reasons, the federal government has not regulated state-level public pensions; see Munnell 1983).

Despite the pay-as-you-go tradition, there are several arguments in support of substantial pension prefunding in the public sector. Funds invested earn the pension plan investment income which "can substantially reduce the employer's ultimate payment for such benefits" (Bleakney, 1972: 16); this may take on special urgency given the aging of the public-sector work force over the next decades (Mitchell, 1991). Also, underfunded pensions impose an implicit future liability on taxpayers, reducing states' and localities' abilities to raise funds in other ways (Epple and Schipper, 1981). Public-sector retiree income security might also be threatened by underfunding; indeed some public employees have sought to offset the risk of underfunded pension promises by demanding higher pay (Inman, 1982, 1986; Mitchell and Smith, 1994; Smith, 1981). Finally, some analysts argue that pay-as-you-go systems decrease savings and impose politically unpalatable redistributive burdens across cohorts (James, 1993).

Despite these arguments favoring prefunding of benefit promises, public-sector pension plans have typically not accumulated the level of assets needed to meet projected liabilities. (cf. Table 4.5). During the 1980s many public employers contributed less to their public employees' pension accounts than they were required to (according to actuarial computations), in part because public tax collections fell in American states and cities during the recession. As a result, some public pensions became (or grew more) underfunded, meaning that plan assets were insufficient to cover benefits promised to retirees. A study of 1989 data showed that state and local employer pension contributions were about 10–15% below target, and the pattern of shortfall was most persistent for systems where unemployment was higher than it had

---

[7] Cessation of benefits has become less likely since ERISA regulations established a government insurance agency for private-sector defined benefit private pensions. On the other hand the pension insurance agency is not completely stable financially, and the risk of private pension underfunding is now borne primarily by groups other than those retirees in the underfunded plan; see Gustman and Mitchell (1992).

Table 4.5
U.S. public pension plan funding ratios

Ratio of Pension Plan Assets to Pension Plan Liabilities	Fraction of Public Plans (%)
State and Local Plans	
< 50%	8
50-74	21
75-99	39
≥ 100%	33

Source: Authors' adaptation of unpublished data from GAO. Market value of assets in numerator, PBO liability measure in denominator. See text.

been for some time. This effect persisted even when controlling for habit persistence, holding constant past cumulative funding levels (Mitchell and Smith 1992, 1994). Therefore a full analysis of funding must take into account the possibility that fiscal stress undermines PERS plans' financial stability.

The structure of PERS boards can also affect pension funding. One possibility is that a board comprised of pension-covered members may meet funding requirements more promptly than one heavily weighted with political appointees.[8] Working counter to this hypothesis is the fact that pension funding is an extremely complex and difficult area, which active and retired workers may be unable to scrutinize fully. Lack of adequate technical training combines with conservatism regarding investment risk, on top of which is the fact that pension participants typically have very poor understanding of their plan's rules and features (Mitchell, 1988). For this reason, having professional representatives rather than relatively nontechnical pension participants on the PERS board could improve funding. Which effect dominates is an empirical matter.

In addition to board composition, other PERS management practices can also influence funding outcomes directly. Specifically, some systems use in-

---

[8] Elements of this were present in the court case recently filed by California state retirees, who protested the governor's effort to reduce state budget deficits by raising the public pension plan's assumed interest rate from 8.5% to 9.5%. Retirees contended that "manipulating the rate of return on plan investments, though within legally 'reasonable limits,' can substantially reduce employer contributions to the point where a pension plan can be substantially underfunded and put at high risk" (Hemmerick, 1991b: 34). When the PERS board refused to implement the governor's proposal, he then moved to dissolve the old board and construct a new board more receptive to his proposals.

house staff actuaries, increasing funding if these staffers are relatively free from political suasion, but decreasing it otherwise. When the PERS board is required to authorize benefit increases, rather than simply passing on increases negotiated by state and local employees independently, this could translate into higher funding rates – after all, authorization to provide future benefits would be required from those managing the funding process. It is also worth investigating whether funding is improved when board members have liability insurance, which, if true, suggests that the private insurance market may enforce funding stringencies on PERS boards when political tensions pull in other directions.

Another set of factors influencing funding may be the reporting requirements to which pension managers respond. While public pension accounting practice embraces some common assumptions and standards across states and localities, the remaining differences make it difficult to compare public plan investment performance and funding outcomes in some cases. This problem has been recognized by many pension analysts over the years, and is slowly being remedied by the Governmental Accounting Standards Board which is devising a framework for public pension financial reporting (GASB, 1992). The majority of large state and local plans now conform to GASB Statement No. 5 (GASB, 1986) which specifies that public pension plans must report assets at market value, with liabilities measured according to a concept known as the pension benefit obligation (PBO).[9] As a result of this increasing standardization, it is now much more likely that stock funding ratios are accurate, by which is meant that pension assets are correctly computed as a fraction of liabilities. This contrasts with the practice a decade ago when most PERS plans reported assets at cost, and used a variety of different methods to compute liability measures (Schmitt, Merck, and Neisner, 1991). Despite this progress, a cross-plan analysis of funding still requires paying attention to different approaches used in reporting assets and funding.

Along the same lines, it might be expected that more frequent reporting would tend to induce standardization, so that better funding would be expected of a PERS required to report to its sponsoring employer and participating members more often. Audits and actuarial valuations are also carried out

---

[9] The PBO includes five types of prospective pension liabilities as noted in Mitchell and Smith (1992): benefits pledged to currently retired employees, benefits pledged to vested terminated employees (based on past service and salary levels), benefits payable to vested active employees (based on current service and salary), benefits payable to nonvested active employees who may vest in the future, and benefits that will be earned by current workers resulting from future salary increases. The plan's PBO changes over time reflecting new expected benefit accruals; these yearly accruals are termed the plan's "normal cost." To be actuarially sound, the employer's annual contributions to the plan must meet normal cost and amortize any past unfunded pension liabilities.

at different intervals, and the reporting standards themselves vary. These different reporting methods may simply affect data quality without altering investment and funding performance, but many fear they have more potent effects altering plan outcomes materially. These cross-plan differences should be controlled in empirical analysis, and examined to see if they influence PERS funding outcomes materially.

Other variations in pension reporting are also important, particularly in the case where flow funding measures are considered. Flow funding is defined as the ratio of *annual actual* employer contributions, to *annual required* contributions. Variations in flow funding measures are due in part to laws governing pension funding practices, which differ across states.[10] A related problem in the reporting context arises when a system uses the PBO measure to report GASB-sanctioned funding measures, but uses some other actuarial method to compute annual required employer contributions. It is possible that a plan would then appear well funded by the officially recommended PBO measure, but would be less than fully funded by the system's own account measure.[11] As a consequence, it is important to investigate whether differences in funding patterns are related to different methods of computing liabilities for reporting, versus for funding, purposes.

Funding differences may also result from other factors. In computing pension obligations, for instance, actuaries employ a variety of assumptions to compute promised future benefits. Unbiased estimates of the factors of central interest require that these assumptions be controlled in the empirical analysis, by including plan-specific estimates of expected future price and wage increases, assumed discount rates and retirement ages, integration of benefits with Social Security, whether benefit levels were guaranteed by law, and portability of pension accruals. Pension systems also have some leeway with regard to their past service liability amortization period, which refers to the time period over which unfunded pension promises from the past are covered from current contributions. Since it is possible that poorly funded

[10] As an example, fire and police pension plans in Portland, Oregon, are governed by a law that sets the public employer's annual contribution rates as a fraction of payroll, and this contribution rate is generally met. Consequently the pension financial statement indicates that the employer's actual contributions are exactly equal to required contributions, resulting in a flow funding rate of 100%. In fact, however, the system is operated on a pay-as-you-go basis; the flow funding figure reported by this plan does not represent the actuarial figures that the accounting standards profession would prefer under its proposed reporting rules.

[11] This has apparently occurred in several instances over the past two years, where employers were able to dramatically cut their contributions after converting to new actuarial methods consistent with the PBO measure. For a discussion of recent efforts by numerous public employers to change public pension funding patterns see Durgin (1991), "Lag Found in Teachers' Pension Contributions" (1991), Hemmerik (1991a, 1991b), Price (1991), and Verhovek (1990).

plans strategically select an amortization period to improve the funding report, this too should be controlled in a multivariate funding analysis.

To this list of pension funding determinants must be joined several indicators of the regulatory and fiscal environment in which PERS board members make funding decisions. Most obviously linked to the pension funding outcome is the existence of state-level legally mandated funding requirements. One would anticipate that if such law is binding, it would enhance funding in those states. A variant of this point is that states experiencing severe fiscal stress tend to reduce funding, suggesting that this too should be taken into account in multivariate analysis. Based on previous work, we include a variable indicating fiscal stress, which is the deviation of the state's unemployment rate from its long-term trend (Mitchell and Smith, 1994). It is anticipated that greater fiscal stress would reduce funding, but perhaps be offset if contributions are derived from a special or dedicated tax. In addition other "political economy variables" are explored, including an indicator of whether a state has a balanced-budget requirement, to assess whether pension underfunding serves as a "safety valve" in cases where the balanced-budget rule is taken seriously. Finally, there may be differences in plan participants' ability to exact full funding rates, so it is important to control for the presence of unionized employees and teachers.

3   Empirical analysis of public pension yields and funding

The data used for empirical analysis are obtained from a cross-sectional survey of 201 pension systems conducted in 1991, covering a total of 269 separate retirement plans. The PENDAT file created from this survey was provided by the Government Finance Officers' Association (Zorn, 1991). As of this writing, there is no larger, more up-to-date, and more representative survey of state and local pension plans in the country; the federal government collects no centralized information of this type (though many have suggested it should).

Respondent systems included in the PENDAT file represented 73% of state and local active pension plan participants, and 71% of state and local plan assets in 1990 (Zorn, 1991). These systems represent the vast majority of the PERS-covered population, but are not necessarily representative of all plans since they are among the largest in the nation, and probably better managed and funded than many smaller plans; as a consequence, interpretation of results must bear this caveat in mind. PERS plans responding to the survey accounted for about a tenth of the estimated universe of state and local pension plans nationally.

The PENDAT datafile is quite extensive, including variables reflecting all aspects of the systems' management, investment, and funding practices as well as plan participant and benefit mixes.[12] The indicator of investment performance is used as a dependent variable for the multivariate analysis (actual investment yield rates) and two measures of pension funding – stock and flow funding patterns.

Taking the investment outcomes first, two different approaches were chosen to measure public system's asset performance. Virtually all PERS report one datum for 1990 – that year's total portfolio return (referred to below as Y1ROR). Most also reported their annualized average return over the period 1986–1990 (referred to below as Y5ROR). Both performance variables are reported in nominal dollars (the analysis therefore assumes that all plans experienced identical inflation rates). The fact that the investment yield is averaged over the 5-year span makes it impossible to compute traditional measures of pension performance variability over time; estimates of this concept must await development of panel data.

Two dependent variables were developed for the funding analysis. The concept that best captures a plan's stock funding rate in the PENDAT survey expresses pension plan assets as a fraction of the pension benefit obligation, and for ease of reference this stock funding measure is termed AST-PBO. An alternative measure focuses on the plan's current funding practices, a concept captured here as FLOWFUND, or the ratio of actual to required employer contributions for the year.

Explanatory variables in the analysis are grouped into five main categories: pension board composition, board management practices, investment practices, reporting requirements and assumptions, and other factors that reflect regulations at the state level governing budget and funding practices. Controls are also included for plan size, type of plan, and covered employees, and in some cases portfolio composition is incorporated on the grounds that plans with less risky holdings will have lower returns.

Most of these variables were directly derived from the PENDAT file, but outside sources were used in a few instances. The variable called TOP10MG indicates whether the pension system used a money manager in the top-10 performance group as identified by Lakonishok et al. (1992). The term UNEMPD represents the degree of fiscal stress experienced by the state

---

[12] When there were missing data, this was handled in several ways. Serious reporting errors in pension statistics were rechecked with the PERS plan representatives directly. A complete list of data checks thus generated is available from the authors on request. For example, the stock funding ratio for Wisconsin was listed in the dataset as 1300%, which the plan representative indicated was incorrect. In the case of missing observations for some of the explanatory variables used in regression models, the variable in question was assigned a value of 0, and concurrently the missing value dummy variable was set to 1. Missing data on the dependent variable (e.g., investment performance or funding) suggested the use of sample selection models to determine whether systems that did report their funding and investment yields had better (or worse) than average outcomes; see section 4.

proxied by the deviation of the unemployment rate in 1990 from the mean of the previous nine years; previous analysts suggest that this type of fiscal stress reduces funding possibilities (Mitchell and Smith, 1994). The variable DEFPOS is also derived from outside sources and indicates whether a state is permitted to carry over a budget deficit from one year to the next. Public pension funding may be seen as an off-budget safety valve, relieving the pressure of having to meet state balanced-budget requirements. Hence pensions may be better funded when state budget deficits can be carried through time, whereas underfunding may prevail more often when state budgets must be balanced, by law, at year's end.[13]

Summarizing this discussion in a multivariate framework, the following model is postulated:

$$Y_1 = a_0 + a_1 X_1 + a_2 X_2 + a_3 X_3 + a_4 X_4 + a_5 Z + e_1 \tag{1}$$

$$Y_2 = b_0 + b_1 X_1 + b_2 X_2 + b_3 X_3 + b_4 X_4 + b_5 Z + e_2 \tag{2}$$

where Y_1 represents a vector of variables reflecting public pension investment performance; Y_2 represents a vector of funding variables; $X_1 - X_4$ represent vectors of variables reflecting pension board composition, board management practices, investment practices, reporting requirements and assumptions; and Z represents a vector of other factors including state regulations governing budget and funding practices, controls for plan size, type, and in some cases portfolio composition. In this section the disturbance terms are assumed to be distributed normally with zero mean; in section 4 this assumption and others, are discussed in more detail.

Evidence on the investment performance of state and local pension systems

In 1990, the annual investment yield reported by the 168 PERS systems was 7.7% (see the appendix Table 4.A.1). This compares favorably with market data showing a 6.8% return for securities that year, and with the 1990

---

[13] If there is a link between state balanced-budget laws and pension funding, it probably arises when state pension contributions are allowed to fluctuate depending on state budget needs, affording politicians on off-budget method of achieving compliance with balanced-budget requirements. This can happen since most state budgets typically do not include public pension systems in their regular budget reports. It has not yet been determined whether the safety-valve argument is empirically important. Certainly balanced-budget mandates are widespread; a majority of states (44) have balanced-budget laws on the books, and most of these (37) require the governor to sign a balanced budget (NASBO, 1992). Only 13 states permit the governor to carry over a budget deficit from one year to the next, providing flexibility that might obviate the need to use the public pension. This latter stance is deemed "most stringent" by NASBO, as represented in the DEFPOS variable developed for this study.

inflation rate of 6.1%. However, not all plans performed this well – one plan reported a −5.5% return that year, while at the other extreme a plan reported a yield of +24.5%. This range is almost certainly due to different portfolio composition patterns across the plans; in the market as a whole, the +6.8% return for securities that year was offset by an average 3.2% yield on bonds, which suggests the importance of holding constant the portfolio composition of pension plans when comparing their investment yields. A narrower frequency distribution of pension yields characterizes Y5ROR, returns averaged over the period 1986–1990. Across the 128 plans reporting the figure averaged 11.6%, with the lowest return reported of −2.5% and the highest being 31%. The overall mean was lower than the annualized return on bonds for the same period of 13.5%, but exceeded the average stock return of 10.1% as well as the annualized inflation rate of 3.3%.[14]

Table 4.6 provides multivariate regression estimates of equation (1), indicating the determinants of pension plan investment yields. The findings show that the composition of the public pension board appears to matter: Specifically, yields in 1990 were about 2% lower if retiree representation on the public pension boards increased by 10%. This may be the result of inexpert board members becoming increasingly activist of late, an explanation buttressed by the fact that the retiree effect was negative but not statistically significant in the 5-year yield equation. This finding is not solely attributable to more conservative investment choices made by retiree board members, since the model controls for the overall fractions of the portfolio held in stocks and bonds.[15] Nevertheless, before concluding that retiree participation on pension boards is necessarily deleterious, it should be noted that appointed members might also depress asset yields if they were improperly selected.

Of the several pension management practice variables used in the investment performance equations, few had a powerful effect on pension yields. One influential practice involved permitting administrative costs to be charged to investment income (ADINVST), rather than being covered from state or local budgets directly. This reduced the 5-year average return figure at statistically significant levels, although the 1990 return was not powerfully affected. Some state and local systems used outside money managers and financial counselors, either in concert with internal management, or exclusively. In any event, plans investing in-house or using external money managers apparently fared about the same, even if the external managers

---

[14] The 1-year yield reported here differs from Zorn's (1991) 6.9% figure, and the 5-year annualized yield reported here is lower than Zorn's 13.9% figure; Zorn uses the PENDAT file but excludes many plans from the analysis (39 and 53 plans, respectively).

[15] More complex risk adjustments could be undertaken in a time series analysis, but cannot be undertaken in this cross-section dataset.

Table 4.6
Determinants of investment returns
In U.S. State and local pension plans
(standard errors in parentheses)

		Dependent Variable	
Explanatory Variable		1990 Return	Five-year Av. Return
A.	Pension Board Composition		
	BDELAC	-0.01	-0.02
		(0.02)	(0.01)
	BDELRT	-0.17**	-0.002
		(0.07)	(0.05)
B.	Pension Management Practices		
	ADINVST	-0.34	-1.24**
		(0.89)	(0.58)
	INVINHS	0.80	0.60
		(1.36)	(0.92)
	TOP10MG	-0.49	-0.32
		(1.32)	(0.86)
	TOP10*EXT	-0.08	1.03
		(1.78)	(1.17)
C.	Pension Investment Practices		
	INSTATE	-0.08*	-0.02
		(0.04)	(0.02)
	PRUDMAN	0.83	0.33
		(1.20)	(0.84)
	STKMAX	-0.03	0.57
		(1.18)	(0.86)
D.	Pension Reporting Practices		
	INDINVPF	-1.16	-0.57
		(1.00)	(0.68)
	FREQVAL	0.70	0.13
		(0.54)	(0.56)
R^2		11.3	12.4
N		158	132

**t ≥ 1.96, *t ≥ 1.65 (< 1.96). Both models also include a constant term as well as controls for plan type (TCHRPLAN), plan size (ASSETS and SSETSW), and the fraction of the plan assets held in bonds and stock (BOND, STOCK). See the Appendix Table for variable descriptions and descriptive statistics.

were drawn from the "top-10" group (as identified by Lakonishok et al. 1992).[16]

Only a few of the rules regarding investment practices proved to affect measured outcomes statistically significantly. In no case was the prudent man requirement statistically linked to returns or investment variability; one explanation is that all pension boards may de facto follow a variant of this policy. The data also indicated no significant effect of state-mandated limits

[16] The PENDAT survey does not indicate whether the systems reported net or gross investment returns, but the negative significant effect of ADINVST suggests that the figures given were net of expenses. Other analysts have suggested that higher gross yields produced by active money managers tend to be equalized after commissions (Ippolito, 1989).

on stockholdings on any of the investment performance variables. More serious is the negative return observed for PERS pensions required to direct a portion of their investments in-state. This policy is often recommended by those who propose to use pension funds to build a stronger job and tax base.[17] The data show that plans following this policy experienced lower investment returns in 1990: The results imply that 10% more in-state investments are associated with a 1% drop in return. This effect was not detected using the 1985–1990 average return data, but should not be ignored since it may reflect recent trends that may not have been observed in earlier years.

Two factors used to quantify pension system reporting practices are included in Table 4.6. It will be recalled that having independent investment performance analysts and more frequent performance valuations could be predicted either to improve or to depress investment yields, depending on whether more reporting is seen as beneficial or harmful (Lakonishok et al. 1991; Lakonishok et al. 1992; Benartzi and Thaler 1992). The data do not support either position, however, since neither variable is strongly statistically significant.

Thus, some pension governance and management factors did affect yields in the major public-sector plans considered here. Three findings stand out:

- Public pension boards having more retiree-trustees experienced lower investment returns.
- Returns did not differ depending on whether a pension board had in-house or external money managers, even if the external managers were drawn from the "top-10" group.
- Public plans required to devote a portion of their assets to state-specific projects earned lower returns.

Funding patterns among state and local pension plans

As noted earlier, many state and local pension plans follow GASB advisory rules when reporting their pension assets and liabilities. This makes it possible to place some credence in funding figures, particularly with regard to the ratio of the pension plan's assets to its promised benefit liabilities (AST-PBO). The stock funding ratio averaged 91% in 1990 (for the 220 plans reporting). There is ample evidence of wide dispersion in funding practice: The minimum stock funding ratio was approximately 0 (for pay-as-you-go plans), and plans were seriously underfunded, having less than half the assets needed to meet pension obligations.[18] On the other hand, the maximum funding ratio was 3.2, and a third of the plans had sufficient assets to meet

---

[17] See, for example, Goldman, Sachs (1993).

[18] Zorn (1991) reports a slightly lower stock funding ratio (89%) but uses a much smaller sample size (30 plans) from the PENDAT survey.

projected benefits. For this reason the average stock funding rates of more than 90% should not be taken as evidence that public plans were uniformly well funded on an accumulated basis.

In contrast to stock funding measures, annual funding statistics capture whether the employer is contributing enough each year to cover new benefit accruals and amortization needs from past unfunded obligations. As mentioned earlier, however, there is reason to believe these annual flow funding figures are biased upward; an employer reporting full compliance with required contribution levels may sometimes receive monies inadequate to meet eventual benefit promises. This probably explains why the average FLOW-FUND ratio in 1990 was 93% (across 187 plans). The range about the mean is large: At one extreme a plan reported receiving 3.4 times the amount required, whereas at the other extreme a plan indicated receiving −4.3 times what was required.[19] On the whole, the vast majority (137 of 187 plans) reported receiving contributions less than 100% of the amount required, suggesting that most public-sector employers' contributions did not meet required levels in 1990.

Multivariate evidence linking public pension governance and funding patterns according to equation (2) is summarized in Table 4.7, where both stock and funding patterns are examined. A first hypothesis was that public pension board composition variables are related to stock funding ratios, and there is support for this position. Specifically, the results show that having more elected members on the board lowered PERS funding rates, with retiree-trustees having a larger depressing effect.[20] No composition effect was found in the flow funding equation, however.

Pension management practice also proved informative in explaining funding patterns: Three of the four variables used were positively related to stock funding patterns. For instance, the plans appeared better funded when a PERS had in-house actuaries, and the effect was statistically significant. Likewise, if the board was required to authorize actuarial assumptions, stock and flow funding were higher. There was a positive significant relationship between funding levels and board members having liability insurance: perhaps this is due to the increased oversight imposed by private insurers. (On the other hand, flow funding was negatively related to liability coverage − which may indicate reverse causality, if plans that underfunded on a flow basis

---

[19] The large negative funding figure was reported by a teachers' plan that changed the actuarial method employed in 1990; a court case concluded in 1993 denied the legality of this change.

[20] It should be noted that fund trustees appointed by politicians may not necessarily ensure that the plan is operated for the sole benefit of the plan participant. For example, the California public employee retirement system sued the governor of that state for proposing to replace the 13-member pension board with a newly appointed 9-member board, as well as appointing the plan's actuary who agreed to the governor's actuarial assumptions (Melbinger, 1992).

Table 4.7
Funding determinants of U.S. State and local pension plans
(standard errors in parentheses)

Explanatory Variable		Dependent Variable	
		Stock Funding Ratio	Flow Funding Ratio
A.	Pension Board Composition		
	BDELAC	-0.20**	0.08
		(0.08)	(0.17)
	BDELRT	-0.61*	0.34
		(0.35)	(0.70)
B.	Pension Management Practices		
	BDBENOK	-1.34	-1.86
		(5.77)	(11.02)
	BDACTOK	13.02*	30.81**
		(7.04)	(14.49)
	LIABINS	13.47**	-19.19**
		(4.89)	(9.33)
	ACCINHS	11.14**	-1.89
		(5.01)	(9.16)
C.	Pension Reporting Practices		
	REPSOLO	4.86	-1.74
		(4.58)	(8.67)
	GIVERPT	8.62	-0.35
		(8.03)	(14.38)
	AMORTPER	-1.25**	-0.18
		(0.20)	(0.37)
D.	Pension Assumptions		
	WDOT	-4.30	1.91
		(3.80)	(7.04)
	PORTABLE	-13.35**	2.20
		(5.25)	(9.82)
	NEXPROR	-0.51	2.16
		(3.59)	(6.49)
	INFL	-3.24	5.13
		(3.42)	(6.10)
E.	Other Factors		
	UNEMPD	-6.07**	0.65
		(2.08)	(3.82)
	FUNDLAW	0.12	-7.49
		(4.94)	(9.22)
	BENNOCUT	3.41	-10.53
		(4.75)	(9.03)
	DEFPOS	7.78	-0.34
		(5.08)	(9.34)
	SPECTAX	3.68	-0.98
		(6.40)	(12.36)
R^2		28.9	18.6
N		217	184

**t ≥ 1.96, *t ≥ 1.65 (< 1.96). Both models also include a constant term as well as controls for plan type and union (TCHRPLAN, UNION), benefit differences across workers (BENTIERS), whether the plan was integrated with social security or indexed (SSINT, COLA), whether the unit credit method was employed (ACTUARUC), the plan's average retirement age (AVRETAGE), and whether the plan reported its retirement age, amortization period, wage growth, inflation, and expected rate of return assumptions (AVRETAGMS, AMORTMS, WDOTMS, INFLMS, EXPRORMS). See the Appendix Table for variable descriptions and descriptive statistics.

were required to purchase insurance in order to induce board members to serve.)

Pension reporting and assumptions also affected funding outcomes as expected. Pension systems differed according to the frequency and format of funding reports, and stock funding ratios were lower where longer amortization periods were selected. It is possible that amortization periods were strategically chosen to influence contribution requirements: In fact, plans that did not report their amortization period appeared to be less well funded than average. Clearly it is necessary to standardize on reporting in order to obtain a clear picture of stock funding practices. Assumptions to compute promised future benefits also played a role in the empirical analysis: The model included variables indicating expected future price and wage increases, assumed discount rates and retirement ages, integration of benefits with Social Security, and portability of pension accruals. Of this set, only the portability factor proved statistically significant at conventional levels, and was negative. This is probably due to the fact that asset accruals did not always follow employees who were permitted to take benefit accruals with them when they changed jobs (usually this is limited to in-state moves). As such, it would be incorrect to conclude that labor mobility per se reduces stock funding ratios; rather, funding was low when systems permitted mobile workers to claim benefits with no concomitant asset accumulation backing up the promise.

Of the other factors controlled in the empirical funding analysis, very few had statistically significant effects. Somewhat surprising was the null effect of state requirements that pension plans had to be funded, requirements that benefit levels had to be guaranteed by law, and requirements that states must balance their budgets from one year to the next. Nor were funding levels different when dedicated or special taxes were earmarked for pension revenue.[21] Employee type (i.e., teachers) and unionization status also had no effect. In fact, only one other variable was found to systematically and powerfully reduce stock funding: namely, fiscal stress, measured here by the deviation of recent unemployment from the levels experienced over the past decade. The effect was substantial, suggesting that a one-point increase in a state's unemployment rate over the long-run average would depress stock funding by 6 percentage points. This effect is consistent with previous studies on public plans (Mitchell and Smith, 1994), and suggests that economic recessions have long- as well as short-term effects on public budgets through pension plan funding.

Because the stock funding data are better than the flow funding data, we emphasize those models and findings. The following conclusions may be drawn:

[21] Thus these data do not support Munnell and Ernsberger's (1989) suggestion that commingling pension funding with other government budgets may exacerbate funding problems. Those authors also suggested that more centralization might improve funding, but this hypothesis is difficult to test in practice since centralization can refer to many different aspects of plan management. Thus, for example, the actuarial assessment may be conducted centrally even though contributions are collected locally, the benefits administration may be managed centrally even though negotiation over benefits is conducted locally, and so forth.

- Better public pension funding was associated with a pension system having in-house actuaries and with board members being required to carry liability insurance.
- Public pension funding was lower when states had experienced fiscal stress, and when employees were represented on the pension system board.
- Funding did not appear sensitive to statutes guaranteeing benefits, or by legal funding requirements, or by the ability of states to carry budget deficits from one year to the next.

4 Sensitivity of results

Several sensitivity tests were conducted to judge the robustness of the results. One concern has to do with potential endogeneity of particular variables in the regression equations. For example, the performance equations included among the vector of control variables the PERS portfolio mix, because the plans' stock and bond holdings were expected to have affected the plan's investment performance. Nevertheless, it could be argued that a system's 1990 return and 1990 portfolio mix are probably simultaneously determined, if one had in mind a more general structural system involving expectations over variables not available in the data set. To test this possibility, these potentially endogenous portfolio composition variables were purged from the equation and the model reestimated. This produced estimates virtually identical to those already reported. In a similar vein, it might be asserted that the pension assumptions in equation (2) are endogenously determined by politicians setting funding targets. Hence a reduced-form equation was estimated that excluded pension assumptions from the model. Here too, coefficient estimates for the remaining variables were virtually identical to those reported here (results available on request). Hence it appears that this form of simultaneity does not exert a potent effect on the outcomes of most interest here, namely the pension governance and authority terms.

An additional question examined in some detail, but summarized here for the sake of brevity, pertained to the issue of biased reporting due to selective missing data. This was handled in two ways. First, if a pension plan had valid data on all but one (or a few) right-hand side variables, the missing datum was assigned a value of 0 and a missing-value indicator was given a value of 1. This permitted maintenance of sample size due to incomplete reporting for pension assumptions, in particular. A second approach was taken if the plan lacked a report for a dependent variable, since this raised a question about whether the data were missing randomly. Specifically, it might be that those plans which were performing less well than the market, or those which were more poorly funded than average might not be reporting. For this reason, several models were also estimated accounting for the probability of some plans not reporting investment yields and funding ratios. In each case, a sample selection term derived from a Probit nonreporting equation (inverse Mills ratio) was incorporated in the regression equations (1 and 2). The selection controls proved to be not statistically significant in general, and other coefficient estimates were quite similar to those reported here (results available on request).

The conclusion from the sensitivity analysis is that the results reported in Tables 4.6 and 4.7 are quite robust to a reasonable range of alternative formulations. They also confirm the important role of several pension governance features in public pension plan outcomes.[22] It must be emphasized that these behavioral patterns are derived from the data at hand, however, and are not necessarily representative of those plans excluded from the PENDAT sample. Specifically, the findings are most applicable to relatively large state-run plans, rather than the smaller local and municipal public plans covering a few officers or other uniformed public sector workers. As a result, the data are not yet good enough to know whether these smaller plans have the same problems, and same strengths, as their larger counterparts.

5   Conclusions and discussion

After a decade of strong growth, public pension plans in the United States are at a crossroads. A few state and local retirement systems are experiencing problems, and some retirees have experienced cuts in anticipated benefits as a result of these developments. In 1991, for instance, cost-of-living clauses in California's public pension plan were disallowed, with funds thus generated earmarked to "reduce employer contributions in fiscal year 1992–92 and subsequent fiscal years until those amounts are depleted" (cited in Melbinger 1992:23). In the future, if public fund assets prove too meager to meet benefit promises, retirees may face other benefit cuts.

In contrast to problems experienced in pension plans where public employers were subject to fiscal distress, many public plans have done quite well. The strong capital markets of the 1980s boosted many pension systems' investment portfolios substantially. Increased assets combined with careful money management and adequate employer contributions covered all or most of the benefits promised to current and future retirees. This research suggests that better performance from public pensions can be attained when plans

---

[22] Several other models were also examined, including one that entered the state budget deficit variable into the returns equations. The coefficient was not statistically significant and all other results were unchanged. Also examined were models where the TOP10MG term was replaced with a term indicating whether any external money manager was used, and results were unchanged.

manage their funds and actuarial computations professionally instead of relying on employee-trustees, and when they do not limit their portfolios to local investments.

These conclusions should be tempered by several considerations. First, additional work is required to control for portfolio risk characteristics, which have only been partly captured in the models examined here. Second, future studies should focus more attention on public pension board activism and its potential effects on pension plan yields as well as risk. A question that is only beginning to be asked is whether the social costs of underfunding and below-market return investments can offset their social benefits. In other words, from a public finance viewpoint, "economically targeted" investments might be justified when the social gains to such investment outweigh the social costs, taking care to note that the costs include potential retiree insecurity if public pension underfunding leads to reductions in anticipated benefits. It would be useful to design and implement such a cost–benefit framework when evaluating public pension asset allocation and performance practices. In order to do this, time-series data must be collected, which can be examined using a common reporting and account framework. Policy makers and re-searchers in the United States have begun to recognize this need, and have recommended standardization of pension data gathering, possibly under the auspices of a federal agency (Melbinger 1992; Mitchell 1991; Munnell 1983).

Because pension systems are extremely complex institutions, a single optimal package of plan practices that is relevant to all systems and across all time periods cannot be identified. Indeed, this research highlights some of the enormously complicated issues that must be confronted when seeking to establish funding norms. If near-full funding of public pension plans is deemed a worthwhile objective, it will be easier to monitor with standardiza-tion of pension reporting practices. This is particularly true of the many assumptions needed to assess a defined benefit plan's promised obligations. Obtaining this information is often a difficult task, inasmuch as rules de-termining pension benefit eligibility and amounts frequently differ from one group of employees to another and across cohorts. Sometimes benefit and contribution regulations have internally inconsistent objectives. For all these reasons, it is a fairly laborious task to improve reporting and disclosure patterns for public plans. The Government Accounting Standards Board in the United States has devoted several years to the development of a standardized framework to be used for reporting public pension plan liabilities and assets, and their work could be beneficially reviewed by those seeking improved public pension plan performance.[23]

---

[23] Fiscal analysts in other countries may profit from the experiences of public pension managers in the United States. A checklist of issues which should be considered is contained in Mitchell (1994).

Outside the United States, it is even more difficult to evaluate pension funding patterns. Data are often insufficient with which to derive assumptions needed for projecting expected labor force patterns, and forecasts of economic trends are also inherently uncertain. Frequently public pension systems are not computerized, making it quite difficult to track investments and participant data. In other cases, there may be significant evasion of public pension payroll taxes, which can make projections of contribution and benefit flows politically disputatious.[24]

This discussion raises a more general question: How should public pension policies around the world be evaluated? Mandated retirement savings programs in most nations are generally subject to a plethora of government restrictions – regarding where the funds can be invested domestically and whether pension funds can be invested abroad, about the fund's exposure to inflation and financial market risk, and related questions. Those contemplating mandating retirement savings programs must recognize that these restrictions are a means of reallocating the risks of retirement income security between the public and private sectors, which should be explicitly acknowledged in designing pension funding and investment policy. Whether the social costs of such programs offset their social benefits should be a question explicitly addressed.

A way to reframe this question is to ask why many U.S. state and local public pensions tend to be relatively well funded, at least as compared with federal plans in many other developed nations that have employed pay-as-you-go financing for some time. One explanation may be that underfunding in the United States is limited because of states' and localities' mobile populations, who respond to the additional tax burdens that underfunded plans must eventually impose. This theory has little empirical support, however, since underfunded pension promises appear to be imperfectly capitalized in property values (Epple and Schipper, 1981). There is some suggestion that public sector workers require a wage premium to compensate them for their underfunded pension promises, and underfunded pensions may also affect government bond ratings (Smith, 1981; Mitchell and Smith, 1994). These and other constraints will probably become increasingly binding with more flexible international labor and capital mobility, and may further restrict governments' ability to underfund public pension plans in the future.

Some analysts suggest that the myriad reporting and funding issues surrounding publicly managed pension plans can be reduced by substituting defined contribution plans in favor of defined benefit plans. In this case, an employer promises only to deposit some contribution rate into an account which then is invested, sometimes with the proviso that funds cannot be withdrawn until retirement. In the United States, deferred compensation plans

---

[24] Mitchell (1994) cites examples of data and tax collection problems in developing countries.

of this sort have become increasingly popular since enabling tax law regarding these plans was clarified during the 1980s. All states currently offer such plans to their public-sector employees, generally in the form of voluntary supplemental tax-deferred savings plans offered in addition to the conventional defined benefit pension plan. A recent study indicated participation rates of about 24% of eligible workers in the public sector. These plans are even more popular among private employees, where 57% of eligible employees participate in 401(k) defined contribution offerings. The difference in participation rates between public and private sectors is attributed to the fact that public employees must make the entire contribution themselves and the limit is currently $7,500 per year (or one-third of compensation), while in the private sector the contribution limit is higher and companies generally offer workers matching funds (EBRI, 1993).

One appeal of these savings plans is that they are self-directed, so participants can frequently tailor their investment portfolios individually. In recent years, however, analysts have become concerned that employees participating in deferred pay plans tend to overconcentrate their investment portfolios in low-risk, low-return assets. As a consequence of their conservative stance, future retirees may find that their retirement income is inadequate to meet needs (EBRI, 1993). This objection is linked to a broader criticism of these plans, which is that they do not necessarily generate subsistence income for retirees, inasmuch as eventual benefit amounts are linked to contributions, not need (James, 1993).

The appeal of mandatory defined contribution plans has been spurred by the recent experiences of Chile's new retirement system. More than a decade ago, a replacement plan for the country's foundering pay-as-you-go social security system was created by formulating a mandatory defined contribution plan, managed by several competing private investment houses. The Chilean system's popularity is in substantial part due to high investment returns during the 1980s, which exceeded those of other public retirement systems in Latin America (James, 1993; Mesa Lago, 1989, 1991). However, little is yet known about how well the Chilean plan performed relative to an internationally diversified portfolio, which is in principle the benchmark that participants would wish to employ. During the first several years of the Chilean pension plan's operation, for instance, the pension system's investment portfolio was limited almost exclusively to government bonds, and only gradually has private domestic equity been permitted. Even more recently, the Chilean defined contribution system has begun to introduce international asset holdings, though these are still limited to a fraction of the pension portfolio.[25]

---

[25] For discussions of the Chilean experience see Baeza (1986), Baeza and Manubens (1988), Cheyre (1991), Diamond (1994), Diamond and Valdés-Prieto (1994), Marcel and Arenas (1992), Myers (1985), Valdés-Prieto (1994), and Wallich (1983).

In sum, policy makers all over the world confront an aging population, and look to pension plans to help meet the growing retirement needs. A key element in meeting these needs will be the improvement of pension plan investment and funding performance. While the U.S. experience cannot be generalized to all countries, it suggests that public pension performance responds to the financial and administrative environment in which these plans operate. Retirement income security for tomorrow requires designing better pension systems today.

APPENDIX TO CHAPTER 4

All variables are derived from the PENDAT file (see Zorn 1991) unless otherwise indicated. Qualitative variables are (0,1) unless specified.

Table 4.A.1
Variable definitions

DEPENDENT VARIABLES

YR1ROR:	Annual (1990) rate of return (%).
YR5ROR:	Average (1986-90) annualized rate of return (%).
AST/PBO:	Reported pension system assets / PBO measure of cumulative plan liabilities (%).
FLOWFUND:	Annual actual / required employer plan contributions (%).

EXPLANATORY VARIABLES

A.	*Pension Board Composition*
BDELAC:	Fraction of pension Board elected by active employees (%).
BDELRT:	Fraction of pension Board elected by retired employees (%).
LIABINS:	Board is covered by liability insurance.
BDBENOK:	Board is required to authorize benefit amounts.
BDACTOK:	Board is required to authorize actuarial assumptions.
B.	*Pension Management Practices*
ADINVST:	Administrative cost charged to pension investment income.
INVINHS:	Investment staff of pension portfolio partly (or fully) managed in-house.
ACCINHS:	Acccounting staff needs of pension system partly (or fully) met in-house.
TOP10MG:	Some investments handled by top 10 performance bracket managers (see text).
TOP10*EXT:	Plan investments exclusively handled by top 10 money managers.
C.	*Pension Investment Practices*
PRUDMAN:	Pension Board required to act according to "prudent man" rule.
INSTATE:	Fraction of pension investments which must be directed in-state (%).
STKMAX:	Maximum limitation on the assets in the pension portfolio.
D.	*Pension Reporting Practices*
INDINVPF:	Pension system obtains indenpendent investment performance evaluations.
FREQVAL:	Frequency of independent performance evaluations.
REPSOLO:	System issues own financial report (not integrated with other budgets).
GIVERPT:	Plan participants receive annual financial report.
AMORTPER:	Amortization period for past service liabilites.
AMORTMS:	Amortization period not stated.
ACTUARUC:	Pension system uses unit credit method of computing pension liabilities.

Table 4.A.1 (cont.)

E.	*Pension Assumptions*
COLA:	Benefits are partially (or fully) indexed after retirement.
WDOT:	Future salary growth assumption required to compute PBO.
WDOTMS:	Salary growth assumption not stated.
PORTABLE:	Employees moving within state may carry benefit accruals to new plans.
NEXPROR:	Interest rate assumption used in computing PBO (%).
EXPRORMS:	Interest rate assumption not stated.
INFL:	Cost of living assumption required to compute PBO.
INFLMS:	Cost of living assumption not stated.
AVRETAGE:	Average retirement age used in computing PBO (yrs).
AVRETAGEMS:	Average retirement age not stated.
SSINT:	Plan integrated with Social Security.

F.	*Other Factors*
FUNDLAW:	State has legal funding standard for pension system.
DEFPOS:	State law does not prohibit carryover of state budget deficit from one year to the next (National Association of State Budget Officers 1992)
TCHRPLAN:	System covers at least some teachers and other school employees.
ASSETS:	Actuarial value of pension system assets, typically at market value ($M).
ASSETSQ:	Squared value of ASSETS.
BOND:	Pension system assets held in corporate and government bonds (%).
STOCK:	Pension system assets held in stock (%).
BENNOCUT:	State has law guaranteeing benefit amounts.
BENTIERS:	Benefits differ according to worker hire date.
ISUNION:	At least some employees covered by the pension system unionized.
SPECTAX:	Special or dedicated tax is source of employer contributions.
UNEMPD:	Recent (1990) level of unemployment minus the long run (1981-89) average level of unemployment level in the state (Mitchell and Smith, 1992).

Table 4.A.2
Descriptive statistics

I. Dependent Variables	Mean	St. Dev.
YR1ROR	7.67	5.0
YR5ROR	11.68	3.0
AST/PBO	90.75	33.1
FLOWFUND	93.79	51.2
I. Explanatory Variables		
BDELAC	31.01	25.3
BDELRT	3.27	6.2
LIABINS	0.42	0.5
BDACTOK	0.83	0.4
BDBENOK	0.72	0.5
ADINVST	0.51	0.5
INVINHS	0.42	0.5
ACCINHS	0.61	0.5
TOP10MG	0.41	0.5
TOP10*EXT	0.18	0.4
PRUDMAN	0.85	0.4
INSTATE	1.45	10.0
STKMAX	0.83	0.4
INDINUPF	0.75	0.4
FREQVAL	1.23	0.8
REPSOLO	0.59	0.5
GIVERPT	0.90	0.3
AMORTPER	22.64	14.0
AMORTMS	0.10	0.3

Table 4.A.2 (cont.)

ACTUARUC	0.10	0.3
COLA	0.79	0.4
WDOT	4.80	2.5
WDOTMS	0.20	0.4
PORTABLE	0.35	0.5
EXPROR	7.75	0.9
EXPRORMS	0.01	0.1
INFL	3.88	2.4
INFLMS	0.26	0.4
AVRETAGE	47.85	23.7
AVRETAGEMS	0.19	0.4
SSINT	0.09	0.3
FUNDLAW	0.58	0.5
DEFPOS	0.35	0.5
TCHRPLAN	0.12	0.3
ASSETS	3252.28	6637.4
ASSETSSQ (*10-6)	54.35	212.2
BOND	33.16	28.1
STOCK	36.09	17.3
BENNOCUT	0.52	0.5
BENTIERS	0.28	0.5
ISUNION	0.69	0.5
SPECTAX	0.14	0.4
UNEMPD90	-1.72	1.2

References

Baeza, Sergio, ed. 1986. *Análisis de la Previsión en Chile.* Chile: Centro de Estudios Públicos.

Baeza, Sergio, and Rodrigo Manubens, eds. 1988. *Sistema Privado De Pensiones En Chile.* Santiago, Chile: Centro de Estudios Publicos.

Beebower, Gilbert L., and Gary L. Bergstrom. 1977. "A Performance Analysis of Pension and Profit-Sharing Portfolios: 1966–1975." *Financial Analysts Journal* 33, May–June: 31–42.

Benartzi, Shlomo, and Richard Thaler. 1992. "Myopic Loss Aversion and the Equity Premium Puzzle." Ithaca, N.Y.: Johnson Graduate School of Management, Cornell University, October. Unpublished manuscript.

Berkowitz, Logue & Associates. 1986. *Study of the Investment Performance of ERISA Plans.* Prepared for the Office of Pension and Welfare Benefits, U.S. Department of Labor, Washington, D.C.

Bleakney, Thomas P. 1972. *Retirement Systems for Public Employees.* Philadelphia: University of Pennsylvania Press.

Brinson, Gary P., L. Randolph Hood, and Gilbert L. Beebower. 1986. "Determinants of Portfolio Performance." *Financial Analysts Journal* 47, July–August: 39–44.

Cheyre, Hernán V. 1991. *La Previsión en Chile Ayer y Hoy.* Santiago, Chile: Centro de Estudios Públicos.

Diamond, Peter. 1994. "Pension Reform in a Transition Economy: Notes on Poland and Chile." In *The Transition in Eastern Europe,* edited by Oliver Blanchard, pp. 243–257. Chicago: University of Chicago Press.

Diamond, P. A., and S. Valdés-Prieto. 1994. "Social Security Reforms." In, *The Chilean Economy,* edited by B. Bosworth, R. Dornbusch, and R. Labán, chap. 6. Washington, D.C.: Brookings Institution.

Durgin, H. 1991. "Politicians Grabbing Pension Assets." *Pensions and Investments* 7, July 8: 1–39.

Employee Benefit Research Institute (EBRI). 1993. *Notes* 14 (1), January.

Epple, Dennis, and K. Schipper. 1981. "Municipal Pension Funding: A Theory and Some Evidence." *Public Choice* 37: 141–178.

Goldman, Sachs. 1993. *The Nature and Scale of Economically Targeted Investments by the 104 Largest U.S. Public Pension Plans.* New York. Unpublished report prepared August.

Governmental Accounting Standards Board (GASB). 1986. "Disclosure of Pension Information by Public Employee Retirement Systems and State and Local Governmental Employers." Statement No. 5. Norwalk, Conn. November.

1992. *Action Report.* Norwalk, Conn. December.

Grinblatt, Mark, and Sheridan Titman. 1989. "Mutual Fund Performance: An Analysis of Quarterly Portfolio Holdings." *Journal of Business* 62(3): 393–416.

Gustman, Alan, and Olivia S. Mitchell. 1992. "Pensions and the US Labor Market." In *Pensions and the US Economy,* edited by Z. Bodie and A. Munnell, pp. 39–87. Pension Research Council. Philadelphia: Irwin.

Hemmerick, Steve. 1991a. "California May Cut Funding." *Pensions and Investments* 19, August 19: 18.

1991b. "Groups Take on California." *Pensions and Investments* 2, December 9: 34.

Hoffman, Arnold, and John Mondejar. 1992. "Pension Assets and Financial Markets, 1950–89." In *Trends in Pensions 1992,* edited by John A. Turner and Daniel J. Beller, pp. 419–448. Washington, D.C.: U.S. Government Printing Office.

Ibbotson Associates. 1992. *SBBI 1992 Yearbook.* Chicago.

Inman, Robert P. 1986. "Appraising the Funding Status of Teacher Pensions: An Econometric Approach." *National Tax Journal,* March 39: 21–24.

1982. "Public Employee Pensions and the Local Labor Budget." *Journal of Public Economics* 19: 49–71.

Ippolito, Richard A. 1989. "Efficiency with Costly Information: A Study of Mutual Fund Performance, 1965–1984." *Quarterly Journal of Economics* 104(1), February: 1–23.

James, Estelle. 1993. "Income Security for Old Age: Conceptual Background and Major Issues." World Bank Public Sector Management and Private Sector Development Working Paper WPS 977. Washington, D.C.: World Bank. September.

"Lag Found in Teachers' Pension Contributions." 1991. *Employee Benefit Plan Review* 45, February: 38.

Lakonishok, Josef, Andrei Shleifer, Richard Thaler, and Robert Vishny. 1991. "Window Dressing by Pension Fund Managers." *American Economic Review* 81(2), May: 227–231.

Lakonishok, Josef, Andrei Shleifer, and Robert Vishny. 1992. "The Structure and Performance of the Money Management Industry." *Brookings Papers on Economic Activity: Microeconomics* 32: 339–391.

Marcel, Mario, and Alberto Arenas. 1992. *Social Security Reform in Chile.* Inter-American Development Bank Occasional Paper No. 5. Washington, D.C.

122   Olivia S. Mitchell and Ping-Lung Hsin

McCarthy, David D., and John A. Turner. 1992. "Pension Rates of Return in Large and Small Plans." In *Trends in Pensions 1992*, edited by John A. Turner and Daniel J. Beller, pp. 543–576. Washington, D.C.: U.S. Government Printing Office. USGPO. 1992.

Melbinger, Michael S. 1992. "The Possibility of Federal Regulation of State and Local Government Retirement Plans." *Employee Benefits Journal* 17(4), December: 23–27.

Mesa-Lago, Carmelo. 1989. *Ascent to Bankruptcy: Financing Social Security in Latin America.* Pittsburgh: University of Pittsburgh Press.

1991. "Portfolio Performance of Selected Social Security Institutes in Latin America." World Bank Discussion Paper No. 139. Washington, D.C.: World Bank.

Mitchell, Olivia S. 1988. "Worker Knowledge of Pension Provisions." *Journal of Labor Economics 6,* January: 21–39.

1991. *Testimony on Public Sector Pensions.* Joint Hearing before the House Select Committee on Aging and the Subcommittee on Investment, Jobs and Prices of the Joint Economic Committee of the U.S. Congress. Washington, D.C. November 20.

1994. "Retirement Systems in the Developed and Developing World: Institutional Structure, Economic Effects, and Lessons for Economies in Transition." Pension Research Council Working Paper No. 94-3. Philadelphia: Wharton School, University of Pennsylvania.

Mitchell, Olivia S., and Emily S. Andrews. 1981. "Scale Economies in Private Multi-Employer Pension Systems." *Industrial and Labor Relations Review* 34, July: 522–530.

Mitchell, Olivia S., and Robert S. Smith. 1992. "Public Sector Pensions: Benefits, Funding and Unionization." In *Industrial Relations Research Association Papers and Proceedings of the 44th Annual Meetings,* pp. 126–133. Madison, Wis.: Industrial Relations Research Association.

1994. "Pension Funding in the Public Sector." *Review of Economics and Statistics* 76, May: 278–290.

Mitchell, Olivia S., Annika Sunden, Ping-Lung Hsin, and Gary Reid. 1993. "An International Appraisal of Social Security Administration Costs." Washington, D.C.: World Bank. Mimeograph.

Munnell, Alicia H. 1983. *Testimony on Public Pensions.* Joint hearing of the Subcommittee on Oversight of the Ways and Means Committee and the Subcommittee on Labor-Management Relations of the Committee on Education and Labor. Washington, D.C. November 15.

Munnell, Alicia H., and C. Nicole Ernsberger. 1989. "Public Pension Surpluses and National Saving: Foreign Experience." *New England Economic Review,* March–April 1989: 16–38.

Myers, Robert J. 1985. "Privatization of Chile's Social Security Program." *Benefits Quarterly* 1(3): 26–35.

National Association of State Budget Officers (NASBO). 1992. "State Balanced Budget Requirements: Provisions and Practice." Washington D.C. June. Mimeograph.

New York Retired Public Employees Association. 1989. "Our Money's Safety: A Response to the Governor's Task Force Report on Pension Fund Investment." Report issued September.

New York State Industrial Cooperation Council. 1990. "Economically Targeted Investments by Pension Funds: A Study of the Feasibility of Implementation of Recommendations Made by the Governor's Task Force on Pension Fund Investment." Report issued February.

1989. "Our Money's Worth: The Report of the Governor's Task Force on Pension Fund Investment." Report issued June.

Pesando, James E., and Douglas Hyatt. 1992. "The Distribution of Investment Risk in Defined Benefit Pension Plans: A Re-Examination." Paper prepared for the Conference on Current Pensions Policy Issues, Miami University, Oxford, Ohio, March.

Phillips, Kristen. 1992. "State and Local Government Pension Benefits." In *Trends in Pensions 1992*, edited by John A. Turner and Daniel J. Beller, pp. 341–392. Washington, D.C.: U.S. Government Printing Office.

Piacentini, J., and J. Foley. 1992. *EBRI Databook on Employee Benefits*. Washington, D.C.: Employee Benefit Research Institute.

Price, M. 1991. "NY Bill Loosens Fund Restrictions." *Pensions and Investments* 10, May 13: 46.

Schmitt, Ray, Carolyn L. Merck, and Jennifer A. Neisner. 1991. "Public Pension Plans: A Status Report." Congressional Research Service Report for Congress #91-813 EPW. Washington, D.C. December.

Smith, R. S. 1981. "Compensating Differentials for Pensions and Underfunding in the Public Sector." *Review of Economics and Statistics* 63: 463–468.

Snell, Ronald K., and Susan Wolfe. 1990. "Public Pension Funds' Investment Practices: Results of a Survey Conducted by the National Conference of State Legislatures and the National Association of Legislative Fiscal Officers." National Conference of State Legislatures, Fiscal Affairs Program, Legislative Finance Paper no. 72. Denver, Colo., February.

Sunden, Annika, and Olivia S. Mitchell. 1994. "An Examination of Social Security Administration Costs in the United States." Pension Research Council Working Paper No. 94-7. Philadelphia: Wharton School, University of Pennsylvania.

Valdés-Prieto, Salvador. 1994. "Administrative Charges in Pensions in Chile, Malaysia, Zambia and the United States." Policy Research Working Paper No. 1372, World Bank, Washington, D.C. (October).

Verhovek, S. H. 1990. "States are Finding Pension Funds Can Be a Bonanza Hard to Resist." *New York Times,* April 22, E8.

Wallich, Christine. 1983. "Savings Mobilization through Social Security: The Experience of Chile during 1916–77." World Bank Staff Working Paper No. 553. Washington, D.C.: World Bank.

Wilshire Associates. 1990. *Report on Funding Levels for State Retirement Systems*. Santa Monica, Calif.

Zorn, Paul. 1990. *Survey of State Retirement Systems Covering General Employees and Teachers*. Washington, D.C.: Government Finance Officers Association, June.

1991. *Survey of State and Local Government Employee Retirement Systems*. Washington, D.C.: Government Finance Officers Association, November.

PART II

Fiscal deficits and private saving in pension reform

CHAPTER 5

Pension reform and growth

Giancarlo Corsetti and Klaus Schmidt-Hebbel

Abstract

This chapter reviews the qualitative macroeconomic and welfare implications of substituting a pay-as-you-go pension system by a fully funded (FF) scheme and summarizes the typically small effects found by the simulations literature based on exogenous growth one-sector models. However, much larger and sustained effects are obtained in the framework of an overlapping-generations model with endogenous growth and formal–informal production sectors, presented in this chapter. Model simulations suggest that a pay-as-you-go-to-FF reform could raise substantially long-term growth rates by eliminating the pay-as-you-go incentives for an informalization of production and employment. A final look at the Chilean reform experience suggests that the structural transformation toward formalization is taking place and that both private saving and growth are rising substantially since 1980. Econometric evidence suggests that the 1981 pension reform could be contributing to Chile's large increase in private saving.

Introduction

Pension system reform is at the forefront of policy discussions and changes in many developing and transition economies. Recent surveys, conferences, and specialized studies attest to this revival of interest in old-age saving arrangements by policy makers and academics (see Felderer, 1993; Arrau and Schmidt-Hebbel, 1994; and World Bank, 1994). It is often argued that substituting state-run pay-as-you-go pension systems by private fully funded schemes could raise saving and eliminate factor market distortions, increasing

We are grateful for comments received from Rodrigo Cifuentes, Alvaro Donoso, and other participants at the Conference on "Pensions: Funding, Privatization and Macroeconomic Policy," Catholic University of Chile, Santiago, January 26–27, 1994. We are particularly indebted to Salvador Valdés-Prieto for outstanding comments and suggestions on an earlier draft. Excellent research assistance by Raimundo Soto is gratefully acknowledged. The usual disclaimer applies.

long-term growth and welfare levels. This chapter evaluates these claims by surveying the existing literature, offering a new approach, and evaluating the empirical evidence limited to the Chilean pension reform experience.

We review first the simulation literature focused on macroeconomic and intergenerational welfare implications of adopting mandatory pension schemes and substituting a pay-as-you-go by a fully funded (FF) system.[1] The existing literature provides a few results on the magnitude of the effects of pension systems and reforms. This chapter compares the output and welfare results obtained in the traditional framework of exogenous growth and overlapping generations (OLG) by Auerbach and Kotlikoff (1987) for the United States and by Arrau and Schmidt-Hebbel (1993), Valdés-Prieto and Cifuentes (1993), and Cifuentes and Valdés-Prieto (1994) for representative economies. Typically, such effects turn out to be moderate at best: Output and welfare are affected only in the very long run and by amounts that normally are not very large.

We show that similar conclusions obtain in the framework of an OLG model of endogenous growth. As is well known, the long-run equilibrium of an endogenous growth model is characterized by stationarity in the rate of growth of output, capital, and consumption. The pure intergenerational transfer-related effect of social security turns out to affect growth rates only slightly – of course, the compounded long-run impact on macroeconomic variables is very large.

In addition to the effect of intergenerational transfers, a pay-as-you-go-FF reform may also affect growth through efficiency improvements in both financial and labor markets. The potential efficiency gains are derived from reform-related incentives to liberalize financial markets or to reduce the magnitude of financial repression. Pension funds, the argument goes, provide particularly valuable financial resources in the process of reforming domestic markets, both because of their magnitude and their encouragement of the development of long-term investment instruments. Efficiency gains in labor markets work through changes in labor supply and resource allocation decisions in response to new incentives in factor and product markets.

This chapter focuses on these mechanisms by making use of a stylized two-sector model of social security and capital accumulation developed in the tradition of the endogenous growth literature. The productive structure of the economy responds to a pension reform as resources can be moved from a

---

[1] An analytical review is offered by Arrau and Schmidt-Hebbel (1993) that discusses the macroeconomic literature of pension systems, initiated by the seminal work of Samuelson (1958) and Diamond (1965) and continued by Samuelson (1975) and Auerbach and Kotlikoff (1987), Breyer (1989), Homburg (1990), Breyer and Wildasin (1993), and Valdés-Prieto and Cifuentes (1993), among others.

formal (taxed and regulated) sector to an informal (untaxed and unregulated) sector. On the one hand, the sectoral reallocation of production generates a Laffer curve, determining the financial sustainability of the pension reform. On the other hand, as efficiency levels of the two sectors differ, output levels and growth rates change with the magnitude of pension-related distortions. As a result, the model highlights conditions under which the long-run impact of the reform can be considerably higher than what is suggested by conventional models that focus exclusively on intergenerational transfers. The issue of financial market liberalization is addressed by varying the mix of labor and capital income taxes financing a pay-as-you-go scheme. Such a mix affects growth through two channels. The first is the distortion in the intertemporal allocation of the accumulated factors; the second is the implicit transfer between people with different propensities to save (young and old).

Illustrative simulations based on this model show that intergenerational transfers caused by a pay-as-you-go-FF pension reform tend to have the least effect on stationary growth. More significant is the financial market effect. The dominating growth gain may stem from reducing the incentive to evade pay-as-you-go contributions in the informal sector when substituting pay-as-you-go by FF.

Only one country has implemented a radical pay-as-you-go-FF reform in which sufficient time has elapsed since its start to assess possible reform effects on economic structure, private saving, and growth. We present some evidence offered by the 1981 Chilean pension reform, focusing closely on the post-1980 changes in economic structure, saving, and growth. Regression analysis explores the evidence on the possible contribution of pension reform to the significant improvement of private saving in Chile.

Section 1 reviews the qualitative macroeconomic and welfare changes of a pay-as-you-go-FF pension reform and compares the simulation results of the existing literature. Section 2 introduces a new two-sector endogenous growth model and applies it to simulate steady-state growth effects of pension reforms. Section 3 looks at Chile's changes in economic structure, saving, and growth and reports regression results for saving.

1 Pension systems, saving, and output levels

1.1 Pension systems and reforms

A pay-as-you-go scheme is an intergenerational social contract of mandatory transfers from workers to pensioners, backed by an implicit government debt or promise to contributing worker cohorts that they will benefit from future worker contributions once they retire. A pay-as-you-go system is said to be financially balanced when pension payments are exactly matched by worker contributions. This is seldom observed in practice. Immature (i.e., recently started) pay-as-you-go systems typically show surpluses, which often turn into deficits when the ratio of pensioners to workers reaches that implied by system maturity. Changing demographic conditions also impinge on pay-as-you-go balances: A rising old-age dependency ratio leads to increasing pay-as-you-go system losses when contributions and pension benefits remain unchanged. Pay-as-you-go surpluses and deficits are typically absorbed by government budgets. Only when the pay-as-you-go system is mature, population growth is constant, and pay-as-you-go is financially balanced are pensioners paid on average a real return on their contributions equal to the real rate of growth of the wage bill or the economy.

There are two reasons why the return on contributions differs from the market real interest rate. First, the growth rate of the wage bill is typically lower than the real return on capital – a feature of dynamically efficient economies a la Diamond (1965). Second, although the growth rate of the wage bill determines the average return on pay-as-you-go contributions, the return obtained by each individual worker is different from the average pensioner's return. The reason is that pay-as-you-go pensions often include a component – unrelated to contributions – that distributes income within cohorts. This distributional component favors (often only in theory) low-income workers or (often in practice) powerful worker groups who are able to secure generous pensions from the political establishment. Hence, a pay-as-you-go scheme is in general actuarially unfair from the point of view of individual workers.

An alternative mandatory pension arrangement is a defined-contribution fully funded scheme that forces workers to save part of their wage income for old age. The average return on old-age saving depends on (domestic and international) market interest rates and rates of return. In principle, an FF system could also include distribution among groups of workers within a given generation, hence weakening the relation between contributions and pensions. As we abstract from this case, pensions in an FF system are actuarially fair for each individual.

A pension reform that substitutes pay-as-you-go by FF involves three changes: The link between worker contributions and benefits is strengthened, the previously hidden pay-as-you-go debt is made explicit, and the distributional function of the old pay-as-you-go system is separated from the new FF scheme. The most generalized feature of pay-as-you-go systems in the real world is pension system losses that grow over time as a result of rising old-age dependency and/or increasing pay-as-you-go system maturity. The fiscal consequences of rising pay-as-you-go system losses are the single most important motivation for reforming pay-as-you-go schemes, typically more important than the potential efficiency and saving–output gains reaped from adopting a FF system (see World Bank, 1994).

Many features determine how starting a mandatory pension scheme or substituting one scheme for another affects an economy's macroeconomic variables and (some appropriately defined criterion of) Pareto efficiency. While we refer the reader to a more extensive survey of the literature (Arrau and Schmidt-Hebbel, 1993), in this chapter we focus on three main features that determine the consequences of substituting pay-as-you-go by FF.[2]

The distortionary nature of pay-as-you-go contributions

Pay-as-you-go pension contributions are typically proportional to wage income and therefore can distort labor market decisions and employment levels. As mentioned earlier, the reason is that the link between worker contributions and benefits is weakened twice by a pay-as-you-go system: Average rates of return on contributions differ from (are typically lower than) market interest rates, and rates paid to individual pensioners on their marginal contributions differ from average rates paid to their cohorts due to intragenerational income redistribution.

Workers attempt to reduce the excess burden of this pure tax by adjusting both the length of their working life and the quantity of labor supplied, or shifting into informal labor markets – the latter response being more likely in developing countries – where all taxes, including the pure tax component of pay-as-you-go contributions, can be avoided. Firms respond to higher pay-as-you-go labor costs by adopting less labor-intensive technologies or by shifting operations to informal markets as well. Overall, pay-as-you-go tends to raise gross labor costs in formal markets while depressing real net wages – a labor market distortion that is avoided by an FF scheme, at least for those workers who are able to assess properly the link between their current contributions and future pension benefits. Loss in employment and economic efficiency due to the pure tax component of pay-as-you-go contributions depends on the relevant supply and demand elasticities for labor and capital (saving and investment).

Form of financing of system transition

The straightforward way to finance the reform transition deficit is by issuing new government debt. The old implicit pay-as-you-go debt is swapped for new explicit government debt so that the government's old pay-as-you-go

---

[2] Other structural features, not considered here, that determine the sign and size of macroeconomic and welfare effects of adopting a mandatory pension system or substituting it by a different scheme are the following: financial openness, intergenerational altruism, the size of mandatory saving relative to presystem voluntary saving, consumer myopia, borrowing constraints, age structure, and incomplete insurance markets for sharing risk.

debt is now explicitly reflected on government books.[3] Debt financing implies that national saving, the capital stock, and the intergenerational distribution of welfare are only marginally affected, by magnitudes that depend on the net efficiency gains of the reform. A very different result is obtained when the transition deficit is financed using current budget surpluses, that is, by raising taxes (and/or cutting public spending). A fully tax-financed transition reverts the initial pay-as-you-go transfer from workers to pensioners – associated with the start of the initial pay-as-you-go scheme – by fully paying off the implicit pay-as-you-go debt. This hurts tax-paying transition generations[4] and benefits nontaxed posttransition generations. Tax financing of the transition – as any restrictive fiscal policy that pays off government debt through taxes and hence shifts resources from current to future generations – encourages higher saving and capital formation, therefore raising future per capita income and wage levels. These first-order effects on saving and capital formation, due to the intergenerational transfer embedded in tax financing, are added to potential second-order effects of the pension reform due to net efficiency changes.

Similar considerations apply to the case of spending cuts, to the extent that currently active workers enjoy less public or publicly provided goods. Note that a reduction in public investment may also affect the path of capital accumulation as well as the efficiency of private capital.

The distortionary nature of general taxation

A debt-financed transition deficit requires raising additional government revenue only to the extent that the interest bill increases when FF substitutes explicit new debt for implicit pay-as-you-go debt. A higher tax rate raises the magnitude of distortions due to general taxation – independently of the underlying tax base. Hence, a shift from pay-as-you-go to FF, while potentially eliminating labor market distortions, induces more widespread tax distortions, which could be permanent (if the transition deficit is debt-financed) or transitory (if it is tax-financed). If general taxation is at the margin less distortionary than payroll taxation, a pension reform brings positive net efficiency gains and can raise the economy's Pareto efficiency.[5]

---

[3] Debt financing in a broad sense can be thought to refer to issuing any public liability or liquidating any public asset to finance the transition deficit. The latter option includes privatization of public enterprises and drawing from government holdings of international reserves or strategic commodity stocks.

[4] These generations could include current pensioners retired under the initial pay-as-you-go system or could comprise only current and future working cohorts.

[5] On the relative efficiency of income taxation (which is the general tax considered by the simulations discussed in this chapter), Auerbach, Kotlikoff, and Skinner (1983) conclude from second-best theory that income taxation will not always be more efficient than wage or payroll taxation; "rather, the relative efficiency of the two taxes will depend on the particular structure

In case of a tax-financed transition – equivalent to a debt-financed reform combined with a contractionary fiscal policy – the new tax-induced distortion is temporary and lasts as long as taxes are required to pay off the initial pay-as-you-go debt. Nonetheless, the literature on tax-smoothing warns that increasing tax rates while shortening the period of contractionary fiscal policy may induce a more than proportional drop in output, labor supply, and welfare.[6]

In conclusion, the distortion-related effects on Pareto efficiency of the way the transition is financed are generally ambiguous. Only under lump sum general taxation – at least theoretically conceivable – does the pay-as-you-go-FF reform raise unambiguously Pareto efficiency by eliminating the distortionary effects of pay-as-you-go taxation.

1.2 Quantitative long-run output and welfare effects of mandatory pension systems and reforms: A look at the literature

Few studies have assessed the short- and long-run fiscal, output, and welfare effects of introducing or substituting mandatory pension systems. Here we discuss the findings of four simulation studies summarized in Table 5.1: one for the U.S. economy (Auerbach and Kotlikoff, 1987), the second for a representative economy (Arrau and Schmidt-Hebbel, 1993), and the third and fourth also for a representative economy (Valdés-Prieto and Cifuentes, 1993, and Cifuentes and Valdés-Prieto, 1994).[7]

of preferences" (Auerbach and Kotlikoff, 1987, p. 80). Auerbach and Kotlikoff's (1987) simulation results for a switch from income to wage taxation (p. 77, table 5.7) show efficiency losses for six and efficiency gains for one of their parameter combinations. This could suggest that efficiency gains are more likely than efficiency losses when substituting payroll by income taxation.

[6] These considerations are also important, although for different reasons, in the presence of short-run price rigidities and liquidity constraints, when the contractionary fiscal policy implied by tax-financing the transition may run against short-run output stabilization policies. The presence of Keynesian market failures thus reinforces the argument in favor of gradualism in addressing the financial costs of the reform.

[7] There are two similar dynamic simulation studies on pay-as-you-go-FF reforms for real-world economies, one for Mexico (Arrau, 1990b) and a second for Chile (Arrau, 1991, 1992). However, they do not report long-run output and welfare effects of the reforms.

The four studies reported here are based on OLG models aimed at assessing the effects on long-term output levels of intergenerational transfers and changes in market distortions. They all share the dynamic general equilibrium framework by Auerbach and Kotlikoff for a closed economy composed of 55 optimizing overlapping cohorts. In all four models intergenerational voluntary transfers and intragenerational distribution are ruled out and mandatory saving always falls short of the amount consumers would voluntarily save in the absence of any pension scheme. Myopia and credit constraints are not considered in the first (Auerbach and Kotlikoff) and the second (Arrau and Schmidt-Hebbel) studies but are introduced in the third (Valdés-Prieto and Cifuentes) and the fourth (Cifuentes and Valdés-Prieto). The main differ-

Table 5.1
Long-run output and welfare effects of pension systems and reforms
(Exogenous growth)

	Output Change	Welfare Change
5.1A Effects at Year 150 after Introducing PAYG in the U.S. Economy		
Under Income Taxation	-5.3%	-6.0
Under Wage Taxation	-4.9%	-6.3
Under Consumption Taxation	-4.5%	-4.8
5.1B. Effects at Year 110 after Substituting PAYG by FF in Representative Economies		
High Population Growth (n=2% per year)		
Debt-Financed Transition Deficit	-1%	-0.3%
Tax-Financed Transition Deficit	+3%	+6.8%
Stationary Population (n=0)		
Debt-Financed Transition Deficit	-4%	-3.5%
Tax-Financed Transition Deficit	+5%	+12.5%
5.1C Steady-State Effects of Substituting PAYG by FF in Representative Economies		
Tax-Financed Transition Deficit		
Without Credit Constraints	+1.9%	+5.9%
With Credit Constraints	+27.1%	+13.5%
5.1.D. Steady-State Effects of Substituting PAYG by FF in Representative Economies		
With Credit Constraints		
75% Debt, 25% Tax-financed Transition Deficit	+7.0%	+3.4%
Full Tax-Financed Transition Deficit	+21.8%	+16.3%

Sources:

5.1A: Auerbach and Kotlikoff (1987), Tables 10.1 and 10.2. The long-run output change is calculated from the percentage changes in capital and labor at year 150 presented in Table 10.1, weighted at a 0.25 capital share.

5.1B: Arrau and Schmidt-Hebbel (1993), Tables 3, 4, and 9. Technical progress is 2% per year, hence stationary GDP growth is 4% or 2%, respectively.

5.1C: Valdés-Prieto and Cifuentes (1993), Table 10 and authors' calculations. Population growth is 2% and technical progress is 2%, hence stationary GDP growth is 4%.

5.1D: Cifuentes and Valdés-Prieto (1994), Table 5, and special calculations provided by those authors. Population growth is 0.5% and technical progress is 0.5%, hence stationary GDP growth is 1%.

ence between the model offered by Auerbach and Kotlikoff and the other frameworks is that both pay-as-you-go and general taxation are distortionary in the former but only general taxation is distortionary in the three latter models, where labor is supplied inelastically. The second study reports sensitivity analyses corresponding to alternative assumptions on critical parameter values – the results are similar to the base-case results summarized here. The first, second, and fourth studies report impact, transition, and steady-state effects on the main fiscal, macroeconomic, and welfare variables. The third study, however, is a model for steady-state equilibria. Here we focus only on long-run or steady-state results reported in the four studies, which often differ strongly from short or medium-term effects.

Starting pay-as-you-go shifts resources from future to current generations. For the United States (Table 5.1A), the start of pay-as-you-go is estimated to reduce long-term output levels by figures close to 5%, with minor differences depending on how general taxes are raised – either on general income, wage income, or consumption. The corresponding long-term welfare losses of future cohorts are 5% to 6%.[8]

The simulations for representative economies by Arrau and Schmidt-Hebbel distinguish between two demographic scenarios (high and zero population growth) and how the transition deficit is financed (debt or taxes). Consider first the case of high population growth at 2% per year. When the fiscal transition deficit is financed by issuing explicit government debt (i.e., the case of a straightforward pension reform), the implicit pay-as-you-go debt is put on government books. Therefore the explicit government debt increases significantly, although this massive debt buildup does not crowd out private investment. The reason is that the reform raises both demand and supply of government debt, as new worker contributions to the FF system are invested in newly issued government debt during the 45 years of fiscal transition deficit.

While direct intergenerational transfers are ruled out by debt financing, higher income taxation imposes a slight but permanent efficiency cost. Hence, long-run saving, capital, investment, and output levels are slightly but negatively affected by debt financing. Output at year 110 is 1% lower than under the initial pay-as-you-go scheme, reflecting the full impact of the modest efficiency loss from higher income taxation. The welfare loss of future steady-state generations is 0.3%, derived from permanently higher income taxation. It is important to note that this loss could be a net gain when labor is supplied elastically and the associated labor market efficiency gain more than offsets the income tax efficiency loss from higher income taxation.

When the transition deficit is financed by taxes, the pension reform is actually combined with a contractionary fiscal policy. This combination hurts tax-paying transition generations and benefits posttransition cohorts. The transfer to future generations raises long-run saving, capital, and output levels. However, long-run output gains of a fully tax-financed pension reform are modest. At year 110 after reform start, output exceeds the level it would have attained under the old pay-as-you-go system by only 3%. Future generations gain 6.8% of their wealth as a result of both the transfer from the tax-paying transition cohorts (which pay off the initial implicit pay-as-you-go debt) and a small efficiency gain due to slightly lower income taxes.

For a stationary population the qualitative results remain unchanged al-

---

[8] The welfare change is computed as the wealth compensation which would have been required to give each cohort to maintain its initial welfare level.

though their size is larger. The reason that the reform effects grow with the old-age dependency ratio is the larger initial pay-as-you-go debt, implying stronger efficiency effects and, in the case of tax financing, a larger transfer toward future generations.

The third and fourth studies – as opposed to the two preceding studies – introduce heterogeneous consumer groups with different degrees of myopia (i.e., dissimilar subjective discount rates) in combination with credit constraints. The latter hit consumers with high discount rates – the young, who expect higher earnings growth, and those with high subjective discount rates – because of the additional restriction that nonhuman wealth has to be nonnegative at any point in time.

The study reported by Valdés-Prieto and Cifuentes allows one to assess the important role played by the group of myopic and credit-constrained individuals when substituting pay-as-you-go with FF (Table 5.1C). Without binding credit constraints or without myopes, the long-term effects of a tax-financed pension reform are modest, similar to the results shown by Arrau and Schmidt-Hebbel. However, when widespread myopia-cum-credit constraints is considered, the pension reform boosts (involuntary) saving significantly, so that the long-term output gain rises 14-fold, from 1.9% to 27.1%. Welfare increases by significantly less because of the involuntary shift of consumption toward the future imposed on credit-constrained myopes. The large size of these effects – and of those reported in the fourth study discussed next – is in part due to the assumption of both studies that FF savings are exempt from income taxation.[9] This assumption, not made in the two preceding studies, provides an additional incentive to saving and hence capital formation when adopting an FF system. However, the results in Chapter 6, where myopes are not considered, show that the impact of tax exemptions is moderate (Table 6.6).

Finally consider the results provided by Cifuentes and Valdés-Prieto, which allow one to distinguish between steady-state and transition effects, and also include a group of myopic and credit-constrained individuals. As this study solves and simulates the entire transition path, its quantitative results are more reliable than those of the preceding study, which is based only on comparisons across steady-state equilibria.

---

[9] The importance of this assumption is borne out by the comparison of steady-state output effects of the reform when pension fund income is and is not exempted from income taxation. This comparison can be inferred from the study by Cifuentes and Valdés-Prieto (table 6) for the case of 75% debt and 25% tax-financed transition deficits. With FF saving exemption from income taxation, the steady-state output increase is 7.0% (as reported in our Table 5.1); it shrinks to only 4.5% without income tax exemption. One may infer that all other long-term output results reported by both the third and fourth studies should be adjusted downward by roughly one-third when evaluating a pay-as-you-go-FF pension reform without the provision of tax exemptions.

Even when debt financing is large relative to tax financing (75% and 25%, respectively), the fourth study (Table 5.1D) reports a significant long-term output gain of 7%. When the transition deficit is fully tax-financed, the long-term output gain rises to 21.8%. The latter figure is quite large, a result due in part to two assumptions: FF savings exemption from income taxation and low stationary GDP growth (1%). However, the main driving force of the reported 21.8% is the presence of a large group of myopes. Chapter 6 shows that in their absence, long-term output gains of a tax-financed pension reform when credit-constraints are present come down to a single-digit figure.

In sum, the simulation results for the four models report modest to moderate long-term changes in output and welfare levels caused by a pension reform. And in the few cases where long-term percentage gains reach double-digit levels, these effects are only reaped decades after the reform has been initiated. Could larger effects be expected when the structure of production is allowed to respond to pension reform? To this question we turn next.

2 An endogenous growth model of pension systems and the size of the informal sector

This section analyzes growth and allocation effects of alternative pension systems within the framework of a stylized overlapping-generations (OLG) model of endogenous growth where capital has an external effect on labor productivity. The structure of the model relates social security to the decision to allocate labor between two productive sectors, using different technologies. The first sector employs both capital and labor and is subject to social security regulation (the formal sector); a second, less efficient sector only employs labor and is totally unregulated (the informal sector). The goal is to provide a stylized model suitable to explore different ways in which pension reforms affect growth, with special reference to the size of the informal sector.

The two main features of the model are the following. First, the social return on capital is sufficiently bounded away from zero and does not decrease with the capital stock. Therefore, the economy can never be dynamically inefficient due to excessive accumulation, as in the traditional OLG model (Diamond, 1965; Blanchard, 1985). Nonetheless, because of the external effect of capital on labor productivity, the social return on capital is not entirely appropriated by private investors. In a long-run equilibrium, the market rate of return may well be lower than the rate of growth of the economy. If this is the case, a pay-as-you-go system pays a higher average pension than an FF system at the current intertemporal price of consumption. Second, as labor moves from the informal to the formal sector in response to a pension reform, both productivity and the rate of return on capital increase.

Because of conflicting income and substitution effects, the change in consumption and growth cannot be determined unambiguously. Nonetheless, our numerical simulations will show the potential importance of the effect under consideration.

The size of the informal sector is surprisingly large not only in developing economies but also in the industrialized world. In Italy, for example, the irregular sector is estimated to produce about 16% of aggregate value added in 1990 (70% in agriculture, 6% in manufacturing, 36% in the building sector, and 22% in services; Rey, 1993). In developing countries, available estimates of informal-sector employment in urban areas vary between an average of 30% for a sample of relatively high-income countries and 50% for a sample of low-income countries (Turnham, 1993). As social security contributions are one of the main components of labor costs, it is well understood that the informalization of production allows firms to reduce their costs substantially. In the case of Latin America, estimates point out that the tax wedge on labor costs imputable to social security is as high as 20% for small firms (Tokman, 1992).[10]

The model focuses on the role of social security in the informalization of production from a macroeconomic perspective. The allocation of labor depends on the perceived marginal degree of appropriation of social security contributions capitalized at the market interest rate. The competitive equilibrium in an economy with an FF pension system provides the base scenario in our simulations. Vis-à-vis this benchmark, we will consider different degrees of appropriation in a pay-as-you-go system. In a world without uncertainty and credit constraints, social security contributions are a component of private saving in the base scenario, whereas they may be perceived as pure taxes in the other cases.

Section 2.1 briefly presents the model and provides a discussion of the basic features of OLG models of endogenous growth. The analytical model is summarized in the appendix (for a full analytical derivation see Corsetti, 1994). Section 2.2 focuses on the quantitative impact of different social security regimes by reporting simulations for different degrees of coverage and equilibrium tax rates.

2.1   The model

2.1.1   Supply: A stylized two-sector model

Our model allows for two sectors, characterized by perfectly competitive markets with free entry. Production technology in the first sector requires

---

[10] A theoretical assessment of the role of social security – together with other forms of regulation – in explaining the emergence of an informal economy is a promising direction of research but is not the purpose of this chapter. All we require is that, at the margin, social security affects the choice to allocate labor between the two sectors.

both capital and labor, whereas production in the second sector is carried out only with labor. Labor in the production functions is measured in efficiency units that do not coincide with labor time. In the tradition of the endogenous growth literature, we assume the presence of an external effect of the existing capital stock on labor efficiency (Sheshinski, 1967; Romer, 1986). Thus, under perfectly competitive markets, firms fail to see the link between their own investment and employment decisions and the efficiency of labor.

Technology in the formal sector is characterized by a standard constant-returns-to-scale production function, with capital and labor (in efficiency units) as productive inputs. Nonetheless, once the external effect of capital on labor is allowed for, aggregate sectoral production will be a linear function of capital (a typical AK model, as in Rebelo 1991), whereas the linear coefficient depends on the share of labor in the formal sector.

In the informal sector, the production function is linear in labor efficiency units, so that the productivity of informal employment determines the net wage rate for the whole economy. Because of the capital-related externality, the social production function in the informal sector is also linear in capital.

The existence of a competitive equilibrium requires the informal sector to be less efficient than the formal sector from the perspective of a social planner. As a result of this feature, shifting labor away from the formal to the informal sector reduces output and the return on capital by diverting the ultimately productive input – embodied capital – from the formal production process to a less efficient one.

2.1.2 Demand

The demand side of the model, which follows Buiter (1992), is derived from a Yaari-Blanchard OLG model (Yaari, 1965; Blanchard, 1985), in a version that differentiates between birth and death rates (Weil, 1989; Buiter, 1988). The endogenous growth version of this model may run into a problem similar to the one pointed out by Jones and Manuelli (1992) with respect to discrete-time OLG models: Technologies that would generate sustained steady-state growth rates in a representative agent model may not do so in an OLG setting. The reason is that the endowment of the young generations may constrain the amount of saving that old generations are able to sell in order to finance consumption in their late days. The technological side of the model provides a strong engine for growth – that is, persistently high productivity of accumulated factors of production. However, the same accumulation process rapidly dwarfs the endowment of newly born people, which becomes a binding constraint on the rate of growth.

In the absence of a proper life cycle, a related issue arises in Yaari-Blanchard models from the fact that accumulated factors are the ultimate source of productivity. In our model, we assume that the capital stock has a positive external effect on labor productivity. If all externalities were internalized, both the social and the private marginal product of raw labor would be zero. In a competitive setting, capital income would exhaust output. Since in the absence of intergenerational bequest and gift motives the newly born generations are endowed exclusively with raw labor, in such a scenario they would not be able to come into play. Each new generation would starve until death, the time of which, luckily enough, is by construction independent of people's diet.

The external effect of outstanding capital on individual productivity captures the idea that capital requires human skills and knowledge. To the extent that these goods are nonrival and nonexcludable, and that they can be freely acquired in proportion to the level of economic activity, new generations see their endowment at birth increase with the size of the economy. Such a feature of OLG models of endogenous growth is often poorly understood. In a representative agent model, any reduction of the share in output of factors that are not productive from a social point of view increases growth and welfare. Thus, to the extent that the productivity of labor hinges on the external effect of capital, it is desirable to reduce the share of labor income.

In our OLG model, factor shares are strictly interwoven with the endowment of new generations at birth. Because of the external effect of capital on their productivity, young generations live out of "rents" from a social planner's perspective. Nonetheless, in early stages of their lives, they also have the highest marginal propensity to save out of labor income. The interaction of these two elements generates a much richer set of possible results than the monotonic relation between factor distribution and the rate of capital accumulation that would characterize a representative-agent version of our model.

2.1.3   Social security and equilibrium

The instantaneous flow of pension benefits is modeled after Saint-Paul (1992), including both an age-dependent and an age-independent component. Benefits are financed through a flat-rate tax on wage income, while the government is required to run a balanced net transfer (benefits minus taxation) budget.

Whereas the net wage rate is technologically determined by productivity in the informal sector, the before-tax equilibrium wage rate in the formal sector depends on the perceived degree of future appropriability of current social security contributions, as determined by law, regulation, and (implicit or explicit, private or political) contracts.

2.2   Simulation results and model discussion

Section 1.2 has reviewed the literature on numerical simulations of OLG growth models, showing that, in general, the steady-state effects of reducing intergenerational transfers with a social security reform tend to be small. The question is therefore how much the long-run macroeconomic impact of pension reforms can vary, once different factors (in addition to the change in pension wealth) are taken into account. By way of example, this section provides a numerical simulation of our model, based on standard parameter values for both preferences and technology.

Endogenous growth models are analytical tools that, of course, are biased toward our goal: Growth rates are permanently affected by any change of parameters. Our exercise is therefore only aimed at capturing qualitative features of the response of economic systems to changing pension regimes, rather than providing a quantitative assessment of the effects under consideration. The simulation results, based on the model discussed in the appendix, are reported in Table 5.2.

The benchmark result is for the model under an FF pension regime (simulation 5.2A, Table 5.2). The following simulations reflect a pay-as-you-go regime that allows for an increase in pensions. In a first run of the model, the pay-as-you-go pension is financed by a lump sum tax and hence there is no informal sector (simulation 5.2B). Pay-as-you-go contribution rates vary between 6% and 20%. Then we let the magnitude of labor market distortions increase with the contribution or wage-tax rate (simulation 5.2C). Now the informal sector emerges as a consequence of the pay-as-you-go system, absorbing up to 47.5% of the labor force. In the next simulation (5.2D), the individually perceived marginal appropriation of future social security benefits is raised from 0 (in simulations 5.2B and 5.2C) to 20%. The final case (simulation 5.2E) substitutes part of the distortionary pay-as-you-go taxation by a distortionary tax on capital (at 0.5%), which lessens somewhat the informalization of the economy but reduces the incentives for capital accumulation.

Note that the simulations allow to distinguish between the intergenerational transfer effect and the distortionary labor market and production effect of pay-as-you-go. The former is reflected by simulation 5.2B, which shows that long-run growth falls from 3.7% under FF to a range of 3.1% to 3.5%, depending on the magnitude of lump-sum taxation and hence the size of the intergenerational transfer. However, when pay-as-you-go taxation is distortionary (simulation 5.2C), growth declines very strongly at high pay-as-you-go contribution rates, as a result of a massive shift of labor from the formal to the informal sector. For instance, at a pay-as-you-go wage rate of 20% (and if the degree by which workers relate current pay-as-you-go contributions to future pensions is 0), stationary growth reaches only 1.8%, much below the 3.1% growth rate achieved when pay-as-you-go is not distortionary. This striking result reflects the much more significant role played by distortionary pay-as-you-go taxation in two-sector economies than by the pay-as-you-go transfer toward older cohorts.

Table 5.2
Long-run endogenous growth effects of mandatory pension systems

Steady-State Simulation Results with and Endogenous-Growth Model

Wage Tax Rate	Formal-Sector Labor Share	Share of Labor in Income	Consump-tion to Capital Ratio	PAYG Pension Rate	Capital and Output Growth
5.2A A FF system					
Any	1	0.75	14.38%	0	3.7%
5.2B A PAYG system financed by lump sum taxation					
6%	1	0.75	14.46%	.11	3.5%
10%	1	0.75	14.56%	.17	3.4%
15%	1	0.75	14.68%	.25	3.3%
20%	1	0.75	14.81%	.34	3.1%
5.2C A PAYG system financed by distortionary taxation: labor shifts from the formal to the informal sector in response to higher tax rates.					
6%	1	0.75	14.46%	.11	3.5%
10%	0.85	0.77	14.76%	.15	3.0%
15%	0.675	0.80	15.01%	.19	2.4%
20%	0.525	0.83	15.10%	.21	1.8%
5.2D A PAYG system financed by distortionary taxation: similar to 5.2.C but at the margin the degree of appropriability of future pension payment at the current capitalization rate is 20%.					
10%	1	0.77	14.55%	.16	3.4%
15%	0.825	0.80	14.89%	.22	2.9%
20%	0.70	0.83	15.11%	.24	2.3%
5.2E A PAYG system financed by distortionary taxation on both labor and capital: similar to 5.2C but, in addition to the PAYG wage tax, there is a 0.5% tax on capital.					
9.7%	0.875	0.77	15.07%	.16	2.7%
14.6%	0.70	0.80	15.35%	.22	2.1%
19.6%	0.55	0.83	15.45%	.24	1.6%

Notes: The simulation model is discussed in the appendix. Parameter values for the simulation are the following: (a) Preferences: elasticity of marginal utility = 1.1, time preference = 0.02; (b) Technology: linear coefficients in the formal and informal sectors: α_1 = 0.2, α_2 = 0.14, the production function in the formal sector is Cobb-Douglas with a capital share of 0.25 and a depreciation rate of 0.02; (c) Demography: birth rate = 0.06, death rate = 0.03, aging rate = 0.03.

Simulation 5.2D introduces a link between current worker contributions and future pension benefits. It shows that a relatively weak link of 20% can substantially lower the pay-as-you-go labor and production distortions induced by high pay-as-you-go contribution rates. At a 20% contribution rate, growth decreases only to 2.3% as compared with 1.8% in simulation 5.2C.

The last simulation (5.2E) is obtained by varying the combination of capital and labor taxation for a given pension rate. Introducing a tax on capital holdings – at a very low rate of 0.5% – allows one to reduce the pay-as-you-go wage tax rate. Lower labor market distortions are matched by higher intertemporal distortions. The net effect (comparing simulation 5.2E to 5.2B) is a further decline in growth rates by an average 0.3 percentage points.

In assessing these numerical results one should keep in mind that, in our model, the long-run impact of a pension reform cannot be determined unambiguously because of the reform-related effects on the degree of labor market efficiency. As the intertemporal price of consumption responds to the pension regime, people revise their saving plans accordingly.

In our analysis, the indicator of labor market distortions is the size of the socially less productive informal sector. Are FF systems the least distortionary of pension systems? In an endogenous growth model with an external effect of capital on labor, a distributional issue arises from the fact that a share of the return on investment goes to capital embodied in labor. Future wages increase with capital accumulation at some rate that may be higher than the market rate (without any adverse consequence for the dynamic efficiency of the economy). Therefore, it is possible that, once law, regulation, and contracts appropriately link contributions to benefits, income incentives to work in the formal sector may be higher in a pay-as-you-go than in an FF system. Of course, this is typically not the case. Whereas the link between current contributions and future benefits is clear in an FF actuarially fair system, it must be carefully built in the design of the social security institutions of a pay-as-you-go scheme.

How are our results affected when allowing for credit constraints, uncertainty, and a pay-as-you-go-FF transition in which outstanding pension liabilities are honored by the government? Credit constraints give workers an incentive to resort to the informal sector in both FF and pay-as-you-go systems. The labor market equilibrium condition includes an extra term in which each additional unit of currently disposable income is weighted by its appropriate shadow price. In an uncertain environment, if workers cannot diversify their portfolio optimally because of missing markets or other inefficiencies, people may expect the government to provide some insurance (either explicitly or implicitly), within the framework of an FF system. To the extent that public insurance weakens the link between contributions and pensions, the (inter- or intragenerational) pay-as-you-go component of the scheme affects the equilibrium net wage in the formal sector, calling for a careful assessment of the moral hazard problem implicit in such schemes. Finally, in the process of switching from a pay-as-you-go to an FF system, the public nature of the implicit pension debt tends to be clearly perceived by currently active workers. As overall fiscal pressure increases, the incentive to tax evasion may be high.

3   Some evidence from Chile

Chile's radical 1981 pension reform substituted a state pay-as-you-go system with a privately managed and nonredistributive FF scheme, complemented by a small state-run redistributive and means-tested minimum-pension transfer program financed by general taxation.[11] The Chilean government had also started other major structural changes since the mid 1970s – including trade liberalization, financial deregulation, privatization, and labor market reform – that were deepened during the 1980s.[12] The economy was also hit by major terms-of-trade and financial shocks during the last two decades. The interaction of different structural reforms and foreign shocks makes it hard to disentangle the effects that can be attributed to the pension reform. The purpose of this section is to focus on the potential effects that pension reform has had on Chile's structure and performance, bearing in mind the difficulties of such an endeavor.

Table 5.3 summarizes the performance of Chile's labor markets, capital markets, public finances, and overall macroeconomy, which were affected, inter alia, by the 1981 pension reform. There is some evidence that the share of formal employment has increased after 1980. A massive improvement in Chile's private saving and overall growth performance has taken place during the past decade. A closer look at the changes in economic structure, private saving, and growth is warranted.

3.1   Economic structure

Chile's pension reform involved a reduction of overall social security contribution rates from 29.3% to 17%, of which the contribution to the new FF scheme is 10% (Table 5.3). The new system provides a close relation between earnings and pension benefits, which was absent under the preceding pay-as-you-go regime. The estimated reduction in the pure tax component of pension contributions – from 16.0% of net wages in 1980 to 6.8% in 1982–1985 and 2.8% in 1990–1992 – may have contributed to higher net wages, lower gross wages, and higher employment in formal labor markets.

Possible efficiency gains in labor markets are suggested by the following

---

[11] For a comprehensive analysis of Chile's pension reform, see Diamond and Valdés-Prieto (1993).

[12] Among recent volumes on Chile's reforms and macroeconomic performance during the past two decades, see Edwards and Cox-Edwards (1987), Morandé and Schmidt-Hebbel (1988), and Bosworth, Dornbusch, and Labán (1994).

changes. The share of independent workers in the labor force (who are not required to contribute to mandatory pension schemes) has declined from 26% before the reform to an average 24.5% after the mid-1980s, signaling an increase of both potential pension contributors and formal labor markets. More direct evidence on the change in the formal–informal structure of labor markets is provided by the significant decline in the relative share of infor-mal-sector employment, from 36.0% in 1980 to 31.1% in 1990–1992.[13] In addition, male labor force participation – which could reflect the incentive effect of the reform on total male employment – has increased slightly during the preceding years. More ambiguous is the behavior of the share of active contributors to pension systems (comprising contributors to both the old and new schemes) in total employment, starting at 62.5% in the early 1980s, declining thereafter, and recovering to an estimated 63% in 1993.

One should be careful in attributing too quickly a causal contribution to pen-sion reform in the formalization of Chile's labor markets evidenced by the preceding figures, as that requires controlling for other intervening factors. Hence we only conclude tentatively that pension reform is a possible explana-tion – among others – for the labor market changes observed in Chile since 1980.

3.2 Private saving

One of the major shifts observed in Chile is the large increase in the private-sector saving rate, from close to zero in 1979–1981 to an average 17.1% of GDP in 1990–1992. The mirror image of the saving boom is a trend decline in the share of private consumption in GDP, from 73% in 1960–1981 to 63% in 1986–1992 (Figure 5.1). This radical departure from the past has made possible both higher investment levels and lower foreign saving flows.

Different policy changes could be behind Chile's saving boom. One of them is pension reform, that could affect private consumption in different ways. We identify next seven channels from pension reform to private saving that may be at work.

(i)   A pay-as-you-go-FF pension reform financed by tax increases (or government expenditure cuts) reduces consumption and saving of tax-paying cohorts and raises consumption and saving of future generations, which benefit from the elimination of the pay-as-you-go debt. The phase of negative effects on transition consumption

---

[13] This formalization of Chile's employment structure stands in marked contrast to the informali-zation observed in other Latin American countries, such as Argentina and Colombia, where pay-as-you-go schemes were prevalent in the 1980s. The latter regional trend is reflected by the average share of informal sector employment in Latin America, which increased from 25.6% in 1980 to 31.4% in 1990–1992 (source: Uthoff 1994, table 1).

Table 5.3
Chile: Pension reform, labor markets, capital markets, fiscal policy, and macroeconomic performance (1979 - 1992)

	1979-81	1982-85	1986-89	1990-92	1979-92
Labor Markets (%)					
Total Social Security Contribution Rate (a)	29.3	17.0	20.0	20.0	
Average Pension Contribution Rate	n.a.	10.0	10.0	10.0	
Average Pure Tax Component of PAYG Contributions (b)	14.6	6.8	4.8	2.8	
Independent Workers / Labor Force (c)	26.0	23.6	24.3	24.7	
Informal Employment / Total Employment (d)	36.0	34.2	n.a.	31.1	
Male Labor Force/Males Aged 15 and above	n.a.	n.a.	74.6	75.3	
Pension Contributors / Employment (e)	n.a.	62.5	57.3	60.0	
Capital Markets (%)					
Real Rates of Return:					
Bank Deposit Rate (90-365 days)	12.0	9.1	4.9	6.7	
Public Debt Yield (f)	n.a.	8.9	5.7	7.7	
Private Pension Fund Return	n.a.	16.7	7.8	22.7	
Private Pension Fund Capitalization/GDP (g)	0.2	7.2	16.3	31.0	
Public Deficit and Debt (% of GDP)					
Overall Public Deficit (h)	-3.5	14.0	-1.3	-0.9	2.7
Pension-Reform Public-Sector Deficit (j)	0.6	3.6	3.9	4.7	3.3
Other Public-Sector Deficit	-4.1	10.4	-5.2	-5.6	-0.6
Public Domestic Debt	2.3	42.7	33.1	40.8	
Investment, Saving and Private Consumption (% of GDP)					
Gross Domestic Investment	20.3	14.3	22.4	23.5	19.9
Foreign Saving	9.0	8.7	3.7	1.3	5.8
National Saving	11.3	5.5	18.7	22.2	14.1
Public Saving	10.5	-3.8	4.7	5.1	3.6
Private Saving	0.8	9.3	14.0	17.1	10.5
Private Consumption	72.2	70.9	62.5	63.5	67.2
Growth (%)					
Per Capita Real GDP Growth	5.4	-3.5	5.7	4.7	2.5
Average Product of Capital (1961-81 = 0.33)	0.38	0.33	0.39	0.44	0.38

Notes:

(a) After 1982 this is the sum of contributions for pensions and health insurance in the new system.
(b) The average pure tax rate (on net wages) implicit in PAYG pension contributions before 1981 is calculated as the excess of the rate of social security contributions over the present value of social contributions after the pension reform, the latter assumed to be equal to the postpension reform social security contribution rate (17% in 1981). (Source: Schmidt-Hebbel 1981). For 1981-1992 it is assumed here that the PAYG pure tax declines linearly, reflecting both the rise in credibility in the new FF system and the gradual shift of contributors from PAYG to FF.
(c) First figure is for 1980 - 1981.
(d) Non-agricultural employment. First figure is for 1980, the second is for 1985, and the third is an average for 1990 and 1992. Source: ILO-PREALC, reported by Uthoff (1994), Table 1.

Table 5.3 (cont.)

(e) Source for 1982-1990: Chamorro (1992). The figure for 1990-1992 is an average of Chamorro (1992) and own estimates.
(f) First figure is for 1983 - 1985.
(g) Source: Diamond and Valdés-Prieto (1994).
(h) Comprises the non-financial and financial (Central Bank) public-sector deficit. Source: Marshall and Schmidt-Hebbel (1994).
(j) Observed public deficit due to pension reform transition. Source: Arrau (1992) and Schmidt-Hebbel (1994).

Other Sources: Central Bank of Chile: Boletín Mensual and Cuentas Nacionales de Chile, various issues; Arrau (1992); Marshall and Schmidt-Hebbel (1994); National Institute of Statistics (INE); and Ministry of Finance of Chile. n.a. Not available

and saving could be protracted before the positive consumption and saving effect on future generations takes place.[14]

(ii) Changes in rates of return derived from the intergenerational transfer effects and efficiency gains of the pension reform could also impinge on private consumption, as long as the intertemporal substitution, income, and human wealth effects of changes in rates of return do not offset each other. Pension reform has allowed contributors to reap very high real returns on their pension fund assets exceeding significantly real rates on bank deposits after and before the 1981 pension reform (see Table 5.3). However, the existing evidence for Chile suggests that interest rates do not affect significantly private consumption or saving levels.

(iii) Higher growth induced by pension reform could reduce consumption ratios to income once growth materializes, when consumers show habit persistence in consumption.

(iv) Anticipation of higher future growth induced by pension reform could raise current consumption ratios to income when consumers anticipate future higher income levels.

(v) The decline and ultimate elimination of the pure tax component of the old pay-as-you-go system reduce the demand for leisure and raise consumption under conventional consumer preferences and labor market conditions.[15]

(vi) Consumer awareness of the need to save for the future could increase (i.e., consumer myopia could decline) with the start of a

[14] See Arrau (1992), Arrau and Schmidt-Hebbel (1993), and Cifuentes and Valdés-Prieto (1994) for illustrative simulations.
[15] That is, when consumer utility depends on both consumption and leisure (and both are gross substitutes) and the labor supply schedule is a positive function of the real wage.

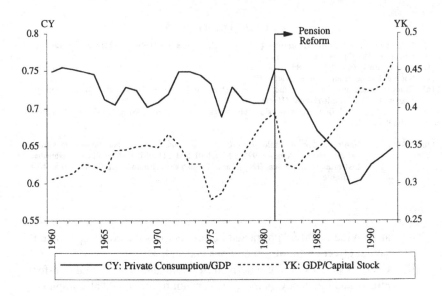

Figure 5.1. Consumption and output ratios in Chile, 1960–1992.

fully funded pension system that provides consumers with regular statements of their pension fund savings, protected by adequate regulation and supervision. This heightened awareness would imply that additional voluntary saving would not be offset one-by-one by the new mandatory saving program.

(vii)   As opposed to the previous group of consumers whose consumption preferences are changed by pension reform, another group of bor-rowing-constrained consumers could be pushed into a corner solution by the pension savings mandated by the new FF pension system, requiring them to save in excess of what they would save voluntarily in the absence of any mandatory saving system. As suggested by the simulations of Cifuentes and Valdés-Prieto (1994) discussed earlier, this may raise overall saving significantly.

It is analytically intractable to derive a structural model for aggregate consumption from an optimizing framework that embeds these seven chan-nels of transmission from pension reform to private consumption. In addition, in the absence of a general equilibrium framework, it is not really possible to identify the precise contribution of pension reform through some of the intervening variables – such as public debt, interest rates, or growth rates –

as the latter may reflect many other policy and structural changes that are contemporaneous to pension reform in Chile.

Hence the approach followed below is to propose and estimate a simple reduced-form consumption model that controls for variables that reflect well-known consumption theories and, in addition, includes proxies for some of the pension reform-induced changes listed here. It combines a framework developed by Corbo and Schmidt-Hebbel (1991) – which discriminates between Keynesian, permanent-income and Ricardian/crowding-out consumption hypotheses – with additional proxies reflecting the pension reform effects. The equation for the ratio of private consumption to private disposable income as the dependent variable is the following linear relation:[16]

$$\frac{C_t}{DY_t} = \beta_0 + \beta_1 \frac{PDY_t}{DY_t} + \beta_2 \frac{PS_t}{DY_t} + \beta_3 \frac{FS_t}{DY_t} + \beta_4\, r_t + \beta_5\, pfs_t + \beta_6\, tax_t \quad (1)$$

where C is private consumption expenditure, DY is current private disposable income, PDY is permanent private disposable income (permanent private gross income plus government transfers minus tax payments), PS is permanent public saving (permanent tax payments minus government transfers minus government consumption), FS is foreign saving, r is the consumption-based real interest rate, pfs is the share of private pension funds in GDP, and tax is the pure tax component of pay-as-you-go contributions.[17] Expected signs of the coefficients are: $\beta_0, \beta_1, \beta_2, \beta_3 > 0$; $\beta_5, \beta_6 < 0$; $\beta_4 \gtreqless 0$.

Equation (1) combines neoclassical determinants (permanent disposable income, the real interest rate), Keynesian variables and liquidity constraints (current income, foreign saving, public saving, and two pension reform-related variables.

Three simple null hypotheses are nested by this specification: Keynesian (or liquidity-constraints) theory: $\beta_0 > 0$, $\beta_1 = \beta_2 = 0$; permanent income hypothesis without Ricardian equivalence: $\beta_1 > 0$, $\beta_0 = \beta_2 = 0$; and Ricardian equivalence or direct crowding-out hypothesis: $\beta_0 = 0$, $\beta_1 = \beta_2 > 0$.[18]

---

[16] All potentially nonstationary variables are scaled to current private disposable income in order to reduce the incidence of spurious correlation. An alternative procedure, based on unit root and co-integration tests and a dynamic error-correction specification, is not feasible due to the short sample period to which the model is applied.

[17] See the notes in Table 5.3 for the definitions of pfs and tax, and the notes in Table 5.4 for the definitions of PDY and PS.

[18] Note that the inclusion of (permanent) public saving reflects two very different hypotheses, among which it is not possible to discriminate: Ricardian equivalence, which states that private consumption increases one-to-one with permanent public saving, and "direct crowding out," which asserts that, under an institutional arrangement by which the public sector captures private saving either directly or through the domestic financial markets, current private saving is crowded out one-to-one by current public saving.

The size of private pension fund savings (pfs) stands here as a proxy for both the growing awareness of one group of consumers to provide for future consumption (the decline in myopia) and the increase in mandatory saving that forces another group of consumers (those with high discount rates and unable to borrow against their future income streams) to save beyond what they would like to do.[19] Finally, the pure tax component of pay-as-you-go contributions – the cause of labor market distortions under pay-as-you-go – should have a negative effect on consumption under normal conditions of consumption–leisure substitutability.

Equation (1) was estimated for Chilean annual data for the 1971–1992 period.[20] Table 5.4 reports results for two-stage least squares estimations under two alternative measures of permanent public saving (forward-looking and static expectations). The results should be taken with caution in view of the small sample size.

The relative size and high significance levels of the first three right-hand variables is consistent with preceding findings for developing countries at large (Corbo and Schmidt-Hebbel, 1991; Easterly, Rodríguez, and Schmidt-Hebbel, 1994) and Chile in particular (Marshall and Schmidt-Hebbel, 1994). Chilean consumers are predominantly Keynesian, with a coefficient for current disposable income (0.75) that is six times as large as the coefficient for (neoclassical) permanent disposable income (0.15). Interestingly, permanent public saving shows a larger coefficient (0.33 to 0.45) than permanent disposable income. The latter finding suggests that borrowing constraints are here more important than Ricardian farsightedness, as the coefficient on permanent public saving is larger than the one on permanent disposable income.

Foreign saving has a very strong crowding-out effect on private saving, with the latter variable (after controlling for possible endogeneity of foreign saving by using instrumental-variable estimation) showing offset coefficients that vary between 0.6 and 0.9. The real interest rate (also instrumentalized) has a small and marginally significantly negative effect on private consumption in one of the equations reported here, suggesting (at least for this case)

---

[19] Note that pfs does not represent here a component or a proxy of total consumer wealth – the latter is included in the consumption function in flow terms as permanent income.

[20] The basic data sources are: C (current-price private consumption expenditure): Central Bank of Chile: *Cuentas Nacionales de Chile*, various issues; current-price GDP, taxes and foreign transfers used in constructing DY (current-price private disposable income): Central Bank of Chile and Ministry of Finance; current-price public saving used for PS (permanent public saving): Ministry of Finance, and Marshall and Schmidt-Hebbel (1994); current-price foreign saving (FS): Central Bank of Chile: *Cuentas Nacionales de Chile*, various issues; nominal interest rate and CPI used in constructing real interest rate (r): Central Bank of Chile; private pension fund savings used in constructing the share to current-price GDP (pfs): Diamond and Valdés-Prieto (1994); and the pure tax component of the pay-as-you-go pension system (tax): Schmidt-Hebbel (1981).

Table 5.4
Chile: Private consumption regressions (1971 - 1992)

$$\frac{C_t}{DY_t} = \beta_0 + \beta_1 \frac{PDY_t}{DY_t} + \beta_2 \frac{PS_t}{DY_t} + \beta_3 \frac{FS_t}{DY_t} + \beta_4 \, r_t + \beta_5 \, pfs_t + \beta_6 \, tax_t$$

5.4A. Forward-looking expectations on permanent public saving (PS)

Model	Constant	PDY/DY	PS/DY	FS/DY	r	pfs	tax	d74	DW	Adj. R^2
1	0.75	0.15	0.45	0.64	0.0002	-0.003	-0.12	-0.11	2.02	0.97
	(15.1)	(4.2)	(3.5)	(5.2)	(-1.0)	(-3.4)	(-1.2)	(-5.4)		
2	0.71	0.15	0.45	0.85	-	-0.002	-	-0.09	2.09	0.96
	(24.6)	(4.1)	(3.5)	(6.5)		(-5.8)		(-5.1)		

5.4B. Static expectations on permanent public saving (PS)

Model	Constant	PDY/DY	PS/DY	FS/DY	r	pfs	tax	d74	DW	R^2
3	0.78	0.14	0.35	0.64	0.0004	-0.004	-0.15	-0.08	2.27	0.98
	(18.2)	(4.9)	(5.1)	(6.2)	(-1.9)	(-4.3)	(-1.8)	(-5.1)		
4	0.73	0.13	0.33	0.92	--	-0.002	--	-0.06	2.27	0.96
	(24.4)	(3.8)	(4.1)	(7.0)		(-5.8)		(-3.5)		

Notes:
(1)   Two alternatives were used for expected permanent public saving. The first is forward looking, defined as the simple average of current-period, one-period-ahead and two-periods-ahead values. The second is static expectations, with a 100% weight given to the current-period value. Permanent private disposable income is estimated from a trend regression.
(2)   All equations are estimated by two-stage least squares. The foreign saving share (FS/DY) and the real interest rate (r) were instrumentalized by a list of instruments comprised by all right-hand side variables other than the two former and the lagged values of all right-hand side variables including the two former.
(3)   t-statistics are reported in parentheses. DW and F are the Durbin-Watson and F statistics, respectively, and Adj. R^2 is the adjusted R^2 coefficient.

that the negative substitution and human wealth effects dominate the positive income effect of a higher interest rate.[21]

---

[21] Recent cross-country saving studies for developing countries (for instance, Giovannini, 1983; Corbo and Schmidt-Hebbel, 1991; and Schmidt-Hebbel, Webb, and Corsetti, 1992), typically report that interest rates are not significant. Schmidt-Hebbel (1981) and Arrau (1990a) estimate elasticities of intertemporal consumption for Chile and fund values close to 1.0, implying that the substitution and income effects offset each other. The latter abstracts, however, from a negative role for the interest rate on consumption, which takes place through the decline in discounted human wealth. Reduced-form consumption equations estimated by Marshall and Schmidt-Hebbel (1994) report a nonsignificant effect of the real interest rate.

Having controlled for the effects of five variables that are consistent with conventional consumption theories, let us focus now on the possible contribution of the two additional variables linked to the pension reform. The relative size of private pension fund savings affects negatively private consumption in Chile, suggesting that part of the positive saving response could be related to financial deepening and a derived reduction in consumer myopia, as well as to the influence of involuntary saving by other consumers suffering from large myopia and borrowing constraints. However, one should be also keenly aware that pfs is highly correlated with other structural and policy changes that took place during the 1980s and early 1990s in Chile – such as the deepening of capital markets at large – that could have had an independent effect on consumption. Hence, the influence of pfs on consumption, explaining on average 10 percentage points of the 21 percentage point decline of the private consumption ratio between 1980 and 1992, should be interpreted as an upper bound of the response of aggregate private consumption to the pension reform effected through the two channels proxied by this variable.

Finally, the pure tax component of pay-as-you-go has a negative effect on consumption – which reaches marginally significant levels in one of the equations in Table 5.4 – reflecting substitution between consumption and leisure. The reduction of the pure pay-as-you-go tax, from 16% of net wages in 1980 to 2% in 1992, accounts at most (according to equation 3 in Table 5.4) for an increase by 2 percentage points of GDP in the private consumption ratio during that time span.

We conclude very tentatively from this evidence that the 1981 Chilean pension reform may have contributed, in conjunction with other structural reforms, to the significant rise in private saving observed during the past decade.

3.3   Growth

Per capita GDP growth has risen significantly since the mid-1980s, exceeding 5% per year. Higher factor productivity explains in part this growth spurt. Figure 5.1 confirms that, in addition to the outstanding private saving improvement, real GDP growth based on rising capital productivity has made a turnaround during the past decade. Whereas the average product of capital was 0.33 during 1961–1985, it started to rise significantly in the early 1980s to reach an average level of 0.44 during 1986–1993.

Chile's radical pension reform may be contributing to less distorted factor markets and, hence, to higher growth. Both the gradual elimination of the pure tax component of pay-as-you-go and the deepening of financial markets resulting from pension reform could have a significant influence on growth. However one should be careful – in the absence of a well-specified framework that distinguishes between different structural growth determinants – in assessing the contribution of pension reform. The reason, again, is that the latter has been approximately contemporaneous with other growth-enhancing structural changes, such as trade reform and financial liberalization.

4   Conclusions

The qualitative effects of pay-as-you-go–FF pension reform on long-term output and welfare hinge crucially on various features of the underlying economy and the way the transition deficit caused by the pension reform is financed. The quantitative effects of the reform via transfers to future generations and efficiency changes on long-term output and welfare are only modest to moderate when long-run growth is considered exogenous and factor market distortions are ruled out.

However, much larger and sustained effects are obtained when considering the impact of pension reform on factor markets, provided long-term growth is endogenous. A new OLG model with endogenous growth and formal–informal production sectors is derived here. Simulations with this model suggest that a pay-as-you-go–FF reform could raise substantially long-term growth rates.

A look at the Chilean reform experience suggests that the structural transformation toward a formalization of labor markets and production is taking place and that both private saving and growth are rising substantially since 1980. Econometric evidence suggests that the 1981 pension reform could be contributing – jointly with other contemporaneous structural changes – to Chile's private saving boom.

APPENDIX TO CHAPTER 5

This appendix briefly describes the model used in the simulations reported in section 2.2. There are two sectors characterized by perfectly competitive markets with free entry. Production in the first sector requires both capital and labor and production in the second sector is carried out only with labor. Denoting by $L(t)$ the total labor force in the economy, measured in labor time, the sectoral allocation of labor $(\sigma_L(t))$ can be summarized by the proportion of workers in the first sector:

$$\sigma_L(t) = \frac{L_1(t)}{(L_1(t) + L_2(t))}$$

where L_1 and L_2 denote employment in sectors 1,2.

Labor in the production functions is measured in efficiency units, which do not coincide with labor time. In the tradition of the endogenous growth literature, we assume the presence of an external effect of the existing capital stock on labor efficiency (Sheshinski, 1967; Romer, 1986). The efficiency of labor time spent in production in the i-th firm in either sector ($J_i(t)$) is therefore defined as:

$$J_i(t) = \epsilon(t)L_i(t)$$

where $\epsilon(t)$ is the economy-wide capital–labor ratio:

$$\epsilon(t) = \frac{K(t)}{L(t)}$$

Production in the first sector is characterized by constant returns to scale in capital and labor efficiency units. Because of the external effect of capital on labor, aggregate production in sector 1 (Y_1) can be expressed as a function of total capital (K) and the share of labor in sector 1:

$$Y_1 = K\sigma_L f\left(\frac{1}{\sigma_L}\right) = \alpha_1 k\Phi[\sigma_L]; \ \Phi'>0, \ \Phi''<0, \ \Phi(0)=0, \ \Phi(1)=1$$

By construction, the newly defined parameter α_1 is the social productivity of capital when the whole labor force is allocated to the first sector. In the case of a Cobb-Douglas production function, we would have:

$$Y = AK^q J^{1-q} = AK^q K^{1-q}\left(\frac{L_1}{L}\right)^{1-q} = A\sigma_L^{1-q}K$$

where A is a productivity parameter and q is the share of capital.

In our specification, capital is the only factor that is ultimately productive, even if part of it is embodied in labor. The preceding expression highlights the fact that moving labor away from the first sector reduces sectoral (and aggregate) output by diverting the ultimately productive input – embodied capital – from the first production process to the second.

The production function in the second sector is linear in labor efficiency units, that is:

$$Y_{2i} = \alpha_2 J_{i2} = \alpha_2 \frac{K}{L}L_{i2}$$

As all output is distributed to labor, the wage rate per efficiency unit is simply equal to α_2, while sectoral output can be easily calculated by aggregating across firms in sector 2:

$$Y_2 \equiv \sum_{i=1}^{M} Y_{2i} = \alpha_2 \sum_{i=1}^{M} J_{i2} = \alpha_2 \frac{K}{L}L_2 = \alpha_2(1-\sigma_L)K$$

Note once again that, because of the external effect of capital on labor efficiency, shifting labor to the second sector is equivalent to reallocating capital away from the first sector.

Overall output which is the sum of gross production across the two sectors, can be expressed in terms of a technology linear in capital – a so-called AK technology. The aggregate productivity parameter is a weighted average of sector productivities, with weights determined by the sectoral allocation of labor:

$$Y_1 + Y_2 = (\Phi(\sigma_L)\alpha_1 + (1 - \sigma_L)\alpha_2)K \equiv A[\sigma_L, \alpha_1, \alpha_2]K$$

We assume that the informal sector is technologically less productive than the formal sector:

$$\alpha_2 < \alpha_1$$

Pensions in our economy are financed by taxing wages in the formal sector at a flat rate t_1. Define γ as the fraction of social security wage tax (per efficiency unit of labor) that, at the margin, makes the present value of lifetime taxes equal to the present value of pension payments paid conditional on past contributions. It is helpful to think of γ as the degree of future appropriation of an additional dollar of social security contributions at the market capitalization rate, as it is determined by pension law, regulation, and (explicit and implicit, legal and political) contracts. For instance, γ will be equal to one in a fully funded system, whereas it will be zero in regimes where a social pension is granted to everybody regardless of past contributions. Equilibrium in the labor market thus implies:

$$w_1(1 - t_1 + \gamma\, t_1) = [f(k_{i1}) - k_{i1}\, f'(k_{i1})](1 - t_1 + \gamma\, t_1) = \alpha_2 = w_2$$

where w_1 and w_2 are wage rates per efficiency unit of labor in the first and the second sector, respectively. Note that the informal sector is (legally or illegally) sheltered from wage taxation and is not granting any sector-specific social security benefits. A positive γ inserts a wedge between cash wage rates net of taxes in the two sectors; the individual future appropriation of current contributions is crucial in assessing the magnitude of labor market distortions associated with alternative pension regimes.

The instantaneous flow of individual pension benefits ($p(s,v)$) is modeled after Saint-Paul (1992) in the following fashion:

$$p(s,v) = \pi_1 e^{\pi_2(t - s)}\epsilon(t)$$

At each instant in time, individual benefits are scaled up to the size of economic activity ($\epsilon(t)$). For a nonzero π_2, pension benefits also increase (or fall) with age. Also, setting public debt equal to zero, the government will be required to run a balanced (primary) budget. Aggregating contributions and transfer over all generations alive at time t and denoting net transfers by NT(t), we have:

$$NT(t) \equiv P(t) - T(t) = e(t)\beta e^{nt}\left[\frac{\pi_1}{\beta - \pi_2} - \frac{\sigma_L t_1 w_1}{(s + \beta)}\right] = 0$$

where P(t) and T(t) are the economy-wide instantaneous flows of pension payments and tax revenue, respectively.

We assume that agents choose their labor allocation at birth. Under this assumption, as both net pension payments and wage income grow with the capital labor ratio, in a long-run equilibrium individuals will supply the same constant share of labor time $\sigma_L(s,t) = \sigma_L(t) = \sigma_L$ to firms in the formal sector.

By referring to a standard Yaari-Blanchard model (Yaari, 1965; Blanchard, 1985), our simulations are carried out by using a system of four equations: the equilibrium condition in the labor market and three differential equations for consumption, capital, and the present value of pension benefits. Each of the three latter equations is associated with the appropriate solvency and feasibility constraints (omitted from the text). The three differential equations are the following:

$$\frac{dc(t)}{dt} = c(t)^2 + \psi c(t) - \eta(\beta + s) - \eta\omega(t)$$

$$\frac{dk(t)}{dt} = A - c(t) - \frac{G}{K} - \delta$$

$$\frac{dw}{dt} = [r + \beta - (A - c(t) - \delta) - \pi_2]w(t) - \frac{\pi_1\beta}{\beta - \pi_2}$$

where:

$$\psi \equiv \left(\frac{r - \rho}{R}\right) + n + s - A + \delta)$$

where η is the consumption to wealth ratio, β is the birth rate, s is the aging rate, ω is the pension wealth to capital ratio, δ is the capital depreciation rate, ρ is the subjective rate of discount, and R is the inverse of the intertemporal elasticity of consumption substitution.

The first two differential equations show the law of motion of consumption per unit of capital c(t) and the rate of growth of capital (i.e., the resource constraint of the economy). The third differential equation describes the evolution of the present value of the aggregate pension wealth to capital ration (π/K). Note that, as steady-state growth rates are positive in endogenous growth models, variables are appropriately expressed per units of capital rather than per person.

References

Arrau, P. (1990a) "Intertemporal Monetary Economics: Evidence from the Southern Cone." Ph.D. dissertation, University of Pennsylvania, Philadelphia.

——— (1990b) "Social Security Reform: The Capital Accumulation and Intergenerational Distribution Effect." Policy Research Department Working Paper no. 512, World Bank, December.

——— (1991) "La Reforma Previsional Chilena y su Financiamiento Durante la Transición." Colección Estudios CIEPLAN 32, June, pp. 5–44.

——— (1992) "El Nuevo Régimen Previsional Chileno." In *Regímenes Pensionales*, edited by L. Witte and M. Cárdenas, pp. 37–65. Friedrich Ebert Foundation of Colombia (FESCOL), Bogotá.

Arrau, P., and K. Schmidt-Hebbel (1993) "Macroeconomic and Intergenerational Welfare Effects of a Transition from Pay-As-You-Go to Fully-Funded Pension Systems." World Bank, June. Unpublished manuscript.

——— (1994) "Pension Systems and Reforms: Country Experiences and Research Issues." *Revista de Análisis Económico,* 9 (1): 3–20.

Auerbach, A., and L. Kotlikoff (1987) *Dynamic Fiscal Policy.* Cambridge University Press.

Auerbach, A., L. Kotlikoff, and J. Skinner (1983) "The Efficiency Gains from Dynamic Tax Reform." *International Economic Review,* 24 (1): 81–100.

Blanchard, O. (1985) "Debt, Deficits and Finite Horizons." *Journal of Political Economy,* 93 (2): 223–247.

Bosworth, B. P., R. Dornbusch, and R. Labán (eds.) (1994) *The Chilean Economy: Policy Lessons and Challenges.* Brookings Institution.

Breyer, F. (1989) "On the Intergenerational Pareto Efficiency of Pay-As-You-Go Financed Pension Systems." *Journal of Institutional and Theoretical Economics,* 145 (4): 643–658.

Breyer, F., and D. E. Wildasin (1993) "Steady-State Welfare Effects of Social Security in a Large Open Economy." *Journal of Economics,* suppl. 7: 43–49.

Buiter, W. (1988) "Death, Birth, Productivity Growth and Debt Neutrality." *Economic Journal,* 98 (391): 279–293.

——— (1992) "Saving and Endogenous Growth: A Survey of Theory and Policy." International Monetary Fund. Unpublished manuscript.

Chamorro, C. (1992) "La Cobertura del Sistema Chileno de Pensiones." M.S. Thesis, Instituto de Economía, Pontificia Universidad Católica de Chile, Santiago, Chile.

Cifuentes, R., and S. Valdés-Prieto (1994) "Pension Reforms in the Presence of Credit Constraints." Instituto de Economía, Pontificia Universidad Católica de Chile, Santiago, Chile, May. Unpublished manuscript.

Corbo, V., and K. Schmidt-Hebbel (1991) "Public Policies and Saving in Developing Countries." *Journal of Development Economics,* 36 (1): 89–115.

Corsetti, G. (1994) "An Endogenous Growth Model of Social Security and the Size of the Informal Sector." *Revista de Análisis Económico,* 9 (1): 57–76.

Diamond, P. (1965) "National Debt in a Neoclassical Growth Model." *American Economic Review,* 55 (5): 1126–1150.

Diamond, P., and S. Valdés-Prieto (1994) "Social Security Reforms." In *The Chilean Economy: Policy Lessons and Challenges,* edited by B. P. Bosworth, R. Dornbusch, and R. Labán. Brookings Institution.

Easterly, W., C. A. Rodríguez, and K. Schmidt-Hebbel (1994) *Public Sector Deficits and Macroeconomic Performance.* Oxford University Press.

Edwards, S., and A. Cox-Edwards (1987) *Monetarism and Liberalization: The Chilean Experiment.* University of Chicago Press.

Felderer, B. (1993) "New Issues in Public Pension Economics." *Journal of Economics,* suppl. 7: 1–15.

Giovannini, A. (1983) "The Interest Elasticity of Savings in Developing Countries: The Existing Evidence." *World Development,* 11 (7): 601–607.

Homburg, S. (1990) "The Efficiency of Unfunded Pension Schemes." *Journal of Institutional and Theoretical Economics,* 146 (4): 640–647.

Jones, L., and R. Manuelli (1992) "Finite Lifetimes and Growth." *Journal of Economic Theory,* 58 (2): 171–197.

Marshall, J., and K. Schmidt-Hebbel (1994) "Fiscal Adjustment and Successful Performance in Chile." In *Public Sector Deficits and Macroeconomic Performance,* ed. by W. Easterly, C. A. Rodríguez, and K. Schmidt-Hebbel. Oxford University Press.

Morandé, F. G., and K. Schmidt-Hebbel (1988) *Del Auge a la Crisis de 1982: Ensayos sobre Liberalización Financiera y Endeudamiento en Chile.* IIMC and ILADES/Georgetown, Santiago, Chile.

Rebelo, S. (1991) "Long Run Policy Analysis and Long Run Growth." *Journal of Political Economy,* 99: 500–521.

Rey, G. M. (1993) "Il frutto proibito dell'Economia Italiana." October. Unpublished manuscript.

Romer, P. (1986) "Increasing Returns and Long-Run Growth." *Journal of Political Economy,* 94 (5): 1002–1037.

Saint-Paul, G. (1992) "Fiscal Policy in an Endogenous Growth Model." *Quarterly Journal of Economics,* 107 (4): 1243–1259.

Samuelson, P. A. (1958) "An Exact Consumption-Loan Model of Interest with or without the Social Contrivance of Money." *Journal of Political Economy,* 66 (6): 467–482.

——— (1975) "Optimum Social Security in a Life-Cycle Model." *International Economic Review,* 16 (3): 539–544.

Schmidt-Hebbel, K. (1981) "El Funcionamiento de los Mercados Laborales en Chile": Un Análisis Preliminar." Documento no. 206, Departamento de Estudios BHC, Santiago, Chile, September.

——— (1987) "Foreign Shocks and Macroeconomic Adjustment in Small Open Economies." Ph.D. diss., Massachusetts Institute of Technology, Cambridge, Mass.

——— (1994) "Pension Reform Transitions from State Pay-As-You-Go to Privately-Managed Fully-Funded Pension Systems." World Bank. Unpublished manuscript.

Schmidt-Hebbel, K., S. B. Webb, and G. Corsetti (1992) "Household Saving in Developing Countries: First Cross-Country Evidence." *World Bank Economic Review,* 6 (3): 529–547.

Sheshinski, E. (1967) "Optimal Accumulation with Learning by Doing." In K. Schell (ed.), *Essays on the Theory of Optimal Economic Growth.* MIT Press.

Tokman, V. (ed.) (1992) *Beyond Regulation: The Informal Sector in Latin America.* PREALC, Lynne Rienner.

Turnham, D. (1993) "Employment and Development: A New Review of Evidence." Development Center Studies. OECD, Paris.

Uthoff, A. (1994) "Some Features on Current Pension System Reform in Latin America." *Revista de Análisis Económico,* 9 (1): 211–235.

Valdés-Prieto, S., and R. Cifuentes (1993) "Credit Constraints and Pensions." Catholic University of Chile, December. Unpublished manuscript.

Weil, P. (1989) "Overlapping Families of Infinitely-Lived Agents." *Journal of Public Economics,* 38 (2): 183–198.

World Bank (1994) *Averting the Old Age Crisis: Policies to Protect the Old and Promote Growth.* Oxford University Press.

Yaari, M. E. (1965) "Uncertain Lifetime, Life Insurance, and the Theory of the Consumer." *Review of Economic Studies,* 32 (April): 137–150.

CHAPTER 6

Transitions in the presence
of credit constraints

Rodrigo Cifuentes and Salvador Valdés-Prieto

Abstract

This chapter quantifies the fiscal impact of a pension reform that shifts financing from the PAYG method to full funding. It uses a simulation model that recognizes that the individual's consumption path is restricted by credit constraints. Specific findings are that (1) this pension reform is feasible with any tax regime only when credit constraints are acknowledged; (2) this pension reform has a much higher positive effect on capital accumulation in the long term, even with 75% of debt financing of the transition deficit, than is gleaned from models that ignore credit constraints; (3) adjustment of the fiscal balance during the transition with a consumption tax or an income tax has almost the same effects, contrary to what is predicted by models that ignore credit constraints; and (4) the income tax exemption granted to the new fully funded pension system has a relatively small effect on capital accumulation, contrary to what is predicted by models that ignore credit constraints, provided workers are not allowed to contribute extra to their individual pension account.

Introduction

Reforms of social security increasingly have come to imply shifts away from the pay-as-you-go financing method toward partial or full funding. The reforms in Chile (1981), Peru (1993), and Argentina (1994) include partial investment in outside assets as an important element of reform.

There is a small literature that attempts to disentangle the short-run from the long-run effects of such a reform, through the use of numerical simulation

This paper is a result of a research project supported by FONDECYT, through grant 0631-92.

models of a dynamic economy.[1] Most of these models are based on Auerbach and Kotlikoff (1987). The version we build upon was initially developed by Arrau (1990b, 1991) and Cifuentes (1993).

Unfortunately, these models assume the capital market is "perfect" in an unrealistic sense, ignoring the large difference in transaction costs between loans secured with physical or financial assets and loans secured with future wage income only. This assumption implies that a shift to full funding[2] is equivalent to a reform that phases out social security, that is, to a reversion to a situation with no mandatory pensions. That assumption implies that introducing a fully funded mandatory pension system has no effect on the economy, either in the short or in the long run. A neutrality result is involved: When mandatory contributions increase, voluntary savings decrease by the same amount, so the paths of consumption and labor supply are not affected.

We model as prohibitive the extra transaction cost of lending when only human capital can be used as collateral. This chapter builds on the work of Mariger (1987), Hubbard and Judd (1987), and Valdés-Prieto and Cifuentes (1993), who characterize optimal consumer behavior through the life cycle in a setting where transaction costs impose credit constraints.[3] A credit constraint is defined as a nonnegativity constraint on net nonhuman assets.

We model the transition path of an economy in response to a set of pension reforms that move social security from pay-as-you-go financing to full funding. As we rule out default on pension promises and pensions already granted, the transition includes both a mechanism to acknowledge hidden debts to those that have not yet retired and another one to continue paying pensions previously issued.

This transition, in the presence of credit constraints, has not been discussed in the literature before. Hubbard and Judd (1987) and Valdés-Prieto and Cifuentes (1993) acknowledge credit constraints, but report comparisons across steady states only. Auerbach and Kotlikoff (1987) study a different pension transition, one associated with the introduction of pay-as-you-go financed social security, and ignore credit constraints. Arrau (1991) considers a pension transition similar to ours, but with a much smaller initial contribu-

---

[1] The existence of a unique transition path is not assured in overlapping-generations economies, but simulation experience shows that the equilibrium path does not depend on initial conditions. The analysis of the eigenvalues of the linearized system performed by Laitner (1990) shows that with the parameter values used here there is always a unique transition path.

[2] If pension funds are not exempted from the income tax. This is discussed in section 4.4.

[3] This chapter also assumes a certainty environment. We ignore uncertainty in the duration of life because, from the point of view of the heir, the resulting bequests would be randomly timed. This makes choice of the optimal consumption path a problem that has not been solved to our knowledge.

tion rate, and ignores tax exemptions to pension funds and credit constraints.

A preliminary but revealing point is whether such a transition is feasible, given the large fiscal cost it entails. We find that ignoring all types of credit constraints, as in standard models, makes it appear that some transitions are infeasible. In particular, this happens when the income tax is raised to finance the transition. However, feasibility returns as soon as credit constraints are acknowledged. This exercise shows dramatically the importance of acknowledging credit constraints, which we do in the rest of the chapter.

We find that the long-term effects of this reform on the capital stock are much larger than what had been found in the previous literature that ignored credit constraints. Even when financing 75% of the transition deficit with new public debt, the positive impact on savings allows an increase of the order of 28% in the capital–labor ratio. The transition path starts with a small consumption boom, which reduces the capital–labor ratio somewhat and lasts 5 to 10 years, and then the interest rate falls monotonically.

The next sections analyze different elements of policy that impinge on the macroeconomic impact of this pension reform. We consider an initial steady state where half of tax revenue is generated by each of two taxes – an income tax and a consumption tax. The first element is which tax is adjusted to finance the impact of the pension reform on the budget. This has the potential to make a difference because the efficiency effects differ and because the impact on intergenerational distribution is expected to be quite different. We find that the difference is small both in the short and the long term. This suggests that credit constraints reduce significantly the inefficiencies associated with an income tax as compared with those related to a consumption tax.

A second element of pension reform policy is the financing approach for the transition deficit. A range of financing policies is possible, according to the degree to which the deficit caused by the transition is financed with public debt. Previous work in this area, such as that by Arrau (1991), does not acknowledge credit constraints. We confirm the standard finding that financing more of the transition with current taxes and less with issue of new public debt leads to increases in the steady-state capital–labor ratio and to increases in the welfare of those generations that live in the long run.

However, we find that when acknowledging credit constraints the degree of debt financing merely adds to an already large positive effect on the capital–labor ratio. The financing policy is not really as critical as it appears when credit constraints are ignored, but it does allow a significant additional improvement. We also find that increasing the share of the deficit that is debt financed from 25% to 75% postpones the year of maximum tax rates by 20 years (from years 2 to 5 to years 20 to 25 since the reform), but the level of the maximum tax rate is only slightly smaller with 25% debt financing. Given the appreciable long-term gains of a higher degree of tax financing, the need to design low-debt financing paths that can survive short-term political constraints becomes apparent.

A third element in pension reform policy involves income tax exemptions for the funded pension system that is being introduced. One standard combination is to exempt contributions and investment income of pension funds, while subjecting benefits to tax. This combination pushes tax revenue to the future, forcing the government to increase other taxes in the meantime, but the pension funds can grow faster and add more to the capital stock. We find that choosing to subject pension fund income (interest) to the income tax, rather than to exempt it, reduces the capital–labor ratio in the steady state by 7.9%. However, an advantage is that the income tax rate can be 3.4 percentage points smaller at its peak during the transition, thanks to the larger tax base.

Section 2 presents our simulation model and the method of analysis. Section 3 discusses the pension transition we consider, emphasizing the different design variables. Section 4 addresses the questions posed, comparing transition paths in dynamic general equilibrium with credit constraints.

2 Credit constraints and the simulation model

This section describes our simulation model, the conditions for macroeconomic equilibrium, and some basic elements of pension economics. This is a life-cycle model with no bequests where consumers are subject to credit constraints. Two missing markets interact here. In the first place, in overlapping generation settings there is no market in which unborn generations may trade. In addition, some consumers find no market in which to exchange their own future labor income (human capital) for current consumption.

2.1 The model

Preferences: There is one representative agent in each generation, which has preferences over sequences of consumption and supplies labor inelastically, as summarized by the following program:

$$\text{Max } U = \sum_{t=21}^{t=75} (1 + \delta)^{-t} u(c(t)) \tag{1}$$

subject to:

$$F(21) = 0; \ F(75) \text{ free.} \tag{a}$$

$$F(t + 1) = F(t) + (1 - \tau_y(t)) \cdot r(t) \cdot F(t) - c(t) \cdot (1 + t_c(t)) + y(t) \tag{b}$$

$$F(t) \geq 0, \text{ all } t. \tag{c}$$

where:

t = age of the individual.

u(c) = utility provided by consumption c. Specifically, we use the functional form $u(c) = (1/1 - 1/\gamma)c^{1 - 1/\gamma}$.

$c(t) \cdot (1 + t_c)$ = real consumption plus the consumption tax rate, which is measured on a tax exclusive base. $c(t)$ is the consumption path, the control variable to be found.

y(t) = net noninterest income, that is, earned income plus pensions after taxes.

Therefore $y(t) = (1 - \chi - \tau_y(t)) \cdot w(t) \cdot 1(t) + p(t)$, where $1(t)$ is the effective units of labor supplied at age t, $w(t)$ is the wage rate, χ is the contribution rate, and $\tau_y(t)$ is the income tax rate. $p(t)$ is total pensions received at age t, which is an amount determined by a benefit formula $p[\chi, w(t), 1(t), r(t),t]$.

F(t) = voluntarily held net nonhuman assets, as of date t.

$(1 - \tau_y(t)) \cdot r(t)$ = the after-tax real interest rate earned by asset F in period t.

The individual lives for 55 periods, of which the first 45 are endowed with labor ability. This can be interpreted as the case of an individual that works from age 21, retires at 65, and dies at age 75.

The utility function used is additively separable across time periods and exhibits constant elasticity of intertemporal substitution in consumption. Parameter γ is the elasticity of intertemporal substitution in consumption, and we use $\gamma = 0.5$. The utility discount factor, or impatience rate, is δ and we use a value of $\delta = 0.02$. These values are chosen to be uncontroversial and are taken from Auerbach and Kotlikoff (1987).

The supply of labor is assumed to be inelastic to wages. This assumption is confirmed by the evidence for males in the United States, but is not representative of the experience of females. In addition, we assume that labor supply drops to zero at age 65. This assumption is consistent with the sharp spike in the retirement frequency observed at that age for males in the United States (Blau, 1994).

The effective units of labor supplied at age t, $1(t)$, depend on a = age, and on t = time of birth, through the function $1(a,t) = 1(a)(1 + x)^t$, where x = rate of labor-augmenting technical progress, and $1(a)$ is the age-earnings profile. This profile indicates that on the basis of experience alone, the labor endowment grows until age 60 and then declines slightly, according to the empirical evidence. We could have used the quadratic profile reported by Auerbach and Kotlikoff (1987) or the fourth-order polinomial reported by Hubbard and Judd (1987). We settled for the age-earnings profile derived by Arrau (1991) from Chilean data. He first estimates a quadratic for the cross-section age-earning function, and then transforms it into an age-earnings profile by using an estimated 2% labor productivity growth for Chile.[4]

Finally, we assume technical progress for labor takes the form of an annual 0.5% increase in the level of the age-earnings profile for each new generation, in comparison to the profile for the previous one. Other types of technical progress are ignored.

Credit constraints: These constraints are represented by condition (c) in program (1). These constraints imply that individuals can only borrow against voluntarily held physical and financial assets, not against their human capital (future earnings) or their pension wealth. Credit constraints allow consumers to borrow for a home mortgage or for a car. Credit constraints merely force consumers to put up positive equity when buying a home.

There are three reasons to introduce credit constraints. First, there are large differences in administrative costs between loans secured with physical or financial assets and loans secured only with future wage income. Indeed, in some cases this differential in costs may be infinite. The main reason is that it is illegal to sign long-term consumer loans secured by human capital, because such clauses are considered akin to slavery. Therefore, consumer loans have to be based on other incentives, such as reputations, and require expenditure on screening, all of which raise transaction costs. If the transaction cost is above a critical level, the consumer will choose not to ask for such credit and will prefer to be "constrained."

A second source of credit constraints is that pension laws prohibit pensioners from mortgaging their future pension benefits. A young worker who is forced to contribute more than what she desires cannot compensate with a consumer loan secured with her future pension. However, if this was the only limit to consumer debt, she could borrow against her wage income when older, which will be large because of rising experience.

The third source of credit constraints is that the tax authorities do not accept interest paid in consumer loans as a valid deduction from income, for the purposes of the personal income tax. This implies that the relevant interest rate for a consumer involved in such debt is the pretax interest rate, potentially much higher than the after-tax rate. Therefore, the rate of interest perceived by an indebted consumer is above the after-tax market rate of return, just as in the other types of credit constraints. In our model, the tax authorities do accept the interest on loans secured by physical or financial assets as a valid deduction from income, but not the interest paid on consumer loans.

---

[4] The age-earnings profile we use is $1(a) = -2.847 \ (1.02)^{a-21} + 0.2373 \ a \ (1.02)^{a-21} - 0.002576 \ a^2(1.02)^{a-21}$. This profile has values of $1(21) = 1.0$, $1(50) = 4.549$, $1(55) = 4.686$, $1(60) = 4.522$ and $1(65) = 3.963$.

Although each of these sources of credit constraints may have a somewhat different impact on its own, accepting the first of these includes automatically the second and the third. The prohibition of securing consumer debt with pensions is dealt with by defining pension wealth to be part of human capital. The tax treatment of interest on consumer debt does not arise when transactions costs prevent that sort of debt from arising in the first place.

Technology: Firms use labor and capital to produce output, with a CES technology with exponential depreciation. Output can be consumed or invested to create capital, with no installation costs. The net production function is:

$$Y = [\beta L^{(\sigma-1/\sigma)} + (1-\beta)K^{(\sigma-1/\sigma)}]^{(\sigma/\sigma-1)} - 0.035K \qquad (2)$$

where

σ = elasticity of substitution in production. In our simulations, $\sigma = 0.80$.

β = income share of labor when $\sigma = 1$. In our simulations, $\beta = 0.75$.

0.035 = depreciation rate of the stock of capital in use.

There is free entry, so firms cannot pay supernormal profits. This implies that the value of firms does not enter separately into the budget constraint of consumers.

Government: The government affects the economy through tax, spending, and debt policies.

1 Government debt. The government has no outstanding net public debt to start with. However, during the transitions the government may issue additional public debt. In this model, the net public debt is the gross public debt minus publicly owned earning assets, such as state enterprises.

2 Government consumption. Following Arrau (1991) we assume that government consumption is 13% of GDP.

3 Taxes. Tax revenue must finance government consumption, interest payments on the public debt, and expenditures linked to the pension reform, minus the issue of new public debt. In our model the supply of capital is elastic in the long run, so an income tax is distortionary. In the general case, a consumption tax whose rate is constant over time is equivalent to a wage tax (Auerbach and Kotlikoff, 1987, p. 62). As labor supply is inelastic in this model, consumption and wage taxes are not distortionary in a steady state. Of course, in a transition where the tax rate changes over time, a consumption tax distorts the allocation of consumption over time.

Again, as labor supply is inelastic in this model, the wage tax that is implicit in mandatory contributions to a pay-as-you-go-financed system is nondistortionary. Therefore, a policy that replaces a wage tax for distortionary taxes, such as a fully debt-financed shift from pay-as-you-go financing to full funding, where income tax rates increase, reduces efficiency and welfare both in the transition and in the steady state. This is not due to pension reform, but to the introduction of new tax distortions. If a reform replaces a wage tax for a constant consumption tax, as it happens in a fully debt-financed shift from pay-as-you-go financing to full funding where consumption tax rates increase, efficiency and welfare are reduced in the transition but not in the steady state.

The assumption that a wage tax that falls on formal labor contracts is nondistortionary is particularly inappropriate for developing countries. However, as the modeling of an informal labor market or household labor would take us too far afield, we will stick to income and consumption taxes in the simulations presented here.

2.2   Macroeconomic Equilibrium

Utility maximization by individuals: Individuals solve problem (1), which includes credit constraints. The objective function is concave and the constraints are convex, so a solution exists and is unique. Valdés-Prieto and Cifuentes (1993) prove that the optimal path for consumption conforms to:

Proposition 1: The optimal consumption path c* under credit constraints follows the law of motion:

$$c^*_{t+1} = [(1 + t_{c,t}/1 + t_{c,t+1})(1 + (1 - \tau_{y,t}) \cdot r(t))/(1 + \delta)]^\gamma \cdot c^*_t \qquad (3)$$
in intervals where $F > 0$.
$c^*(t) = y(t)$ in intervals where $F = 0$.

In addition,

(i)   All resources are consumed in the life cycle.
(ii)   Consumption does not jump along the optimal path.

The junction times where consumption enters and leaves constrained intervals are found using the forward-looking computational procedure developed by Valdés-Prieto and Cifuentes (1993).

Optimization condition (3) can also be used to find the minimum size for the transaction costs of securing debt with human capital, above which the consumer will choose to be "constrained" rather than asking for credit. Measured in percentage points that must be added to the after tax market interest rate, this transaction cost is:

$$\text{min trans. cost (t)} \equiv [d^*(t) - (1 - \tau_{y,t}) \cdot r(t)] \qquad (4)$$

where $d^*(t)$ is the consumer's discount factor in period t. According to (i),

$$d^*(t) = [(c^*_{t+1}/c^*_t)^{1/\gamma} \cdot (1 + \delta)] \cdot [(1 + t_{c,t+1}/1 + t_{c,t})] - 1$$

Profit maximization by firms: We assume there are no corporate taxes that are not fully deductible from personal taxes by the individual owners. This implies the following marginal conditions:

$$\partial Y/\partial K = r + \text{depreciation rate}; \ \partial Y/\partial L = w \tag{5}$$

Both these marginal productivities can be expressed as a function of a single parameter, the capital–labor ratio. The marginal conditions imply the following factor demands:

$$L^d = (w)^{-\sigma}(\beta)^{\sigma}(Y)^{(\sigma/\sigma-1)}; \ K^d = (r + 0.035)^{-\sigma}(1-\beta)^{\sigma}(Y)^{(\sigma/\sigma-1)} \tag{6}$$

Market clearing: Every period, asset market equilibrium equates savings demand from firms (K^d) and the government (B) with savings supply by individuals, both measured as stocks. This condition determines endogenously the real rate of return for each period of the transition path. The asset market equilibrium equation in each period is:

$$K^d(t) + B(t) = \sum_{a=1}^{a=55} F(t,a) \cdot (1+n)^{-a} + \sum_{a=1}^{a=55} A(t,a) \cdot (1+n)^{-a} \tag{7}$$

where:

$K^d(t)$ = stock demand in t for physical capital by firms.

 $B(t)$ = stock of outstanding government bonds in t.

$F(t,a)$ = savings supplied voluntarily by an individual of age a in year t.

$A(t,a)$ = pension fund owned by an individual of age a in year t. Before the reform this amount is zero for all individuals.

 n = rate of population growth (we use $n = 0.005$).

Labor market equilibrium requires real wages to adjust until firms' demand for labor be equal to the supply of labor by all households, in each period. The aggregate supply of labor is influenced by the age-earnings profile, the rate of population growth, and the rate of technical progress in labor productivity:

$$L(t) = \sum_{a=1}^{a=55} l(a) \cdot (1+n)^{-t} \cdot (1+x)^{-t} \tag{8}$$

where:

 $L(t)$ = demand for labor by firms in period t.

 $l(a)$ = supply of effective labor units by the generation of age a. This is given by the age-earnings profile used by Arrau (1991). The normalization that fixes the size of the economy is that $l(21) = 1$.

 n = rate of population growth (we use $n = 0.005$).

 x = rate of labor productivity growth (we use $x = 0.005$).

Simulation methodology: The numerical simulation method we use can be separated in two parts. The first is a routine that finds the individual's optimal consumption path, subject to credit constraints, given some paths for interest rates, wage rates, and the tax rates. The second part of the model aggregates individual decisions and searches for the general equilibrium. In this part, the computer solves a set of nonlinear equations, by which equation (8) determines a path for L, and then (7) and (2) are solved together for paths of K and Y.

The rational expectations equilibrium path is such that the path of the capital–labor ratio and tax rates expected by consumers is ultimately consistent with market and budget equilibrium in each period. To find this equilibrium path, we first find the steady state before the pension reform. The capital-labor ratio from this steady state is used as an initial guess for the next 200 years. With these initial guesses, plus the reforms to contribution rates and the pension benefit formula, and the reforms to tax rates required to keep the budget in equilibrium given the pension reform, we obtain the full optimal consumption path and the associated supply of voluntary and forced savings for the representative individual of each generation.

Next we use the discrepancy between the supply and demand for capital to improve the guess for the path of the capital–labor ratio. The capital–labor ratio after year 110 is fixed to be the same as the value observed for year 110. With this guess a new iteration is started. The government budget is kept in equilibrium in response to the changes in tax bases by adjusting the path of tax rates. The tax rates after year 110 are fixed to be same as the value observed for year 110. Iteration continues until criteria of convergence for the path of the capital–labor ratio and the path of tax rates are met simultaneously. This method is originally due to Auerbach and Kotlikoff (1987), but we based our programming on the GAUSS version developed by Arrau (1991).

3   The pension reform

Transitions to funding exhibit several design features that are choices available to the policy maker. Some of these choices, such as the degree of financing through the issue of public debt, the tax rate that adjusts over time to keep the budget in equilibrium, and the availability of tax exemptions for pension funds, are the object of detailed analysis in section 3. The other design variables are assumed to follow policies discussed in this section.

3.1   Recognition of past contributions or (partial) default

The first assumption is that those who contributed to the old pension system receive some financial recognition, in the new system, for contributions made in the old system. The justification is that default on pension obligations is politically impossible, given the fact that public opinion is inhabited almost exclusively by people that have contributed to the old system – all voters have contributed in the past except those who are 21 years old – and will benefit from such an acknowledgment. Partial default can be modeled by varying the size of the financial recognition received by each cohort.

There are several ways to offer this financial recognition. One approach is the "recognition bond," which is issued by the government when the individual shifts to the new system and is paid in one lump sum when the individual reaches the standard retirement age of 65. The amount of the bond is proportional to the contributions in the old system, plus interest from the date of system shift until retirement date.

An alternative is the one adopted by the Argentinian pension reform of 1993, which acknowledges past contributions by paying a "compensatory pension." This is proportional to the amount of years contributed to the old system and is a fraction of the benefit that would apply if the person had continued in the old system until retirement. The main fiscal difference with the recognition bond is that it avoids paying a lump sum when the worker retires, and instead pays a pension over time. In other words, the compensatory pension approach implies no prepayment of the obligations to contributors.

The policy adopted in the Chilean pension reform of 1981 is a mix of the previous two, as those already pensioned by the date of reform receive a compensatory pension (the continuation of their pension) instead of recognition bond, which would be a lump sum equal to the present expected value of remaining pension obligations. Those pensioned after the reform date receive a recognition bond.

3.2   Detailed design of a recognition bond

In our simulations we adopt the recognition bond approach. Rather than inventing a policy ourselves, we simply apply the recognition bond policy followed in the Chilean reform of 1981: In the year where the transition starts, the basic amount of the recognition bond is calculated as the present value (at the market interest rates of the transition path), as of the reform date, of the pensions that a worker who retires in year one of the reform would have obtained in the old pay-as-you-go-financed system if no reform had existed. Those pensions are defined by the continuation of the initial steady state.

For workers that retire after the reform years, this basic amount is reduced by a fraction that is the number of years of contribution to the old system divided by 45 (the maximum number of years of contribution). To take into account that workers who were young at the reform date contributed on the basis of relatively low earnings, the basic amount is adjusted also by the ratio of earnings at the age the worker had in the year before the transition and the projected earnings for that same worker in the last year of work before retirement, in the event no reform had taken place.

During the years between the transition date – the date of issue of all recognition bonds – and retirement, recognition bonds earn tax-exempt interest at a statutory rate, which we assume to be 4% per year. The recognition bond is a zero-coupon bond that comes due at retirement. The worker does not receive this amount as a lump sum, but rather is forced to hold it in a special account, which earns the market interest rate, is exempt from income taxes, and pays out a constant real pension during the retirement years. The pension is set at a level such that after the last payout the account balance reaches zero. The pension is subject to income taxes.

This arrangement implies that during the transition there exists a set of financial intermediaries who receive maturing recognition bonds and invest the funds, increasing the supply of savings to the capital market. These intermediaries are necessary to ensure that those pensioned before the reform date are treated in the same way as those pensioned after, in the sense of receiving a flow of pension rather than a lump sum. This may make a difference due to credit constraints. These intermediaries may be thought of as pension fund management companies, where each member keeps an individual account with his contributions plus interest, and to which the final value of his recognition bond is added at retirement date. Even in the extreme case where the reform eliminates all mandatory pensions (the new system has a zero contribution rate), these intermediaries will hold some funds during the first 55 years since the reform.

3.3   Degree of debt financing

The second assumption is about the time path of the public debt. As explained before, this pension reform entails acknowledgment of a large fiscal obligation to those who contributed in the past. The reform creates a large fiscal "deficit" because the pensions owed to those generations already pensioned as of the reform date must continue to be paid, but the contributions to the old pay-as-you-go-financed system have disappeared. We put "deficit" in quotation marks because strictly speaking these payments are debt amortization, so they belong in the capital account. As discussed in section 3, two polar financing policies are possible, namely full tax financing and full debt financing. In the general case of partial debt financing, a time path for the national debt must be chosen. This time path can be characterized in terms of the share of the transition deficit that is financed with debt in each year, and of the way in which the debt–GNP ratio is set in a final value.

Let us define as the "transition deficit," the sum of payments of pension already granted and maturing recognition bonds. The transition deficit lasts for 45 years, until the last recognition bond is paid. One possible assumption, used by Arrau (1991), is that new debt is issued only to finance the recognition bonds that mature, but not the pensions already granted at the time the transition started. This results in a growing share of the transition deficit financed with debt, with the share reaching 100% in year 11 since the start of the transition. Instead, we assume that the share of the transition deficit financed with debt is constant over time. Most of our simulations assume that this share is 75%.

More important for the path of the macroeconomy is the assumption regarding the way in which the debt–GNP ratio is set in a final value. One possible rule is that, once the last recognition bond has matured, the public debt outstanding that results is kept constant as a proportion of GDP. This approach allows the debt–GNP ratio to fall during the years 40–45 since the transition started, because during those years the volume of maturing recognition bonds as a share of GNP is below the growth rate of the economy. In this period the required tax rate falls steeply. The associated bulge in the path of the public debt introduces a significant macroeconomic shock that makes interpretation of the pension reform more difficult.

To avoid this hidden fiscal shock, we assume the final value of the debt–GNP ratio is fixed at the highest level it achieves. In other words, we allow the debt–GNP ratio to rise according to the assumption about the share of the transition deficit that is financed with debt, but once these financing needs diminish we keep the debt–GNP ratio fixed at the highest level it reached. This generates extra revenue that allows tax rates to fall more moderately.

3.4   Size of the new funded system

The third assumption concerns the contribution rate to the new funded system. In the initial steady state, the contribution rate is 15% but the individual rate of return is $n + x = 0.5 + 0.5 = 1.0\%$ per annum. In the new funded pension system, a lower contribution rate is feasible without sacrificing the pension benefit, because the rate of return available in the capital market is larger than the growth rate of the economy. On the other hand, maintaining the 15% contribution rate will increase substantially the supply of funds to the capital market, pushing interest rates down in the long run, which in turn will reduce pensions. These conflicting effects are summarized in Table 6.1.

On the basis of Table 6.1, we will assume that the pension reform entails a reduction in the contribution rate from 15% to 10%. This reduction is justified because smaller reductions in the contribution rate do not improve the replacement rate materially in the long run. Higher reductions may be feasible, but run a higher risk of not achieving the desired replacement rate.

Table 6.1
Replacement rates for different contribution rates
(Pension as a % of the average wage during the last ten years of work)

	Initial PAYG	New Pension System (Partially Funded)				
Contribution Rate	15%	6%	8%	10%	12%	14%
Replacement Rate	69%	99%	108%	114%	116%	115%
Interest Rate (% before tax)	8.44	5.61	4.93	4.32	3.75	3.14

Other Assumptions: The public debt rises from zero to 100% across steady states; in the initial and final steady states the government revenue is raised by an income tax alone; the retirement age is 64 years.

Another justification for this choice is that the Chilean reform of 1981 reduced the contribution rate from 22% to 13%, which is a similar proportional reduction.

3.5   Gradual phase-in of the pension reform

A final important design variable is the degree to which the pension reform takes place over time. At one extreme is a one-shot shift of all active workers to the new fully funded pension system. This implies only pensioners remain in the old system. However, one may also think of a graduated shift of active workers. It may be possible to offer the option to switch pension systems only to those below age 50. This was achieved in the Chilean and Peruvian reforms by inducing people above age 50 not to shift to the new system. This implies that active workers over age 50 continue contributing to the pay-as-you-go system, which helps to reduce the transition deficit.

It is also possible to obtain a partial phase-in by channeling a part of the contribution, say one-third, to the new funded system and retaining the rest in the old system, so that everybody would have pensions from two sources during the transition. The part of the contribution channeled to the new pension system could be raised to two-thirds by year 5 and to three-thirds by year 10. This is similar to the approach followed in Australia to introduce a funded pension system. This approach produces a postponement in the financing needs of the transition till after the current government yields office, so it may be very attractive politically. Spreading the reform over time mitigates intergenerational redistribution, but also postpones the increase in national savings associated with the reform.

In order to facilitate interpretation and analysis, in this chapter we model the extreme case of a one-shot reform, with no gradual phase-in. As all active workers switch to the new system, even those of age 64, the transition deficit is initially very large. The transition deficit includes both the continuation of payment of pension to those already pensioned and the recognition bonds that are owed to those that retire in the second year after the transition started. The first item is roughly the share of labor in GDP, 78% with our parameter assumptions, times the contribution rate to the old system, 15%, whose revenue was used to pay these pensions, which amounts to 11.7% of GDP. The second item is the recognition bond of the first generation that retires in the new system, which is the present value of 10 years of pensions, discounted at market interest rates, which amounts to 8–9% of GDP. The total transition deficit starts close to 20% of GDP. After 10 years, the first item disappears and the transition deficit falls to some 10% of GDP. Then it falls gradually to zero by year 45.

In this setting, the assumption that new public debt finances 75% of the transition deficit allows tax rates to increase more gradually in response to growing interest payments.

4   Simulation results

4.1   The importance of credit constraints

This section studies whether a transition from pay-as-you-go financing to full funding is feasible, given the large fiscal cost it entails. A natural first approach to this issue is to ignore all types of credit constraints, as standard simulation models do, and to attempt a transition.

The case we study first is one in which 75% of the transition deficit is financed with the issue of public debt, the tax rate that adjusts is the income tax rate, and the new pension funds are exempt from income taxes. Figure 6.1a shows the evolution of the path of the income tax rate for iterations 1 and 2. In iteration 1 the income tax rate rises to 33% in year 35, but in iteration 2 it rises to 52%. Iteration 3 is not shown because the required income tax rates for some years goes above 100%.

This is not due to a failure in the numerical convergence method. There is no equilibrium path for this transition. Figure 6.1b shows that the required income tax rates rise for a fundamental economic reason: The base of the income tax, as a percentage of GDP, becomes lower and lower as the iterations proceed, for years 25 to 40 since the start of the transition. In turn, the tax base falls because aggregate voluntary assets are negative – and very large – during those years.

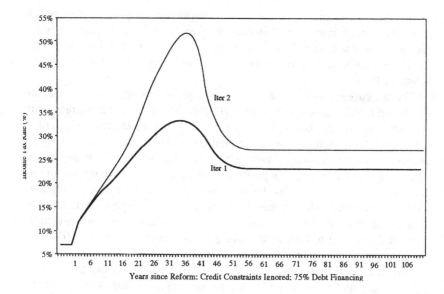

Figure 6.1a. Income tax rate.

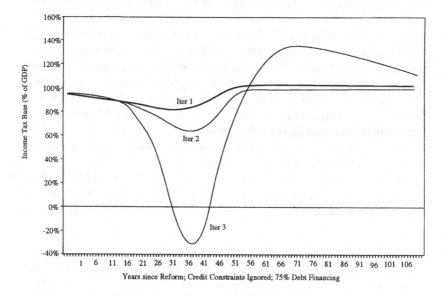

Figure 6.2b. Income tax base.

As credit constraints were ignored, the implicit assumption is that the tax authorities accept interest paid on consumer debt as a deduction from income for the income tax. The simulation shows that this deduction becomes huge in the aggregate during the critical years, reducing the income tax base substantially.

The tax base drops because of tax arbitrage by forward-looking consumers. When looking forward from year 20, they see that income tax rates will rise substantially and then will fall by year 45. Planning 25 years ahead, they realize that their savings into the pension funds will grow at the tax-exempt interest rate, while voluntary savings will be taxed strongly. Driving voluntary savings to a very negative position appears as an attractive option for the generations alive at this point, because this maximizes current consumption, while consumption when retired is financed out of the pension funds that accumulate free of the abnormally high income taxes. If the simulation allowed the worker to contribute more than the mandatory rate of 10%, this tax arbitrage would be even more dramatic.

Summing up, in this setting there is a dynamic Laffer curve that prevents an equilibrium path from existing.[5] There are several ways around this problem. The first is to reduce the share of the transition deficit that is financed with the issue of public debt, for example from 75% to 25%. Figure 6.2a shows that an equilibrium path exists for the 25% case.[6] However, this avenue is not satisfactory because, as shown by Figure 6.2b, the income tax base still falls to an unrealistic 55% of GDP in year 36, because of the incentives described earlier. A second approach is to change the tax that adjusts during the transition to be the consumption tax. This recovers existence for any degree of debt financing of the transition deficit, but this "solution" is not general because in many countries the main revenue earner is the income tax, and the consumption tax is also subject to exemptions not considered in this model. A third approach is to subject pension funds and individual retirement accounts to income taxes, as in Australia, but even in Australia pension funds pay a lower rate, so this would not be representative of international experience.

The problem with all these approaches is that they derive policy implications from a simulation approach that is flawed. In practice, the tax authorities do not accept interest paid in consumer credit as a valid deduction of income,

---

[5] This problem was not reported by Arrau (1991) because he considered a much smaller initial contribution rate (5% instead of 15%) and ignored the tax exemptions to pensions funds. This second point occurs because Arrau modeled the reform as an elimination of contributions. In Arrau (1990b) he considers briefly the issue of tax exemptions, but for a miniscule system with a contribution rate of 0.3%.

[6] Convergence to the equilibrium path was reached in iteration 22. An equilibrium path does not exist for a debt financing share as low as 30%.

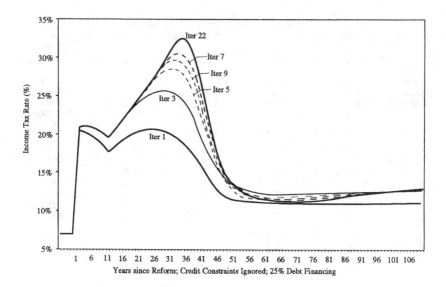

Figure 6.2a. Income tax rate.

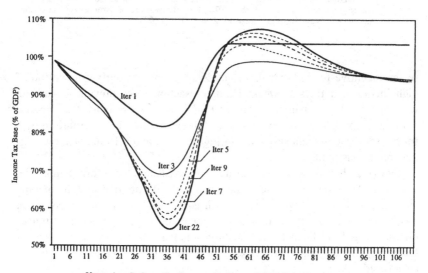

Years since Reform; Credit constraints Ignored; 25% Debt Financing

Figure 6.2b. Income tax base.

Table 6.2
The equilibrium path exists with credit constrains
(75% of transition deficit financed with debt; pension funds exempt from income taxes)

Years Since Reform	Income Tax Rate (%)	Income Tax Base (% of GDP)	Years Since Reform	Income Tax Rate (%)	Income Tax Base (% of GDP)
Before	6.95	93.5	25	23.15	97.1
			30	21.08	98.1
1	9.58	97.5	35	18.97	99.4
2	12.20	97.6	40	16.90	100.7
3	13.21	97.7	45	15.49	101.6
4	14.16	97.6	50	15.93	102.2
5	15.06	97.5	55	16.60	101.3
10	18.52	97.7	60	16.87	100.1
15	21.43	98.0	80	16.38	99.8
20	23.45	97.4	100	16.51	100.0
			110	16.48	99.8

Note: The income tax base increases by 4% of GDP in the year of the reform, because the contribution rate falls from 15% to 10%, leaving 5% more of earnings subject to the income tax. Wage income is close to 80% of GDP.

so the incentive for individuals to get deeply into debt during the period of high income tax rates is weak. High transaction costs prevent consumers from offering future wages as collateral on a big scale, so individuals choose not to attempt this sort of tax arbitrage. Table 6.2 shows the equilibrium path for the same parameters simulated in Figures 6.1a and 6.1b but acknowledging credit constraints.

Table 6.2 shows that an equilibrium path exists and the reform is feasible. The base of the income tax never falls below 97.5% of GDP, and the income tax rate never goes above 23.5%, which is high but much lower than when credit constraints are ignored. This pension reform – even though its transition deficit is front loaded and very high – is feasible for any degree of debt financing, and any degree of tax exemption, as soon as credit constraints are acknowledged.

This exercise shows that ignoring credit constraints is a big drawback of standard simulation models, because the quantification sought can be severely biased. The rest of the simulations presented in this chapter acknowledge credit constraints.

4.2 The taxes that adjust during the transition

Recall that in the initial steady state two taxes coexist, namely an income and a consumption tax. Their rates are set in such a way that half of revenue is collected by each tax in the initial steady state. During the transition and thereafter, either one of the two tax rates adjusts. This setup allows a quantification of the impact of selecting different taxes to adjust the budget during the transition. This quantification takes into account that changes in tax rates occur in the presence of other taxes.

In the initial steady state there is a third tax, namely a hidden wage tax associated to the contributions to the old pay-as-you-go pension system. This tax arises because contributions earn a rate of return equal to the growth rate of the economy, much lower than the market rate of return.

As explained in Chapter 7, from a fiscal point of view the pension reform is equivalent to the substitution of the wage tax (implicit in the low returns to pay-as-you-go contributions) for the tax rate that adjusts the budget during the transition, plus an acknowledgment of the hidden public debt. If the consumption tax adjusts the budget in the transition, the pension reform is equivalent to a shift from wage taxes to consumption taxes. If the income tax adjusts during the transition, the pension reform is equivalent to a shift from wage taxes to income taxes. If public debt is issued in the transition, these shifts are delayed in time, but the pattern remains.

Existing theory about this policy choice stresses that an increase in any tax that falls more heavily on the elderly is equivalent to a wealth tax on them. The share of wages earned by the elderly is zero, the share of income received by the elderly is positive, and the share of consumption obtained by the elderly is the highest of these three. This is because the elderly finance part of their consumption by drawing down assets.

Therefore, existing theory predicts a switch to consumption taxes will fall more heavily on the elderly than a switch to income taxes. The implication is that adjusting the budget through a consumption tax increases the efficiency of the tax regime, because a tax that does not induce substitution is like a lump sum tax. In addition, this choice leaves future generations better off as it encourages more capital accumulation, but leaves the elderly worse off (Auerbach and Kotlikoff, 1987).

Simulation results in the literature, such as those in Auerbach and Kotlikoff (1987, p. 66) evaluate the impact of fiscal reforms of this sort, which substitute a wage tax by consumption taxes, or a wage tax by an income tax. For example, in their base case they find that substituting a wage tax for a consumption tax increases the capital–labor ratio by 14.8% in the long run. Similarly, substituting a wage tax for an income tax, reduces the capital–labor

Table 6.3A
The equilibrium path when the income tax rate adjusts
(75% of transition deficit financed with debt; pension funds exempt from income taxes;
consumption tax rate = 8.26%, tax-exclusive basis)

Years Since Reform	Income Tax Rate (%)	Interest Rate (bef. tax) (%)	Wage Rate (%)	Consumption GNP	Public Debt GNP (%)	Pension Funds Total Assets (%)1	Capital Labor Ratio (%)2
Before	6.95	8.07	0.946	0.7866	0	0	2.231
1	9.58	8.07	0.946	0.8003	0	0	2.231
2	12.20	8.14	0.945	0.7980	0.0876	0.0404	2.217
3	13.21	8.21	0.943	0.7973	0.2292	0.1135	2.204
4	14.16	8.27	0.942	0.7966	0.3637	0.1796	2.192
5	15.06	8.33	0.941	0.7958	0.4910	0.2399	2.181
10	18.52	8.50	0.937	0.7914	1.0124	0.4827	2.149
15	21.43	8.48	0.937	0.7810	1.3751	0.6671	2.152
20	23.45	7.99	0.948	0.7567	1.6902	0.8240	2.248
25	23.15	6.93	0.973	0.7309	1.9248	0.9297	2.478
30	21.08	5.82	1.002	0.7269	2.0697	0.9749	2.777
35	18.97	5.12	1.022	0.7426	2.1387	0.9838	3.003
40	16.90	4.89	1.029	0.7630	2.1477	0.9798	3.085
45	15.49	5.03	1.025	0.7802	"	0.9670	3.034
50	15.93	5.39	1.015	0.7855	"	0.9534	2.913
55	16.60	5.69	1.006	0.7787	"	0.9488	2.816
60	16.87	5.78	1.003	0.7695	"	0.9511	2.789
70	16.61	5.62	1.008	0.7647	"	0.9580	2.839
80	16.38	5.51	1.011	0.7680	"	0.9579	2.872
90	16.43	5.55	1.010	0.7698	"	0.9563	2.860
100	16.51	5.59	1.009	0.7689	"	0.9564	2.849
110	16.48	5.57	1.009	0.7683	"	0.9566	2.854

Note 1: Total Assets is the sum of physical capital and the net public debt, or equivalently, the sum of voluntary savings and pension funds.

Note 2: As aggregate labor supply follows a fixed path in this model, the capital/labor ratio is a good indicator of capital accumulation.

ratio by 7.4% in the long run. Of course, these numbers are not directly applicable to our transition exercise because the public debt rises considerably.

For our specific parameter assumptions, the standard prediction[7] is that substituting a wage tax for a consumption tax, which is used to service a public debt that increases from zero to 215% of GDP,[8] increases the capital–

[7] The results reported in this paragraph were obtained with PREVIMACRO, a prepackaged simulation model for steady states developed by the authors.

[8] This level of the public debt is taken from the simulations presented in Tables 6.3A and 6.3B. In both cases the public debt rises from zero to a level close to 215% of GDP in the long run.

Table 6.3B
The equilibrium path when the consumption tax rate adjusts
(75% of transition deficit financed with debt; pension funds exempt from income taxes; income
tax rate = 6.95%)

Years Since Reform	Consumption Tax Rate[1] (%)	Interest Rate (bef. tax) (%)	Wage Rate (%)	Consumption GNP	Public Debt GNP (%)	Pension Funds Total Assets (%)[2]	Capital Labor Ratio (%)[3]
Before	8.26	8.07	0.946	0.7866	0	0	2.231
1	11.55	8.07	0.946	0.7932	0	0	2.231
2	14.82	8.11	0.946	0.7904	0.0876	0.0404	2.223
3	16.07	8.13	0.945	0.7884	0.2288	0.1129	2.219
4	17.24	8.14	0.945	0.7867	0.3628	0.1780	2.217
5	18.31	8.14	0.945	0.7852	0.4892	0.2370	2.218
10	22.13	8.02	0.947	0.7805	1.0033	0.4680	2.241
15	25.24	7.82	0.952	0.7751	1.3580	0.6340	2.281
20	27.79	7.42	0.961	0.7619	1.6720	0.7740	2.365
25	28.27	6.75	0.978	0.7442	1.9176	0.8800	2.523
30	27.35	5.91	1.000	0.7345	2.0740	0.9400	2.749
35	24.83	5.26	1.018	0.7427	2.1458	0.9620	2.954
40	21.70	4.98	1.027	0.7595	2.1539	0.9650	3.052
45	19.48	5.04	1.025	0.7756	"	0.9550	3.032
50	19.83	5.31	1.017	0.7816	"	0.9410	2.940
55	20.55	5.56	1.009	0.7770	"	0.9350	2.857
60	20.89	5.65	1.007	0.7697	"	0.9360	2.827
70	20.68	5.56	1.010	0.7650	"	0.9410	2.858
80	20.43	5.47	1.012	0.7672	"	0.9420	2.887
90	20.47	5.48	1.012	0.7690	"	0.9410	2.881
100	20.56	5.52	1.011	0.7684	"	0.9410	2.871
110	20.54	5.51	1.011	0.7681	"	0.9410	2.874

Note 1: The consumption tax rate is expressed on a tax-exclusive basis.

Note 2: Total Assets is the sum of physical capital and the net public debt, or equivalently, the sum of voluntary savings and pension funds.

Note 3: As aggregate labor supply fixed in this model, the capital/labor ratio is a good indicator of capital accumulation.

labor ratio by 3.5% in the long run. Substituting a wage tax for an income tax, which is used to service a public debt that increases from zero to 215% of GDP, reduces the capital–labor ratio by 16.0% in the long run. However, these results do not consider credit constraints.

Our simulations of the full transition quantify these effects but also acknowledge credit constraints. The simulations in Tables 6.3A and 6.3B differ in the tax rate that adjusts. Both assume that 75% of the transition deficit is financed with debt. and that the income of pension funds is exempt from income taxes.

The first obvious difference in results is that the capital–labor ratio rises by 28.8% in the long run when the consumption tax adjusts and by 27.9% when the income tax adjusts. These effects are much larger than when ignoring credit constraints. This is the first conclusion of this section.

In addition, macroeconomic and fiscal indicators are also very close during *each* of the years of the transition. In other words, the performance of the income tax improves considerably when credit constraints are acknowledged. The second conclusion is that it does not make a big difference for the macroeconomy whether the consumption or the income tax rate adjusts the budget.

One possible explanation is that, for the individuals who are credit-constrained, wages, income, and consumption are identical, so there is less difference in tax bases and tax incidence than in models that ignore credit constraints. There are two explanations for the overall increase in the capital–labor ratio: First, the reform is 25% tax-financed, adding to national savings. Second, the new pension system forces those that are credit constrained to save and the resulting funds increase supply in the capital market.

The transition itself is also quite interesting. A notable element is the consumption boom experienced during the first 3 years of the transition, which can be attributed to credit constraints. Recall that the pension reform reduces the contribution rate from 15% to 10%. This increases the taxable wage by 5.88%. Given a share of 78% of wages in GDP, this amounts to a potential increase in worker consumption of 3.90% of GDP, if all workers were constrained.[9] On the other hand, the transition deficit is close to 19% of GDP in the second year, and 25% of this must be financed with an increase in taxes, part of which are borne by pensioners. This dampening effect amounts to 4.75% of GDP as a first approximation. In the equilibrium transition path the first effect dominates, when taking into account other static and intertemporal effects.

Another important aspect is the path of the public debt and of the growing pension funds. As 75% of the transition deficit is financed with new public debt, the debt outstanding increases rapidly in both cases, reaching 170% of GDP by year 20. More important, the new pension funds grow even faster, because the real interest rate is initially high and because there are few cash outflows during the first decades.

In addition, the stock of voluntary savings is substituted by mandatory savings at an uneven rate. The net impact on the supply of capital to firms becomes significantly positive by year 20 to 25 and thereafter the capital–

---

[9] This effect was predicted by Diamond and Valdés-Prieto (1994) when analyzing the Chilean reform. In that reform, however, the government built a fiscal surplus of 5% of GDP before the reform date, so no tax was raised in the year of the reform. The net impact on aggregate demand was substantial in 1981, helping to explain the puzzle of the large current account deficit observed in that year.

labor ratio rises. This happens only when the pension funds reach a share over 80% of the net outstanding assets, which from the demand side are capital demanded by firms plus the net public debt of the government. For smaller shares, substitution between forced and voluntary savings is very high. This unevenness can be attributed to the existence of just one representative agent per generation. As discovered by Valdés-Prieto and Cifuentes (1993) dispersion in impatience rates would produce much smoother substitution and a much smaller share of pension funds in net outstanding assets.

The tax rates rise above the new long-run levels from year 20 to 40, because tax revenue must cover simultaneously 25% of the transition deficit and the interest cost of a public debt that has grown to 170% of GDP and more. At the peak of the high taxes (year 20 or 25), consumers anticipate that tax rates will fall, so they postpone consumption. In the case when consumption taxes are adjusting, they postpone consumption to avoid consumption taxes. In the case when income taxes are adjusting, consumers postpone consumption because they expect the after-tax return on voluntary saving to increase, so it pays more to build up voluntary savings.

As consumption falls, savings increase and investment increases, leading to an increase in the capital–labor ratio. Unlike saving, investment in this model without adjustment costs is determined by short-term interest rates alone. In the equilibrium path, these factors that encourage savings are so powerful that they lead to overshooting of the capital stock. Later on, from year 45 to 60, consumption increases in response to very low real interest rates, until the capital–labor ratio reaches its long-term level.

4.3   The degree of debt financing of the transition

This section presents the results of the stimulation for cases in which the degree of debt financing is 75%, 25%, and 0. In all cases the tax rate that adjusts is the income tax, and pension funds are exempt from income taxes.

The conventional wisdom in this matter is that a lower degree of debt financing permits a larger increase in physical capital in the long term. The cost is higher taxes for those generations living during the transition. More concretely, conventional simulation models suggest that our pension reform would yield increases in the capital–labor ratio of 11.2%, 14.8%, and 30.7% for final steady states in which the public debt–GDP ratio rose to 215%, 70%, and 0 respectively.[10] However, these estimates ignore credit constraints.

Tables 6.4 and 6.5 show that the macroeconomic impact of the financing

---

[10] These numbers are taken from Table 6.5. These simulations were conducted in PREVI-MACRO.

Table 6.4
Impact of the degree of debt financing on the transition deficit
(income tax rate adjusts; pension funds are exempt from income taxes)

Years Since Reform	Required Income Tax Rate			Real Interest Rate (before tax)		
	75% debt (%)	25% debt (%)	0% debt (%)	75% debt (%)	25% debt (%)	0% debt (%)
Before	6.95	6.95	6.95	8.07	8.07	8.07
1	9.58	15.77	18.92	8.07	8.07	8.07
2	12.20	21.82	26.70	8.14	8.04	7.95
3	13.21	21.81	26.24	8.21	7.96	7.78
4	14.16	21.72	25.69	8.27	7.86	7.57
5	15.06	21.55	25.05	8.33	7.74	7.35
10	18.52	19.47	20.63	8.50	7.06	6.22
15	21.43	19.35	19.57	8.48	6.40	5.32
20	23.45	19.02	18.69	7.99	5.60	4.47
25	23.15	17.67	16.95	6.93	4.77	3.73
30	21.08	15.66	14.67	5.82	4.12	3.22
	18.97	13.54	12.19	5.12	3.78	2.93
40	16.90	11.44	9.87	4.89	3.69	2.79
45	15.49	9.70	8.10	5.03	3.76	2.73
50	15.93	9.57	7.90	5.39	3.86	2.70
55	16.60	9.68	7.95	5.69	3.91	2.69
60	16.87	9.74	7.98	5.78	3.90	2.68
70	16.61	9.76	8.01	5.62	3.89	2.68
80	16.38	9.75	8.01	5.51	3.89	2.68
90	16.43	9.75	8.01	5.55	3.89	2.68
100	16.51	9.75	8.01	5.59	3.89	2.68
110	16.48	9.75	8.01	5.57	3.89	2.68

policy for the transition is very different when credit constraints are acknowledged. The actual changes in the capital–labor ratio are 27.9%, 57.0%, and 87.3% in the three cases discussed here. The main explanation for the difference is that credit constraints assure that the new pension system increases the supply of savings, rather than having no effect, as implicitly assumed in models that ignore credit constraints.

The degree of debt financing per se does not make much difference. This can be seen from the fact that the increment in the capital–labor ratio derived from passing from 75% to 25% debt financing is $1.148/0.888 = 29.3\%$ when ignoring credit constraints and $1.57/1.279 = 22.8\%$ when acknowledging them. These figures are of the same order of magnitude. The conclusion is that financing policy per se has, at the margin, a similar impact as expected from the previous literature, but is less important overall because

Table 6.5
Steady-state effects of the degree of debt financing
(income tax rate adjusts; pension funds exempt from income taxes)

Degree of Debt Financing	Before Reform	75%	25%	0%
Capital/Labor Ratio	2.2313	2.854	3.5041	4.1797
% Increase in K/L	-	27.9%	57.0%	87.3%
Real Wages	0.9464	1.009	1.0624	1.1084
Real Interest Rate (%)	8.07	5.57	3.89	2.68
Public Debt/GDP	0	2.148	0.694	0
Consumption/GDP (%)	78.66	76.83	75.06	73.23
Gross Investment/GDP (%)	8.34	10.17	11.94	13.77
Pension Funds/Net Assets (%)	0	95.66	93.50	84.37
Income Tax Rate (%)	6.95	16.48	9.75	8.01
Consumption Tax Rate (%)	8.26	8.26	8.26	8.26
Growth Rate of GDP (%)	1.00	1.00	1.00	1.00

the impact will be substantially positive for any degree of debt financing below 75%.

We also find that increasing the share of the deficit that is debt financed from 25% to 75% postpones the year of maximum tax rates by 20 years (from year 2 to 5 to year 20 to 25 since the reform), but the level of the maximum tax rate is only slightly smaller with 25% debt financing.

Another interesting result uncovered by these experiments is that for very low degrees of debt financing the capital accumulation effect is so large that interest rates fall to levels such that the pension paid by the pension system falls significantly. This induces households to increase their saving for old age, increasing the supply of voluntary savings. In turn, this increased supply of savings reduces the market interest rate still more. This effect may be large here because there is just one representative agent per generation, with a single impatience rate.

4.4   Exempting pension funds from the income tax

Even when ignoring credit constraints, phasing out pay-as-you-go-financed old-age pensions is different from a shifting to full funding. Voluntary and forced savings are imperfect substitutes because the latter usually enjoy tax exemptions. There are three possible tax exemptions for social security.[11]

---

[11] See Kingston and Piggott (1993) for a partial equilibrium exposition.

(a) Contributions may be exempt from the income tax.
(b) The pension paid by the new system may be exempt from personal income taxes.
(c) The capital income of the pension fund may be exempt from corporate income taxes.

Up to now we have assumed that exemptions (a) and (c) applied, while (b) did not. This section explores the macroeconomic consequences of abandoning exemption (c).

The conventional theory emphasizes that application of exemptions (a) and (c) delays taxation and therefore the required tax rate must be larger during a significant transition period. The counterpart is that a larger pension fund can be accumulated. However, those individuals who are already retired – who dissave – do not enjoy this tax break and instead must pay the higher tax rate that will be imposed in the transition. Therefore, this exemption policy is equivalent to a substantial fiscal saving effort during the transition and leads to a higher level of physical capital in the final steady state at the cost of lower welfare for those retired in the transition period.

Exemptions also have substitution effects, because individuals are induced to save more in the tax-free vehicles. These effects do not apply here, because we assume individuals are banned from saving more than 10% of earnings in their individual pension account.

This section presents three alternative approaches to tax exemption. These three cases differ by the percentage of pension fund assets that are exempt from income taxes. This interpretation is useful because in most countries that grant income tax exemptions to pension funds there is no tax credit for the corporate income taxes paid by the firms whose equity is held by pension funds. Therefore, we can take as the central case the one with 50% of the economic income of the pension fund (interest, dividends, and capital gains) subject to income taxes. The differences with the results when 100% is exempt can be interpreted as the impact of granting pension funds a tax credit for the corporate tax paid by the firms in which they hold equity. The results for the case of 0% exemption have the straightforward interpretation.

As seen in section 4.1, a problem with conventional models is that they exaggerate the impact of tax exemptions, because they allow for unrealistic levels of tax arbitrage by consumers that issue large volumes of consumer debt backed only by future pension income. Our simulation results avoid this by acknowledging credit constraints.

Table 6.6 shows that choosing to exempt fully pension fund income (interest) to the income tax, rather than the central scenario with 50% exemption, implies an increase in the capital–labor ratio of 4.3% in the long run.

Table 6.6
Macroeconomic effects of tax exemptions for pension funds
(income tax rate adjusts; 75% of debt financing)

A. Comparison of Steady States

	Before Reform	Final Steady State		
Exemption from Income Tax on Pension Fund Income:		100%	50%	0%
Capital/Labor Ratio	2.2313	2.854	2.737	2.6296
% Increase in K/L	-	27.9%	22.7%	17.9%
Income/Labor Ratio	1.1695	1.2331	1.2223	1.2119
% Increase in Y/L	-	5.4%	4.5%	3.6%
Real Wages	0.9464	1.009	0.9985	0.9881
Real Interest Rate (%)	8.07	5.57	5.96	6.34
Public Debt/GDP	0	2.148	2.179	2.214
Consumption/GDP (%)	78.66	76.83	77.16	77.48
Gross Investment/GDP (%)	8.34	10.17	9.84	9.52
Pension Funds/Net Assets (%)	0	95.66	94.84	93.80
Income Tax Rate (%)	6.95	16.48	15.61	14.80
Consumption Tax Rate (%)	8.26	8.26	8.26	8.26
Growth Rate of GDP (%)	1.00	1.00	1.00	1.00

B. Comparisons of Transitions

Income Tax Rate in Year 5		15.06	14.73	14.41
Income Tax Rate in Year 10		18.52	17.51	16.64
Income Tax Rate in Year 15		21.43	19.74	18.35
Income Tax Rate in Year 20		23.45	21.41	19.68
Income Tax Rate in Year 25		23.15	21.61	20.05
Income Tax Rate in Year 30		21.08	20.33	19.36
Income Tax Rate in Year 35		18.97	18.53	17.99

Going in the opposite direction, and fully taxing pension fund income leads to a fall in the capital–labor ratio of 3.9% in the long run. This range of outcomes is not very large.

An advantage of taxing pension fund income fully is that the income tax rate can be 3.77 percentage points smaller at its peak during the transition (year 20), thanks to the larger tax base. Again the range is not very large.

One may have expected that tax-exempt pension funds would grow to be significantly larger because of the higher rate of return. However, when taking into account the endogeneity of real interest rates, as in the simulations, we find that the share of pension funds in total net assets does not change by more than 1.86 percentage points due to exemption.

We expect exemptions to have a larger impact in settings where individuals have freedom to increase the amount they can save in tax-free vehicles, at least within some bounds set by the tax law.

5   Concluding remarks

This chapter discusses the macroeconomics of mandatory pensions, for which we use an overlapping-generations, life-cycle simulation model where consumers must meet credit constraints. These are defined as the condition that voluntary assets must be nonnegative.

The first policy lesson is that a pension reform that replaces pay-as-you-go financing for full funding is entirely feasible from a fiscal point of view, as soon as we acknowledge the existence of credit constraints.

The second lesson is that the long-term gains from such a reform are much higher than previously known, because the mandatory funded pension scheme forces an increase in saving rates during the transition period. The capital–labor ratio increases 28% even when 75% of the transition deficit is financed with new public debt. This occurs because a significant share of the population – those below 35 years of age, in most years – are restricted by credit constraints and are forced to reduce consumption, while the capital income of pension funds accumulates. Of course, this means that the generations alive during the transition will be forced to consume even less (save more) than previously known.

We also find that reducing the degree of debt financing has a marginal impact similar to that already known from the literature that ignores credit constraints. On the other hand, changing the tax base for the taxes that adjust during the transition, from income to consumption basis, has only marginal effects, contrary to what is found in the literature that ignores credit constraints. Finally, exempting pension funds from income taxes has secondary effects in the long run, although it requires higher tax rates during the transition.

Familiarity with the numbers, obtained with these simulations, suggests that the main problem with this pension reform is the dramatic increase in tax rates that is required during the transition, even with 75% debt financing. In this base case, the income tax rate rises from 7% before the reform to 12.2% in year 2 to 23.5% in year 20 and then falls to 16.5% in the long run. The problem is how to design low-debt financing paths that can satisfy short-term political pressures, such as the drive to improve the probability of reelection.

From a short-term political point of view, an attractive policy is to ban the switch to the new pension system of workers above age 50, while financing with new taxes 25% of the payments of pensions to those already pensioned at the date of the reform. The rest would be financed with contribution revenue from those above age 50 and with the issue of new public debt. This requires an increase in income tax rates from 7% to 10% by year 5.

An alternative, with universal switching to the new system, would be to break up the transition deficit in two parts: the payments of pensions to those already pensioned at the date of the reform, which would be entirely financed with new public debt; and the payment of a recognition for past contributions, in the form of partial pensions, to those that have not retired yet, which would be financed 50% with new debt and 50% with new taxes and smaller general expenditure. The fiscal implication of this arrangement for the first 5 years is an increase in revenue needs on the order of 0.75% of GDP in each year, which requires an increase of the income tax rate to just 11% by year 5.

Both setups may enable the government that introduces the reform to claim that it assured funding of future pensions and faster capital accumulation, while still avoiding an increase in tax rates during its tenure.

References

Arrau, P. (1990a) "Intertemporal Substitution in a Monetary Framework: Evidence from Two Latin American Countries." World Bank, January. Mimeograph.

(1990b) "Social Security Reform: The Capital Accumulation and Intergenerational Distribution Effect." Working Paper WPS-512, World Bank, October, 53 p.

(1991) "La Reforma Previsional Chilena y su Financiamiento durante la Transición." Colección Estudios CIEPLAN, 32, June 5–44.

Auerbach, A., and L. Kotlikoff (1987) Dynamic Fiscal Policy. Cambridge University Press.

Blau, D. (1994) "Labor Force Dynamics of Older Men." Econometrica 62, no. 1, 117–156.

Cifuentes, R. (1993) Efectos Macroeconómicos y Distributivos de los Sistemas Previsionales: Un Enfoque de Equilibrio General. Thesis for the Degree of Master in Economics, U. Católica de Chile, Santiago.

Diamond, P., and S. Valdés-Prieto, (1994) "Social Security Reforms." In B. Bosworth, R. Dornbusch, and R. Labán, editors, The Chilean Economy, chapter 6. Brookings Institution, Washington, D.C.

Hubbard, G., and K. Judd (1987) "Social Security and Individual Welfare: Precautionary Saving, Borrowing Constraints and the Payroll Tax." American Economic Review, 77, no. 4, 630–646.

Kingston, G., and J. Piggott (1993) "A Ricardian Equivalence Theorem on the taxation of pension funds." Economic Letters, 42, 399–403.

Laitner, J. (1990) "Tax Changes and Phase Diagrams for an Overlapping Generations Model." Journal of Political Economy, 98, no. 1, 193–220.

Mariger, R. (1987) "A Life-cycle Consumption Model with Liquidity Constraints: Theory and Empirical Results." Econometrica, 55, no. 3, 533–557.

Valdés-Prieto, S., and R. Cifuentes (1993) "Credit Constraints and Pensions." Instituto Economía, U. Católica de Chile. Mimeograph.

CHAPTER 7

Financing a pension reform toward private funded pensions

Salvador Valdés-Prieto

Abstract

This chapter studies financing policies for the portion of a pension system that mandates actuarially fair insurance and savings. We show first that a reform to switch from pay-as-you-go to funding does not have to impose a double burden on the transition generation. The "fiscal cost" of the transition can be met by applying the following four measures simultaneously: reduction of the contribution rate, introduction of compensatory pensions for the generations alive during the transition, gradual increase of the public debt–GDP ratio during the transition, and creation of a new permanent payroll tax. Then we analyze a second reform that grants pension institutions the freedom to rebalance their investment portfolio away from government bonds. Using a general equilibrium model and simulation, we show that this reform may achieve valuable diversification of aggregate risk in a small open economy. The chapter argues that achieving these gains requires both division of the pension institution into many and independence of these institutions from political pressures. Both of these requirements can be met by privatization.

1 Introduction

This chapter explores the welfare impact of financing policies for the portion of a pension system that mandates actuarially fair insurance and savings. This focus leaves out issues of redistribution from rich to poor in the same generation. The two options discussed are pay-as-you-go financing and full funding.

The literature on overlapping-generations economies where technical progress is exogenous shows that funding a pension system that was pre-

I am grateful for the comments of Peter Diamond, Gert Wagner, and an anonymous referee.

viously financed with the pay-as-you-go method leads to an increase in savings (i.e., implies faster capital accumulation) during a transition period. This same process also implies a redistribution, since those generations alive during the transition are worse off whereas future generations are better off. The conclusion is that, unless dynamic growth effects are triggered, moving to funding cannot lead to a Pareto improvement (Blanchard and Fischer, 1989). In political terms, a reform of the financing method that increases the degree of funding would be unacceptable for the living generations. This prediction is specially relevant in Europe, where the pension systems are largest.

The focus of this chapter is a less ambitious reform, which does not attempt to increase national saving, but is politically more attractive because living generations are not burdened. This reform may nevertheless allow for economic and political benefits. Among the economic benefits mentioned in the literature are positive externalities in the capital market (Valdés-Prieto and Cifuentes, 1990), a reduction of wage taxes, which reduces negative externalities in the labor market (Corsetti and Schmidt-Hebbel, Chapter 5, this volume), and access to international risk diversification (this chapter), all of which allow better pension benefits in the long term. The political benefits are more transparent fiscal accounting (Diamond and Valdés-Prieto, 1994) and less exposure of pension benefits to political risk (Godoy and Valdés-Prieto, Chapter 3, this volume).

The chapter proceeds in several steps. Section 2 identifies pension reforms that adopt fully funded schemes but also leave the budget and national savings untouched. These reforms do not impose a double burden on the transition generation. This section shows how neutral relabeling of cash flows can be done to achieve contractual documentation of debts of the government to the pension institution, paying market interest rates and enjoying constitutional protection for property rights.

Such a neutral switch to funding does not merely require the issue of public debt to pay off the pension promises associated with the pay-as-you-go financing system, as it is commonly thought. That is not enough because the public debt must pay market interest rates while the hidden pension debt costs the government a smaller rate, equal to the growth rate of the economy.

It is found that the following four measures must be applied simultaneously to achieve neutrality: (1) permanent reduction of the contribution rate, which keeps pensions the same because pension reserves will earn market rates of return; (2) creation of a new permanent tax on covered earnings to leave take-home wages and the public finances unaltered; (3) introduction of supplementary pensions for the generations that were still working at the date of the transition, to be added to the partial pension the worker will finance with the contributions made after the reform; and (4) a gradual issue of public debt during a transition period, according to a specific program that is identified. This keeps all markets in equilibrium without forcing changes in interest rates.

This section also offers numerical simulations that quantify the required new tax on covered earnings and the reduction in the contribution rate. These show that for an initially balanced system where the contribution rate is 15%, the reduction in the contribution rate is quite large, between 3 and 10 percentage points, depending on the parameters of the economy. The new tax on covered earnings must be of the same size. These magnitudes show the importance of avoiding simple debt finance to cover the transition deficit.

Section 3 discusses how this reform, which would be a mere relabeling in a certain world, has important implications for risk sharing and the transparency of the political process in a context of uncertainty. Missing insurance markets imply that pension reforms may have first-order welfare impacts (Enders and Lapan, 1982, 1993; Gordon and Varian, 1988; Green, 1988; Richter, 1993).

One risk without a market is the risk that the political system may redefine (default upon) legislated pension promises and reduce benefits. Taxes and pensions are adjusted ex-post, according to a political bargaining process whose outcome is modeled as a random variable. This is different from the models available in the previous literature, such as Gordon and Varian (1988), where the outcome of political bargaining is fixed ex ante and with certainty, according to some constitutional rule.

This section also discusses the implications of taking these pension reforms one step further, which is allowing the pension institution(s) to trade the contractual government debt they hold in order to improve their portfolio composition. This section considers several settings in which this reform may happen, such as closed and open economies. The implications for efficiency, fiscal stability, and intergenerational equity are potentially significant.

The most interesting implication is a link between portfolio freedom for financial institutions and privatization of those institutions. It is argued that granting the freedom for portfolio rebalancing requires division of the pension institution into several units to prevent the creation of monopoly power in the government debt market. On the other hand, these pension institutions can be relied upon to reach the risk–return frontier only if they are independent from political pressures to buy government bonds at low rates. These two requirements point toward privatization of these institutions.

Conversely, this section shows that privatization does not require true funding of pension liabilities. Only apparent funding is enough. The critical requirement is freedom to rebalance the investment portfolio, which generates a welfare improvement.

A specific case is the one of a small open economy for which international interest rates and rates of return are stochastic. When the pension institutions are allowed to sell part of their government bonds, they can acquire private assets whose returns are set in international capital markets and offer scope for higher returns and higher pensions. If they do so, the government cannot guarantee pensions without putting up equity, which we rule out. This implies that pensioners must bear investment risk in this option, which is proportional to the share of the portfolio not invested in government debt. In addition, as the interest rate for traded public debt is set in international capital markets, there is a new source of fiscal risk that causes fluctuations in the tax burden.

Section 4 brings these ideas together in a general equilibrium model of a very small open economy. In this model, political risk appears explicitly and several sources of fiscal risk are considered. This model allows simulation of the ex ante welfare level for specific preferences and distributions. It is found that welfare can be improved by 3% to 4% of GDP if portfolio rebalancing is allowed to a number of pension institutions that compete to reach the risk–return frontier.

2 Reforms to the financing method of mandatory pensions

This section provides a public finance framework and outlines the features that a reform to the financing method of a pension system must have in order to be neutral for capital accumulation.

2.1 The meaning of funding

The degree of funding of a pension system is usefully separated into three components:

(a) The sector of the economy that gives backing to the promises to the pension institution. The conventional sectors are the government, the private sector, and foreigners. The distinction is important as the probability of full payment to the pension institution is governed by different processes in each sector, opening the issue of risk diversification across these processes.

(b) The degree to which pensions are backed by contractual investments, as opposed to legislated promises of paying benefits. We say that pension promises are "apparently funded" when an accountant finds that explicit pension reserves can be identified. Other types of promises, such as legislated promises that the government will cover any shortfall in the pension institution's cash flow, or mandated benefits such as a legislated obligation of employers to pay certain severance payments, may be apparently unfunded or not. This concept is useful because a reform to the financing method of pensions can achieve a switch from unfunded (pay-as-you-go) to apparently funded status, without imposing a double burden on the transition generations.

(c) The degree to which promises to the pension institution are backed by a stock of outside assets, such as physical capital or international assets. We define this as "ultimate funding." A government promise is ultimately unfunded when its backing is the ability of the government to tax the economy in the future. A private sector promise is ultimately unfunded when it is backed by future earnings ability alone, as in consumer credit. This concept is directly linked to the stock of savings in the economy.

2.2   Accounting identities in the short and in the long run

Consider a standard unfunded social security system that has already matured. Let us define:

g_t = growth rate of the covered wage bill and of GDP in period t. The covered wage bill is the revenue base for social security contributions. We assume it is the same as the growth rate of GDP.

r_t = real rate of return paid out by investments in capital (physical or financial) in period t. This return may be contracted in the previous period, as in the case of fixed-income debt instruments.

C_t = flow of contributions during period t.

P_t = flow of pension payments due according to the benefit rules.

Q_t = flow of net government transfers to the pension institution, which may be positive or negative.

T_t = flow of tax revenue, net of transfers to the private sector.

G_t = flow of other government expenditures, including consumption and investment.

Y_t = flow of gross income of the private sector, excluding return from assets.

X_t = flow of final demand from the private sector, including consumption and investment.

D_t = stock of obligations of the pension system at the beginning of period t.

B_t = national debt outstanding at the beginning of period t, net of government-owned assets valued at market prices.

A_t = net privately owned assets outstanding at the beginning of period t.

The flow budget constraints for the private sector and the government are the following:

$$Y_t + r_t \cdot B_t + r_t \cdot A_t + P_t = Xt + T_t + C_t + (A_{t+1} - A_t) \text{ (private sector) (1)}$$

$$T_t + (B_{t+1} - B_t) = Q_t + G_t + r_t \cdot B_t \qquad \text{(government) (2)}$$

As tax revenue grows with the economy, the government can afford to let the debt grow and still keep constant the ratio of the national debt to GDP.

Therefore, it can choose its path to be $B_{t+1} = B_t \cdot (1 + g_t)$. Assuming the government adopts this debt policy, replacement in (2) yields:

$$T_t = G_t + Q_t + (r_t - g_t) \cdot B_t \tag{2'}$$

The flow budget constraint of the pension institution is:

$$C_t + Q_t = P_t \tag{3}$$

Equation (3) is valid because the pension institution is financed with the *standard* unfunded approach with no reserves, or "pay as you go" approach. As it is unfunded, its cash flow does not include investment income. The government supports pensions by mandating contributions C_t and by direct cash transfers of size Q_t. Q_t is zero if the pension system is "balanced."

A pension institution financed with this method can be thought of as having a balance sheet. The outstanding liability, defined as D_t, is the real present discounted value of pensions already promised (at the beginning of period t). This includes both pensions due to current pensioners and the deferred pensions that would be owed to current workers even if they stopped contributing now.

This pension institution has two assets available to meet obligations in case workers stopped contributing. They are the present value of its two main sources of income. First is the present value of future government transfers Q_t, which we call PV(Q). The second asset is the authorization to the pension institution to raise taxes to pay the pensions owed by the pension system, which we call H_t (hidden government debt in t). If contributions stopped, the pension institution would have to tax labor earnings explicitly to pay its liabilities. The difference between PV(Q) and H is the following: PV(Q) is the value of the continuation over time of a currently explicit government transfer, while H_t is the value of the hidden wage tax implicit in pay-as-you-go contributions. For example, the wage tax would be raised in case of a reduction in the ratio of workers to pensioners. The balance sheet identity for the pension system as of time t is:

$$D_t = H_t + PV(Q)_t \tag{4}$$

In a pension institution with partial or full funding, a third and a fourth asset exist, namely contractual government debt and claims on the private sector, including the foreign sector.

Equation (4) can also be derived from the flow budget constraint (3) by decomposing C_t between the wage tax implicit in a pay-as-you-go system with transfer Q, and the contribution C'_t that a funded system would require to pay the *same* benefits. Adding the flows from different time periods discounted at rates r_t, simplifying the C'_t with the discounted pensions financed by them, and using (4) leads to H = PV (implicit wage tax revenues).

The flow accounts of the pension system and the government do not change if hidden pension liabilities are acknowledged. Let d_t be the growth rate of pension liabilities outstanding, in real terms. This definition is that $D_{t+1} = (1 + d_t) \cdot D_t$. If the share of explicit government transfers as a share of pension payouts is held constant, then both $PV(Q)_t$ and H_t must grow at rate d_t to meet the balance sheet of the pension system. That is:

$$PV(Q)_{t+1} = (1 + d_t) \cdot PV(Q)_t; \quad H_{t+1} = (1 + d_t) \cdot H_t \tag{5}$$

Using (4) and (5), equations (3) and (2') can be rewritten as:

$$\begin{aligned} P_t &= C_t + Q_t + 0 \\ &= C_t + [Q_t + d_t \cdot H_t - (H_{t+1} - H_t)] \end{aligned} \tag{6}$$

$$\begin{aligned} T_t &= G_t + (r_t - g_t) \cdot B_t + Q_t + 0 \\ &= G_t + (r_t - g_t) \cdot B_t + [Q_t + d_t \cdot H_t - (H_{t+1} - H_t)] \end{aligned} \tag{7}$$

Equations (6) and (7) show that the absence from (3) of terms such as $(D_{t+1} - D_t)$ and $r_t \cdot D_t$ is due to the simple fact that they cancel out. They also show that the special feature of the hidden pension liability is that its "rate of return" is d_t, rather than the market rate of return r_t.

There are two arguments that bound d_t: First, the pension system's liabilities must meet the non-Ponzi game condition for this path to be sustainable in the long run; in the long run the rate of growth of the pension system's liabilities (d_t) cannot be larger than the rate of growth of the economy (g_t). Second, if the pension system's liabilities grew at a smaller rate than the economy, then the size of the pension system would diminish in relation to the economy and would dissappear in the long run; to avoid this, the rate of growth of the pension system's liabilities (d_t) cannot be smaller than the rate of growth of the economy (g_t) in the long run.

These two arguments imply that:

$$\lim_{t \to \infty}[d_t - g_t] = 0 \tag{8}$$

This means that in a standard pension system, the magnitudes D, PV(Q), and H must grow with the economy, at rate g, in the long run. They also show that the special feature of the hidden pension liability is that its rate of return tends to g_t, rather than being equal to r_t, the market rate of return.

2.3   Review of some related results in public finance

To close this section, we review briefly some results in public finance that allow a better understanding of the pay-as-you-go financing system.

This chapter assumes that $r > g$. As Tirole (1985, p. 1507) argued, if an economy reached a steady state with $r < g$, those assets whose dividends grow with the economy (at rate g) would attain an infinite price, offering an arbitrage opportunity to private investors. For example, firms that serve markets protected from entry where demand grows at rate g can be expected to pay dividends growing at rate g. The owners of such a firm would earn arbitrage profits by issuing debt yielding rate r. The same happens to the government if market interest rates fall below g, because tax revenue can be expected to grow at rate g. The government can earn arbitrage profits by issuing explicit public debt or hidden public debts (by moving to pay as you go financing of pension benefits) that yield rate r. However, massive issues of private and public debt would push market yields above g.

Another issue is the rate of return on pension contributions. This is commonly defined as the internal rate of return, for a given individual that is entering the labor force, of the cash flows associated to contributions and pension benefits.

In the case of pension institutions financed with the pay-as-you-go method, the calculation of this internal rate of return is straightfoward only when it is balanced and is expected to continue in balance for a long period. In this case, as the assets of the pension institution yield g in the long run, it follows that the pension system pays a return on g on its liabilities, that is, on contributions. The difference $(r - g) > 0$ can be interpreted as an implicit tax on the rate of return of contributions, which in turn translates into an implicit tax on the earnings on which contributions are levied.

This internal rate of return is harder to pin down when transfers Q are different from zero. If Q is positive, then pensions are higher for the same contributions, and the pension system appears to offer a rate of return on contributions better than g. Q may be large enough to allow the pension system to yield more than the market rate of return on contributions (see Diamond, 1981). However, a positive transfer Q has to be financed with higher taxes or lower spending on valued public goods. When transfers Q are different from zero, the internal rate of return calculation should include the extra taxes (or reduced public goods) needed to finance Q. If Q grows at rate g in the long run, the extra taxes must also grow at rate g, which implies that a pension institution financed with the pay-as-you-go system yields g even if Q is positive.

In the other extreme, if the pension institution is financed with the fully funded method, the internal rate of return on contributions is r, the market rate of return in the long run.

Regarding the optimal size and sign of Q, it should be chosen to minimize static inefficiency in the standard public finance sense, by allowing the use of the least distortive set of taxes.

This allows an interpretation of the contradictory results of Breyer and

Straub (1993) and Arrau (1991). The first show that a gradual shift from pay-as-you-go to funding allows a Pareto improvement, whereas the second finds that the result is a Pareto worsening. The difference lies in that Breyer and Straub assume availability of lump sum contributions, which are less distortionary than proportional contribution rates, whereas Arrau assumes the opposite: that only income taxes are available, which are more distortionary than contribution rates because in his model economy they are levied on inelastically supplied labor.

If taxes on covered earnings are more distortionary than other taxes, as Breyer and Straub assume, then it is optimal to reduce contribution rates, to raise other taxes, and to finance the pension institution with a positive Q. If taxes on covered earnings are less distortionary than other taxes, as Arrau assumes, then it is optimal to increase contribution rates, to reduce other taxes, and to have the pension institution give regular transfers to the government through a negative Q. Both essays ignore that a pension reform is not a prerequisite for optimization of the set of tax rates, including those that fall on covered earnings.

2.4   A preliminary reform: Replace legislated promises for debt contracts

This section considers a preliminary reform. In this reform, legislated promises of the government to back the pension system are replaced with tradeable financial contracts between the government and the pension institution. In these debt contracts, which may be perpetual bonds, the government promises to pay the pension institution: (a) Q_t in the first year, and similar amounts that will grow at rate g thereafter; and (b) a rate of return g on the stock of previously hidden government liabilities to the pension institution. The total contractual commitment of the government would add up to D_t, the pension institution's liabilities. Recall that rate g is below the market return r. We will assume for now that the pension institution does not trade its assets and keeps the entire stock of newly issued securities.

This reform has no fiscal cost, because the government can sell new debt paying interest g to the pension institution in each period. With this revenue, the government can pay the interest on the stock outstanding, and still keep the ratio of this debt to GDP constant. The pension institution will use the interest earned on its securities to buy more each year, without affecting the other flows in the economy.

In a certainty environment, such a reform is a mere relabeling of existing agreements. However, under uncertainty and political risk, this preliminary reform may have value in its own right, if some insulation of the pension institution from politics and the government budget is valued by workers.

This insulation may occur because changing contracts require consent from both parties to be valid before the courts, whereas legislation requires the decision of only one side: the coalition of parties that control the government. With just legislated promises, that coalition suffers a conflict of interest, as it must trade off both the debts of future taxpayers and the claims of current pensioners and voters, but its selection of a particular compromise affects the probability of its continuation in power (reelection). There is a plausible presumption that the political system will resolve a conflict between future taxpayers and current pensioners in a different way than courts would enforce a contract between debtors and creditors.

This difference is very clear in the case of the United States, where the Constitution prohibits default on the federal debt (except through inflation, when the debt is expressed in nominal terms). However, the Supreme Court held in a 1960 decision, *Flemming v. Nestor,* that retirees have no contractual right to their promised social security benefits despite their past payments to the system, and that Congress has the power to reduce the program's benefits.[1]

The case of the Philippines (Tiglao, 1990) shows that the presence of financial contracts forced at least some public discussion about the terms of government support to the pension institution, even in a setting where the government designates the managers of the pension institution. The case of many Latin American countries suggests the same (Mesa-Lago, 1978).

2.5   Switching from pay-as-you-go to full funding without fiscal cost.

This section shows how to switch from pay-as-you-go to full funding without imposing a double burden on the transition generation. The "fiscal cost" of the transition can be met without provoking intergenerational redistribution. This is done through meticulous relabeling of the obligations and cash flows associated with a balanced pay-as-you-go-financed standard pension system.

A simple way to start this relabeling exercise is to consider that the reform discussed in section 2.3 has been implemented. Now a second reform is offered, whereby the government begins to pay market interest rate r on a growing portion of its debts to the pension institution, rather than the growth rate g. We analyze first the long-run implications of this reform, that is, we analyze the situation when this reform has been fully implemented.

It is clear from (6) and (7) that this change affects the flow budget constraints of the government and the pension institution. In the new steady state, the flow of government interest payments for its previously hidden debt to the pension institution, as a share of GDP, increases from $g \cdot H/GDP$ to $r \cdot H/GDP$. Obviously, this must worsen the budget balance. Considering the

[1] See Ferrara (1985), p. 193.

issuance of new debt at rate $g \cdot$ H/GDP, the government's cash flow worsens only by $(r - g) \cdot$ H/GDP.

In the new steady state, this increase in government expenditure must be made up in some way. Note first that the government's cash flow deficit is matched by a cash flow surplus in the pension institution. According to (6), one of its sources of funds increases from $[Qt + (g - g) \cdot Ht]$ to $[Qt + (r - g) \cdot Ht]$. Therefore, other sources must decrease or the use of funds must increase to keep the accounting identity of the pension system. The two options are to decrease contributions or to raise pensions.

If pensions were raised, neutral relabeling would require that a new tax on pensions be introduced, as mentioned by Kotlikoff (1994, p. 18). Such a new tax would take away the pension increase and leave pensioners with the same original net pensions. However, this option appears difficult to make compatible with insulation of the pension system from the political process. This is because one important facet of insulation is that pension benefits should not be taxed differently from other income. If pensions could be taxed at discriminatory rates, say in response to temporary budget pressures, then no pension system would ever be insulated from politics. Private pension arrangements such as corporate pensions and annuities would be subject to arbitrary interference.

Therefore, we consider the other option, where contributions are reduced. This affects the private sector budget constraint: The young (active workers) will improve their take-home salary, unless they are subject to a new tax. If this new tax is just enough to compensate the budget worsening, then workers will be left with the same take-home salary as before reform. The next question is whether this approach can be made compatible with insulation of the pension system from the political process. This appears feasible because the new tax is based on income from wages, not on contributions to the pension institution. The fact that the base for this tax is not related to pensions makes a political difference. If budget pressures lead the political system to change this tax rate later on, this does not affect the functioning of the pension system. The cash flows of the pension institution become independent from the annual budget process.

The exact base of the new tax is important to achieve neutral relabeling at the moment of the reform. The new tax must be imposed on exactly the same base as social security contributions. Therefore it must be a proportional tax on taxable labor earnings, to be paid by all those who have the obligation to contribute to social security. This avoids redistribution between workers who participate in the uncovered and covered labor markets, and between individuals who work a different number of hours.

Note that there is no intergenerational redistribution associated with this reform, as no sector is forced to change its budget constraint. This implies that the stock of physical capital is not affected. The labor market distortion created by mandatory contributions continues to have the same size as before, although it now originates in the new payroll tax. Asset prices are not affected because the pension system is not allowed to trade the contractual debt it holds now. The gain from such a relabeling cannot come from an increase in savings and capital. However, this reform has achieved some insulation from the political process, which may prove valuable when considering uncertainty, as discussed in section 3.

2.6 The size of the new tax on covered earnings

This section offers simulations regarding the size of the new tax on earnings, as a proportion of the initial contribution rate. We only discuss mature and balanced pay-as-you-go pension systems, in which direct government transfers Q are zero. Consider the following definitions:

c = contribution rate in the initial pay-as-you-go system (% of earnings).

t = new tax on covered earnings, or wage tax (% of earnings).

$c' = c - t$ = contribution rate in the final apparently funded system.

p = pension payout per pensioner (resources per period).

According to the previous discussion, the required rate for the new tax is the revenue need, $(r - g) \cdot H_t$, divided by the revenue base, which is the covered wage bill. There are no substitution effects due to this new tax because it merely replaces implicit for explicit taxes. Neutrality assures no income effects are present.

As Q is zero, then $PV(Q) = 0$ and $H_t = D_t$. Therefore:

$$t = [(r - g) \cdot D/\text{Covered wage bill}] \tag{9}$$

$$t/c = [(r - g)/c] \cdot [D/\text{Covered wage bill}] \tag{9'}$$

The first parenthesis shows that the difference $(r - g)$ is a major determinant of the relative size of the new tax t. The second parenthesis is a function of demographic and life-cycle parameters such as the population growth rate, the shape of the age-earnings profile, the way in which increases in labor productivity are distributed throughout the working population, and the growth rate of pensions after they are first granted.

Comparing across steady states, an alternative approach to calculate the same ratio is to exploit the notion that, for an individual, the final pension must be the same when contributing c and earning return g as when contributing c' and earning the return r.

We present simulations for a steady state where individual workers contribute for 40 years and retire for 15 years. We also assume that the pension remains flat in real terms once granted. Define:

Eo = covered earnings when first contributing, say at age 25.

w = growth rate of covered earnings across the working life, assumed to be constant for simplicity.[2]

The pension obtained before the reform was:

$$p = c \cdot [Eo(1+g)^{39} + Eo(1+w)(1+g)^{38} + \dots Eo(1+w)^{39}]$$
$$\cdot [g/(1-(1+g)^{-15}]$$
$$= c \cdot Eo \cdot (1+w)^{39} \cdot \{[(1+g/1+w)^{40} - 1]/[(1+g/1+w)-1]\}$$
$$\cdot [g/(1-(1+g)^{-15})]$$
$$= c \cdot Eo \cdot A(g,w,40,15)$$

The pension obtained after the reform will be:

$$p' = c' \cdot [Eo(1+r)^{39} + Eo(1+w)(1+r)^{38} + \dots Eo(1+w)^{39}]$$
$$\cdot [r/(1-(1+r)^{-15})]$$
$$= c' \cdot Eo \cdot (1+w)^{39} \cdot \{[(1+r/1+w)^{40} - 1]/[(1+r/1+2)-1]\}$$
$$\cdot [r/(1-(1+r)^{-15})]$$
$$= c' \cdot Eo \cdot B(r,w,40,15)$$

For the reform to be neutral, we need $p' = p$, which in turn requires $c' \cdot B = c \cdot A$. As $t = c - c'$, we find that:

$$(t/c) = 1 - [A(g,w,40,15)/B(r,w,40,15)] \tag{10}$$

Table 7.1 shows the value of t for different parameters, assuming that the initial contribution rate is $c = 15\%$. Table 7.1 also shows that the size of the new wage tax may be considerable, ranging from 3 to 10 percentage points of the wage rate. It is also clear that the size of the required new tax depends primarily on the size of $(r-g)$. Conversely, this table also shows that the contribution rate may be reduced dramatically in response to a slight increase in the annual rate of return available to pension savings.

2.7   A neutral transition path

Up to now we have compared steady states. This section discusses the transition, and more precisely the reform path that yields a neutral relabeling of cash flows. This will identify a time path for the gradual increase in the portion of the previously hidden debt that pays market interest rates. This section finds that to manage the transition a further measure is needed: introduction of a set of compensatory pensions for the generations alive during the transition.

At the date of the reform, several groups can be identified:

---

[2] The empirical evidence for the United States shows that the age-earnings profile follows a quadratic or a polynomial of the fourth order (Hubbard and Judd, 1987). The assumption of a constant growth rate used in the text is adopted for simplicity.

Table 7.1
New tax on covered earnings and new contribution rate
(entry is t = new wage tax, in % of earnings. It is assumed
that the initial contribution rate is 15%)

(r-g)	g = 1.5%		g = 4.0 %	
	w = 3.0%	w = 4.0%	w = 3.0%	w= 4.5%
0.0%	0.0	0.0	0.0	0.0
1.0%	3.4	3.2	3.6	3.4
2.0%	6.0	5.8	6.4	6.1
3.0%	8.2	7.9	8.5	8.2
4.0%	9.8	9.6	10.2	9.8

(a) the generations that already retired. As reform involves changes in contribution rates and taxes on earnings, they will not be affected directly. They must continue receiving their pensions as if no reform had happened.

(b) the generations that had not entered the covered labor market as of the date of the reform. When they enter in the future, they will find that contribution rates have already been reduced to c' and that the new tax on covered earnings is in place, but that their contributions will earn return r rather than g. As national savings will not have been affected by the reform, the calculations offered in the section 2.5 apply directly to these generations, and they are not affected by the transition.

(c) the generations that have already contributed for "k" years as of the date of the reform, with k = 1,2, . . . 39. During those k years, they contributed at rate c. For the next (40-k) years they will contribute at rate c' and pay the new tax on earnings, so they will keep the same take-home salary. Still, to achieve neutral relabeling during the transition, we need to assure that they get a pension of the same size they would have obtained if no reform had occurred.

The difference between the pension p they would have obtained without reform, and the partial pension they can finance out of their contributions after the reform can be defined as a pension supplement. This supplement acknowledges the contributions made before the reform. Using the previous notation, the partial pension "p'" is:[3]

---

[3] We use the notation Eo(k) to represent the earnings when first entering the covered sector. It may be a function of the number of years of contributions k registered by the individual as of the date of the reform, probably because of technical progress in labor productivity.

$$p' = c' \cdot Eo(k) \cdot (1+w)^k [(1+r)^{39-k} + (1+w)(1+r)^{38-k}$$
$$+ \ldots (1+w)^{39-k}] \cdot [r/(1-(1+r)^{-15})]$$

After some algebra, we find the size of the required pension supplement "s" as a ratio of p simplifies to:

$$(s/p) = [1 - (1+r/1+w)^{-k}]/[1 - (1+r/1+w)^{-40}]$$
$$\text{for } k = 1, 2, \ldots 39. \tag{11}$$

This simple expression exhibits the expected characteristics: The required pension supplement is large for generations that have contributed a large number of years before the reform, and small for those that had contributed for just a few years before the reform.[4]

Now we discuss the options for a neutral financing of the required supplements. Recall that the new tax on earnings and the new contribution rate are implemented immediately. The new rate of return on debt outstanding can be phased in gradually or not. Budget balancing for the pension institution requires that it can produce a transitory cash surplus large enough to pay the pension supplements identified previously. This cash surplus is obtained by liquidating H, the initial stock of assets.

The initial stock H of debt that yields g can be allocated between the different groups that have claims on the pension institution. A part of it is held by the generations that are already pensioned. This portion of H can go on yielding g, but the face value outstanding will drop to zero in 15 years (lifetime of the youngest group of pensioners) as principal is liquidated to meet promised pensions to this group.[5]

The remainder of the initial stock of debt H is held by those generations that contributed before the reform but have not yet retired. These claims, plus interest earned at rate g, must be exactly enough to finance the supplementary pensions discussed earlier. The rest of the pensions to be received by this group will be financed by their own future contributions, which will be capitalized at r, the market rate of return.

During the first year after the reform, the fiscal accounts move as follows: (1) it continues paying interest g on debt H outstanding; (2) part of debt H is not renewed, as the pension institution must liquidate some of it to pay its pension obligations; (3) it receives new revenue from the new tax on earnings.

[4] The only determinant of the shape of this curve is $(1 + r/1 + w)$, which is due to the simplifying assumptions that r is constant over time and that w is constant for all ages. In a practical application, more precise assumptions should be used, plus data on the differential in life expectancy of men and women and on the expected number of surviving dependents, which are specific to the covered population.

[5] An alternative would be for the government to prepay this portion of debt H in cash, while requiring pensioners to use the cash to buy real annuities from approved intermediaries. This option is not discussed because of its administrative complexity.

The result must be a cash deficit, equal to the new contributions at rate c'. This must be covered by issuing new financial debt yielding r, which must be bought by the pension institution. Thus, the portfolio of the pension institution changes composition. Recall that the pension institution is not yet allowed to trade the new government debt it is buying.

The accounting shows that the path of financial debt B outstanding at the beginning of each period, which yields r, is given as follows:

$$B(0) = 0 \tag{12a}$$

$$B(t) = B(t-1) \cdot (1+r) + c' \cdot \text{Wage Bill}(t) - \sum \text{partial}$$
$$\text{pensions} \quad t = 1, \ldots 39 \tag{12b}$$

$$B(t) = B(t-1) \cdot (1+g) \quad t = 40, \ldots \tag{12c}$$

During the first 39 years the pension institution pays only partial pensions with the reserves B that earn r, because the rest are supplementary pensions paid with H, the reserves that earn g. Starting in year 40, the pension institution pays full pensions with reserves that earn r and the reserves H that yield g are exhausted. Thereafter, the stock of reserves B grows at rate g, with the economy.

This exercise shows that a reform that moves the pension system toward apparent funding is entirely feasible without imposing a double burden on the transition generations. As this reform is a neutral relabeling of previous arrangements, it does not induce an increase in the saving rate.

Finally, it is informative to compare the financing of the Chilean pension reform of 1981 with the neutral financing option discussed in this section. (For a detailed reference, see Diamond and Valdés-Prieto, 1994.) In the Chilean reform there is a strong reduction in contribution rates, from 22% to 14%, and acknowledgment of contributions of transition generations to the old system, in the form of a "recognition bond" that earns an interest rate similar to the expected growth rate of the economy (4% real).

However, in Chile the new tax on covered earnings was absent. Instead, the Chilean government built a primary surplus of 5.5% of GDP *before* the reform, over 1979–1980, and used it to finance the reform. This fiscal effort may be decomposed in two parts: the first is the primary surplus that is equivalent to the missing new tax on earnings. This part would represent the fact that the new tax on earnings was replaced by a reduction in public spending. The second part of the primary surplus is the excess over the amount needed for a neutral reform. This excess prevented a sizable increase in the net public debt, increased national saving, and forced the transition generations to pay a double burden. It should be pointed out that the size of the double burden appears to have been near 1.5% of GDP, much less than what would be needed in European countries, which have larger benefits, higher total coverage, and older populations. Another difference is that the Chilean reform granted the pension institution(s) the freedom to reshuffle their growing portfolio away from government debt. They have chosen to hold around 40% of their growing investment portfolios in government debt.

3   Neutral pension reforms and risk sharing

The previous section has shown that in a certainty environment there is a large set of pension systems with the same implications for savings, the budget, take-home pay, and pensions. This section extends the analysis of neutral pension reforms to a risky environment and finds that the elements of this set of arrangements are no longer equivalent.

3.1   Transparency and missing insurance markets

Neutral reforms make risk more transparent and, in some cases, may affect risk sharing and welfare. For example, consider the fiscal problems caused by a demographic transition. A pension institution using the pay-as-you-go financing method comes under pressure when this event occurs, because the reduction in contribution revenue (generated by the young) comes together with a fixed pension expenditure (owed to the old). The government should make good its guarantee to the pension institution, but in a bad moment: The demographic transition also reduces general tax revenue (generated by the young) while increasing the public debt–GDP ratio because the growth rate of the economy has fallen, ceteris paribus. In this setting,the government can easily say that the pension institution is in trouble, and may legislate a reduction in pension benefits. The absence of a contractual guarantee in favor of the pension institution may affect the political outlook and legislation.

After a neutral pension reform toward apparent funding, the same demographic transition would have a different impact: The imbalance would show up in the fiscal accounts and not in the accounts of the pension institution. This is because a funded institution responds to a reduction in contributions with a liquidation of assets, or at least a growth of its assets below GDP growth. The smaller demand for bonds forces the government to pay part of the principal of its debt to the pension institution. From a political point of view, it is the government that must adjust. From an economic point of view, the property rights of the pension institution are transparent, and therefore are more likely to be respected.

Of course, the government may attempt to legislate a reduction in its debt to the pension institution. However, that will not be easy because of constitutional protection for debt contracts. The government may attempt to renegotiate the interest rate on the *new* debt it sells to the pension institution each period, and may succeed as long as the pension institution is forced to hold only government debt. Even in this case the manager of the pension institution can appeal to the voters, showing that their pensions would suffer and asking them to press the government not to renegotiate. Such processes have been observed in the Philippines (Tiglao, 1990).

For other shocks the pay-as-you-go financing method provides risk sharing across generations. For example, if a young generation is unusually lucky and is endowed with high income when young, the pay-as-you-go method generates a cash surplus in the pension institution. Part of this may be spent in higher pensions for the previous, less lucky, generation. An alternative is for the surplus to be passed along to the government budget, maybe to be used in public debt reduction, public investment, transfers, or public consumption. The allocation may be influenced by the fact that the pension institution has the cash surplus, suggesting it should be spent on pension-related items.

After a neutral reform that moves the financing method to apparent funding, the same shock would force the pension institution to buy more government debt, if that is the only asset it may hold. Therefore, all the cash surplus is captured by the government, by issuing more debt. The question of how to allocate the government's cash surplus will be influenced by the fact that the government has increased its contractual debt to the pension institution, a fact that may favor investment over consumption.

The conclusion is that some "relabeling" reforms make risk allocation much more transparent than other reforms. In turn, this may allow a better design of mechanisms to cope with risk. The pay-as-you-go financing mechanism has important insurance features embedded into it, but so does the apparently funded system that emerges after a neutral reform. This suggests a general conjecture: Relabeling is not neutral in a risky world.

This conjecture can be true only if some insurance markets do not exist. This is necessary to allow pension arrangements to have some impact on risk sharing and welfare. Without this assumption, endowment and fiscal risk could be absorbed at minimum social cost using these markets, achieving a Pareto superior allocation, as shown by Peled (1982).

This requirement suggests that the concept of transparency and missing insurance markets are linked. It is possible that the neutral reforms that yield more transparency are precisely those that rely to a greater extent on existing insurance and risk markets, whose prices facilitate understanding of the economic trade-offs involved in each policy choice.

The absence of some insurance markets may be due to various factors. Standard arguments refer to moral hazard, adverse selection, and positive loads. It is useful to add factors associated with the design of the pension system. For example, in the standard social security system financed with the pay-as-you-go method, political risk may be defined as the uncertainty about how the political system will allocate fiscal shocks among the generations alive at each point in time. This definition recognizes that pension benefits in an unfunded pension system are adjusted ex post, according to a political bargaining process whose outcome may be modeled as a random variable.[6] This random variable is hard to insure because there is no sizable market in it.

The contractual nature of government debt increases demand in some insurance markets. For example, in the apparently funded pension system, fiscal shocks must be borne by the young generation alone, because pensions are not touched. As it is hard to imagine where insurance for young taxpayers could be bought, this suggests that some risk diversification is lost when adopting an apparently funded system.

Neutral reforms will not have an impact either if the capital markets span an asset whose return is perfectly correlated with the endowment risk. If such an asset was supplied, we would find, as Richter (1993) did, that holding it allows as much intergenerational risk sharing as a pay-as-you-go financed pension system. In Richter's model for a closed economy, each generation can save by holding an infinitely durable consumer asset (urban land, rural land). This asset is in fixed supply, so if the current generation of young is unusually numerous, the price of the long-lived asset is pushed up and the older generation is allowed to consume more when selling the asset. Endowment risk generates a perfectly correlated risk of holding the durable asset, which can be traded between generations. Risk is shared across generations even though each one has a finite horizon. He finds that introducing a pay-as-you-go-financed program in this setting is Pareto inefficient.

Thus, our conjecture may be correct if enough insurance markets are missing. In this case, the pay-as-you-go financing method has scope to allow Pareto improvements (Enders and Lapan, 1982, 1993; Gordon and Varian, 1988; Green, 1988), but a reform towards apparent funding may allow an even better outcome. In such a setting, the size of the pension system, measured by the size of the contribution rate, is important as it influences the degree of risk sharing.

3.2   A further reform: Allowing portfolio rebalancing

The pension reform discussed in section 2 introduced just two of the traits of funding, namely contractual promises and market rates of return, while preserving balance in all budget constraints in the certainty case. This achieves some insulation of the pension system from the political process.

---

[6] This approach to politics is more realistic than models such as Gordon and Varian (1988), where political bargaining is replaced by a constitutional rule, which in turn is optimized by a benevolent planner-king who maximizes welfare behind a veil of ignorance.

This section discusses the implications of taking these reforms one step further, which is allowing the pension institution(s) to trade their holdings of contractual government debt. One justification for this policy is that the pension institutions may improve their portfolio allocation, achieving a better combination of risk and return, which may raise benefits or allow a reduction in contribution rates or both. Another justification is that this freedom is necessary for credible insulation of the pension system from the political process. Both arguments rely on considerations of risk.

A "portfolio rebalancing" reform does not have to create panic in the financial markets as long as timely information is provided. An appropriate information strategy may include the following steps: (a) before this reform, change the reporting practices about the public debt, including in it the hidden pension debt and making clear it is not tradable; and (b) when this reform starts, stress that the total public debt, including financial and hidden portions, will not increase.

In addition, the government may adopt the strategy of making its debt to the pension institution to be tradable *gradually,* avoiding a one-shot tradability reform. To achieve this, the authorization to trade can be granted at the start of the transition, which may take some 40 years, such that it affects only the flow of new debt B which replaces the old debt H.

The discussion that follows assumes that domestic government debt and claims on foreigners are not perfect substitutes in a portfolio. If they were, a portfolio reallocation by the pension institution would have no effect on domestic or international interest rates. In that situation, the single interest rate would be given solely by the stock of savings supplied to the economy, and a portfolio reallocation would not affect that stock.[7]

Consider the implications of making the assets of the pension institution tradable, in several settings. In the case of a *very* small open economy, the market interest rates at which the government may borrow and at which the pension institution may invest are set by the international capital market at levels that are not affected by an authorization to the pension institution to reallocate its portfolio. In this setting such an authorization would have beneficial effects for all generations of pensioners if the pension institution is able to move the allocation toward the risk–return frontier. In addition, there would be no effect on the cost of government debt.

The cases of a large open economy, defined as one whose actions may alter the interest rates offered to it by the international capital markets, and of a closed economy, are more complicated. Now the authorization to the

---

[7] In the case of pension reforms that do have an effect on net savings, not studied here, the analysis can be guided by the results of Breyer and Wildasin (1993). They show for a large open economy that can affect world interest rates, the welfare impact of an increase in savings depends on whether the country has a net debtor or net creditor position.

pension institution to reallocate gradually its portfolio should affect at least some interest rates. If other (foreign) investors were initially in portfolio equilibrium, and the pension institutions wish to diversify away from the corner allocation in which 100% of their portfolio is in government debt, the market interest rate charged on public debt should increase, while the interest rate offered by the international capital market to the pension institution might fall. The impact on these two interest rates may be different in magnitude. The impacts depend on the size of the market for each of the assets in which the pension institution invests.

One interpretation of these changes in market interest rates is that the initial pay-as-you-go financing scheme contains a second implicit tax on the rate of return offered to contributors. The first implicit tax was the difference between r, the market rate of return in the public debt, and g, the growth rate of the economy. The second implicit tax would be the difference between d, the expected rate of return on public debt after asset reallocation is authorized to the pension institutions, and r, the expected rate of return on public debt before such authorization, both for the same level of risk.

This implicit tax should have efficiency implications, as the supply of labor to the covered sectors – subject to mandatory contributions – should be sensitive to it in the general case. In addition, the supply of voluntary savings may change.

At this point the importance of dividing up the pension institution into many independent units, rather than having just one, becomes apparent. This precaution avoids granting monopoly power over the price of government debt to a single pension institution. On the other hand, these pension institutions can be relied on to reach the risk–return frontier only if they are independent from political pressures to buy government bonds at low rates. An obvious way to meet these two requirements is to privatize these institutions. The implication is that there is a link between the efficiency gains of portfolio freedom for pension institutions and privatization of those institutions.

Another implication of an authorization to reallocate assets is that it may redistribute wealth toward future generations, while living generations are forced to pay more net taxes. Higher net taxes are needed initially either to service debt at higher interest rates or to reduce the debt outstanding (in a closed economy). If the government adjusts by increasing taxes or reducing expenditures, or both, living generations are worse off. On the other hand, future generations are made better off even though they must pay higher net taxes, because they enjoy better pensions thanks to the higher expected rate of return obtained by the pension institutions for the same level of risk. Of course, this redistribution may be less evident if the authorization to reallocate assets is granted gradually.

One way to escape this redistribution between generations is for the government to adjust by increasing the volume of the public debt during the period in which reallocation is occurring. The workers and pensioners alive at the beginning of the transition can be spared from an increase in net taxes. In the final steady state, workers would enjoy better pensions, but they would have to pay higher net taxes to finance the service of a higher public debt, given a rate of return.

A reasonable conjecture is that the net effect on the welfare of workers living in the final steady state would still be positive, because the initial portfolio of pension institutions (100% government debt) was *inside* the risk–return frontier. The pension institutions should increase their rate of return and the level of pensions, at a same level of risk, which is a free lunch.

However, avoiding redistribution through increased public debt has dangers, as the issue of more public debt may increase the rate of return required by international investors, according to a supply curve of funds, which may be quite steep. It is conceivable that this approach could take a government to the unstable side of its debt Laffer curve. This possibility warrants further research and empirical estimates.

3.3   Risk sharing and portfolio rebalancing

Consider an open economy with overlapping generations. Several sources of uncertainty, as seen from before the birth of a generation, may be considered. The first is about the income that a generation will be able to produce while young (endowment risk). The second is about the fiscal expenditure that the country will confront during the periods in which it will be alive (fiscal risk). These two risks are unavoidable. However, they may be diversified partially by linking the pension system to the international capital market. The return available to the pension institutions by investing in international assets is random, so it should help to diversify the other risks.

The additional gains offered by portfolio rebalancing of pension institutions may be small, however, because voluntary saving in the international capital market is possible. Access to international asset markets implies that the generations can trade over time and can trade risk among themselves even in the absence of a government and pension institutions. Moreover, if the pension institutions rebalance their portfolios away from government debt, individuals may react, changing the portfolio composition of their voluntary stock of saving with little overall impact on risk sharing.

In any of these settings, the rate of return required by investors other than the pension institutions to hold government debt could be stochastic if their preferences or alternatives are stochastic. This is the source of a new fiscal risk. For example, if the international capital markets increase permanently the rate of return required to hold the domestic country's public debt for some exogenous reason, this would impose an increase in net taxes or the level of the public debt. The issues are whether this risk can be partially diversified with other sources of fiscal risk, and which taxpayers will absorb the residual risk.

The stochastic nature of this rate of return also has implication for the pension institutions' budget. There are two aspects to consider. The first is present even if the pension institutions invest only in fixed-income government securities. Although the rate of return enjoyed by different generations may be different, for each one of them the rate can be known at the moment of contribution if the government offers debt of all maturities. In such a setting each generation can be promised a defined benefit or a fixed rate of return when young.

Even in this case the government is exposed to the risk that a given generation turns out to be poor and contributes less than average. In that case the pension institutions must liquidate assets in the aggregate, forcing the government to repay its debt, unless foreign investors replace the pension institutions. If not, this process feeds back into an uncertain tax burden.

The second aspect appears if the pension institutions invest a positive amount in the international capital market. If the rate of return paid by the international capital markets to the pension institutions turns out to be smaller than anticipated, either pensions are cut (defined contribution) or the guarantors cover the loss. In the latter case the pension institutions are insurance companies and the guarantors are their shareholders.

Alternatively, defined benefits may be kept by purchasing a rate-of-return guarantee in the international capital markets, whose cost would have to be added to the contribution rate. However, the market in rate-of-return guarantees at horizons of 30 years or more seems to be small.

If the government legislates a guarantee for those defined benefits, the guarantee is not protected by constitutional priorities in favor of contracts, so the pension institutions return to political dependence. If the government offers to sell a contractual guarantee, risk is shifted back to taxpayers. In this case, a transparency rule should be useful, whereby estimates of the present expected value of this hidden contingent subsidy would be clearly reported alongside figures for the public debt.

4   Risk sharing in a very small open economy

This section offers a model for the case of a very small open economy, bringing together the implications for risk sharing of the different reforms discussed up to now. After these reforms, risk may be distributed in a different way. We restrict policies to those that have no effect on saving and compare steady states only.

This model describes two alternative pension systems under uncertainty of the endowment and of nonpension government expenditures. These systems are compared from the point of view of a benevolent planner-king who can choose among them through a constitutional mandate and seeks to maximize ex ante welfare from behind a veil of ignorance.

In the pension system with pay-as-you-go financing, there is the risk that the political system may redefine (default upon) legislated pension promises and reduce benefits. Taxes and pensions are adjusted ex post, according to a political bargaining process whose outcome is modeled as a random variable.

In the apparently funded option, constitutional protection of debt contracts eliminates political risks. As pensioners are insulated from fiscal risk, all fiscal risk falls on young taxpayers. In addition, the pension institution is allowed to rebalance its portfolio of government bonds, so it can acquire private assets whose returns are set in international capital markets. If it does so, pensioners must bear investment risk, which is proportional to the share of the portfolio not invested in government debt. In addition, as the interest rate for traded public debt is set in international capital markets, and is random, there is a new source of fiscal risk.

As the country is very small, the rate of return required by the international capital market for holding government bonds is not affected by sales of bonds by the pension institution, or by new issues of the government. We assume that the return available to the pension institutions by investing in other international capital markets is random but is not a function of the amount invested.

This model is dramatically simplified by assuming voluntary saving in the international capital market is impossible. This can be the result of individual myopia, meaning higher impatience rates than the one used to choose the size of each pension system. This size, measured by the contribution rate, is chosen to maximize expected welfare from behind the veil of ignorance.

4.1   The model

4.1.1   Individual behavior
There is one representative individual per generation, who lives for two periods. His preferences are represented by the expected utility $EV(C1,C2)$. As seen after birth, consumption in the second period is stochastic. For simplicity, population growth and productivity growth are zero. The expected utility is assumed to have a specific form:

$$EV(C1,C2) = u(C1) + (1/1 + \delta) \cdot Eu(C2) \tag{13}$$

where δ is the utility discount rate and u is per-period utility.
The budget constraints which the individual must meet ex post are:

$$t = 1: \quad C1 = Y \cdot (1 - c) - Ty - Tw - S \tag{14a}$$

$$t = 2: \quad C2 = P + S \cdot (1 + r) \tag{14b}$$

where:

C_t = consumption in period t. Second period consumption is random.

Y = lifetime income, all of which is earned while young. This is an endowment whose value becomes known after being born.

c = contribution rate to the pension system, paid when young. This rate is fixed at the constitutional level.

Ty = tax paid when young.

Tw = wage tax, that is, the new tax on earnings introduced to preserve expected fiscal neutrality.

S = amount of voluntary savings in the international capital market.

r = rate of return on voluntary saving.

P = actual pension received when old, random. It may be different from original pension promises.

This formulation contains the implicit simplification that the old do not pay taxes. The purpose is to make starker the comparisons we are interested in.

The most dramatic simplification we adopt is that the individual does not have voluntary saving, so $S = 0$. This may be explained as the result of myopic behavior of individuals, which can be represented by a utility discount rate higher than δ, in combination with consumer credit constraints. As the individual chooses a corner solution where $S^* = 0$, pensions are the only source of income when old. In this interpretation, δ is the utility discount rate used by a benevolent constitutional assembly that sets c, the size of the pension system.

4.1.2 A standard pay-as-you-go pension system

The selection of pension system sets the shapes of the fiscal budget constraint, the budget constraint of the government and of the individual's budget. Fiscal expenditure in nonpension items, G, is a stochastic variable. The contribution rate is set at some level "c," and explicit taxes on the young absorb the full variation of the budget. Tw is zero with pay-as-you-go financing.

In the standard pay-as-you-go pension system, the political system legislates pensions and taxes. They must be reconciled so that there is an overall balanced budget in each period. In any period, the government and the pension institution must meet the following budget constraint ex post:

$$Ty_t + c \cdot Y_t = G_t + P_t \quad \text{for all t} \tag{15}$$

We assume that contractual government debt is zero in all periods. The pension institution does not have debts either. There is hidden debt because the government has promised backing to the pension institution to pay legislated pension benefits. The pay-as-you-go financing mechanism implies the pension institution has a joint budget constraint with the government, allowing funds to flow in either direction. If the pension institution suffers a deficit and nonpension expenditure is low, then the government insures pensions. In this sense, this is a "defined benefit" pension system.

The "state of the budget" before the political process adjusts taxes and pensions is summarized with the variable Z:

$$Z_t \equiv G_t + (LPB - c \cdot Y_t) \tag{16}$$

where: LPB is the legislated pension benefit to the current old before the political process adjusts taxes and pensions, $c \cdot Y_t$ is the contribution revenue of the pension system, and the difference in parenthesis is the net requirement of the pension institution. $LPB = c \cdot Y_{t-1}$ because population and productivity growth are zero.

However, a change in legislation may reduce or increase legislated pension benefits – for example, through a change in the legal pension age – to keep budget equilibrium.

The question is how does the political system divide up the net needs Z among taxpayers and pensioners. The timing of the political bargaining game is the following:

> *period* $-\infty$: The expected values EZ and ETy are determined. This is the "baseline scenario," which affects the outcome of political bargaining.
>
> *period* $t-1$: Legislated benefits for $t = 1$ are determined according to contributions in that period. $LPB = c \cdot Y_{t-1}$.
>
> *period* t_a: Most period-one variables are revealed, including Y_t and G_t.
>
> *period* t_b: Now θ_t is revealed by politicians. We impose $E\theta = 0$.

Variable θ defines how the fiscal burden is distributed. This is shown by the distributional equations. Random variables as of *period* t_a are shown in italics:

$$Ty = ETy + (1 - \theta)(Z - EZ) \tag{17a}$$

$$P = LPB + \theta(EZ - Z) \tag{17b}$$

where: θ = percentage of the unexpected component of the fiscal burden allocated to the old. It is a random variable whose support is [0,1].

Equation (18) assures that ex post budget equilibrium is always met. It also identifies each individual's budget constraint. These timing definitions, and the ex-post budget constraint, lead to the following values of taxes and pensions:

$$Ty_t = Z_t + (1 - \theta_t)(Z_t - E_{-\infty}Z) \tag{18a}$$

$$P_t = cY_{t-1} + \theta_t(E_{-\infty}Z - Z_t) \quad \text{where } E_{-\infty}Z = EG \tag{18b}$$

Now we introduce the notion that the stochastic behavior of the political system is correlated with the state of the budget. We study a case such that, when the budget is short of funds, the political allocation tends to increase the share of the burden passed to pensioners. However, when the budget is flush with funds, the share of abundance passed on to young taxpayers tends to increase.

Put in a different way, there are two states of nature for the political system: In the "fair state," the allocation of fiscal risk is symmetric in the sense that gains and losses are distributed equally between the young (taxpayers) and the old (pensioners). However, in the "unfair state," the old get a larger share of the losses and a smaller share of the gains.

This can be modeled in mathematical terms, by choosing the following conditional distribution of θ:

$$\theta \text{ given } Z_t > EG = \begin{cases} \beta & \text{with probability 0.5 (fair state)} \\ \beta + k & \text{with probability 0.5 (unfair state)} \end{cases}$$
$$\text{(Deficit)}$$

$$\theta \text{ given } Z_t < EG = \begin{cases} \beta & \text{with probability 0.5 (fair state)} \\ \beta - k & \text{with probability 0.5 (unfair state)} \end{cases}$$
$$\text{(Surplus)}$$

We assume k is positive, and that both $\beta - k$ and $\beta + k$ belong in [0,1]. Parameters β and k are an exogenous feature of the political process, which is not the object of policy design. Still, we choose parameter β to be close to 0.5, that is, to a 50% allocation of losses between old and young in the fair state.[8]

The welfare achieved by the representative member of a generation depends on the point in time in which the expectation is assessed. From the point of view of constitutional design, it is natural to take expectations unconditionally behind a veil of ignorance, that is, the year before a given generation is born. Using the preceding equations, and recalling that $S = 0$, it

---

[8] To assure that the unconditional expectation of θ is 0, it is enough to impose the condition that Z has a symmetric density function around EZ. The expectation of θ conditional on $Z > EZ$ is $\beta + 0.5k$, but conditional on $Z < EZ$ is $\beta - 0.5k$.

is easy to show that the expected utility with a pay-as-you-go-financed pension system of size c is:

$$EV(C1,C2) = E[u(Y_1 - G_1 - c \cdot Y_0 - (1 - \theta_1) \cdot (G_1 - EG + c \cdot (Y_0 - Y_1)))]$$
$$+ (1/1 + \delta) \ E[u(c \cdot Y_1 + \theta_2 \cdot (EG - G_2 + c \cdot (Y_1 - Y_2)))] \tag{19}$$

The subindices 0, 1, and 2 indicate the period in which each random variable is realized. Equation (19) shows, for example, that the income of the previous generation is important for consumption of the current young because it affects promised pension benefits and, through the state of the budget, affects the level of taxes on the young.

4.1.3   The apparently funded pension system
We model now a pension system where government support to the pension institution is of contractual nature. The government pays a market rate of return on its debts, either on average or year by year. As discussed in section 2, this system can be compared with the pay-as-you-go one only if an earnings tax is imposed to preserve fiscal neutrality. The take-home earnings of the young are preserved in expected value because the contribution rate is reduced to c'.

The government's budget constraint is:

$$Ty_t = G_t + (d_{t-1} \cdot B_{t-1} - Tw_t) + B_{t-1} - B_t \tag{20}$$

where:

d_{t-1} = the real interest rate, set in $t-1$ but paid in t, that the government promised on the bonds it issued in period $t-1$. The government cost is the difference between the real interest rate it promised to pay and the growth rate of the economy, which is zero in this model.

B_t = the amount of the bonds issued in period t.

Tw_t = the revenue from the new earnings tax.

In this arrangement, all the fiscal risk is borne by the young through their taxes, because pensions are untouchable by legislators. The pension institution's aggregate budget constraint is:

$$c' \cdot Y_t + R_t A_{t-1} + A_{t-1} = P_t + A_t \tag{21}$$

where:

P_t = actual pension benefits paid in t.

A_t = assets of the pension institution at the beginning of period t.

R_t = rate of return earned by the pension institution, paid in t.

This rate of return depends on the portfolio composition chosen by the pension institution:

$$R_t = \alpha(1 + r_t) + (1 - \alpha)(1 + d_{t-1}) \quad = 1 + d_{t-1} + \alpha(r_t - d_{t-1}) \qquad (22)$$

where:

α = share of pension funds invested in the international capital markets. The rest is invested in government debt.

r_t = rate of return obtained from the investments in the international capital markets.

Note that α does not appear in the government's budget constraint, because the government owes the same amount regardless of whether the pension institution exchanged assets with foreign investors or not. As all the assets of the pension institution are owed to individual account balances, the institution's balance sheet identity requires that:

$$A_t = c' \cdot Y_t \quad \text{for all } t \qquad (23)$$

Equations (23) and (22) together imply that $Pt = c' \cdot Y_{t-1}[1 + d_{t-1} + \alpha \cdot (r_t - d_{t-1})]$ as expected.

Although the budgets of the government and the pension institution are not linked after portfolio rebalancing, they were linked at the moment of reform. At that point in time, 100% of the portfolio of the pension institution was invested in government bonds. In order to allow a meaningful comparison with the pay-as-you-go-financed pension system, we must rule out intergenerational redistributions. To achieve this, we assume that the government follows the rule of keeping its public debt in line with the assets of the pension institution – that is:

$$A_t = B_t \quad \text{for all } t \qquad (24)$$

This allows determination of the total tax burden of the young, namely Ty + Tw. Using (24), (23), and (20), we find that:

$$Ty_t + Tw_t = G_t + c' \cdot d_{t-1} \cdot Y_{t-1} + c' \cdot (Y_{t-1} - Y_t) \qquad (25)$$

This shows that in an apparently funded system the young taxpayers bear three types of risk, which may diversify each other. The first is fiscal risk for nonpension sources. The second is the risk that the rate of return required by the international capital market be different from "normal," in combination with the eventually correlated size of the debt. The third source is the risk of being forced to reduce the size of the public debt in response to a reduction in the endowment of the young generation as compared with that of the old one. This third source of risk is present also in the pay-as-you-go-financed system, but this risk is smaller here if $c' < c$ which will occur if $Ed > 0$.

Bringing all this together, the level of ex-ante welfare achieved in an apparently funded system by a representative member of a yet-unborn generation is:

$$EV(C1,C2) = E[u(Y_1 - G_1 - c' \cdot Y_0 \cdot (1 + d_0)]$$

$$= + (1/1 + \delta)E[u(c' \cdot Y_1 \cdot [1 + d_1 + \alpha \cdot (r_2 - d_1))]$$

The subindices 0, 1, and 2 indicate the period in which each random variable is realized. Period 1 is when this generation is born.

The size of the new earnings tax is reported for completeness. As the role of this tax is to cover the interest expense of the government debt, which pays a market return, we assume it is set at the constitutional level, so it does not vary over time. The rate of this tax must be such that:

$$E[Tw_t] = E[t \cdot Y_t] = E[d_{t-1} \cdot B_{t-1}] \tag{27}$$

But as $B_{t-1} = c' \cdot Y_{t-1}$ we find that:

$$t = c' \cdot E(d \cdot Y)/E(Y) \tag{28}$$

The "normal" rate of return required by the international capital market is $E(d \cdot Y)/E(Y)$, which takes into account the eventual correlation between d and Y.

Thus, this model produces expressions for the welfare level of a representative generation in steady state, as seen from behind the veil of ignorance, for sizes c and c' of each pension system.

4.2   Assumptions for a simulation

In the first place, we must choose values for c and c'. If we accept the result of section 2, derived under certainty, that $t = c - c'$, where c is the contribution rate of the equivalent pay-as-you-go pension system, then:

$$c' = c/[1 + E(d \cdot Y)/E(Y)] \tag{29}$$

We will not use this result although we refer to it again later, but use instead an alternative procedure. It is not interesting to compare badly designed pension systems. Therefore, it would appear reasonable to search for optimal values for parameters c and c', which presumably would be determined by the benevolent constitutional assembly. This is the method we use for choosing c and c'.

Parameter α, the portfolio allocation in the funded system, is assumed to be chosen optimally by the pension institutions.

For simulation, we use the following discrete-value distributions:

Y_0, Y_1, Y_2: i.i.d. binomials:

$$Y_t = \begin{cases} 0.95 \text{ with probability } 0.5 \\ 1.05 \text{ with probability } 0.5 \end{cases}$$

G_1 and G_2: i.i.d. binomials:

$$G_t = \begin{cases} 0.15 \text{ with probability } 0.5 \\ 0.25 \text{ with probability } 0.5 \end{cases}$$

r_t: i.i.d. two conditional binomials:

$$r_t \text{ given } Y_t = 0.95 = \begin{cases} -1\% \text{ per year} = -0.26 & \text{prob. } 0.5 \\ 2\% \text{ per year} = 0.81 & \text{prob. } 0.5 \end{cases}$$

$$r_t \text{ given } Y_t = 1.05 = \begin{cases} 1\% \text{ per year} = 0.35 & \text{prob. } 0.5 \\ 4\% \text{ per year} = 2.24 & \text{prob. } 0.5 \end{cases}$$

d_t: independent from Y_t. Therefore $E(d \cdot Y)/E(Y) = E(d)$.d is an i.i.d. binomial:

$$d_t = \begin{cases} 0.5\% \text{ per year} = 0.16 & \text{prob. } 0.5 \\ 1.5\% \text{ per year} = 0.56 & \text{prob. } 0.5 \quad E(d) = 0.36 \end{cases}$$

As is usual in overlapping-generations models with two-period lives, the annual rates of return used were compounded for 30 years, leading to the numbers already presented.

Political risk:

$$\theta \text{ given } Z_t > E_{-\infty}Z = \begin{cases} 0.5 & \text{with probability } 0.5 \\ 0.7 & \text{with probability } 0.5 \end{cases}$$

$$\theta \text{ given } Z_t < E_{-\infty}Z = \begin{cases} 0.5 & \text{with probability } 0.5 \\ 0.3 & \text{with probability } 0.5 \end{cases}$$

Preferences: The simplest function is considered, with unit elasticity of intertemporal substitution in consumption and unit relative risk aversion:

$$V(C1,C2) = Ln(C1) + (1/1 + \delta)Ln(C2) \tag{30}$$

where $\delta = $ is the annual rate of time preference, compounded for 30 years. We discuss two values for δ. The first one is $\delta = 0$, which is deemed useful for paternalist legislators that care a lot about future consumption. The other one is $\delta = 2\%$ per year, that is, $\delta = 0.81$ in 30 years.

4.3   Simulation results

We can see in Table 7.2 that the socially optimal contribution rates c^* for the pay-as-you-go system are 38% for $\delta = 0\%$ per year and 28% for $\delta = 2\%$ per year.

As explained in section 4.2, the requirement of neutrality for the reform determines c' from c, through formula (29). This has an interesting consequence for a country that switches pension systems. If the economy starts with an optimally sized pension system c^*, as it switches to $c'(c^*)$, the new

Table 7.2
Welfare in the pay-as-you-go pension system

δ = 0 % per year		δ = 2% per year	
Contribution Rate c	Welfare	Contribution Rate c	Welfare
0.44	-1.874	0.32	-1.376
0.42	-1.862	0.30	-1.370
0.40	-1.856	0.28*	-1.368*
0.38*	-1.855*	0.26	-1.370
0.36	-1.861	0.24	-1.378
0.34	-1.872	0.22	-1.390
0.32	-1.888	0.20	-1.409

Source: Own calculations.

contribution rate may be inefficient from the point of view of risk sharing in the reformed pension system. If c' could be optimized further, without changing the size of the public debt, then there would exist gains available to be distributed.

Given that $E(d) = 0.36$, equation (29) suggests that the contribution rates in an apparently funded system with the same public debt must be $c' = 27.9\%$ if $\delta = 0\%$ per year and 20.6% if $\delta = 2\%$ per year. The differences with c^*, namely 10.1% and 7.4%, must be the rates of the tax on earnings that keeps the government financed. It was surprising to find in our simulations that $c'(c^*)$ is efficient in the reformed pension system. If this were a general property of neutral pension reforms, there would never be gains from changing the size of the pension system. However, this may be a result of the special functional forms and distributions used here.

We report the simulations for the apparently funded pension system, for these contribution rates, in Table 7.3. Comparing the welfare levels achieved with pay-as-you-go (Table 7.2) with those achieved with apparent funding (Table 7.3), we find that for this set of distributions the apparently funded pension system can be superior or inferior to the pay-as-you-go system, depending on the degree α of diversification away from government bonds. If pension institutions are forced to hold government debt only, the apparently funded system is marginally inferior for these distributions. This may be interpreted as that the welfare gain coming from reduced exposure to political risk is more or less canceled out – in this example – by the welfare loss of increased exposure to fluctuations in d, the rate of return required by investors to hold government debt.

Table 7.3
Welfare in the apparently funded pension system

| δ = 0.0 % per year | | δ = 2.0% per year | |
α	c' = 27.9 % Welfare	α	c' = 20.6 % Welfare
0.0	-1.873	0.0	-1.377
0.4	-1.776	0.4	-1.323
0.6	-1.748	0.6	-1.308
0.8	-1.733	0.8	-1.300
0.98*	-1.728*	0.98*	-1.297*
1.2	-1.735	1.2	-1.301

Note: The optimization of c' is not reported.

However, the apparently funded system can be allowed to diversify its backing by exchanging assets with other investors. We expect a pension system that works in the best interest of its members to increase α above zero. Table 7.3 shows that by doing so the apparently funded pension system can achieve a significantly higher welfare level.

To measure the welfare increase in the context of this simulation, we search for the equivalent variation of passing from a pay-as-you-go system to an apparently funded one. T* is the permanent lump sum tax, expressed as a percentage of expected income, that may be levied on the young in the apparently funded system, to keep their welfare the same as in the pay-as-you-go system. The results are shown in Table 7.4, and suggest that the gain can be sizable.

5   Concluding comments

This chapter brings together some well-known results and introduces new ones. Public finance has shown that in the certainty case it is possible to design a neutral pension reform toward funding such that no generation suffers a double burden. In this reform, legislated pension promises are transformed into public debt that earn the market rate of return. It has not been realized always that neutrality may require large reductions in the contribution rate and imposing substantial new wage taxes. The chapter also contributes a methodology to find the supplementary pension required by the transition generations, and identifies a neutral time-path for transforming the

Table 7.4
Equivalent variation of switching to an apparently funded system

	$\delta = 0.0\ \%$ per year $c' = 27.9\ \%$			$\delta = 2\%$ per year $c' = 20.6\ \%$		
	$\alpha = 0\%$	$\alpha = 60\%$	$\alpha = 98\%$	$\alpha = 0\%$	$\alpha = 60\%$	$\alpha = 98\%$
T*:	-0.7%	4.0%	4.8%	-0.5%	2.9%	3.5%

(T* = largest lump sum tax that can be charged on the young in the apparently funded system without making it desirable to remain in the pay-as-you-go system)

hidden debt to the pension system into explicit public debt that yields the market interest rate.

Although this reform does not improve welfare by itself, it sets the stage for a second reform with a substantial potential for Pareto improvement. This may be achieved when the pension institutions are allowed to rebalance their portfolio and move away from 100% allocation to government debt. The chapter discusses a number of implications for risk sharing of this shift, in a variety of settings ranging from a very small open economy to a closed economy. These welfare gains may be a significant aspect of optimal pension policy.

This chapter also introduces a new type of general equilibrium model, in which political risk is modeled explicitly and several sources of fiscal risk are considered. The model allows simulations to be performed. The simulation results show the size of the steady-state gains from a pension reform that abandons pay-as-you-go finance in favor of funding, without imposing a double burden on a transition generation. The gains stem from diversification away from 100% government backing of pensions.

The results can also be interpreted as identifying the conditions for privatization of pension institutions. Privatization does not require true funding of pension liabilities, as apparent funding is enough. The critical requirement for privatization is freedom to rebalance the investment portfolio. On the other hand, it seems difficult to grant this freedom *and* achieve the gains of rebalancing without privatizing. This freedom can be granted without creating monopoly in the government debt market only if there are many pension institutions buying independently. The gains may be achieved only if each of the pension institutions attempts to move toward the risk–return frontier, which leaves out government-managed pension institutions because they are sensitive to political pressures to overinvest in government bonds.

References

Arrau, P. (1991) "La Reforma Previsional Chilena y su Financiamiento durante la Transición." *Colección Estudios CIEPLAN*, 32, June, 5–44.

Blanchard, O., and S. Fischer (1989) *Lectures on Macroeconomics.* MIT Press, Cambridge, Mass.

Breyer, F., and M. Straub (1993) "Welfare Effects of Unfunded Pension Systems When Labor Supply Is Endogenous." *Journal of Public Economics* 50, 77–91.

Breyer, F., and D. E. Wildasin (1993) "Steady-State Welfare Effects of Social Security in a Large Open Economy." *Journal of Economics (Zeitschrift für Nationalökonomie)*, Supplement 7, Springer Verlag, 43–50.

Diamond, P. A.(1981) "Comments." In F. Skidmore, ed., *Social Security Financing*, 164–169. MIT Press, Cambridge, Mass.

Diamond, P., and S. Valdés-Prieto (1994) "Social Security Reforms." In B. Bosworth, R. Dornbusch, and R. Labán, editors, *The Chilean Economy: Policy Lessons and Challenges*, chap. 6. Brookings Institution, Washington, D.C.

Enders, W., and H. E. Lapan (1982) "Social Security Taxation and Intergenerational Risk Sharing." *International Economic Review* 23, 647–658.

——— (1993) "A Model of First- and Second-Best Social Security." *Journal of Economics (Zeitschrift für Nationalökonomie)*, Supplement 7, Springer Verlag, 65–90.

Ferrara, P. ed. (1985) *Social Security: Prospects for Real Reform.* Cato Institute, Washington, D.C., August.

Gordon, R., and H. Varian (1988) "Intergenerational Risk Sharing." *Journal of Public Economics* 37, 185–202.

Green, Jerry (1988) "Demographics, Market Failure and Social Security." In Susan M. Wachter, editor, *Social Security and Private Pensions*, 3–16. Lexington Books.

Hubbard, G., and K. Judd (1987) "Social Security and Individual Welfare: Precautionary Saving, Borrowing Constraints and the Payroll Tax." *American Economic Review* 77, no. 4, September, 630–646.

Kotlikoff, L. (1994) "A Critical Review of the World Bank's Social Insurance Analysis." World Bank, Washington, D.C. Mimeograph.

Mesa-Lago, C. (1978) *Social Security in Latin America: Pressure Groups, Stratification and Inequality.* University of Pittsburgh Press, Pittsburgh.

Peled, D. (1982) "Informational Diversity over Time and the Optimality of Monetary Equilibria." *Journal of Economic Theory* 28, 255–274.

Richter, W. F. (1993) "Intergenerational Risk Sharing and Social Security in an Economy with Land." *Journal of Economics (Zeitschrift für Nationalökonomie)*, Supplement 7, Springer Verlag, 91–104.

Tiglao, Rigoberto (1990) "Pinched Pensions: Government Institutions Called on to Help Phillipine Cash Squeeze." *Far Eastern Economic Review* 48 (November 29), 48–49.

Tirole, J. (1985) "Asset Bubbles and Overlapping Generations." *Econometrica* 53, no. 6 (November), pp. 1499–1527.

Valdés-Prieto, S., and R. Cifuentes (1990) "Previsión Obligatoria para la vejez y Crecimiento Económico." Working Paper no. 131, Instituto de Economía, Univ. Católica de Chile, Santiago, November.

PART III

Macroeconomic policy and private pensions

Pension funds, capital controls, and macroeconomic stability

Helmut Reisen and John Williamson

1 Introduction

It is well known that high capital mobility introduces an important constraint on macroeconomic policy. The question therefore arises as to whether free international investment by pension funds might have a macroeconomic cost that needs to be weighed against its presumed microeconomic advantages in terms of permitting retirees to enjoy the benefits of international diversification (an improved combination of risk and return). If so, the further question arises of whether a novel form of exchange control – for example, a requirement that foreign investment by pension funds be allowed only when there is equal inward investment by foreign pension funds – might help to overcome the macroeconomic costs without losing the microeconomic gains.

This chapter starts with an analysis of the impact of a small country opening up its stock (equity) market for investment from abroad, focusing on the question of the extent to which this will constrain macroeconomic policy. It then proceeds to examine the investment strategies of, and the restrictions imposed upon, privately managed pension funds in the OECD area. This is followed by a discussion of U.K. experience after the liberalization of capital controls in 1979.

The chapter then turns to normative issues. We argue that since the diversification of pension funds fosters stock market integration rather than interest linkages, it does little to limit short-term monetary sovereignty. We conclude that the case for regulating this form of capital mobility is weak once a country has got to the point where it does not need to fear a major net loss of savings. The remainder of the chapter discusses various techniques by which the foreign investment of pension funds could be regulated, were our main conclusion regarding the pointlessness of such regulation to be rejected. For example, one possibility would be to limit domestic pension funds to

Research supported by the Ministry of Finance, Chile. Copyright Institute for International Economics: all rights reserved.

portfolio swaps with foreign pension funds. We also discuss whether there is a case for transitory controls on pension funds while the size of their portfolios is growing particularly rapidly.

2   The implications of stock market integration

A classic result of the international monetary theory developed by Robert Mundell in the 1960s states that high (strictly speaking, perfect) capital mobility and fixed exchange rates preclude the use of monetary policy to stabilize the economy (Mundell, 1968, chap. 18). To express the same point in another way, a way that has been made familiar in the debate on European monetary integration: Fixed exchange rates, free capital mobility, and monetary independence constitute an "impossible trinity." Note that in this context a "fixed exchange rate" does not mean just an unalterably pegged exchange rate: It includes also an exchange rate whose value is determined by the authorities, even if subject to a crawling peg and guided by a target for the real exchange rate.

However, as shown in later sections of this chapter, pension funds invest primarily in stocks (equities) rather than the bonds that are hypothesized to be perfect substitutes in the Mundell-inspired literature. Standard macroeconomic models do not contain a stock market[1] (despite the fact that in some countries a larger part of personal wealth is held in the form of equities than of bonds), so that one cannot simply appeal to familiar results to understand the implications of stock market integration. We therefore attempt to think through the implications from first principles. With apologies to those economists who find such informality aesthetically offensive, we do this without constructing a formal model.

The interesting case to analyze is that in which capital mobility would be perfect in the conventional sense (i.e., bonds are perfect substitutes) but for the continued existence of capital controls.[2] The question is then what effect the elimination of controls on cross-border flows of equity capital would have on a country's monetary independence.

Consider the simplest possible model, in which arbitrage between the bond and stock markets equilibrates rates of return in the two markets. The bond market is conventionally modeled as trading short-term assets with a known nominal interest rate r, while the rate of return on equities consists of

---

[1] Macroeconomic models that include a stock market are Blanchard (1985), Buiter (1987), and several papers by Michael Gavin (1989, 1991a, 1991b).

[2] If bonds are perfect substitutes and there are no effective controls on the movement of bond capital, then we know that the country has no monetary independence whether or not the movement of equity capital is restricted. If bonds are imperfect substitutes, then it will have a degree of monetary independence whether or not the movement of equity capital is restricted. Hence the interesting case is the one discussed in the text.

the sum of the divident yield and capital gains. Let dividends per share be d, let the price of a share be e, assume perfect foresight, and use a hat to denote a rate of change. Then perfect arbitrage between the two markets implies:

$$r = \frac{d}{e} + \frac{\hat{e}}{e}.$$

If the right-hand side is equated to the equivalent expression for the world market, and that is in turn equal to the foreign rate of interest r^*, then arbitrage through the equity market would indeed ensure the equality of domestic and foreign interest rates, that is, it would result in the loss of the monetary sovereignty.

Now ask whether the assumptions needed to establish that result constitute a useful first approximation to reality. Ask in particular whether it is sensible to assume perfect foresight in the rate of change of share prices, given that the theory of portfolio diversification that is used to explain and guide equity investment is based on *inability* to foresee changes in share prices correctly. The answer is clearly that it is not useful even as a first approximation, and the implication is that one should not expect to find arbitrage equating yields between equity and bond markets. It follows immediately that linking equity markets should not be expected to equate interest rates or, therefore, to eliminate monetary sovereignty.

Of course, one should still expect that opening the equity market will have an impact on aggregate demand unless this is deliberately prevented by the central bank. Consider the case in which both inflows and outflows of equity investment are liberalized. Suppose that this results in a net inflow of equity investment.[3] This will bid up the value of the stock market, producing a positive wealth effect and a lower cost of capital, both of which will tend to increase demand. In order to hold the exchange rate constant, the central bank will have to supply more domestic money to the foreign buyers of stocks, which they will of course pass on to the domestic sellers. If the central bank wishes to hold the money supply (or, indeed, aggregate demand, in either real or nominal terms) constant, it will have to increase the interest rate. The result will be contrasting movements in the expected return on equities (lower) and on bonds (higher); thus the possibility of sterilizing the impact of an inflow of equity capital indeed depends upon arbitrage between the equity and bond markets not being too high.

The final part of this theoretical section examines what difference the existence of equity capital mobility makes to the response of an economy to

---

[3] Note that liberalizing only the inflow of equity capital would have the same qualitative effects as are identified here, whereas liberalizing only the outflow would have a converse set of consequences. (The effects of liberalizing outflows when inflows are already liberalized are more debatable, as discussed subsequently.)

various shocks. It is again assumed that equity capital is the only form of capital that is internationally mobile. The shocks that we examine are (a) a tightening of monetary policy, and (b) a decreased desire to hold local equities as a result of less optimistic expectations of their future yield.

Consider first the impact of a tighter monetary policy. The higher interest rate on bonds must be expected to depress the local equity market as well, which will raise holding yields and thus attract an inflow of equity capital from abroad. This will tend to limit the effectiveness of monetary policy, just as does any other form of capital mobility. The imperfection of arbitrage between bond and equity markets will, however, limit the extent to which monetary policy is undermined.

Consider next the impact of a portfolio shock in the form of a sudden decrease in the desire to hold local equities, say as a result of a downward reevaluation of the likelihood of future earnings growth in the domestic economy. It is of crucial importance to specify also *whose* expectations undergo revision. There are three possibilities: foreigners, local investors, and both.

A pessimistic revision of expectations by foreigners obviously has no impact on the domestic economy in the case where there is no capital mobility.[4] When there are foreign holdings, attempted liquidation of those holdings will drive the stock market down; since domestic holders do not by assumption share the pessimistic reevaluation that initiated the sales of stock, they will buy up shares from the foreigners who will use their receipts to buy foreign exchange, thus placing pressure on the reserves and/or the exchange rate, depending on the exchange rate regime.[5] If the central bank attempts to defend the exchange rate and sterilize the impact on the money supply, it will have to reduce interest rates, thus aggravating the loss of reserves but diminishing the decline in the stock market. Mobility of equity capital is in this case destabilizing.

If local investors revise their expectations downward but foreigners do not, then the fall in the stock market will tend to induce additional inward investment that will limit the size of the stock market decline relative to the case of no capital mobility. Reserves will rise, and even a central bank that tried to stabilize might decide not to sterilize this inflow as the increased

[4] The same analysis applies where foreigners want to liquidate their holdings for other reasons, e.g., a stock market collapse at home. This is prone to spill over into declines in stock prices in other markets where foreigners are allowed to hold shares, but not into those that prohibit foreign shareholding. Compare the behavior of the Japanese and Korean stock markets on Black Monday: the former, which had large foreign holdings, followed Wall Street down, while the latter, which at that time prohibited foreign holdings, actually rose.

[5] This case is analyzed in Corbo and Hernández (1993, p. 6), although without recognizing the crucial importance of the implicit assumption that it is only foreigners who make a pessimistic reevaluation of the country's prospects.

money supply and lower interest rates would tend to offset the negative impact on demand of a lower stock market. Mobility of equity capital is in this case unambiguously stabilizing.

However, both of these cases seem rather unconvincing, at least as responses to "a disappointing political development, a sudden decrease in the price of the main exportable good or an increase in the price of the main importable good" (Corbo and Hernández, 1993, p. 5). A more neutral assumption would be that the expectations of both foreign and local investors undergo a similar downward revision. In that case there is no reason why there would be any capital outflow: The stock market will decline to the degree needed to persuade investors as a group to continue holding the existing stocks, but that will involve no net sales by foreigners. (This assertion needs to be qualified to the extent that a group of domestically based market makers automatically increases its portfolios in a declining market, but this can surely not be a major factor.) Indeed, the impact of a given downward revision of expectations will be *less* in the case in which portfolios are internationally diversified, because that part of domestically owned wealth that is invested abroad will be protected against the capital loss from the fall in the domestic stock market. (See Gavin, 1991a, for a rigorous demonstration of this proposition.)

3 Investment strategies of pension funds in the OECD area

Individual wealth in the OECD area is increasingly managed by institutional investors. Fully funded, privately managed pension funds have so far been important (as a percentage of financial assets and GDP) in only a handful of OECD countries, such as the United States, the United Kingdom, the Netherlands, Switzerland, Canada, and Australia (see Table 8.1). Elsewhere, private funded schemes have seen their development hampered by the scale of state social security pension provision (Davis, 1992). State social security in the OECD mostly provides a compulsory, indexed, defined benefit, and unfunded pension scheme. However, aging populations, with a rising proportion of retirees, will further strain existing social security systems. Policy makers are thus faced with the unappealing choice of either decreasing benefits or of increasing social security taxes. At the same time, the need to tackle unemployment is exerting strong pressure to control labor costs.

These pressures can be expected to stimulate strong growth in private funded pensions and create incentives to seek maximum returns on pension fund assets (Davanzo and Kautz, 1992). According to the European Federation for Retirement Provision (see the *Guardian*, October 5, 1993), every 1% improvement in pension funds' investment returns will reduce employers' costs by 2% to 3% of the payroll. The need for high returns on pension

Table 8.1.

Pension funds assets in selected OECD countries

	1988 Assets		1992 Assets			
	Billion dollars	Percentage of GDP	Total (billion dollars)	Thereof Private (billion dollars)	Total as percentage of GDP	Foreign asset share, percentage of total
1. United States	1646.7	33.8	3315	2265	56.4	4.6
2. Japan	134.1	4.6	728	362	19.8	8.2
3. United Kingdom	475.9	57.0	644	544	61.9	28.0
4. Netherlands	177.4	77.9	242	147	75.5	13.8
5. Canada	130.9	26.7	230	108	40.9	9.2
6. Switzerland	121.1	68.0	188	125	78.2	7.7
7. Germany	41.1	3.5	114	85	6.4	4.3
8. Sweden	51.2	28.4	81	0	33.0	1.0
9. Australia	51.3	18.9	67	34	23.3	14.6
10. France	–	–	41	n.a.	3.1	1.9
11. Denmark	–	–	40	21	28.1	4.0
12. Ireland	–	–	16	n.a.	32.8	35.0
13. Italy	–	–	11	n.a.	0.9	4.1
14. Norway	–	–	6	4	5.3	0
15. Spain	–	–	5	n.a.	0.9	1.0
16. Belgium	–	–	4	n.a.	0.2	31.1
17. Portugal	–	–	2	n.a.	2.4	3.2
Total OECD			5740			
Memos:						
Chile	3.6	16.5	12.5		34.5	

Source: Intersec Research Corp., London Representative Office. European Federation for Retirement Provision (as reported in *The Guardian*, 5 Oct. 1993). OECD, Main Economic Indicators, September 1993.

assets implies a need for global diversification. Pension assets will dominate investment trends and capital flows around the world.

Before we examine how pension funds *actually do invest* their assets, it is useful to spell out how pension funds *should invest* to maximize return for a given risk. Modern portfolio theory (see, e.g., Solnik, 1988) and its major tool, the capital asset pricing model (CAPM), hold that the world market portfolio is the optimal risky portfolio in a full efficient and integrated international capital market. For any portfolio underinvested in foreign assets (as a percentage of world market capitalization) there is the prospect of a free lunch: International diversification can lower risk by eliminating nonsystemic volatility without sacrificing expected return.[6] Alternatively, global diversification will raise the expected return for a given level of risk. The diversification benefits consist of reduced risk, usually measured by the annualized standard deviation of monthly returns, by investing in markets that are relatively uncorrelated (or even negatively correlated) with the investor's domestic market. International diversification reduces risk faster than domestic diversification because domestic securities exhibit stronger correlation as a result of their joint exposure to country-specific shocks. International diversification should cover both stocks and bonds; efficient portfolios made up of only stocks display a substantially higher risk for the same level of return than efficient portfolios made up of both stocks and bonds (Solnik and Noetzlin, 1982).

Since OECD stock markets are already highly integrated,[7] their monthly returns display correlation coefficients on the order of 50% to 90%. By contrast, stock markets in Latin America and Asia still display negative or very low correlation with those in the industrialized countries. Note, however, that equity returns in those developing countries that have opened their markets to foreign portfolio investment have become more closely correlated with the returns in developed markets in recent years, with coefficients around 40% (Mullin, 1993). Of course, investment in emerging markets not only reduces risk, it is also likely to raise the mean return of portfolios.

Growth in the OECD has proved to be and is expected to remain substantially below growth in many non-OECD countries. Through 1994, the OECD (1993) predicts growth to average 2.7% in the OECD area, 6.9% in the so-

---

[6] The CAPM claims that the world market portfolio must be on the *efficient frontier* and that it is thus impossible to beat the market, whence the idea of a passive index fund approach. Such a portfolio strategy can be self-destroying when markets are not efficient. A case in point is the Japanese stock market bubble when in late 1989 the Tokyo market was worth 45% of world market capitalization. For those investors following the index approach, this meant an extreme degree of concentration, not risk-reducing diversification, and subsequent tears.

[7] Roll (1992) finds that different stock market returns among OECD markets are due to differences in the countries' industrial structure and the behavior of exchange rates.

called dynamic Asian economies, and 6% to 7% in both Argentina and Chile. Stock market prices cannot outpace GDP growth in the longer run: Share prices cannot rise faster than the dividends that give them their value, nor can dividends rise faster than the profits from which they are paid. Profits in turn can scarcely rise faster than the economy, as that would mean shareholders winning consistently at the expense of someone else. Investment in high-growth non-OECD countries thus promises higher returns than it does for slow-growth OECD countries as long as the market is less than perfectly efficient at arbitraging away such differences.

Pension funds are long-term contractual savings institutions, unlike investment funds, which need to stand ready to meet, at short notice, requests for reimbursements. The portfolio choice of pension funds will thus not only be guided by optimizing risk–return trade-offs, but will have to be aligned to the structure of their liabilities. The definition of retiree benefits (nominal vs. real, and defined contribution vs. defined benefit schemes), the maturity structure of receipts, and expenses will feature prominently among the determinants of portfolio investment.

In most OECD countries, quantitative limits to international investment still constrain the portfolio management of pension funds (see next section). How do pension funds invest when such limits are absent? Coote (1993) has recently looked at this question by examining *in-house investment guidelines* of life insurance and pension institutions in Australia, the Netherlands, Switzerland, and the United Kingdom. The investment behavior of these largely unconstrained institutions may be indicative of the future for those countries that decide to relax their official restrictions on international investment. Here is a short summary of Coote's findings:

(1) Pension funds take a *conservative* approach to international investment, which is motivated more by risk-reducing portfolio diversification than by expectations of superior long-term returns. The emphasis on diversificaton benefits is reflected in the fact that in-house guidelines specify both *minimum and maximum* limits to foreign investment; it is considered just as imprudent not to have a minimum foreign exposure as to hold too many foreign assets (see Table 8.2).

(2) Investment guidelines usually specify benchmarks for the purpose of defining a neutral long-term investment position, with a breakdown for the three major international asset classes, namely equities, fixed-interest instruments, and real estate. Limits to foreign equity holdings are usually the highest, those for foreign property holdings the lowest among the three asset classes. The preference for equities reflects the advantage to participants in defined contribution pension funds of acquiring assets of long duration with high yields and an

Table 8.2
Maximum guideline limits for foreign investment of pension
funds and life insurance companies
(percentage distribution)

Class Intervals	All Sample Pension Funds	Australia	Netherlands	Switzerland	United Kingdom
<10	15	10	33	40	9
11-20	33	30	13	27	36
21-30	30	20	27	27	18
>30	22	40	27	7	36

Source: Coote (1993).

expectation that their price movements will broadly offset inflation, a role for which equities are ideally suited. Bonds are suitable as a core holding for defined benefit pension funds with liabilities defined in nominal terms.

(3) Regional specifications cover in most guidelines minimum and maximum investment limits in three major regions – Europe, North America, and Asia Pacific. The benchmark here is often a commonly reported index such as the Morgan Stanley Market Capitalization Weighted Accumulation Index.[8] The share of countries in this benchmark depends on the capitalization value of their respective stock markets; countries may not be overweight or underweight by more than 5% of their share in the benchmark. (Note that neither Latin America nor Africa was mentioned by Coote.) The development of forward currency markets has now led most pension funds to recognize that investment in a foreign asset and investment in a foreign currency involve two separate investment decisions.

(4) Pension fund portfolios nonetheless often continue to display a home bias. Goldstein and Mussa (1993, p. 24) list the possible explanations as "transaction costs, externally-imposed prudential limits on foreign assets, uncertainties about expected returns, higher (than warranted) risk perceptions about foreign assets due to relative unfamiliarity with those markets and institutions," and express their own belief that the latter factor is the most important. Moreover, currency matching requirements sometimes obligate the holding of excess

[8] This finding contradicts an earlier study by Davis (1991) based on interviews with U.K. pension fund managers who mostly appeared unwilling to use global indexation even as a benchmark.

reserves when the currency composition of assets and liabilities is mismatched; such requirements make foreign investment less attractive.[9] Another factor, which militates particularly against pension fund investment into emerging markets, is liquidity risk (Davis, 1991). Yet a further explanation is the role of employee representatives, who typically favor investment at home because of a protectionist assumption that home investment promotes social welfare. In some countries, like Germany, the track record of (positive) inflation-adjusted returns on domestic government bonds and the strength of the domestic currency have also made foreign investment look less compelling. However, while pension funds have not so far pursued diversification into foreign assets to the extent predicted by modern portfolio theory, namely to the global portfolio, there is currently a clear trend to reduce the home bias of pension fund investment, so that those funds with low foreign exposure are now rapidly investing abroad, foremost in equities.

(5)   There is a strong tendency for portfolio behavior to conform to industry norms, a result of the principal–agent problem. For a pension fund manager, a strategy of low personal risk is to do what the others are doing. If they are all wrong in their choices, the manager will not be held *personally* accountable. But for the principal, the sponsoring companies and the pension beneficiaries, the damage will be done.

It should be noted that future investment behavior may be less conservative than that described by the Coote report. An increasing number of U.S. and U.K. companies are turning away from traditional defined benefit retirement plans, which guarantee employees a specific pension by investing their cash in a company-wide fund, towards defined contribution pensions, which give employees the chance to choose from a variety of investment options, most of which are mutual funds. In the future, therefore, pension funds are likely to stress return objectives more than in the past, especially while risk-free assets (such as deposits) yield returns as low as currently in the United States.

There is currently widespread enthusiasm about the long-run prospects for portfolio flows into emerging markets based on the calculation of risk–return trade-offs. Yet, the enthusiasm may easily be overdone. It seems obvious that

[9] Solnik (1988) categorizes the concern as a "misconception." Pension funds need to worry about the real purchasing power of their assets, and long-term deviations from purchasing power parity have been widely observed. But currency risk gets partly diversified away in a well-diversified portfolio, or it can be hedged. Furthermore, foreign-currency assets can protect the real purchasing power of pension assets since foreign goods represent a sizable part of any consumption basket, as well as reducing domestic monetary risk.

in a large, well-diversified economy such as the United States there should be enough opportunities to find poorly correlated equity returns and hence more potential for *domestic* diversification benefits than in a small, monostructured economy. To compare standard deviations of monthly returns of a joint U.S. index (such as the Standard and Poors 500) and their correlation with smaller counterparts is thus to exaggerate the benefits of foreign diversification, because one U.S. index would hide the domestic diversification potential for the U.S. investor. Diversification benefits can also be overstated by the common use of monthly returns, since the correlation of stock returns falls with the frequency of observation. Since performance checks for pension funds occur often on a quarterly basis, an efficient frontier based on quarterly or longer observations (not readily available from International Finance Corporation) is likely to provide a more realistic and lower estimate of the risk reduction implied by foreign investment. Standard deviations of monthly returns may also be a poor risk guide to the extent that *event risk* becomes more important (Howell, Cozzini, and Greenwood, 1992). Diversification will not eliminate systemic risks such as the 1987 crash when all markets are likely to be correlated. Finally, the low correlation of stock returns between mature and emerging markets that is currently observed cannot persist with heavy flows between these markets. The flows will help break down the historically low correlations between OECD and non-OECD stocks, just as happened with intra-OECD correlations, which strengthened during the 1980s (Mullin, 1993).

To the extent that economic development requires a long period of permanent (as opposed to temporary) capital inflows, this survey of investment strategies reveals pension funds as a particularly suitable vehicle for such inflows. In contrast to managed funds (country and mutual funds) and private domestic and foreign investors who switch assets rapidly in the search for short-term returns (Gooptu, 1993), pension funds (like life insurance companies) can be taken as a risk-averse group interested in participating in long-term investment. Pension funds are usually not forced to withdraw their assets suddenly due to a short-term demand for funds. Moreover, unlike money market funds and bond houses, pension funds are primarily interested in foreign equity investment. Pension funds in OECD countries are huge potential sources of financing for developing countries. Yet, as will be shown in the next section, regulations in many OECD countries still constitute a barrier to releasing that flow.

4   Restrictions on foreign investment

Many OECD countries still retain restrictions on international investment by pension funds (Table 8.3). Although most capital-account items have been

Table 8.3
Regulatory constraints on foreign investment by
pension funds in selected OECD countries

Country	Regulation	Source
Australia	No governmental limits to foreign investment.	Coote, 1993
Austria	No more than 20 per cent of assets in bonds, domestic bank deposits and cash reserves denominated in foreign currencies. No more than 10 per cent of employed funds in foreign real estate.	Gusen, 1993
Canada	The ceiling (formerly 10 per cent) is progressively raised to reach 20 per cent for 1995 and thereafter. A tax of 1 per cent per month is levied on excess foreign property holdings.	Gusen, 1993
Denmark	Must hold at least 60 per cent of assets in domestic debt instruments (real estate, investment trusts, and shares limited to 40 per cent). Only "small proportion" can be invested internationally.	Davis, 1992
Germany	4 per cent limit on foreign asset holdings.	Gusen, 1993
	5 per cent of assets can be invested in foreign bonds.	IMF, 1993
Japan	Nonbinding at 30 per cent of assets in the general account.	World Bank, 1993
Netherlands	No more than 5 per cent of the General Civil Service Pension Fund. 'Prudent man' rule for private funds.	Gusen, 1993 Davis, 1992
Norway	Foreign investment prohibited.	Gusen, 1993
Portugal	No more than 20 per cent of the EC listed securities.	Gusen, 1993
Switzerland	25 per cent limit on equity holdings of foreign-based companies; 20 per cent limit on foreign currency cash or bonds. Total foreign investment limit 30 per cent.	Coote, 1993
United Kingdom	No ceiling; 'prudent man' concept.	Davis, 1992
United States	No ceiling; 'prudent man' concept.	Davis, 1992

brought within the full discipline of the OECD Code of Liberalization of Capital Movements[10] and have been effectively liberalized during the 1980s, investment abroad by pension funds still remains outside the scope of the code. Restrictions are not only incorporated in exchange controls, but also in tax laws and in legislation covering financial institutions.

These restrictions can be classified by the type of investment instrument (limits on foreign real estate, bonds, shares), by issuer (government vs. private), by country of origin of the issuer, by whether the instruments are traded on recognized exchanges, and by the currency in which the instrument is denominated. Restrictions can take the form of outright prohibitions, limits for particular categories of investment, or incentives offered for particular investments.

For pension funds (and other institutional investors, such as life insurance companies or mutual funds), the distinction between capital controls and restrictions is to a certain extent muted. Prudential concern is often cited as a major motive for imposing government restrictions on investment by pension funds, both at home and abroad. Authorities feel a duty to protect the financial interest of individuals who have entrusted their savings to funds. Foreign investments come under particular scrutiny in some countries, because of deficiencies in information about local business and financial conditions, including regulatory standards for the issuance of securities, settlement risk, transfer risk, and sovereign (default) risk. But these risks can be dealt with by the market; and other motivations for government restrictions on foreign investment closely resemble those for the more "classical" capital controls, such as the retention of domestic savings and of monetary autonomy (see Gusen, 1993, pp. 18–20).

Restrictions on foreign investment by pension funds are often motivated by the desire to retain domestic savings for investment at home. True, it is sometimes argued that capital controls are so porous that their removal would do little to increase the export of capital. However, the mere fact that it is always possible for owners of wealth to place their funds abroad retail, at a premium, through a parallel market does not imply that controls that prevent institutions from exporting capital wholesale, at the official rate, have no effect in limiting the export of capital. Capital controls can prevent the placement abroad of long-term institutional savings. Tight restrictions, such as found in Germany, are mirrored by a low proportion of foreign assets in the portfolio of pension funds. The same observation holds for a number of

---

[10] The codes commit OECD member countries to eliminate any restrictions on capital movements between one another on operations listed in the codes. Not listed so far, and thus not under a general liberalization commitment, are mortgage and consumer credits and investment abroad by institutional investors, such as life insurance companies and pension funds.

other OECD countries, such as Denmark, France, Norway, Sweden, and, with regard to public pension funds, the Netherlands.

The ceilings on the share of foreign assets imposed by other OECD countries where pension funds are of any significance are generally considered to be nonbinding. Examples are Japan and Switzerland, where such ceilings have been set at 30%. Australian, Canadian, U.K., and U.S. pension funds are subject to a "prudent man rule." That rule gives pension funds considerable latitude with their portfolio investments provided they can demonstrate to authorities that their investment behavior as a whole is "prudent." A prudent approach to investment is interpreted to imply avoidance of excessive concentration and self-investment, as well as speculative investments.

When pension funds are free to invest abroad, they tend to extend the foreign asset share up to around 20% to 30%, as seen with private Dutch and U.K. funds.[11] Most empirical work on efficient frontiers displays minimum risk (for given return) in precisely the range chosen by unconstrained pension funds, that is, at a foreign assets share between 20% and 30% (e.g., Greenwood, 1993). Although U.K. and private Dutch funds have already arrived at that level, pension funds in most of the other OECD countries have only started their portfolio diversification towards optimal risk–return trade-offs. The process of portfolio adjustment does not occur overnight but stretches out over a decade or so.

In Europe, the drive toward foreign investment by pension funds could be threatened by European Community (EC) regulation (see the *Guardian,* October 5, 1993). A draft directive, originally proposed by Sir Leon Brittan as a measure to liberalize capital markets and create a level playing field for financial institutions, runs the risk of emerging as a protectionist measure: A majority of EC governments are now pushing for a limit of 20% on the proportion of assets that may be invested abroad,[12] where "abroad" is interpreted to include the rest of the European Union. The proposed directive would establish a European norm that could encourage or even oblige future governments to order the repatriation of foreign investments where they exceed the 20% limit (as is already the case in the United Kingdom, Belgium, and Ireland).

---

[11] As discussed earlier, the higher potential for diversification within large economies such as the United States and Japan will result in a smaller share of foreign assets held by pension funds domiciled there.

[12] As a compromise between the differing attitudes among OECD countries, OECD's CMIT/ CMF Joint Working Group recently recommended allowing institutional investors to place at least 20% of their assets abroad, and to match liabilities in foreign currencies with foreign currency assets up to at least equal value.

5 Abolition of capital controls: the U.K. experience

In the United Kingdom pension funds already accounted for an important proportion of personal savings and of GDP (around 20%) when capital controls were dismantled in October 1979. The U.K. experience may thus provide some insights relevant to countries considering dismantling capital controls in the presence of domestic institutional investors.

On theoretical grounds, it is usually expected that liberalizing capital inflows, and even outflows, will produce a net capital inflow, a positive wealth effect, and an appreciation of the real value of the domestic currency (Fischer and Reisen, 1993). Kenen (1993) shows that, in a two-period model, the liberalization of outflow controls may lead to the repatriation of domestic assets – a net capital inflow – because controls on outflows "tax" the option of reexporting capital later, and so reduce the incentive to repatriate capital now. Similarly, Labán and Larraín (1993) show that a liberalization of outflows – specifically, a reduction in the minimum capital repatriation period for foreign investment – reduces the irreversibility of inward investment and therefore the option value of waiting before moving funds in, thus potentially increasing net inward investment. Realignment of portfolio structures and the once-and-for-all attempt by foreign and domestic investors to increase their claims on a newly liberalized economy have sometimes created a spending boom, caused by the wealth effect due to the (at times euphoric) revaluation of domestic assets. All these forces will lead to a real appreciation of the domestic currency, in particular when liberalization is followed (rather than preceded) by a stabilization policy that drives real interest rates up.

In contrast to these hypotheses, the abolition of U.K. capital controls in the presence of important domestic institutional investors (notably pension funds) generated a wealth loss due to the disappearance of the "investment currency" premium and heavy net outward portfolio flows, with new foreign demand for sterling assets significantly lower than the demand by U.K. residents for overseas assets. The net effect of portfolio flows was to raise interest rates and to depreciate sterling, even though the currency appreciated heavily in real terms due to other factors. (Although a definite decomposition of sterling's appreciation during 1979–1982 has never been achieved,[13] with the development of North Sea oil, the second oil price shock, and sweeping policy changes under Margaret Thatcher coinciding with the abolition of capital controls, the fact that net portfolio flows became strongly negative implies that the abolition of capital controls limited rather than intensified the appreciation.)

---

[13] Despite the efforts of Bean (1988) and Buiter (1988).

The Bank of England (1981) argued that a net outflow was to be expected in the British context, given the importance of the investment currency premium over the long period when capital controls had been in place. With respect to portfolio investment, the U.K. controls had limited residents' purchase of foreign exchange for the purpose of investment overseas to the proceeds from the sale of existing foreign securities or from foreign currency borrowing. This constituted the "investment currency" market, in which there was a premium over the official exchange rate, which was mostly in the range of 30% to 50%, or on occasion even higher (Artis and Taylor, 1989). The size of the premium demonstrates the effectiveness of capital controls in locking in domestic savings.

The Bank of England (1981) argued that their removal triggered portfolio adjustment through four channels. First, the loss of the "investment currency" premium constituted a *reduction in the wealth* of investors who had previously been holding overseas securities, and a disruption to their previous portfolio balance. Attempts to restore the preabolition share of foreign assets in portfolios would give rise to capital outflows. Second, the abolition of the premium directly reduced the *sterling price* of foreign securities, which would induce investors to raise the desired portfolio share of foreign assets beyond preabolition levels, as long as foreign currency yields and risks remained unchanged. Third, some *refinancing in sterling* of investment originally financed with foreign currency borrowing was to be expected. Fourth, on top of the three stock-adjustment effects, a continuing *flow effect* was required to maintain portfolio balance as wealth increased.

Once controls were abolished, U.K. pension funds became the driving force for important net capital outflows. Net outward portfolio flows, which had been virtually nil when controls were still in place, cumulated to £36 billion during 1980–1985. As shown in Table 8.4, the net overseas share of the assets of nonbank financial institutions rose from 5.9% in 1979 (equivalent to £8.9 billion) to 14.3% in 1985 (£67.6 billion). Pension funds invested almost exclusively in foreign equities, withdrawing funds from illiquid property and low-return government bonds. The foreign asset share of pension funds rose to 15% in 1985, up from 7% in 1979, and rose further to around 30% by 1993. The switch in portfolio flows and the rise of foreign asset shares in portfolios can be put down as the "effect" of abolishing capital controls (Artis and Taylor, 1989 – implying that controls had been very effective in preventing global diversification of U.K. portfolios as long as they existed. The OECD (1990) noted a further stimulus to outward portfolio investment from 1988 on, when the government started retiring debt, creating a lack of suitable domestic investment assets.

Measures of financial market integration usually focus on interest rate

Table 8.4
United Kingdom: Pension Funds and Portfolio Flows, 1979 and after

	1979	1985
1. Portfolio of Pension Funds		
- foreign assets, %	7	15
- government bonds, %	22	18
- property, %	18	10
2. Portfolio of Nonbank Financial Institutions		
- gross overseas, %	7.3	16.4
- net overseas, %	5.9	14.3

	1975-1979	1980-1985
3. Portfolio Flows, net outward, £ bn. per annum	-0.3	6.0

Sources: Davis (92); Artis and Taylor (89).

parity conditions. Such a focus is justified by the concern that high capital mobility erodes the effectiveness of monetary policy as an instrument to manage the domestic economy under a regime of fixed (or managed) exchange rates. U.K. capital controls had indeed inhibited full interest arbitrage (a further indication of their effectiveness); their removal subsequently had a dramatic effect in eliminating deviations from covered interest parity (Artis and Taylor, 1989).[14] But it is unlikely that pension funds contributed in any great measure to short-term interest arbitrage, since their postabolition portfolio shifts mainly involved replacing property and government bonds by foreign equity purchases.

Pension funds, as the driving force of postabolition portfolio outflows, could nevertheless be held responsible for changes in the sterling exchange rate and interest rate *levels*. The Bank of England (1981) concluded that capital controls had contained the demand for foreign currency, and that removing them depreciated the pound and increased interest rates. Evidence

---

[14] Liberalization also reduced sharply the elasticity of long-term rates in response to short-term rates within the United Kingdom, while the correlation with foreign long rates increased (Blundell-Wignall and Browne, 1991). The weakened liquidity effect implied a further loss of power for monetary policy to influence private spending.

in favor of this position can be found in the behavior of onshore–offshore interest differentials: preabolition differentials in favor of offshore rates fell after abolition (Artis and Taylor, 1989).

The global integration of the U.K. stock market has undoubtedly been fostered primarily through pension funds after capital controls were dismantled. While no significant increase in the correlation of *short-run* stock market returns could be detected, the U.K. stock exchange became co-integrated with continental Europe and Japan, although not with the United States (Taylor and Tonks, 1989). The cointegration of different sets of stock market returns suggests that in the long run these returns are highly correlated, with the implication that the benefits from international diversification will be reduced. It is revealing for the importance of U.K. pension funds in fostering stock market integration to compare Taylor and Tonk's findings with the development of the asset mix of U.K. pension funds over the 1980s (Davis, 1991). While the share of U.S. assets (for which no rise in integration was detected) fell from 56% to 30%, the share of Japanese and European assets rose from some 30% to 59%.

6   Capital mobility and macroeconomic management

The evidence thus indicates that the global diversification of pension fund assets fosters stock market integration rather than interest rate linkages. This justifies the attempt to analyze the implications of equity capital mobility in section 2: Although pension funds will doubtless undertake marginal investments in fixed-interest assets, they are primarily equity investors and their main impact on monetary autonomy will come as a result of arbitrage between the stock and bond markets. Since that arbitrage is very imperfect, stock market integration does little to curb short-term monetary autonomy. The fear that allowing pension funds to place their assets abroad would further limit the ability of the Central Bank to conduct an autonomous monetary and exchange rate policy is thus misplaced.

Are the other arguments in favor of limiting capital mobility more persuasive when applied to the specific case of pension funds? The most important of these arguments relates to the desire to keep funds at home, in order to finance the domestic investment that is needed to promote growth. This can be a legitimate consideration at an early stage of the development process, or under conditions of great political uncertainty, since foreign investors cannot be expected to place even a small part of their portfolio in local assets in return for a modest premium on their expected rate of return if the economic risks of investing in the local economy are supplemented by political risks specific to foreign investors. In the absence of offsetting inward investment, a liberalization of outflows does indeed imply a net loss of savings to finance local investment. In contrast, once a country has got to the stage of being able to reassure foreign investors that they face no additional risks simply on account of being foreign, the potential exists for mutual gain through two-way investment that diversifies the portfolios of both parties, with local investors gaining greater security for a modest cost in lower expected yields, and the foreign investors gaining a greater expected yield for a modest cost in terms of less security. Indeed, a developing country can expect net inward investment, simply because the capital–labor ratio is relatively low and hence profit opportunities are likely to be relatively high.

Reasonable assumptions suggest, for example, that Chile could expect to have a net balance of inward investment under a scenario of full liberalization. In the not too distant future, OECD pension funds could hold 20% of their assets abroad (as described earlier, this is the ceiling now being discussed at the EU, a compromise found in OECD discussions, and a number close to the mean and mode of in-house investment guidelines). Respecting market weights within that 20% limit, $79 billion would have been invested in emerging markets and $3.2 billion of it in Chile, on the basis of 1992 assets. If OECD pension funds held a global portfolio as suggested by modern portfolio theory, they would hold $16 billion in Chile and almost $400 billion in all 20 emerging markets.

Table 8.5 compares the preceding estimates for pension-related inflows to the outflows likely after further liberalization. Currently, net foreign assets related to pension funds are negative (a net inflow), since Chile's pension funds are only starting to invest abroad. Even if the current 3% limit for outward investment was fully exploited, this would mean only $375 million held abroad, still short of the $500 million estimated to be currently invested in Chile. If Chile's pension system was allowed to invest 20% instead of 3% abroad, and OECD pension schemes behaved likewise, nothing much would change in *net* flow terms compared with the current situation. Under the unrealistic assumption that both Chile's and the OECD pension fund would end up with a global portfolio, Chile would enjoy net pension-related inward investment of $3.6 billion. All these numbers apply to estimated end-1992 assets, and extrapolation assumes implicitly that Chile's pension fund assets do not grow at a faster rate than do those of OECD pension funds. Chile's net foreign asset position would, of course, be raised by faster relative growth of its pension assets and reduced by relatively faster growth of its stock market capitalization.

It has been argued that it would be a mistake to vary capital controls with a view to trying to fine tune the flow of capital, because of the possible perverse effect whereby a liberalization of outflow controls could stimulate a net inflow (Williamson 1993). Our analysis in section 4 also pointed to this possibility. However, one context in which this analysis seems of question-

Table 8.5
Chile: Pension-related asset position

	Inward	Outward	Net Foreign Assets
1. End 1992	0.5	0.0	-0.5
2. Assuming 20% ceiling on foreign assets for both OECD and Chile's pension funds	3.2	2.5	-0.7
3. Assuming investment along World Stock Market Capitalization	16.0	12.4	-3.6

Note: Applies to estimated pension fund assets end 1992, when Chile's pension funds held assets of $12.5 billion.

Source: Banco Central de Chile, *Boletín Mensual*; IFC, *Emerging Stock Markets Factbook*, 1993.

able relevance concerns outward investment by domestically based pension funds (as opposed to the right of foreign funds to repatriate their holdings at will). Specifically, it is difficult to see any reason why legalizing foreign investment by pension funds should encourage inward investment (except insofar as it reduces domestic asset prices and thus increases the incentive to buy domestic assets). Thus liberalization of outward investment by pension funds would seem a rather sensible response to embarrassingly large capital inflows that threaten the ability to maintain a competitive exchange rate.

Another problem with liberalizing capital outflows is that this may erode the tax base, but this also hardly seems a relevant consideration with regard to foreign investment by pension funds.

We therefore conclude that foreign investment by pension funds, both inward and outward, should be one of the first components of the capital account to be liberalized. The fact that a number of OECD countries still maintain regulations that limit outward investment by their pension funds is both anomalous and harmful to the interests of developing countries, and the discussion within the European Union of changes that would roll back past liberalization is even more regrettable. In addition, once a developing country has got to the point of appearing sufficiently reassuring to foreign investors that they perceive no risk of being treated less favorably simply because they are foreign, there is no reason for the country to fear a net loss of savings as a result of liberalizing investment by pension funds. In particular, we have argued that at that point the desirability of maintaining a degree of monetary autonomy and a competitive exchange rate do not imply any need to prohibit foreign investment by pension funds.

It was suggested during the conference that an important reason for delaying the liberalization of outward investment by pension funds was the positive externalities that these funds provide for the widening and deepening of capital markets. For example, Vittas (1992) suggests that contractual savings institutions, essentially pension funds and life insurance companies, play a crucial role in mobilizing long-term financial resources and developing equity and bond markets (government, corporate, and mortgage). They thus fill the gap in the supply of long-term finance that exists in most developing countries, as well as facilitating the privatization of state-owned enterprises and promoting greater dispersion of corporate ownership. We would regard this argument as reinforcing the caveat expressed in the preceding paragraph, that liberalization should not be undertaken prior to a situation where foreign investors can be expected to replace any outward flow of savings by domestic pension funds.

7 Techniques for regulating foreign investment by pension funds

For completeness, we add a brief discussion of various techniques by which the foreign investment of pension funds could be regulated, were our main recommendation regarding the inadvisability of such regulation to be rejected.

1. One possible technique would be to limit domestic pension funds to portfolio swaps with foreign pension funds.[15] If the exchange control regulations prohibited reinvestment of dividends, then the only impact of the pension funds on the foreign exchange market would be the difference between the realized returns on inward versus outward investment over the period in question.

Unlike many proposals for capital controls, this one appears to be administratively feasible. Pension funds are well-defined legal entities that are in any event regulated, and it would not seem difficult to ensure that they undertook all foreign investments through a swap market.

This proposal would achieve complete insulation of the domestic economy from changes in the portfolio preferences of foreign investors. Consider, for example, the sort of shock which we established at the end of section 2 was capable of destabilizing the domestic economy, namely a downward revision of expectations for domestic earnings that was not shared by local investors. Under this scenario foreign pension funds would start to sell shares, but in

---

[15] This possibility was first suggested by Alan Gelb of the World Bank.

order to get their funds out they would have to find a national pension fund that was willing to liquidate some of its foreign holdings and repatriate its funds. Since the national pension fund would invest its earnings in the domestic stock market, there would be no reason for any major change in the price of domestic equities; the price that would adjust to reequilibrate the market would be the premium/discount on the foreign exchange rate at which pension fund swaps were undertaken. Some spillover on domestic markets could still occur, but only to the extent that the foreign pension funds decided to invest in other assets like bonds, and even then a move that would depress stock prices would tend to increase bond prices so that there would be no first-order effects on aggregate demand. Hence this proposal would provide an effective solution, though one to a problem that we argued to be nonexistent.

The big disadvantage of the proposal is that it would preclude developing countries financing a net resource transfer from investment by pension funds. Of course, there are times when inward investment is excessive and hence a mechanism that repels an inflow of reserves can be helpful. But if one believes that long-term investments on an equity basis provide a superior form in which to tap foreign capital, then foregoing net pension fund inflows is a high price to pay for solving a nonexistent long-run problem even if there may sometimes be an incidental short-run benefit in limiting unwanted inflows as well, especially when one recognizes that it is equally likely that the inflows may at other times be very much wanted on short-run grounds.

2. Another idea is to create a special foreign exchange market for capital movements by pension funds, with its own freely floating exchange rate. Except for legal form, this proposal appears to be identical to the preceding one; in both cases an investment by a pension fund would have to be matched by an equal investment in the opposite direction, at an exchange rate determined by supply and demand of pension funds alone. Hence it too would be administratively feasible, conjuncturally pointless, and developmentally damaging.

3. It has also been suggested that it might be advisable to subject pension funds to capital controls during a transitional period when such funds were growing particularly rapidly. Presumably the fear is that there is a danger that without such controls pension funds will be net outward investors during this transitional period.

This fear does not seem very likely to be justified. Pension funds in many OECD countries have already reached maturity, so that their investments in a newly liberalizing developing country are likely to build up much more quickly than the foreign investments of that country's pension funds. We would not object strenuously if a country decided that it wished to liberalize gradually, as many of the OECD countries have done, from time to time raising the ceiling for the proportion of assets that a pension fund was entitled to hold abroad. On the other hand, we are doubtful whether such gradualism is likely to have much impact on behavior, given the evidence that pension funds themselves tend to respond to newfound freedom to invest abroad rather cautiously.

References

Artis, M. J., and Mark P. Taylor (1989). "Abolishing Exchange Control: The UK Experience." *CEPR Discussion Paper* No. 294. London.

Bank of England (1981). "The Effects of Exchange Control Abolition on Capital Flows." *Quartely Bulletin,* September, pp. 369–373.

Bean, Charles R. (1988). "Sterling Misalignment and British Trade Performance." In R. C. Marston (ed.), *Misalignment of Exchange Rates: Effects on Industry and Trade,* pp. 39–69. University of Chicago Press, Chicago.

Blanchard, Oliver (1985). "Debt, Deficits, and Finite Horizons." *Journal of Political Economy,* 93, April, pp. 223–247.

Blundell-Wignall, Adrian, and Frank Browne (1991). "Macroeconomic Consequences of Financial Liberalisation: A Summary Report." *OECD ESD Working Papers* No. 98. Paris.

(1987). "Fiscal Policies in Open Interdependent Economies." In A. Razin and E. Sadka (eds.), *Economic Policy in Theory and Practice,* pp. 101–144. Macmillan, London.

Buiter, Willem H. (1988). Comment (on Bean). In R. C. Marston (ed.), *Misalignment of Exchange Rates: Effects on Industry and Trade,* pp. 69–75. University of Chicago Press, Chicago.

Coote, Robin (1993). "Self-Regulation of Foreign Investment by Institutional Investors." OECD/DAFFE/INV(93)18. Paris. Mimeograph.

Corbo, Vittorio, and Leonardo Hernández (1993). "Macroeconomic Adjustment to Capital Inflows: Rationale and Some Recent Experiences." Paper presented to a World Bank Symposium on Portfolio Investment in Developing Countries, Washington, D.C., September 9–10.

Davanzo, Lawrence, and Leslie B. Kautz (1992). "Toward a Global Pension Market." *Journal of Portfolio Management,* Summer 1992, pp. 77–85.

Davis, E. Philip (1991). "International Diversification of Institutional Investors." Bank of England, London, Discussion Papers (Technical Series) No. 44.

(1992). "The Structure, Regulation and Performance of Pension funds in Nine Industrial Countries." Bank of England, London. Mimeograph.

Fischer, Bernhard, and Helmut Reisen (1993). *Liberalising Capital Flows in Developing Countries: Pitfalls, Prerequisites and Perspectives.* OECD Development Centre Studies. Paris.

Gavin, Michael (1989). "The Stock Market and Exchange Rate Dynamics." *Journal of International Money and Finance,* 8, pp. 181–200.

(1991a). "Animal Spirits, Terms of Trade and the Current Account." Columbia University, New York. Mimeograph.

(1991b). "Equity Markets in the World Economy: Capital Flows, Asset Prices, and the Transfer Problem." Columbia University, New York. Mimeograph.

Goldstein, Michael, and Michael Mussa (1993). "The Integration of World Capital Markets." Paper presented to the Conference on "Changing Capital Markets:

Implications for Monetary Policy," sponsored by the Federal Reserve Bank of Kansas City at Jackson Hole, Wyoming, August 19–21.

Gooptu, Sudarshan (1993). "Portfolio Investment Flows to Emerging Markets." World Bank Research Working Paper WPS 1117. Washington, D.C.

Greenwood, John G. (1993). "Portfolio Investment in Asian and Pacific Economies: Trends and Prospects." *Asian Development Review*, 11.1, pp. 120–150.

Guardian (1993). *EC Set to Put Ceiling on Pension Funds' Foreign Holdings.* October 5, London.

Gusen, Peter (1993). "Investment Abroad by Institutional Investors." OECD/DAFFE/ INV (83) 14. Paris. Mimeograph.

Howell, Michael, Angela Cozzini, and Luci Greenwood (1992). *Cross Border Capital Flows: A Study of Foreign Equity Investment.* 1991–1992 Review. Baring Securities, London.

Kenen, Peter (1993). "Financial Opening and the Exchange Rate Regime." In H. Reisen and B. Fischer (eds.), *Financial Opening: Policy Issues and Experiences in Developing Countries.* pp. 237–261. OECD, Paris.

Labán, Raúl, and Felipe Larraín (1993). "Can A Liberalization of Capital Outflows Increase Net Capital Inflows?" Working Paper No. 155, Instituto de Economía, Univ. Católica de Chile, Santiago.

Mullin, John (1993). "Emerging Equity Markets in the Global Economy." *Federal Reserve Bank of New York Quarterly Review,* 18.2, pp. 54–83.

Mundell, Robert A. (1968). *International Economics.* Macmillan, London.

OECD (1990). *OECD Economic Surveys: United Kingdom.* OECD, Paris. *Economic Outlook* No. 53. OECD, Paris.

Roll, Richard (1992). "Industrial Structure and the Comparative Behaviour of International Stock Market Indexes." *Journal of Finance,* 42.1, pp. 3–42.

Solnik, Bruno (1988). *International Investments.* Addison-Wesley, Reading, Mass.

Solnik, Bruno, and Bernard Noetzlin (1982). "Optimal International Asset Allocation." *Journal of Portfolio Management,* Fall, pp. 11–21.

Taylor, Mark, and Ian Tonks (1989). "The Internationalisation of Stock Markets and the Abolition of U.K. Exchange Control." *Review of Economics and Statistics,* 71.2, pp. 332–336.

Vittas, Dimitri (1992). "Contractual Savings and Emerging Securities Markets." World Bank Research Paper Working Paper WPS 858. Washington, D.C.

Williamson, John (1993). "A Cost-Benefit Analysis of Capital Account Liberalisation." In H. Reisen and B. Fischer (eds.), *Financial Opening: Policy Issues and Experiences in Developing Countries,* pp. 35–34. OECD, Paris.

CHAPTER 9

Are there (good) macroeconomic reasons for limiting external investments by pension funds? The Chilean experience

Juan Andrés Fontaine

Chile, as have most countries, has had a long experience with exchange controls. In general, they have been imposed during foreign exchange crises to prevent "capital flight" and then kept (in some looser form) once normal conditions have been reestablished. Exchange controls entered Chile as a key macropolicy instrument during the Great Depression and remained in the 1940s and 1950s not only as such, but also as a flexible, "friendly" protectionist tool. After a brief experiment with freer convertibility, exchange controls were reinstated in 1961, during a new and severe balance-of-payments crisis. They underwent many changes in the following 28 years, but, interestingly enough, despite the wide and deep liberalization of the economy in the 1970s and 1980s, the essential principles of the 1961 law on exchange controls remained intact. In 1989 the new Central Bank law limited its powers to impose effective exchange controls, and created the legal conditions for their elimination. Since then, the Central Bank has been slowly advancing in that direction.

Progress has been particularly slow in two areas: in allowing funds to invest abroad and in removing certain restrictions to capital inflows. This is a consequence of old and new concerns about an "excessive" capital mobility. The former ones are based on the fear that further opening of the capital account could lead scarce domestic savings to flow outward, whereas the latter are connected to the presumed loss of macropolicy sovereignty that a fully open economy would bring about.

A small country like Chile would benefit greatly from having a fully open capital market. On the one hand, the inflow of foreign financing would reduce the cost of capital in Chile, thus fostering investment growth. On the other hand, allowing greater international diversification to domestic investors would clearly reduce their exposure to Chilean country risks. Chilean exports amount to around one-third of GDP and they are highly concentrated in a few commodities. National income is thus subjected to frequent and large terms-of-trade shocks. If pension funds were allowed to diversify these risks in the international capital market, they would not only be able to reduce the volatility of their returns, but contribute to greater stability in national income.[1]

This chapter reviews the macroeconomic arguments for capital controls, with a special focus on those restricting international diversification by pension funds. The analysis is based on the Chilean experience and the Chilean economic policy debate. The conclusions are valid though for a variety of countries undergoing similar processes of financial opening and development of private pension funds systems.

The chapter is organized as follows. The first section summarizes the recent Chilean experience with pension funds and exchange controls. Section 2 presents and discusses the three macroeconomic arguments for establishing exchange or capital controls. Section 3 takes the third of those arguments, exchange rate stability, and analyzes its implications for macropolicy and discusses the merits of such objective. Section 4 discusses whether pension funds deserve "special treatment" with regard to capital controls.

1   Pension funds and exchange controls in Chile

Pension funds are the most important "institutional investor" in Chile. The size of the assets they manage is equivalent to 35% of GDP and growing fast. The story began in 1980 with the privatization of old-age, disability, and survivors state pension systems.[2] The reform involved the creation of a new, fully funded, competitive, and privately administered system that replaced the old, pay-as-you-go system. Social security contributions are mandatory (10% of gross wage for old-age benefits, plus 2% to 3% for commissions and disability and survivors insurance) and the state guarantees a minimum pension and a minimum relative return (defined as a function of the industry average). As a counterpart, pension funds face strict regulations and tight supervision in a variety of areas, including "investment grade" and portfolio diversification requirements.

The social security reform gave rise to a rapid expansion of the capital market. Financial savings (or M7 in the Chilean financial jargon) grew from 28% of GDP in 1980 to 68% in 1993; pension funds were nonexistent in 1980 and now make close to a third of financial savings. Initially, the expansion was concentrated on fixed-income securities, because shares were

---

[1] The benefits pension funds would draw from international diversification are discussed by Valente (1988, 1991).

[2] For a complete description of the new Chilean Pension Funds System, see Cheyre (1991).

not an authorized investment for pension funds. It is interesting to note that despite the great uncertainty prevailing during the macroeconomic crisis of 1982–1983 and the inflationary climate of 1984–1985 (see Table 9.1), the process of financial deepening started by pension funds was not undermined. Pension funds invested most of their resources in CPI-indexed government securities, bank certificates of deposit (CDs), and mortgage bonds. Terms were initially short, but then gradually extended: 10 years after their creation pension funds were avidly buying 12–20 year Central Bank bonds, mortgage bonds, and debentures.

In 1985 pension funds were allowed to invest in shares, on a very limited basis. The restrictions were subsequently eased and now some 30% of their assets are devoted to shares. Pension funds have been very important players in the stock market and have contributed to its extraordinary growth in the past 10 years. Market capitalization stands at about 90% of GDP in end-1993, after being only 32% of GDP 5 years earlier.

The growth of the capital market has performed a number of important macroeconomic functions. Financial liberalization is desirable because it stimulates savings and improves its allocation among the different investments projects, as emphasized by the literature on "financial repression."[3] Financial liberalization also produces some positive *macroeconomic* consequences that are seldom as emphasized.

In my view, the Chilean experience shows that a deep capital market is extraordinarily useful in facilitating internal resource transfers. In Chile, as in the rest of Latin America, the most pressing problem in the 1980s was generating the external net transfer needed to serve (partially) foreign debts to international banks. Given that the debt was or became public (in Chile private external debts of the financial system ended being guaranteed by the state), this also caused an internal transfer problem: Net savings generated in the private sector had to be transferred to the public sector to be used in servicing foreign debts.

The internal transfer problem was addressed in Chile, as in most other Latin American countries, with a strong dose of fiscal adjustment.[4] The tax burden was increased, and fiscal transfers to the private sector were cut. But the Chilean public sector had an option that was not available to other Latin American countries: to tap the domestic capital market in order to finance the external transfers. Chile's need for fiscal adjustment was substantially eased by the use of this expedient. Domestic residents were able to lead substantial amounts to the public sector without demanding extraordinarily high interest rates, as observed in similar attempts in Argentina, Brazil, and Mexico.

---

[3] McKinnon (1973) and Shaw (1973) were extremely influential in Chile.

[4] For an analysis of the Chilean adjustment process, see Fontaine (1989a).

Table 9.1

Key macro-economic indicators (1)

	1980	1981	1982	1983	1984	1985	1986	1987	1988	1989	1990	1991	1992
GDP (annual growth %)	7.9	6.2	-13.6	-2.8	5.9	2.0	5.6	6.6	7.3	10.2	3.0	6.1	10.3
Unemployment Rate (%)(2)	10.4	11.3	19.6	14.6	13.9	12	8.8	7.9	6.3	5.3	5.7	5.3	4.4
Inflation Rate (%)	31.2	9.5	20.7	23.1	23	26.4	17.4	21.5	12.7	21.4	27.3	18.7	12.7
Real Interest Rate (%) (3)	8.42	13.16	12.13	7.83	8.44	8.17	4.13	4.25	4.58	6.77	9.44	5.43	5.25
Real Wages (annual growth %)	8.6	9.0	0.3	-10.9	0.2	-4.5	2.0	-0.2	6.5	1.9	1.8	4.9	4.5
Current Account Deficit (as % of GDP)	7.1	14.3	9.8	5.7	10.9	8.1	6.4	3.9	0.7	2.7	2.0	-0.4	1.4
Fiscal Deficit (as % of GDP) (4)	7.4	5.5	-2.0	-2.9	-1.9	-0.9	0.8	2.1	5.1	7.2	4.9	4.4	5.4

(1)   Series including GDP in their calculation are not homogeneous due to changes in National Accounts from 1985 on.
(2)   October-December survey.
(3)   90-365 day bank deposit rate. Only banks until 1983.
(4)   Treasury savings.

Source: Banco Central de Chile.

Domestic public-sector debt (most of it in the form of Central Bank short- and medium-term bonds) increased from 5% of GDP in 1980 to 28% in 1990. In late 1993 it still stands at 28%.

This was also crucial when authorization was given to buying back external debt paper at a discount in the secondary market. The debt conversion program applied in Chile between 1985 and 1989 involved the discounted *prepayment* of external debts by original debtors.[5] In order to do this the debtors had to raise funds in the domestic market. Debt conversions amounted to approximately U.S. $10 billion in 5 years at face value, and discounts averaged some 15%. Therefore, original debtors had to raise the peso equivalent an average of U.S. $1.9 billion per year, or 8% of average GDP. Again, this was feasible – and noninflationary – only because of the depth of the Chilean capital markets. And note that 40% of the debts prepaid were originally owned by public-sector entities, so this was also a cause of the growth of internal public debt referred to above.

There are several explanations of why this option was available to the Chilean government and not to other highly indebted ones in Latin America. Chile was able to manage its debt negotiations with international banks in a less confrontational fashion than other countries and was quick to put in place a credible economic program under the seal of the International Monetary Fund and the World Bank. Also, the Chilean government never lost its good credit reputation among domestic investors, as was the case – and dramatically so – in Argentina and Peru. But, in my view, pension funds were also very important in explaining the difference.

By 1985, for example, pension funds had already accumulated a significant stock of assets (equivalent to almost 11% of GDP) and they were continually growing with the flow of monthly contributions. Pension funds are particularly avid investors in low-risk securities, such as those offered by the Central Bank. As indicated, these notes were in general CPI-indexed, and the government retained sufficient credibility to convince pension funds that the indexing formula was not going to be altered (and, to date, despite complaints of mortgage debtors, it has never been changed).[6]

The set of regulations faced by pension funds also played a part. During the 1980s pension funds were generally constrained in their permitted invest-

---

[5] Debt-conversion schemes in Chile have been intensely analyzed. See, for example, Fontaine (1988) and Larraín and Velasco (1990).

[6] The Unidad de Fomento (UF), the CPI-indexed unit of account in which most medium- and long-term financial assets and liabilities are denominated in Chile, has performed a crucial role in the development of the Chilean capital market. Based on failed experiences elsewhere, financial indexation does not enjoy a good reputation in the profession. In my opinion, the Chilean experience shows that this view may be incorrect, but I know of no systematic study attempting to undo this unjustice.

ments, public bonds, mortgage bonds, and CDs being their primary options. Shares and privately issued bonds were only very gradually authorized. The regulations never *forced* pension funds to hold a given proportion of their assets in public debt (on the contrary, limits were placed on their *maximum* holdings), but by reducing the menu of permitted investments, they indirectly induced them to do so.

These regulations not only constrained investment options within the domestic market, but until 1989 they banned any international portfolio diversification by pension funds. This was a crucial factor explaining why the Chilean domestic capital market grew so much in size and depth, despite an internal climate of debt crisis and great uncertainty. In March 1990 the pension law was amended to allow some international portfolio diversifications. As of late 1993, pension funds could invest up to 3% of their portfolio in fixed-income securities issued by low-risk sovereign debtors and banks. The limit can be gradually raised by the Central Bank to 10% in 7 years. A recently approved new amendment (mid-1995) allows investments in foreign shares and raises that limit to 12%.

In Chile, during the past decade, not only were pension funds subject to specific restrictions on international capital movements, but most foreign exchange operations were subject to strict Central Bank control.

The old Chilean legal framework for exchange controls stated that only the foreign exchange operations authorized by the Central Bank were legal. An illegal, parallel market took care of the rest. The 1989 Central Bank Law abolished this principle and replaced it by the opposite: All exchange operations are legal and free, except those specifically restricted by the Central Bank.[7] In order for these restrictions to be applied, the specific operation has to be restricted to the "formal" or bank exchange market and subjected there to a number of possible limitations (the "informal" market, by definition, is made of all other transactions and is legally free). The tightest restrictions are only allowed under "critical balance-of-payments conditions."

Since 1988–1989, Chile and most other Latin American countries have experienced a dramatic improvement in balance-of-payments conditions.[8] The turnaround has been so dramatic that central bankers, after spending the previous years lamenting the critical scarcity of foreign exchange, have found themselves accumulating huge amounts of international reserves. Ironically, the "dollar glut" has become the number-one macroeconomic "problem" in Chile and other countries. This has been caused by a number of factors, of both external and internal origin: high export growth, low international interest rates, high domestic interest rates, relatively successful stabilization pro-

---

[7] See Fontaine (1989b).

[8] See Calvo, Leiderman, and Reinhart (1992) and Labán and Larraín (1993).

grams and structural reforms, freer legal environment for foreign exchange transactions.

Monetary authorities have become increasingly uncomfortable with the dollar glut. They fear it is creating an appreciation of the peso that would undermine export-propelled economic growth. Attempts to offset this by accumulating international reserves may cause excessive monetary expansion or cost too much. Furthermore, capital inflows are thought to reduce the effectiveness of monetary policy to control inflation and can aggravate distortions caused by excessive bank credit.[9]

These concerns have led the Central Bank to restrict capital inflows to Chile,[10] and the measures taken are of three classes. First, in 1991 the government extended the stamp tax previously applicable only to domestic credits to all credits, with the only exemption of export financing. The stamp tax increases borrowing costs by an annualized 1.2% for loans up to 1-year maturity and becomes increasingly less costly for longer maturities. The second measure, also passed in 1991 and strengthened in 1992, was the imposition of nonremunerated reserve requirements on all external credits and foreign exchange deposits received by Chilean banks, firms, and individuals. All these borrowers are required to deposit with the Central Bank an amount equivalent to 30% of the external credits or deposits for a 1-year period, independently of the maturity of their liabilities. This mechanism makes it extremely dear (almost prohibitive) to borrow short term from abroad, but is significantly less costly for long-term loans. Reserve requirements are, of course, a kind of tax collected by the Central Bank.[11]

These taxes have the effect of introducing a wedge between domestic and international interest rates. A higher wedge is placed on short-term rates, because short-term rates are the ones most influenced by the antiinflationary monetary policy followed and because "hot money" is deemed more dangerous.

A third measure has gradually gained importance as international capital markets have become more willing to take Chilean risks. Chile is now considered an attractive "emerging market" and Chilean companies are being offered highly attractive opportunities for raising capital either through equity (via American depositary receipts, ADRs) or medium-term international bonds. The Central Bank has been extremely cautious in allowing these operations. ADRs issues are allowed only for companies willing to expand their equity base, a minimum amount of U.S. $50 million is required and good credit ratings from both an international agency *and* the essentially

---

[9] Calvo et al. (1993) deal with these problems.

[10] The Chilean Central Bank's arguments are best stated by Zahler (1992).

[11] Taxation of international capital flows has been advocated by Tobin (1978) and others.

state-controlled Comisión Clasificadora de Riesgos are needed.[12] Bond issues face similar restrictions. In practice, both mechanisms are starting to be exploited by the few companies able to meet the requirements.

It could have been expected that concerns over the macroeconomic effects of an overabundance of foreign exchange would have led to the elimination of restrictions on capital outflows. In fact, restrictions on external investments by nonfinancial entities have been lifted and the repatriation of capital invested by foreigners in Chile is now allowed at earlier dates than before. However, restrictions on international diversification by financial institutions such as banks and pension funds have been essentially maintained. In the case of banks, the argument has been to avoid Chile's good international credit standing being used to transfer resources to less creditworthy countries. Banks are seen as particularly prone to this behavior, given the explicit or implicit state guarantees on their liabilities. As mentioned already, pension funds have been limited until recently to 3% of their portfolio in their foreign investments, as mandated by the corresponding law.

2   The economic foundations of exchange controls

In this section we review the use of exchange controls as a macropolicy instrument. There are, of course, many other reasons why exchange controls may have been used in Chile or elsewhere (e.g., as noted earlier, as an import protection device), which are of no relevance for us here.

What can Chile's long experience with exchange controls teach us about their rationale for macropolicy objectives? I see three different arguments supporting the use of such controls: protecting the tax base, insulating the domestic economy from certain capital market imperfections, and avoiding exchange rate instability.

Protecting the tax base

In Chile probably the oldest and most frequent rationale for exchange controls is preventing the "capital flight" caused by taxation. Economic policy in the 1940s, 1950s, and 1960s was very much guided by redistributional aims, taxing capital in favor of certain politically influential groups. It is well known that under capital mobility private capital is able (legally) to escape much of such taxation, shifting the tax burden to the less mobile factors (land, but also labor). Exchange controls were thus used to make such escape illegal.

---

[12] In April 1994 some of these restrictions were relaxed: The minimum issue for ADRs was lowered to U.S.$50 million and now the (still very strict) credit ratings required are to be produced by an international entity instead of the "Comisión Clasificadora de Riesgos."

Of course, "taxing capital" has to be understood in an ample sense. Chile did not exhibit in the 1940s to 1960s extremely high *open* tax rates. But it did show a substantial amount of regulations (of prices, wages, etc.) that were in essence taxes in disguise. Also Chile made intensive use of the inflation tax.

Is the tax argument still relevant in Chile? As it is well known, the free-market reforms of the 1970s and 1980s reduced substantially open and disguised taxation of capital in Chile. So they rendered exchange controls less important from the tax point of view. Anyway, the tax argument is still present because fiscal authorities tend to fear that an open capital account would facilitate tax evasion, in the sense that profits earned abroad would simply evade domestic taxes.

I think this is a valid concern and it militates against an extreme version of exchange deregulation in which even the registration of capital movements is eliminated. But capital mobility can be essentially free, even if exchange transactions are carried through authorized dealers (e.g., banks) and/or subject to the requirement of filling some forms that the tax collector can access, and in such case the tax argument will cease to be valid.[13] This is the purpose of articles 42 and 40 of the current Chilean Central Bank Law, stating, respectively, its power to dictate that certain transactions can only be carried through the "formal exchange market" (i.e., banks or other authorized dealers) and that even transactions carried outside this market may be subject to the requirement of being informed, ex post, to the Central Bank.

Market failure

As in other areas one can justify capital or exchange controls as a means to rectify certain market failures. The standard argument is directed at controlling capital inflows rather than outflows: Given the absence of a global judiciary system, there is such a thing as sovereign debt and "country risk." This in turn may create a negative externality in the sense that any individual considering the possibility of raising capital abroad does not take into account

---

[13] Another tax-related concern is the existence of certain peculiarities in the tax structure. Personal income tax rates are high (the top marginal rate is 48%) and the corporate income tax rate is low (15%). Dividends are included in the personal income tax base and corporate income taxes paid by them are a tax credit. The distortion this generates vis-à-vis foreign investors in Chile is eliminated by a special 35% tax on profit remittances. The incentive to evade taxation of dividends by realizing capital gains is dealt with through a special 15% tax on capital gains. This latter special tax would come under trouble in a totally open financial environment: How would capital gains earned on transactions of Chilean shares abroad be taxed? This problem is already present with ADR transactions. Anyway, it is not relevant for pension funds, which are not subject to the capital gains tax in Chile.

the effects of his decision on the overall credit rating of the country. Of course, the actual significance of this externality is debatable. Anyway, in principle, it can provide the foundation for monitoring private external indebtedness as a relevant macropolicy concern and even for establishing some exchange or capital controls.[14] For example, it is on these grounds, that the Central Bank of Chile imposes certain "investment grade" or minimum quality standards to Chilean private securities placed abroad through ADRs and Eurobonds.

It has also been argued that the distortions created by the "moral hazard" introduced by cost-free explicit or implicit state guarantees for bank liabilities may be aggravated by capital inflows to banks.[15] Also, if capital inflows are volatile and intermediated through the financial system, they may accentuate financial instability and even create costly financial crises.

It is much more difficult to find a good reason for using the market failure argument to limit capital outflows, such as those one would expect if Chilean pension funds were allowed to invest abroad. But looking back at the Chilean experience since the privatization of the social security system in 1980, one can find one scenario that, in my opinion, justifies such capital controls. In 1982 Chile, as other Latin American countries, suffered a severe balance-of-payments crisis. Such problems arise from a specific market failure: When many investors and creditors (either resident or nonresident) decide, for any reason, to reduce their exposure to a given country, it pays to do so quickly, before others do the same. This creates a sharp increase in capital outflows that in principle calls for an overshooting of the real exchange rate. If the authorities are interested in keeping the exchange rate on line with its long-run equilibrium level, they will intervene selling reserves while they last. Exchange controls might be the only tool left when reserves are coming close to exhaustion.

In my view this is an important argument for taking a cautious view with respect to complete elimination of exchange controls. It is totally unreasonable to expect that during a crisis of confidence, such as that of 1982, the authorities will be willing to tolerate a real devaluation of the currency of the magnitude needed to restore short-run equilibrium, with the ensuing inflationary impact and real wage drop. But note that this argument is confined to the specific case of times of crises. Therefore, it provides a rationale for empowering some authority, for example, the Central Bank, to impose ex-

---

[14] Harberger (1985) and Edwards (1986).

[15] Calvo et al. (1993) seem to overemphasize this point. For example, they argue that foreign investment is less harmful than loans because the former does not rely on domestic intermediation. However, if foreign investors buy real assets, someone – a domestic resident – has to sell them! This portfolio shift presumably also increases financial intermediation.

change controls under abnormal, critical, balance-of-payments conditions.[16] The Chilean Central Bank Law of 1989 has such a provision (articles 49 and 50), establishing that exchange controls must be explicitly justified in the need to preserve "monetary stability" or securing "adequate financing" for the balance of payments. They must also follow an exceptional approval procedure and have a (renewable) duration of less than a year. Exchange controls are then for exceptional times, not for normal ones.

The distinction between exceptional and normal times is not always very clear.[17] But I think that reasonable central bankers can in general agree about when the balance-of-payments situation has really turned critical. In the Chilean situation of 1982–1988, the case was clear: Chile had to suspend debt service and engage in a lengthy process of nonvoluntary debt rescheduling and refinancing. Exchange controls were an inescapable corollary of this process.

Exchange rate stability

Central Banks, political authorities, and the general public tend to dislike exchange rate instability. *Nominal* exchange rate instability is considered undesirable because it may create price-level fluctuations and may increase cross-border transactions costs. *Real* exchange rate volatility is considered detrimental to export-propelled growth.

This poses two problems to economic policy. One, insulating the balance of payments from the exogenous fluctuations of international capital flows. The other, trying to neutralize the impact on capital flows coming from domestic policy decisions.

The first problem is valid if international capital flows are inherently volatile. We discussed earlier the critical case in which a change in perceptions might create a run against the local currency. But we can also find a similar behavior when the change in perception is a positive one. We have seen it happening time and again in Latin America: A positive change in perceptions gives rise to a dramatic surge of capital inflows. This is frequently linked to some informational deficiencies or irrational behavior ("herd instincts") on the part of investors.[18] But it need not be so: Changes in

---

[16] It must be admitted that the likelihood of exchange controls being imposed in times of crises may in itself exert a destabilizing effect on capital movements, precipitating massive capital outflows as soon as fundamental conditions show a slight deterioration. I am aware of this problem, but, is there a solution to it?

[17] In fact, many restrictions have been kept in Chile, despite obvious indications that their relaxation would not cause any inflationary or balance-of-payments problem whatsoever.

[18] Krause (1991) argues strongly in this sense, using both rational expectations models creating "destabilizing speculation" and irrational behavior. See also McKinnon (1991).

exposure, by their very nature, involve a change in a desired *stock*, and, in the absence of controls and other restrictions, they typically take place through large, sudden, once-and-for-all changes in *flows*.

The observed instability of capital inflows is often an argument for limiting short-term capital movements, while leaving foreign investment and medium- and long-term loans under freer conditions. The implicit presumption is that the former are "hot money," that is they conform a less stable form of capital flows. I do not see much basis for this presumption. Long-term loans are, of course, less liquid than short-term ones. But, they can typically be prepaid or sold at a discount, and, in any case, when a country has accumulated a significant amount of international debt, the size of the amortizations quotas coming due in the short run are at least as hot as short-term debts. Similar considerations can be made about foreign investments: Despite being less liquid, they can accrue substantial repatriation rights over undistributed past profits.

The second problem is generally posed in terms of either conserving or relinquishing sovereignty over monetary policy. Changes in monetary policy typically induce changes in interest rates and, under free capital mobility, in capital flows and exchange rates. Exchange rate stability would then require either relinquishing monetary independence (as in a standard "currency board" monetary regime) or massive sterilized Central Bank interventions in the foreign exchange market. If such interventions are not able to neutralize large swings in capital flows, exchange controls would serve as a complementary tool. Therefore, restrictions on inflows (outflows) would be graduated so as to offset any appreciating (depreciating) pressures that would undermine exchange rate stability.

The argument for placing exchange controls has been important in Chile. Chile has followed a policy of stable real exchange rates and also desires to maintain some monetary policy sovereignty. Therefore, it has relied, among other things, on exchange controls.

3   Real exchange rate policy and capital mobility

As indicated already, policy makers in general show a strong preference for nominal exchange rate stability. Fixed exchange rate regimes are of course the purest expression of this preference. There are good reasons for adopting such regimes, such as imposing price discipline and fostering international trade. And it is well known that under a fixed exchange rate regime, such as the Argentine one, money supply is clearly endogenous, so macroeconomic policy loses a powerful instrument. This is also the case when the devaluation rate is preannounced by a "tablita" (as in Mexico until 1993).

Since the abandoning of the fixed exchange rate regime in 1982, Chile has followed a policy of stabilizing the real exchange rate (RER) as a key component of its export-oriented growth strategy. Unlike some Asian tigers, export promotion in Chile has not taken the shape of microeconomic interventions by the government. Instead, it has chosen a market-based approach that stresses the remotion of policy-induced antiexport biases and the stabilization of the RER around its estimated long-term equilibrium level.[19] The Central Bank has been put in charge of the complex task of ascertaining the level and the arduous one of implementing the corresponding policy measures.

A RER policy may also be inconsistent with an independent monetary policy aimed at the stabilization of the RER. For example, a monetary contraction either directly (through a reduction in absorption) or indirectly (by increasing domestic interest rates and capital flows) tends to cause an appreciation in the RER. A "RER policy" may thus also involve the relinquishing of an autonomous monetary policy.

It would be beyond the scope of this chapter to explain the different fiscal, commercial, and external debt policy measures taken in Chile with the aim of stabilizing the RER around its estimated long-term equilibrium level and, at the same time, preserving the monetary sovereignty needed to fight domestic inflation. Of course, central banks do not have much power to influence RER by only manipulating nominal exchange rates. Still, it is useful to present the menu of policies applied:

(a) Substantial fiscal adjustment: A nonfinancial public-sector deficit of 4.4% of GDP in 1984 was turned into an average surplus of 2.9% of GDP in 1988–1992. Fiscal austerity was helped by the creation in 1985 of the Copper Stabilization Fund, which ensured that windfall profits accrued to the government from its copper company (CODELCO) in the high-price period of 1988–1992 were saved.

(b) Adjustments in import tariffs: During the 1983–1984 balance-of-payments crises, import tariffs were raised from a quasi-uniform level of 10% to 35% in two steps. They were taken back to 20% in 1985 to accommodate a real devaluation of the peso. When balance-of-payments prospects improved, tariffs were again reduced in 1988 to 15% and in 1991 to 11%.

(c) Exchange controls: As explained in section 1, controls on capital outflows were stepped up in 1982–1984 to implement the external debt rescheduling process. Later, when the problem became the exact opposite one, restrictions were placed on capital inflows and certain outflows were liberalized.

(d) External debt prepayments: Capital repatriations and foreign invest-

---

[19] For the concept of "equilibrium" RER, see Edwards (1989).

ments were allowed through debt conversion mechanisms in 1985. Since the allowed quota of debt conversions was set by the Central Bank, the pressures over the exchange rate market could be managed. Later, the Central Bank engaged in official buyback operations in 1988–1989 and in 1993.

(e) Accumulation of international reserves: In order to prevent an excessive appreciation of the peso in real terms the Central Bank accumulated substantial reserves. On average, the yearly balance-of-payments surpluses amounted to U.S.$1.5 billions or 5% of GDP in 1988–1992, taking the stock of international reserves to a level equivalent to 22% of GDP by end-1993. The monetary impact of reserve accumulation has been systematically sterilized.

(f) Direct Central Bank intervention in the exchange market:[20] (1) An exchange rate policy sets a currency band or zone around a moving central parity; (2) the central parity is adjusted on a daily basis so as to keep constant the RER of the peso against a basket of currencies; (3) the width of the band started at +/−0.5% in 1984 and has been amplified in several steps to +/−10%; (4) the Central Bank modifies in a stepwise fashion the central parity level as its perception of the long-term equilibrium RER level changes.

The combination of policies listed here has been successful in stabilizing the real exchange rate, despite fluctuations in terms of trade, interest rates, and capital flows. The observed stability of the RER has been considered a key factor in the strong growth shown by exports during the past eight years. Inflation was kept at around 20% per year in the second half of the 1980s and gradually reduced to about 12% in 1992–1993. Monetary policy has been quite active. Somehow, it seems that pursuing the real exchange objective has not meant a significant loss of monetary sovereignty. Domestic interest rates have fluctuated following monetary policy changes, with some independence from changes in international rates.

Despite this essentially successful experience, I would like to discuss some of the costs and benefits of these policies aimed at stabilizing the RER and preserving monetary independence. The costs are associated with sterilized interventions and exchange controls; the benefits, with export-oriented growth.

Sterilized foreign exchange interventions are often discredited as either useless or counterproductive. Their usefulness cannot be denied when facing a balance-of-payments deficit: As long as they last, international reserves can be used as a buffer stock preventing steep depreciations; but, of course, in "a

---

[20] Chilean exchange rate policy since 1984 is notably similar to that advocated by Williamson (1985) and recently studied by Krugman (1992) and others.

speculative attack," reserves typically become exhausted quite rapidly. In the opposite situation, when there is a surplus of foreign exchange to be absorbed by the Central Bank, sterilized intervention will be useless only if the country faces a perfectly elastic supply of foreign capital. Then any attempt to keep interest rates above the level at which such supply becomes horizontal will be totally futile: Capital will keep on flowing and reserves will grow explosively. But in more realistic cases, when capital flows are limited by an upward sloping supply curve or by adjustment costs, interest differentials can be maintained by appropriate sterilized interventions.

The question still arises whether the costs of sterilized interventions outweigh their benefits. The costs are equivalent to the difference between the domestic currency cost of funds to the Central Bank and the return it gets on its holdings of reserves. In some cases, weak domestic capital markets or bad reputation prevent the Central Bank from issuing domestic debt at reasonable costs to fund reserve accumulations. In such cases, monetary control can only be kept through rather limited coercive measures, such as reserve requirements or the use of a fiscal surplus for monetary sterilization purposes.

But Chile enjoys a deep capital market, so reserve accumulation can be funded with domestic debt. In principle this can be done in large proportions: In Chile internal Central Bank debt amounts to 26% of GDP and a third of financial savings. There are no signs its creditors are feeling uneasy. This is not public debt used to finance fiscal spending, but to acquire an outside asset, namely, international reserves. Still, the cost of funds of the Chilean Central Bank has been higher than the return on international reserves. This is what one would expect if domestic interest rates are above international ones. I estimate that the yearly cost to the Central Bank of holding "excess international reserves" has been of the order of U.S.$130 million or 0.3% of GDP in 1993.[21] But, of course, this cost is very dependent on its funding and investment strategies. My feeling is that costs can be substantially reduced if the Central Bank, acting more like a private bank or investment fund, paid more attention to optimal funding and investment strategies.

When foreign exchange interventions are deemed impotent or too costly, the Central Bank has resorted to exchange controls. As described in section 1, in the mid-1980s, when there was a deficit of foreign exchange and reserves were scarce, these controls restricted capital *outflows*. This is the case referred to earlier in which controls are applied in a crisis situation. But in the early 1990s things changed and the Central Bank introduced capital

---

[21] This estimation assumes "normal" reserves at 6 months of imports and thus "excess reserves" at U.S.$4,700 million; their real peso return is estimated at 3.8% – that is, LIBOR plus a devaluation of the peso equal to domestic inflation – and marginal cost of funds to the Central Bank is estimated at 6.5%. Of course, this computation is very sensitive to changes in the RER.

controls to limit *inflows*, and thus reduce the size of its foreign exchange interventions and associated costs. Have these restrictions performed their objective? Have they been too costly?

It would be beyond the scope of this chapter to provide a full answer to these questions. Of course, the counterfactual analysis of how the Chilean economy would have performed without these restrictions is highly difficult to do. Anyway, we know that despite their implementation by mid-1991, capital inflows continued very strong in the second half of that year, and in the following 2 years. The nature of the flows though did change: less short-term credits (now heavily taxed) and more portfolio investments (exempted from restrictions). Also, in the current account, nonfactor services improved significantly, probably as a consequence of some disguised (and untaxed) capital inflows.

The costs of these measures have not been insignificant. Trade financing has become dearer, something that damages the competitiveness of exports. Project financing, although to a smaller extent, has also been affected. Firms allowed to raise equity abroad have been granted a competitive advantage. Firms willing to receive capital inflows through the informal exchange market have also been given a competitive advantage. Foreign portfolio investment has been given a better treatment than debt and, consequently, the stock market has boomed. In sum, resource allocation distortions have been intro-duced in order to ameliorate the quasi-fiscal cost of sterilized foreign market interventions.

Were there less costly options? In my view, there indeed were two routes that were to some extent explored, but with insufficient emphasis. One is the further opening of the capital account. Private capital outflows can replicate sterilized interventions. Instead of the Central Bank being in charge of raising resources domestically to invest abroad, that task is left to private firms, banks, or fund managers. Private incentives probably ensure that the funding is done at the minimum cost and that the mix of investments is efficient. Central banks do not typically face the right incentives.

The big question is whether such options will actually cause private capital outflows. For example, lifting restrictions on debt prepayments or early repatriations of foreign investment, as was done in Chile in 1991–1992, may end up stimulating more capital inflows, as their risk is reduced.[22] On the other hand, domestic investors may not be very interested in sending their capital abroad if returns are higher at home than abroad. For example, the cautious steps taken in Chile to allow some international portfolio diversifica-tion by banks and pension funds (i.e., allowing them to invest in fixed-income instruments of low-risk countries) have resulted in negligible capital outflows.

---

[22] See Labán and Larraín (1993) for an elegant proof based on irreversible investments.

However, it all depends on the attractiveness and variety of the allowed foreign investment options. For example, direct foreign investment abroad by Chilean companies has lately become a significant outflow of capital. Similar results could be expected if commercial banks were allowed more room to lend or invest abroad. Pension funds could also be willing to forgo high domestic returns in order to achieve a more diversified portfolio, were they allowed to.

Aside from lifting restrictions on capital outflows, the other option to capital controls is, in my opinion, to tolerate more volatility in exchange rates. As said earlier, the root of the loss of monetary sovereignty can be found not in capital flows per se, but in a Central Bank's decision to stabilize exchange rates. This may be a reasonable intermediate objective for a country that is starting an export-oriented growth strategy, in which private investors must be given some sense of stability in export incentives[23] (and if not given by the RER, then probably some distortionary subsidies would be called for). But the required RER stability need not be absolute and, over time, may well be replaced by more flexible formulas.

The route followed by the Chilean exchange rate policy has been consistent with the above considerations. As explained, the Central Bank provides stability for the RER within a band, one that has been gradually increased to +/−10%. In principle such a band allows great exchange rate flexibility. In addition, the central parity and the upper and lower bounds of the currency band for the U.S. dollar fluctuate on a daily basis according to the changes in the international parity of the U.S. dollar vis-à-vis the German mark (DM) and the yen (Y). This provides an additional source of nominal exchange rate uncertainty in Chile, one that is particularly relevant when the market exchange rate is close to the "floor" or the "ceiling" of the currency band.

Exchange rate flexibility is important on two grounds. First, in the presence of capital movements, changes in exchange rates act as a sort of automatic stabilizer. A significant appreciation (depreciation) of the currency tends to diminish capital inflows (outflows) because, at some point, it induces the expectation of a future devaluation (revaluation). This, of course, is the well-known argument in favor of "stabilizing speculation" and floating exchange rates.[24] It is also the basis for the exchange rate overshooting its long-term level when monetary policies change.[25]

This automatic stabilizing property is, of course, far from perfect. The

[23] See Labán and Larraín (1993) for a list of authors showing that RER stability has promoted export growth. Larraín and Vergara (1993) provide evidence supporting their contention that RER stability stimulated investment in Southeast Asian countries.

[24] Friedman (1953).

[25] Dornbusch (1976).

overshooting model assumes agents have a view of the long-run equilibrium exchange rate which is inelastic relative to current realizations of this variable.[26] In practice, market expectations may be positively correlated with spot prices, for some range of exchange rate fluctuations. If this is the case, the exchange rate swings needed to stabilize capital flows can be very significant. But, in the end, they do work. This seems to be the experience from the long and wide fluctuations of the main international currencies since 1971.

In addition to the stabilizing function, exchange rate volatility by itself increases the risks associated with uncovered interest arbitrage. This risk can be hedged through futures, forwards, and other arrangements, but this involves a cost. Historically, this cost has been an argument for eliminating exchange risks and pegging the exchange rate: Financial integration seems better served by fixed exchange rates. But, on the other hand, financial integration may induce undesired movements in real exchange rates and, as said, in order to prevent them central banks may end up erecting artificial barriers, such as capital controls.[27] Therefore, the "natural" barrier to capital movements provided by some real exchange rate volatility may not be a bad solution.

In the Chilean exchange rate mechanism, this is the role that should be performed by the amplitude of the currency bands and their link to the highly volatile international parities. This latter measure was adopted in mid-1992, when – due to strong capital inflows – the spot rate was close to the "floor" of the currency band. The system was in essence operating under a crawling peg to the U.S. dollar. Once linked to DM/U.S.\$ and Y/U.S.\$ rates, the "floor" became volatile and the cost of interest arbitrage increased correspondingly.[28] This seems to be one factor – there are others[29] – explaining why spot rates have never since come to the floor of the band.

[26] Dornbusch's model of exchange rate overshooting starts from the interest parity condition, $i - i^* = x$, where i and i^* are, respectively, the domestic and external interest rates and x the expected rate of devaluation. Such rate can be defined as $x = e' - e$, where e' stands for the (log of the) expected long run or fundamental exchange rate level and e for the (log of the) spot exchange rate. The model converges only if $dx/de < 0$, which requires $de'/de < 1$.

[27] Put in other words, fixed exchange rate systems or RER stabilization policies introduce a sort of implicit insurance against exchange risks. In such regimes even if RERs do change, they do it slowly and thus leave ample room for speculators to adjust portfolios. Elsewhere I have argued this was a prime cause of excessive capital inflows to Chile in the late 1970s (see Fontaine, 1983, 1989a). Valdés-Prieto (1992) stresses this point also. In my opinion this problem is also quite relevant for understanding recent capital inflows to Argentina and Mexico.

[28] See Fontaine (1992) for a full exposition of the arguments in favor of linking the Chilean exchange rate policy to a basket of currencies.

[29] Other factors are additional regulations limiting open foreign exchange positions held by banks, increased frequency of Central Bank interventions, and, since early 1993, a moderate change in expectations due to the deterioration of the trade balance.

This consideration must be taken into account by monetary authorities when engaging in foreign exchange interventions. In Chile the Central Bank has increasingly become involved in intervention at interior points of the band. These are supposed to iron out "unjustified," short-run movements in exchange rates. But if this is done too frequently, then a de facto peg is born, with corresponding implicit exchange rate insurance. In such a case, all the functions of exchange rate fluctuations cease and interest arbitrage is again made costless and with no automatic stabilizer.

In the end, as in so many areas of economic policy, there is a trade-off: financial openness versus real exchange rate stability. The trade-off can be avoided only at the expense of costly sterilized interventions. If such costs are deemed excessive, either financial openness must be sacrificed through capital controls or some degree of real exchange rate volatility accepted. My point is that without abandoning a general concern for some broad stabilization of the RER at its long-term equilibrium, economic policy should allow the market to determine short-term deviations around that level.

4 Are pension funds a special case?

In the previous two sections we have come to the conclusion that "normal" fluctuations in capital flows should be dealt with through a mix of sterilized interventions and foreign exchange volatility, and "abnormal" or "critical" fluctuations should be handled with temporary exchange or capital controls in order to avoid major disturbances in exchange or financial markets. The issue addressed in this section is whether some specific controls should be placed on capital movements by pension funds.

To some extent, pension funds are indeed a special case in the initial stages of a social security reform, as in Chile in the early 1980s or in Peru now. In such cases, placing some restrictions on external investments by newly created pension funds may serve two purposes: to develop a (typically lethargic) domestic capital market, and to help the public sector ease the "fiscal cost" of moving from a pay-as-you-go system to a fully funded one. The second function can be crucial. Social security reform typically not only faces formidable political pressures, but also has to deal with fiscal conservatives. For example, IMF missions, which conceivably could be natural allies for pension reform, by insisting on fiscal measures to offset transitional fiscal costs may end up blocking it. The possibility of having pension funds financing the transition between the two social security systems should eliminate such concerns, because the resulting fiscal deficit would not "crowd out" private spending.

Important as this reason is for placing some capital controls on pension funds, it does not necessarily call for full prohibition as in Chile up to 1990. It is also of a temporary nature. In time, if one purpose of the social security reform is to increase aggregate savings, its fiscal cost has to be dealt with through fiscal austerity measures. So a sound proposition might be to start with some restriction on external investments by pension funds (say, a 10% limit), which can be gradually lifted as the fiscal situation improves and the capital market matures. In Chile, for example, where the fiscal position is strong and the domestic capital market is well developed, I would argue that such a limit is not justified.

Aside from their role during the transition, are there other arguments for specific capital controls on pension funds? In general, as I will explain below, I feel pension funds should be subject to the same rules as any other economic agent with regard to foreign exchange regulations. However, given the authorities' preoccupation with RER stability and the large size of Chilean pension funds, one can argue that, under critical balance-of-payments conditions, they could be subjected to a specific restriction. The idea would be for the Central Bank – only under those critical conditions – to establish a limit to the amount capital pension funds can remit abroad in a given period of time, say, a month. In principle, the same restriction should be applied to capital inflows, but it may come into conflict with their obligation to liquidate their investments when facing net withdrawals. The monthly quota can be established for the whole pension fund industry, with individual portions of it allocated through auction. If this is not feasible, a second best would be to determine noncumulative individual monthly quotas.

The purpose of this restriction would be to reduce the volatility of capital flows originated in pension funds' decisions only in times of balance-of-payments crises. Of course, under normal circumstances any volatility in such flows should be permitted and the restrictions would not apply. The fundamental reason why these emergency restrictions would be specific to pension funds is none other than their large size and their ease of control. Our discussion in the previous section suggests that in general central banks should be prepared to accept some volatility in capital flows and exchange rates, but that their reluctance to tolerate extreme swings in these variables is understandable. Also, that under critical conditions, when a crisis of confidence arises, markets may act on the basis of erroneous information. Because of the size of pension funds, sudden changes in their portfolio can greatly disturb exchange markets. The purpose of the suggested restriction would be to introduce some sluggishness on such adjustments.[30] Note that the sug-

---

[30] A connected reason is that pension funds in Chile are committed to get a return on the portfolios they manage of at least a minimum between 50% of the pension fund industry-wide average or that average minus 200 basis points. This has created a strong tendency for them to choose similar portfolios: Deviations from the average portfolio are risky. Therefore, if pension funds are free to invest abroad one would expect all of them simultaneously to be moving capital inward or outward. I owe this comment to Salvador Valdés-Prieto who tells me this was pointed out to him by Alvaro Donoso.

gested "emergency" restriction would act on *flows* and not on *stocks,* as the current pension funds legislation envisages.

The two restrictions proposed here are the only ones I could justify as specific capital controls for pension funds.[31] Otherwise pension funds should follow general rules regarding capital movements.[32] And I prefer those rules to be quite liberal, except under critical conditions in the balance of payments. Of course, this does not mean that their investments abroad should be exempted from prudential risk diversification requirements similar to those applied to their domestic investments. The point is that (except under crises conditions), there are no (good) macroeconomic reasons to treat international investments by pension funds differently from local ones.

5   Summary

In this chapter we have discussed the macropolicy arguments for establishing exchange or capital controls, especially as they relate to pension funds. It has

---

[31] It may be argued that the preference of pension funds for long-term paper makes them less sensitive to short-run interest differentials, such as those that weaken monetary policy. This argument is highly debatable because it is not clear that monetary policy should concentrate only on short-term interest rates. After all, spending decisions, and thus inflationary pressures, are also affected by long-term rates. The construction industry, for example, is typically a victim of monetary contractions and is particularly sensitive to long-term rates. But even if that were the case, the long-term nature of pension funds as investors needs to be examined. This may be true for pension funds that offer a precommitted pension level (as life insurance companies). They have to match long-term liabilities with long-term assets. Chilean pension funds do not work that way: They simply manage their members' savings, and pension levels are ultimately determined by the accumulated funds (except for the minimun relative return referred to in note 30). Conceptually, they face as liabilities the withdrawls from their members who come to retirement age and the net flows lost to other pension funds. Since there is strong competition among pension funds and people can move from one to another on a 3-month notice, this latter liability is of short maturity. Thus, Chilean pension funds are not long-term investors. Their fixed-income portfolio has an average maturity of 3.5 years. They do hold, though, a significant proportion of their portfolio in shares (nearly 30%, the authorized maximum), which are often seen as a long-term investment, but given the booming stock market in Chile, this can also reflect short-term motivations. Therefore, I would not favor giving pension funds a special prerogative to invest abroad based on the hypothesis that they would not undermine monetary sovereignty.

[32] This conclusion is inconsistent with the spirit (if not the letter) of article 48 of the Central Bank Law. This article exempts foreign exchange operations by pension funds from administrative restrictions imposed by the Central Bank, other than those specified by law. Ironically, this precept was fiercely fought for by pension fund lobbies in order to get guaranteed access to foreign exchange and international diversification. But in doing so it created a privilege that can be regulated only by law. And legislators have been extremely cautious in this respect. In my opinion, had not the precedent been established that pension funds are a special case that deserves legislative level treatment, the Central Bank would have allowed them as much freedom to invest abroad as presently enjoyed by industrial firms and individuals.

been taken for granted, and presumed well known, that financial opening is in general a worthwhile objective. The discussion has been conducted against the background of the recent Chilean experience with capital controls and large pension funds.

General macroeconomic arguments for restricting capital flows are based on limiting tax avoidance, compensating certain market failures, and reducing exchange rate fluctuations.

In the current economic environment in Chile, the tax argument is not particularly relevant, and is clearly not applicable to pension funds. An important market failure can be identified in times of balance-of-payments crises, of a run against the domestic currency. Capital controls can then be a less costly option than a sharp overshooting in the exchange rate. Such capital controls should be strictly proportional to the depth of the crises and of a temporary nature. Ideally, they should be publicly justified on these grounds by the Central Bank, to stimulate a technical discussion on their applicability. They should be applied as across the board as much as possible, and include pension funds.

The prevention of real exchange rate volatility leads to a trade-off between relatively costly sterilized interventions and loss of monetary policy sovereignty. In my view, the trade-off can be eased if the private sector is allowed to perform some of the stabilization, which requires enabling it to invest abroad. Pension funds can help in this respect because they should be naturally inclined to maintain international diversification. On the other hand, the size and frequency of Central Bank foreign exchange interventions can be significantly reduced if some exchange rate volatility is allowed to remain, so interest arbitrage becomes more costly.

In a country like Chile, with a deep capital market (where sterilized interventions can be funded) and a strong export base (which can afford some RER fluctuations), I think general capital controls are not needed, except in times of balance-of-payments crises. Some monetary sovereignty can be maintained by a carefully balanced mix of sterilized interventions and exchange rate volatility.

In general, I see no reason for treating pension funds as a special case with respect to capital controls. But I would admit two exceptions to this conclusion. The first one is that limiting foreign investments by pension funds in the initial stages of a private social security system allows stimulation of the development of the domestic capital market and helps the state to finance the transition from a pay-as-you-go system to a fully funded one. The second justifies placing some quantitative restriction on capital movements by pension funds (specifically outflows) only under very critical balance-of-payments conditions, because by their large size pension funds can disturb the domestic exchange market. In the Chilean case, the first exemption is no longer valid, while the second may be in the future. Present regulations, imposing a (low) limit on the *stock* of foreign investments and not on the *outflow* generated by them, are not consistent with the argument presented here.

References

Calvo, A., Leiderman, L. and Reinhart, C. (1992). "Capital Flows to Latin America: The 1970s and the 1990s." IMF Working Paper. Washington, D.C., IMF, October.

(1993). "The Capital Inflows Problem: Concepts and Issues." Washington, D.C., IMF, June. Mimeograph.

Cheyre, H. (1991). *La Reforma Previsional en Chile*. Santiago, Chile, Centro de Estudios Públicos.

Dornbusch, R. (1976). "Expectations and Exchange Rate Dynamics." *Journal of Political Economy,* 84, no. 6, December, pp. 1161–1176

(1989). *Real Exchange Rates, Devaluation, and Adjustment.* Cambridge, Mass., MIT press.

Fontaine, J. A. (1983). "¿Qué pasó en la economía chilena?" *Estudios Públicos,* no. 22, Winter, pp. 11–73.

(1988). "Los mecanismos de conversión de deudas en Chile." *Estudios Públicos,* no. 30, Autumn, pp. 137–158.

(1989a). "The Chilean Economy in the Eighties: Adjustment and Recovery." In S. Edwards and F. Larraín, (eds.) 1989. *Debt, Adjustment and Recovery,* pp. 208–233. Oxford, Basil Blackwell.

(1989b). "Banco Central: autonomía para cautelar la estabilidad." *Cuadernos de Economía,* 26, no. 77, April, pp. 65–90.

(1992). "Una alternativa cambiaria." *Punto de Referencia,* Centro de Estudios Públicos, no. 98, June.

Friedman, M. (1953). "The Case for Flexible Exchange Rates." In *Essays in Positive Economics,* pp. 157–203.

Harberger, A. (1985). "Lessons for Debtor-Country Managers and Policymakers." In G. Smith and J. Cuddington (eds.), *International Debt and the Developing Countries.* Washington, D.C., World Bank.

Krause, L. (1991). *Speculation and the Dollar: The Political Economy of Exchange Rates.* Boulder, Colo., Westview Press.

Krugman, P. (1992). "Exchange Rates in a Currency Band: A sketch of the new approach." In P. Krugman and M. Miller (eds.), *Exchange Rate Targets and Currency Bands.* Cambridge, Cambridge University Press.

Labán, R. and F. Larraín (1993). "Twenty Years of Experience with Capital Mobility in Chile." April. Mimeograph.

(1994) "The Chilean Experience with Capital Mobility." In B. Bosworth, R. Dobusch and R. Labán, eds. *The Chilean Economy: Policy Lessons and Challenges,* pp. 117–163. Washington, D. C., Brookings Institution.

Larraín, F., and A. Velasco (1990). "Can Swaps Solve the Debt Crises? Lessons from the Chilean Experience," *Princeton Studies in International Finance* no. 69. Princeton University. Princeton N.J. November.

Larraín, F., and Vergara, R. (1993). "Investment and Macroeconomic Adjustment: The

Case of East Asia." In L. Lassen and A. Solimano (eds.), *Striving for Growth after Adjustment,* pp. 229–274. Washington, D.C., World Bank.

McKinnon, R. (1973). *Money and Capital in Economic Development.* Washington, D.C., Brookings Institution.

(1991). *The Order of Economic Liberalization: Financial Control in the Transition to a Market Economy.* Baltimore, Johns Hopkins University Press.

Shaw, E. (1973). *Financial Deepening in Economic Development.* New York, Oxford University Press.

Tobin, J. (1978). "A Proposal for International Monetary Reform." *Eastern Economic Journal* 4, July–October.

Valdés-Prieto, S. (1994). "Financial Liberalization and the Capital Account: Chile 1974–84." In G. Caprio, I. Atiyas and J. Hanson (eds.), *Financial Reform: Theory and Experience.* chap. 12. Cambridge, Cambridge University Press.

Valente, J. R. (1988). "Diversificación Internacional: Una Alternativa para las Necesidades de Inversión de los Fondos de Pensiones." Centro de Estudios Públicos. Documento de Trabajo no. 109, December.

(1991). "Inversión de los Fondos de Pensión en el Extranjero." Centro de Estudios Públicos. Documento de Trabajo no. 159, August.

Williamson, J. (1985). *The Exchange Rate System.* Washington, D.C., Institute for International Economics.

Zahler, R. (1992). "Política Monetaria en un Contexto de Apertura de Cuenta de Capitales." *Boletín Mensual* 771, pp. 1169–1180. Santiago, Banco Central de Chile, May.

PART IV

Policy and regulation of pension systems

CHAPTER 10

Pension choices and pensions policy in the United Kingdom

David Blake

1   Introduction

The United Kingdom has one of the richest and longest experiences of
pension provision anywhere in the world: The earliest recorded pension
scheme dates back to 1375. Largely because of this early lead, there have
been few significant outside influences on the development of British pensions. The outside influences that have occurred have been far between – for
example, the introduction of group life pension schemes from the United
States in the 1920s and the European Community's[1] various rulings on the
equal treatment of men and women from the 1970s.

The single most important influence on the development of U.K. pensions
and pension schemes has been the state itself. Historically, the state has provided pensions for the poor and for the mainly lower-paid workers who have
not had an employer's pension scheme to join; and it has provided, through
generous tax breaks and through the example of having good pension schemes
for its own employees, incentives for the private sector to establish reasonably
good occupational pension schemes; and more recently it has allowed individuals to set up their own personal pension schemes independent of the employer.

In other countries, people have looked to their employer or even to their
trade union to provide retirement benefits. But it seems doubtful in the U.K.
context of strong social class stratification whether the private sector would
have provided pensions much above the subsistence level without state
intervention. And for similar reasons, trade unions have not been involved in
providing pensions or indeed other personal finance services, given their
historical assertion that it is the responsibility of the bosses to provide decent
pensions in retirement.

I am extremely grateful for the very detailed and inciteful comments and suggestions made by
Salvador Valdés-Prieto on earlier drafts of this chapter.
[1] On November 1, 1993, the European Community became the European Union.

277

So the state's role has been paramount. But also of great importance has been the legal framework that has been used to operate occupational pension schemes, namely trust law. Trust law was originally established to protect the assets of medieval knights who had gone off to fight in the Crusades. Subsequently, discretionary trusts became the legal vehicle through which employers ran their occupational pension schemes. More recently, trust law was used as a framework for establishing personal pension schemes.

The development of the British pension system has therefore taken place under a common legal framework within the context of a stable long-term political environment. We are therefore in a position to discuss U.K. pensions free from the pitfalls often common to international comparisons. In this chapter, we analyze the pension choices currently available in the United Kingdom and the public policy issues facing the government both now and in the near future. In the light of this analysis, we draw conclusions relevant for consideration in other countries.

2   Pension choices

In this section, we examine and compare the extensive range of pension choices offered by the state, by companies, and by private-sector financial institutions. We find that the main choices are between a state pension system, which offers a relatively low level of pension that is fully indexed to prices after retirement; an occupational pension system, which offers a relatively high level of pension (partially indexed to prices after retirement), but, as a result of poor transfer values between schemes, only to workers who spend most of their working lives with the same company; and a personal pension system, which offers pensions that are based on uncertain investment returns (but again are only partially indexed to inflation) and benefit from complete portability between contracts of employment, but are subject to very high setup and administration costs, inappropriate sales tactics, and very low early-surrender values.

2.1   The range of available choices

Individuals in employment and in receipt of earnings subject to National Insurance contributions (NICs)[2] will build up entitlement both to the flat-rate basic state pension[3] and to the State Earnings-Related Pension Scheme

---

[2] NICs also build up entitlement to health service, sickness, and invalidity benefits and to the job seeker's allowance (formerly unemployment benefit).

[3] In 1994–1995, this was £57.60 per week for a single person and £92.10 per week for a married couple.

(SERPS pension).[4] These pensions are paid by the Department of Social Security (DSS). The self-employed are also entitled to a basic state pension, but not to a SERPS pension. Employees with earnings in excess of the lower earnings limit (LEL)[5] (the minimum earnings level for entitlement to membership of SERPS) will automatically be members of SERPS, unless they belong to an employer's occupational pension scheme[6] or to a personal pension scheme[7] that has been contracted-out of SERPS. In these cases, both the individual and the employer contracting-out receive a rebate on their NICs (1.8% of earnings for employees and 3.0% for employers) and the individual forgoes the right to receive a SERPS pension. However, there is no obligation on employers to operate their own pension scheme, nor, since 1988, is there any contractual requirement for an employee to join the employer's scheme if it has one.

There is now a very wide range of private sector pension schemes open to individuals. They can join their employer's occupational pension scheme (if it has one), which can be:

(i) a contracted-in final salary scheme (CIFSS),
(ii) a contracted-in money purchase scheme (CIMPS),
(iii) a contracted-out final salary scheme (COFSS), or
(iv) a contracted-out money purchase scheme (COMPS).

A CIFSS is a defined benefit scheme that has not been contracted-out of SERPS and so provides a salary-related pension in addition to the SERPS and basic state pensions. A CIMPS is a special type of defined contribution scheme that will be discussed in more detail. COFSSs must provide guaranteed minimum pensions (GMPs) equivalent to the value of SERPS benefits replaced; while COMPSs must make guaranteed minimum contributions (GMCs) equivalent to the contracted-out rebate. Individuals can also top up their schemes with additional voluntary contributions or free-standing additional voluntary contributions (up to limits permitted by the Inland Revenue).

---

[4] The basic state pension scheme began in 1927, although its present structure dates from 1948, whereas SERPS began in 1978.

[5] In 1994–1995, this was £57 per week: The LEL is always set equal to the nearest full £1 below the basic state pension.

[6] Occupational schemes began in the mid-19th century, although pension schemes provided by guilds of skilled artisans can be traced back to the late 14th century. Such schemes are generally administered by the companies themselves but the companies typically appoint a professional fund management group to invest scheme assets.

[7] Personal pension schemes began in 1988. There are three main types: endowment-linked schemes, deposit administration schemes, and unit-linked schemes. Such schemes are provided by, respectively, insurance companies, banks and building societies, and unit trusts (mutual funds). The pension annuity itself (the size of which depends on the value of the accumulated fund at retirement) must be provided by an insurance company.

As an alternative, employees now have the following personal pension choices that are independent of their employer's scheme:

(i) an appropriate personal pension scheme (APPS), which is contracted out of SERPS and provides protected rights that stand in place of SERPS benefits (also known as a minimum contribution or rebate-only personal pension scheme since the only contribution into it is the combined 4.8% rebate on NICs with the employee's share of the rebate grossed up for basic rate tax relief [of 25%]), or

(ii) an appropriate personal pension scheme that is also contracted out of SERPS but, as a result of additional contributions (although usually only from the employee), provides more generous benefits than under (i).

Individuals can be members of occupational schemes *and* have personal pensions only in the following circumstances:

(i)   the occupational scheme provides only a spouse's pension and/or a lump sum on death-in-service,

(ii) the occupational scheme is contracted-into SERPS and provides benefits in addition to those of SERPS but an appropriate personal pension scheme, based only on minimum contributions, is used to replace SERPS benefits only (this is the contracted-in money purchase scheme to which we referred earlier), or

(iii) members of occupational pension schemes can use personal pension schemes for the purpose of receiving transfer payments from previous schemes (in the case where the receiving scheme will not convert the transfer payment into an equivalent number of added years of service in the receiving scheme),[8]

(iv) individuals can be members of personal pension schemes while retaining deferred pensions in former occupational schemes.

In 1995, there were 21.5 million employees in work in the United Kingdom and another 2.5 million people who were self-employed. The pension arrangements of these people were as follows:

(i)   6.75 million employees entitled to a state pension but not members of a company pension scheme,

(ii) 1.5 million employees in SERPS plus a company pension scheme,

(iii) 9.5 million employees in a company pension scheme that is contracted out of SERPS (almost all of these employees belong to COFSSs),

(iv) 3.75 million employees in personal pension schemes (mainly APPSs),

---

[8] They can also use deferred annuity contracts (called section 32 buyout policies) provided by life companies for this purpose.

(v)   1.25 million self-employed in personal pension schemes,
(vi) 1.25 million self-employed without a personal pension other than the
      basic state pension.

This means that in 1995, about 70% of pension scheme members in the
United Kingdom were members of SERPS or an occupational pension
scheme and 30% were members of personal pension schemes. What factors
motivated these choices?

2.2   The choice between SERPS and an occupational pension
         scheme

All employees with sufficient NICs are entitled to the full basic state pension,[9] which for a single person is currently equal to about 20% of national
average earnings.[10] On the other hand, SERPS provides a maximum pension
of only 25% of an individual's average revalued earnings (up to the upper
earnings limit or UEL)[11] when the scheme matures in 1998.[12] This, in turn,
implies that the maximum SERPS pension will equal about 20% of national
average earnings. So the total current maximum pension available from the
combined state schemes is only 40% of national average earnings.[13]

---

[9] Payment of the full rate of pension requires NICs to have been paid for a minimum number
   of qualifying years between the age of 16 and the year of retirement. The number of
   qualifying years is related to the length of working life. For example, if the length of working
   life since age 16 is 10 years or less, the number of qualifying years is the length of working
   life less 1 year, whereas if the length of working life is more than 41 years, the number of
   qualifying years is the length of working life less 5 years. A reduced rate pension may be paid
   if someone has at least one-quarter of the required number of qualifying years; otherwise the
   individual will have to rely on a subsistence state benefit called income support.

[10] In 1994–1995, national average earnings were £317 per week or around £16,500 per year.

[11] In 1994–1995, this was £430 per week.

[12] The SERPS pension is equal to 1.25% of the individual's average revalued earnings (or
   earnings factors) within the earnings band between the LEL and UEL for each year of
   membership of SERPS from 1978 up to a maximum of 20 years. The best 20 years' earnings
   within the band are revalued by the annual increase in national average earnings up to
   retirement. The maximum SERPS pension is therefore 25% of average revalued earnings. The
   contribution conditions are the same as for the basic state pension. After retirement, both the
   basic state pension and the SERPS pension are fully indexed to the retail price level.

[13] The 1986 Social Security Act reduced the value of the SERPS program for those retiring after
   1999 to an estimated maximum of 16% of national average earnings. This is because the
   SERPS pension will then equal 1% of career-revalued earnings within the earnings band
   between the LEL and UEL for each year of membership of SERPS until state pension age.
   The maximum SERPS pension would therefore fall to 20% of an individual's career-revalued
   earnings. In addition, contributions have to be paid throughout the career. The 1995 Pensions
   Act has reduced the value of the SERPS pension even further for those retiring after 2000 by
   reducing the size of the earnings band on which the final pension is based. By 2050, the
   maximum SERPS pension will fall to only 7% of national average earnings.

Apart from the relatively low pension at retirement, SERPS has a number of other potential disadvantages. For example, SERPS does not provide:

(i)   income tax relief on employees' contributions,
(ii) a transfer value to take to a private-sector scheme,
(iii) a return of contributions on death before retirement,
(iv) the opportunity to make additional voluntary contributions into SERPS (although it is possible to take out a separate personal pension to supplement the SERPS pension),
(v)   any possibility of early retirement before state pension age (65 for men and 60 for women),[14]
(vi) a tax-free lump sum at retirement (in return for a lower pension),
(vii) a widow's pension if the widow is under age 45 (unless there is a dependent child).

The main advantage of the state pension is that it is fully indexed to retail price inflation. Another advantage is that there is an automatic right for a member of an occupational scheme to recontract back into SERPS on payment of a *transfer premium* from the occupational scheme, which is calculated by the DSS and which extinguishes the obligation of the scheme to provide a GMP for that member; this is useful in the event that the occupational scheme is wound up following the insolvency of the sponsoring company.

A contracted-out occupational pension scheme, on the other hand, offers a maximum pension of 67% of final salary[15] (together with the security of an accumulated fund). But this has only limited price indexation (LPI) up to a maximum of 5% per year, although companies can, if they have the resources, provide more generous increases, including full indexation to retail prices (although they may not provide more than full indexation – so they could not, for example, index the pension to earnings, which in the United Kingdom grow at about 2% per annum more than prices). Furthermore, occupational pension schemes provide all the seven benefits listed previously.

In return for these pensions, the employee's contribution rate is 1.8% of earnings for SERPS membership (i.e., the implied contribution rate is equal to the employee's contracted-out rebate on NICs) and about 5.5% of earnings for membership of an occupational scheme.[16] The employer's contribution rate is 3.0.% of earnings for SERPS membership (i.e., the employer's contracted-out rebate on NICs) and about 9.75% of earnings for an occupa-

---

[14] As a result of the 1995 Pensions Act, the state pension age for women is being raised progressively to 65 over a 10-year period between 2010 and 2020.

[15] The pension accrual rate is 1.67% of final salary for each year of service up to a maximum of 40 years' service.

[16] The employee's take-home pay is raised by the amount of the contracted-out rebate but then lowered by more than this because of the higher contribution into the employer's scheme; the rebate does not go directly into the employer's scheme.

tional scheme.[17] Therefore the total cost of SERPS membership is 4.8% of earnings, while the total cost of an occupational pension scheme is 15.25% of earnings on average, more than three times as much.

So contracted-out schemes provide more generous benefits than contracted-in schemes, but at much higher cost. The state scheme was designed to provide only a minimum level of benefits for those on below-average salaries who were not able to join an employer's scheme. Nevertheless, the SERPS pension is provided at very low cost to SERPS members. In fact, the SERPS pension currently has a very high implied real rate of return on contributions of 6.7% per annum, which is double that on contributions toward a typical occupational pension scheme (3.3% per annum).[18]

When comparing SERPS and an occupational scheme, we can draw the following conclusions. SERPS is a suitable pension scheme for employees on modest salaries or for employees who tend to change jobs frequently. It is also suitable for small firms without a system of administration for handling an occupational scheme. But, for more highly paid employees and for larger companies, the benefits of an occupational scheme dominate the simplicity of SERPS.

However, membership of occupational pension schemes has been voluntary since 1988. The evidence from a National Association of Pension Funds survey in July 1993 indicates that 19% of new employees who would have accepted automatic membership of their company's pension scheme have not bothered to do so given that this now has to be a positive decision that immediately reduces their current disposable income. For many, this is clear evidence of myopia, but some indicated that they were aware that this was not a sensible long-term decision, although natural inertia often prevented them joining the pension scheme for some time after they joined the company.[19] The consequence of this is that such individuals remain members of SERPS by default. This means that individuals in aggregate may now save less for their pensions than before.

2.3   The choice between SERPS and a personal pension scheme

It is difficult to compare SERPS and a personal pension scheme because so many assumptions have to be made about likely investment returns, earnings

---

[17] The employer's contribution into an employee's pension scheme is not regarded as additional employee earnings for tax purposes. However, the employer does enjoy tax relief on its contributions to exempt-approved schemes.

[18] This is demonstrated in Appendix A.

[19] This means they are aware of time inconsistency, the (impossible) wish, once they are old, that they had saved more when they were young, but nevertheless discount this temporarily.

growth, and inflation. However, it is important to take the following list of factors into account:

(i) age – the younger an individual is, the greater the time that there is for personal pension contributions and the returns on them to accumulate;

(ii) sex – state pensions for men begin five years later than for women;[20]

(iii) special bonus – there was a special incentive in terms of an additional contracted-out rebate for those taking out personal pensions between 1988 (the year in which they first became available) and 1996;

(iv) anticipated investment performance – a return is expected to be generated on personal pension savings, especially in relation to inflation and after taking into account commissions and management costs;

(v) risk – SERPS provides an earnings-related pension at retirement that is guaranteed, whereas a personal pension offers the chance of a higher pension (with no limit to the maximum pension permissible) but at the risk that the investment performance is disastrous and with the further possibility that the insurance company offering the subsequent pension annuity might become insolvent;

(vi) inflation indexation – the SERPS pension is fully indexed whereas the personal pension has only LPI up to a maximum of 3% per year; individuals can choose to have a fully indexed personal pension, but the starting value of the pension is reduced accordingly.

Table 10.1 presents estimates of the pension (as a proportion of earnings) that could be expected for men and women at different ages from membership of, respectively, a personal pension scheme and SERPS for the same contributions. The assumptions made are listed at the bottom of the table. The table shows that, with these assumptions, men older than 45 years and women older than 35 years are better off staying in SERPS. Employees below these ages can expect to receive larger pensions as a proportion of pay by opting for personal pensions. However, this is not guaranteed. On the other hand, there is no limit to the maximum personal pension that can be achieved. But, unlike the SERPS pension, the personal pension only has to be partially indexed to inflation up to 3% per year.

Many members of personal pension schemes will make contributions higher than those implied by Table 10.1. Members of SERPS are not able to do so. On average, contributions into those personal pension schemes that are not simply rebate-only are about 6% of earnings (in addition to the NI rebate). The expected personal pension (as a proportion of earnings) in this case is therefore

[20] However, see note 14.

Table 10.1
Comparison between personal pensions and SERPS
(no previous contributions into any other pension scheme)

Age in 1988	Men		Women	
	Personal Pension(a) (% of salary)	SERPS (% of salary)	Personal Pension (a) (% of salary)	SERPS (% of salary)
20	25.4	14.7	18.5	14.6
25	21.9	13.1	15.9	12.8
30	18.7	12.5	13.4	12.0
35	15.9	12.0	11.2	11.5
40	13.3	11.5	9.0	10.7
45	10.7	10.7	6.9	9.6
50	8.1	9.6	4.8	8.9
55	5.6	8.0	2.6	4.0
60	3.1	4.0	-	-

(a) Contributions comprise NI rebate plus 2pc special bonus for five years.

Assumptions: salary increases by 6.5p.c. p.a.; National Insurance lower earnings limit/upper earnings limit increases by 6.5p.c. p.a.; investment return 8.5p.c. p.a.; personal pension increases by 3p.c. p.a.; personal pension expenses 10p.c. p.a.; inflation 5p.c. p.a.; allowance is also made for a reducing rebate and tax relief on employee contributions.

Source: Wolanski & Co., *Daily Telegraph*, October 18, 1986.

much higher than indicated in Table 10.1. This is likely to make personal pension schemes much more attractive than SERPS for higher paid workers.

2.4 The choice between an occupational pension scheme and a personal pension scheme

Perhaps the most important choice that has to be made in terms of pensions is the one between a defined benefit occupational pension scheme and a defined contribution personal pension scheme. It is also the most difficult choice to make, because the outcome will not be known before the time of retirement, when it is too late to do anything about it.

The main advantages of an occupational pension scheme are:

(i)   the pension is guaranteed to be related to salary at or near retirement; this is beneficial for people who expect rapid promotion or if there is substantial wage inflation;

(ii) the employer is obliged to contribute to the scheme[21] as well as the employee; the average employee contribution is 5.5% of salary, but

---

[21] If it has one, although there is no obligation for the employer to have a scheme.

the average employer contribution is 9.75% of salary and most employees appear not to be aware of this additional tax-free element to their remuneration package;

(iii)   additional benefits such as early retirement on the grounds of ill-health and death-in-service benefits are automatically provided.

The main disadvantages of an occupational pension scheme are:

(i)   the pension is limited to a fraction of preretirement income, at most two-thirds of final salary;

(ii)   the pension is linked to a particular contract of employment;

(iii) preserved pension rights or transfer values between schemes tend to be very poor, thereby reducing the overall pension available at retirement (this is probably the most serious disadvantage of occupational schemes);

(iv)   the member has no control over the investments in the scheme;

(v)   the accruing pension assets cannot readily be used as security for a loan; in other words, the pension assets are almost completely illiquid until retirement, although this is beginning to change as a result of competition from personal pension schemes;

(vi)   an individual can be fired or made redundant in which case the pension will be linked to the salary at the time of firing or redundancy, not at retirement.

The main advantages of a personal pension scheme are:

(i)   there is no limit to the size of the pension at retirement;

(ii)   the pension scheme is not linked to a contract of employment;

(iii) the pension scheme is portable and so can be taken with a person when he or she changes jobs; so there is no problem with transfer values between schemes as with occupational pensions;

(iv)   the member has some influence over the investments in the scheme and can choose the scheme provider;

(v)   the accruing pension assets can be used as security for a pension loan or pension mortgage;

(vi)   there was a 2% special bonus for individuals taking out personal pensions between 1988 and 1993, then 1% between 1993 and 1996 (as long as they had not been contracted out of SERPS before);

(vii) the pension scheme is very flexible in terms of changed circumstances – for example, it is possible to reduce or stop making contributions altogether in the event of being made unemployed;

(viii) there is a carry-forward facility, so that it is possible to make higher than permitted tax-relieved contributions in the current year based on unused contribution limits over the previous six years;

(ix)   there is a carry-back facility, so that it is possible to make contribu-
       tions in a year when there are no net relevant earnings (say as a
       result of unemployment or maternity leave) and to have the contribu-
       tions set against earnings in the previous tax year.

The main disadvantages of a personal pension scheme are:

(i)   the size of the pension is not guaranteed and if the investments
       perform badly, the pension will be low;
(ii)   the employer is not obliged to and is also not likely to contribute to
       a personal pension scheme;[22]
(iii) additional benefits such as early retirement on the grounds of ill-
       health and death-in-service benefits require additional contributions
       (in total up to 5% of earnings can be used to provide for these
       benefits);
(iv)   there is no automatic right to rejoin the employer's scheme;
(v)   the full cost of administering the pension scheme is borne by the
       member; this cost (which may be disguised) can be quite high,
       between 10% and 20% of premiums in contrast with between 5%
       and 7% of premiums for occupational schemes;[23]
(vi)   the costs of transferring between personal pension schemes is quite
       high: This could be important if there is dissatisfaction with the
       investment performance or administration of the current personal
       pension scheme;
(vii) because of their recent introduction, there is no long-term data on
       the adequacy of personal pension schemes.

One of the most important factors determining whether it is financially
beneficial to join a personal pension scheme is the age at commencement of
the scheme. Table 10.2 shows the contributions to a personal pension scheme
at different commencement ages needed to achieve a pension of two-thirds of
final salary at retirement. Only someone taking out a personal pension scheme
before the age of about 35 is likely to be able to afford the necessary
contributions, while anyone taking one out after the age of 40 would not be
permitted to make the required contributions. These examples suggest that
only very young people are likely to get a pension from a money purchase
scheme that is close to the two-thirds of final salary available from an
occupational scheme and even then this pension is not guaranteed.

The choice between an occupational scheme and a personal scheme will

---

[22] It is also unlikely that employees would be able to negotiate higher pay to compensate for
this. The fact that employees are prepared to forgo the employer's contribution without any
compensating increase in their gross pay provides evidence of either ignorance or irrationality
on their part.

[23] A complete analysis of costs in personal pension schemes is provided in Appendix B.

Table 10.2
Contributions needed to achieve a pension of
two-thirds final salary
(no previous contributions into any other pension scheme)

Age at Commencement (male)	Required Contributions (% of salary)	Maximum Contributions (% of salary)
25	10.90	17.5
30	13.41	17.5
35	16.81	17.5
40	21.66	20.0
45	28.92	20.0
50	40.81	25.0
55	64.15	30.0
60	129.83	35.0

Assumptions: Male retiring at age 65; no previous contributions into any other pension scheme; salary increases by 3 p.c. p.a.; investment return 6 p.c. p.a.

Source: Save and Prosper, *Daily Telegraph*, November 13, 1993.

be determined mainly by the age of the individual,[24] the anticipated number of job changes during the career, and the individual's attitude to risk. Personal pension schemes will be favored principally by young mobile people with a low degree of risk aversion. For people who work for a company with a good occupational pension scheme and who intend to remain with the company for the remainder of their careers, the occupational scheme is likely to be the better choice.

There is also evidence that high-pressure sales tactics have been used to persuade members of occupational pension schemes (especially older long-serving members) to switch into inappropriate personal pension schemes: Sales agents had sought too little information from potential clients to be able to give them proper advice. In October 1993 the Securities and Investments Board (SIB) reprimanded the North of England Building Society following a routine inspection of 600 schemes, which revealed that one-third of clients

---

[24] Although the starting age of the individual when he or she joined a personal pension scheme would not be so important if it was possible for the personal scheme to receive a fair-value transfer from the occupational scheme. One of the great weaknesses of the entire British pension system is the lack of transparent transfer rules between SERPS, occupational, and personal pension schemes.

had been wrongly advised to switch out of occupational schemes. In November 1993 LAUTRO (the Life Assurance and Unit Trust Regulatory Organisation, which has now been replaced by the Personal Investment Authority) conducted a survey of personal schemes taken out during the third quarter of 1992 and found that 50,000 schemes had lapsed within one year. In December 1993 the SIB announced it would undertake a more general review of the personal pension schemes of up to 500,000 individuals who had transferred £7 billion out of occupational schemes since 1988. Both LAUTRO and the SIB had established working parties to consider possible compensation, which may run into hundreds of millions of pounds. The initial evidence suggested that as many as 90% of these individuals had been given inappropriate advice.

The great flexibility offered by personal pension schemes is offset somewhat by the high costs (often disguised) charged by the organizers of the schemes.

With pension schemes arranged by insurance companies, the costs fall into three parts: initial commissions, annual management fees, and early surrender values. Annual management fees are similar to those charged elsewhere in the U.K. fund management industry, although there can be quite large relative differences between different management groups: The typical range is between 0.5% and 1.5% of the fund value. The big differences arise over the methods for extracting initial commissions and for calculating early surrender values. For example, in Appendix B we found that pension schemes extracting initial commissions using capital units would end up delivering pensions that were 10% lower than schemes involving recurring single premiums. We also found that surrender values for with-profits endowment schemes were on average 27% below maturity values when cashed in just 1 year to maturity. On top of this, charges can be imposed in a bewildering variety of ways. Apart from initial commissions and annual fund management fees, there can be fixed monthly "administration" charges and a "nil allocation" period of up to a year during which none of the member's contributions are allocated to investments. Most of the money collected during the nil allocation period is used to pay sales agents' commissions. Most of the charges are disguised in the small print of the policy documentation.

Pension schemes organized by unit trusts have much simpler charging structures than those organized by insurance companies. Nevertheless, charges can be imposed in a misleading way. This is because unit trusts are required to publish four different prices for their units: the offer price (the price that new investors pay for their units), the bid price (the price at which existing investors can sell their units), the cancellation price (the minimum bid price), and the initial charge (the quoted front-end cost of investing in unit trusts).

The initial charge is loaded into the offer price, but if the bid–offer spread (the difference between the bid price and the offer price) is greater than the initial charge, then the "effective" initial charge is greater than the "quoted" initial charge. The average quoted initial charge on unit trusts is 5%. But if a unit trust's bid price is 85p and its offer price is 93p, then the effective initial charge is 8.60% (of the offer price). In other words, this is the loss that would be incurred if a unit trust was purchased and immediately resold. In July 1993 69.7% of the 1,438 unit trusts operating in the United Kingdom had bid–offer spread exceeding the initial charge (according to a survey by Singer and Friedlander). The worst cases were Barclays Unicorn Property, Morgan Grenfell Genesis, and New Court Smaller Companies with spread of 8.60%, 8.39%, and 8.19%, respectively. Further, it is possible for the "effective" bid price (i.e., the cancellation price) to be below the "quoted" bid price, so that investors do even worse when they sell their units. In July 1993 51.4% of unit trusts had cancellation prices below bid prices.

There is a simple solution to these deceptive practices and that is to adopt a policy of single pricing. Both buyers and sellers face the same buying and selling price and there is in addition a fixed charge for sellers only. Single pricing is already used by some unit trusts such as Singer and Friedlander and Fidelity to sell offshore unit trusts in the United Kingdom.

The new disclosure rules that came into force at the beginning of 1995 will force insurance companies to simplify their charging structures for fear of losing out to unit trusts. But unit trusts, which in principle have the clearest and most straightforward charging structures, will sooner or later have to adopt single pricing if they are to avoid misleading investors.

2.5   The choice between a personal pension scheme and a contracted-out money purchase scheme

An employer's contracted-out money purchase scheme (COMPS) has a number of potential advantages over a personal pension scheme taken out by an individual employee, even though both are defined contribution schemes and both are contracted out of SERPS. The main advantages are as follows:

(i)   the employer's group scheme is likely, as a result of economies of scale, to be cheaper to administer on a per capita basis than a personal pension scheme. The government itself has assumed administrative expenses of 7% of premiums for a COMPS and 10% for a personal scheme;

(ii) National Insurance rebates for a COMPS can be paid into the pension fund at the same time that wages or salaries are paid, that is, on a weekly or monthly basis. This is because with this type of scheme, NICs are paid net of the rebate. However, with personal pensions,

NICs are paid gross, and the rebate does not become available for reinvestment until some time after the end of the tax year. On average, there is a delay of about 9 months before the rebates are invested in a personal scheme;

(iii) it is more likely that employers will make additional contributions into their own schemes (in addition to the employer's NI rebate) than into a personal pension scheme, especially if those taking out personal schemes are regarded as likely early leavers;

(iv) additional benefits such as death-in-service benefits may be provided automatically in a COMPS; they would cost extra to provide in a personal scheme.

2.6 *The choice between contracted-out money purchase schemes, group personal pension schemes, and industry-wide portable pension schemes*

Small employers who would like to operate contracted-out money purchase schemes for their employees can choose between the following:

(i) contracted-out money purchase schemes (COMPS) based on the guaranteed minimum contribution (GMC) test, or

(ii) group personal pension schemes (GPPS).

A COMPS has quite cumbersome administrative arrangements in respect of National Insurance rebates. The GMCs into a COMPS provide protected rights for members of the scheme and so are designed to replicate the rights under SERPS. As a result, a two-tiered administration system is necessary to handle the reduced NICs for employees contracted out under the COMPS and the full NICs for employees who have chosen to remain in SERPS. If the employer makes only the minimum level of contributions, the payments under the two schemes have to be reconciled on a monthly basis. On the other hand, if the employer pays more than the minimum contributions, rebate reconciliations can be made at the end of the tax year. Similarly if employees join or leave a COMPS part of the way through the tax year, the employer is required to identify the minimum contributions for that individual immediately. There are additional problems when an employee wishes to join the company's additional voluntary contributions scheme, because the company has to ensure that excessive benefits are not paid.

A group personal pension scheme is simply a collection of individual personal pension schemes organized by the same employer. The individual schemes are completely portable, so employees can take them when they change jobs. They can also decide on an individual basis whether to use their schemes to contract out of SERPS. The main advantage from the employer's position is administrative convenience. It can decide which employees belong to the group scheme and how much to contribute to the schemes of different employees (e.g., instead of profit sharing), automatically deduct employee contributions from payroll, and make a single payment to the company providing the scheme. The only information that the employer needs to provide on individual employees to the scheme provider is:

(i)   their age, sex and salary,
(ii)   the proportion of salary contribution from employee and employer, and
(iii)   their expected retirement age.

Another advantage is that the employer need make no further contribution to an individual's scheme once that individual has changed employers.

The group plan allows each employee to build up his or her own portable fund independently of how often that employee changes jobs. A typical group fund will be invested in a range of subfunds, such as a smaller companies fund, an investment trust fund, or a managed fund. However, because they are fully portable, there are few economies of scale in administration costs and so explicit commissions are broadly similar to those for individual schemes.[25] Group personal pension plans are designed for the employees of small companies with fewer than about 100 employees. There are about half a million such companies in the United Kingdom and they employ most of the 6.75 million of what have been called Britain's "great unpensioned."

One disadvantage with a GPPS is that the rebate from the DSS is not usually recovered until 9 months after the end of the tax year, unlike the case with a COMPS where the rebate is available immediately for investing. In addition, GPPSs, as with all personal pensions, come under the know-your-client rule of the 1986 Financial Services Act, so advisers must conduct a financial profile of every potential member of the GPPS to confirm that membership constitutes best advice for the financial circumstances of the applicant. Also employers are not obliged to contribute to a GPPS. So the choice between a COMPS and a GPPS depends on whether the employer's payroll system is sophisticated enough to handle the NI rebates. If not, a GPPS may be preferred.

Industry-wide portable pension schemes are designed for employees working in small companies who prefer to have a portable company pension scheme rather than a portable personal pension scheme. Examples are the Engineering Industry Pension Scheme (EIPS) and the British Clothing Industry Association's Pension Scheme (BCIAPS), both launched in 1988. The EIPS is open to about half a million employees in engineering

---

[25] The cost savings are on marketing and other one-off set-up costs.

companies not operating occupational pension schemes. It is a money purchase scheme and is administered by insurance company Friends' Provident. The contributions from both employers and employees are invested in with-profits endowment-linked schemes, which attract annual bonuses until pension age. Death-in-service benefits are a lump sum equal to two years' earnings and a pension to the surviving spouse. If death occurs after retirement, the surviving spouse receives a 50% pension. Employees moving from one participating employer to another will be able to take the full transfer value of their pension with them. Employees leaving the industry will be able to put the full transfer value into their new employer's scheme or into a personal pension scheme. The BCIAPS is open to around 200,000 employees. It is also a money purchase scheme and is administered by unit trust group Save and Prosper. The contributions from both employers and employees will be invested in unit trusts, ranging from a fixed-interest trust to an equity trust. As with standard unit trusts, there is an initial charge of 5% and an annual charge of 1.25%.

Proponents of industry-wide schemes claim that they have advantages over personal pension schemes. The main advantage is that economies of scale can lead to lower marketing and operating costs. Also employers are more likely to make contributions to an industry-wide scheme than to an individual employee's personal pension scheme. Another advantage is that with the industry-wide scheme, the National Insurance rebate is paid monthly, whereas with personal pensions the payment of the rebate takes about 9 months from the end of the tax year. Further, industry-wide schemes usually involve free death-in-service benefits, whereas personal pension schemes do not.

3   Pension policy

Governments have a crucial role to play in the provision of pensions in any country, both directly through the schemes that they themselves run and indirectly through the establishment of the framework of incentives and controls in which private-sector pension schemes operate. In this section we examine the U.K. government's policy toward pensions (especially in respect of private-sector provision), both historical and current.

3.1   The historical influences of the state on pension provision

3.1.1   Tax breaks
The state has done much to influence the development of private-sector pension schemes because tax breaks have only been available to schemes approved by the Inland Revenue. With the high level of progressive taxation

experienced in Britain for much of the 20th century, the tax concessions have made approved pension schemes a more efficient way of remunerating workers than paying them higher salaries and allowing them to save for their own retirement out of these. Indeed, pension schemes are an extremely tax-efficient savings vehicle. However, the state has also been concerned to prevent pension schemes being used as vehicles for tax avoidance.

The tax treatment of occupational pension schemes is governed by the Finance Acts of 1970 and 1989 and the 1988 Income and Corporation Taxes Act. Only exempt-approved schemes are eligible for tax relief. An exempt-approved scheme is one that has been established under an irrevocable trust and has been approved by the Pension Schemes Office of the Inland Revenue. An exempt-approved scheme has the following set of tax reliefs. Both the employee's and the employer's contributions attract tax relief at the highest marginal tax rate respectively of the employee and employer so long as the contributions of the employee do not exceed 15% of the employee's salary and so long as the combined contributions of employee and employer do not exceed 17.5% of the employee's salary.[26] In addition, the employer's contribution is not treated for tax purposes as the employee's income. Further, the investment income and realized capital gains from the fund are exempt from income and capital gains taxes (so long as the fund does not engage in trading or property development). Finally, any lump sum payable on retirement is also tax free and any lump sum payable to a beneficiary on the death of the scheme member is free from inheritance tax. Only the final pension itself is taxable as earned income. There is an earnings limit on which a final salary pension can be based, which is set at £60,000 (in 1989 prices or £76,800 for 1994–1995), implying a maximum pension, at two-thirds of final salary, of £40,000 (in 1989 prices). The maximum lump sum that can be commuted at retirement is £90,000 (in 1989 prices).

However, since August 1989, occupational schemes have been able to offer top-up schemes on top of their main schemes. The top-up schemes can provide additional pension benefits above the tax-approved limits but do not enjoy any tax advantages on contributions or investment income above the tax-approved limits.

The tax treatment of personal pension schemes is governed by the 1987 (no. 2) and 1989 Finance Acts. The 1987 act allows full tax relief on contributions up to 17.5% of salary as the maximum combined employer and employee contributions. The Inland Revenue also allows unused tax relief on employee contributions to be carried forward for up to six years. The investment income and realized capital gains from the fund are exempt from income and capital gains

---

[26] Higher combined limits apply to employees over 50, ranging from 20% for a 51-year-old to 27.5% for a 74-year-old.

taxes respectively. The lump sum payable on retirement is tax free, while the annuity pension is taxed as earned income. The 1989 act introduced new limits on contributions that qualify for tax relief in personal pension schemes for those aged 36 and over, ranging from 20% of earnings for a 36-year-old to 35% for someone above 56 years. The earnings limit on which contributions qualify for tax relief was set at £60,000 (in 1989 prices).

In tax terms, pension fund savings are treated more favorably than any other savings vehicle. But there is an anomaly in the present system in respect of the tax-free lump sum. If this was taxed at the same rate as the pension annuity, then it would not matter what the size of the lump sum was, although there is evidence that pensioners tend to spend the lump sum in about two years. If it were not for the tax-free lump sum, the tax treatment of pension schemes would simply be one of tax deferral. In other words, all the inflows into the scheme are tax relieved but the resulting higher outflows from the scheme when it matures would be taxed. The tax liability would merely be deferred and not avoided if the lump sum was also taxed. The position is slightly more complicated than this because of the possibility of tax arbitrage, that is, it is possible for individuals to transfer the tax liability from a period where they face a high marginal tax rate (i.e., when they are in work) to a period where they face a lower marginal tax rate (i.e., when they are retired).

Nevertheless, tax reliefs are a subsidy that can cause distortions elsewhere in the system. In particular, by making savings through a pension scheme more attractive than other forms of saving, tax reliefs discriminate against the direct holding of shares by individuals. Whereas they hold shares indirectly through their pension funds, individuals can exercise no direct influence on the activities of companies by this means. Instead they have to rely on the pension funds themselves to exercise this influence on their behalf. And, of course, it is not clear that, as investors, individuals would take the same view as their pension funds about the activities of the companies whose shares they own.

Another distortion is that employees become imprisoned within their own occupational schemes. The tax system locks them into a particular scheme and makes it very expensive to move to another one. This reduces labor mobility and so leads to wider inefficiencies in the economy. The introduction of personal pension schemes was designed to overcome this.

As a final example of the distortions caused by tax reliefs, it would, of course, be possible for the current rate of income tax to be lower if the tax subsidies were absent. It has been estimated that in 1993 the tax relief on pension schemes was worth £15 billion, equivalent to 10p in the pound off the standard rate of income tax. This would increase current disposable income and might actually increase pensions savings (if the positive effect of increasing disposable income outweighed the discouraging substitution effect of a lower net rate of return on pensions savings).

On balance, the tax reliefs appear to be justified. Most people, especially the young, appear not to think too much about their pension. By the time they reach retirement, it is too late. Using tax reliefs to encourage people to save for their retirement is on the whole a good thing.

3.1.2   The rights of early leavers

In recent years, the state has done much to improve the rights of early leavers. These were first established by the National Insurance Act 1959 and subsequently reinforced by the Social Security Acts of 1973, 1985, and 1990, and the Health and Social Security Act of 1984.

The 1973 Social Security Act, for example, required that pension schemes provide deferred pensions to those early leavers who were at least 26 years of age and who had accumulated at least 5 years' service; those with less than 5 years' scheme membership could have a refund of employee contributions. However, the deferred pension was not indexed for inflation between the date of leaving and the date of retirement. The huge inflation of the 1970s showed the inadequacy of the 1973 act. The position was improved first by the 1985 act and subsequently by the 1990 act. These acts required the deferred pensions of early leavers with at least 2 years' scheme membership to be uprated each year by the annual rate of inflation up to a maximum of 5% per annum compound from April 1978 for those leaving occupational schemes after January 1991. And as an alternative to a deferred pension, the 1985 act allowed early leavers to take their pension entitlement with them. This is achieved through a transfer value calculated as the cash equivalent of the accrued rights under the scheme. The transfer value is paid to another scheme (either occupational or personal) or into an insurance policy known as a "section 32 buyout policy" after section 32 of the 1981 Finance Act which first permitted buyouts. Depending on the scheme, the transfer value is used to provide added years in the new scheme or now, increasingly, a money purchase pension at retirement.

3.1.3   Investor protection

Finally, the government has been concerned with investor protection. Trustees had a fiduciary duty under the 1925 Trustee Act to preserve the trust capital and to apply the capital and its income according to the trust deed.[27] Without specific provision in the trust deeds, the 1925 act limited the authorized investments of the pension fund to British government or government-guaranteed securities and to the stocks of local authorities and certain railways and

---

[27] The role of the trustees is to operate the pension scheme for the benefit of its members. They have to act in accordance with the trust deed and rules of the scheme, within the framework of law. They also have to act prudently, conscientiously, honestly, and with the utmost good faith.

utilities. The 1925 act was superseded by the 1961 Trustee Investments Act, which considerably widened the scope of authorized investments to include company securities and unit trusts. Trustees are required to *invest* in assets for the long-term benefits of their pensioners and not to *trade* in assets for short-term speculative gains. However, the 1990 Finance Act exempted from tax pension funds' trading income from futures and options contracts. This allows pension funds to use futures and options contracts for risk management purposes without fear of a tax charge.

Despite their wide investment powers, trustees do still face a few restrictions on their investments. For example, the 1990 Social Security Act placed limits on the amount of self-investment by pension funds in parent companies to 5% of fund assets. The 5% ceiling covers shares, loans, property, and also money owed by the company to the scheme. The ceiling is designed to protect pension schemes from the failure of the parent company and also from hostile takeovers.[28]

When personal pension schemes first started, the categories of eligible securities that could be selected were quite restrictive, mainly quoted U.K. shares and investment trusts. This was changed by the 1989 Finance Act. It became possible to invest in overseas shares, unquoted U.K. shares, unit trusts, gilts, and commercial property.

A new regulatory framework (involving the setting up of the Securities and Investments Board along similar lines to the Securities and Exchange Commission in the United States) was established by the 1986 Financial Services Act, as part of the wider changes in the City of London, known as the Big Bang. The act requires the authorization of everyone carrying on investment business or giving investment advice. The way in which the act affects pension schemes was contained in a guidance note entitled *Pensions Advice and Management Authorisation Under the Financial Services Act* issued by the SIB in February 1987.

Pension scheme trustees and employers can advise employees on the merits of joining a scheme without being authorized. They can also compare the advantages and disadvantages of scheme membership versus other forms of pension provision such as personal pensions without being authorized. This is because discussing a class of investment (and personal pensions are regarded as a class of investment) is not regarded under the act as giving investment advice. However, trustees and employers could not advise or recommend specific pension plans without being authorized, as this does constitute investment advice under the act. As far as managing the invest-

---

[28] However, the government has not yet implemented the self-investment provisions. Once implemented pension funds are given 2 years to divest themselves of stocks listed on the Stock Exchange and loans to the sponsoring company, and 5 years to divest themselves of stocks listed on the Unlisted Securities Market and property.

ments of the fund are concerned, trustees will not have to be authorized if all the day-to-day investment management decisions are taken on behalf of the trustees by an authorized person. If this is not the case, then the trustees themselves will have to be authorized.

In most occupational pension schemes, the trustees are chosen by the employer. Trustees therefore face a potential conflict of interest because they are supposed to act in the best interests of the beneficiaries but may find themselves under intense pressure from the employer. We can consider some possibilities. Unscrupulous employers could pressure trustees into making disguised loans to parent companies via affiliated companies, thereby breaching any limits on self-investment. Employers could also take part in front-running, whereby the company is informed about asset purchases and sales that are about to be executed by the scheme and could transact beforehand. Similarly, the pension scheme could be induced to purchase assets from the employer at inflated prices.

The inadequacy of the trust status of pension schemes was exposed in a major way by Robert Maxwell in 1991. On November 5, 1991, Maxwell died at sea off the Canary Islands. Within a month, his business empire had collapsed. On December 4, 1991, the Serious Fraud Office launched an investigation into how the pension schemes of Maxwell's public companies, Mirror Group Newspapers (MGN) and Maxwell Communication Corporation (MCC), had incurred potential losses of £400 million on loans to his main private companies, Headington Investments and Robert Maxwell Group. In total, during the 6 months before his death, Maxwell had taken £700 million in cash and securities from his public companies and their pension funds. MCC had made loans of £240 million and MGN had made loans of £45 million. The MCC pension fund was owed £65 million, while the MGN pension fund was owed £350 million.

Accountants Coopers and Lybrand Deloitte, auditors to all the Maxwell companies, discovered that the pension funds had been lending shares to the private companies for some time. Initially, the private companies put up collateral to the pension funds of between 125% and 150% of the value of the borrowed shares. But in the 6 months before he died, Maxwell began to sell the collateral. The proceeds should have been used to repay the pension funds but they were used to shore up a collapsing business empire. The pension funds had been in surplus prior to the stock lending. By December 1991, they needed £150 million to meet their liabilities to pensioners. The MGN pension fund, for example, had been valued at £520 million and had a surplus of £150 million. This had been turned into a deficit of £200 million. By December 1991, the MGN pension fund had assets of £170 million and liabilities of £370 million.

The House of Commons Social Security Committee published its report on the Maxwell affair in March 1992. It was strongly critical of the roles played by the regulatory authorities, financial institutions, professional bodies, and pension fund trustees, and it called for the members of the Maxwell pension funds to receive compensation, mainly from the banks holding the pension fund assets as collateral for their loans to Maxwell. In particular, it criticized the actuaries, auditors, and lawyers for having a "strict compartmentalised view" of their responsibilities and for failing to communicate with each other, despite growing evidence of malpractice: "Pontius Pilate would have blushed at the spectacle of so many witnesses washing their hands in public before the committee of their responsibilities in this affair." The report was also critical of the system of self-regulation operating in the City, stating that the way in which IMRO (the Investment Managers Regulatory Organisation) carried out its duties suggested "that this aspect of the system of self-regulation is – when the chips are down – little short of a tragic comedy. . . . In other words, the system works in those circumstances where there is in fact little need for a regulatory system at all."

In June 1992, the Social Security secretary Peter Lilley announced the establishment of the Pension Law Review Committee under the chairmanship of Professor Roy Goode QC of Oxford University. The Goode Committee submitted its report entitled *Pension Law Reform* (CM 2342) in September 1993. In total there were 218 recommendations. The principal recommendations were as follows:

(i)   Trust law should continue to provide the foundation for interests, rights, and duties arising in connection with occupational pension schemes but should be reinforced by a Pensions Act administered by a *pensions regulator.*

(ii) Freedom of trust should be limited so as to ensure the reality of the pension promise, to protect rights accrued in respect of past service and to allow members to elect up to one-third of the trustee board in the case of final-salary schemes and up to two-thirds of the trustee board in the case of money-purchase schemes. Trustees should also receive formal training.

(iii) The security for members' entitlements should be strengthened by minimum funding requirements, monitoring by the pensions regulator and scheme auditors and actuaries, restrictions on withdrawals from surplus, and, as a last resort, a *compensation scheme* to cover scheme deficits arising from fraud, theft or other misappropriation.

(iv) The administrative burdens imposed on employers and scheme administrators should wherever possible be reduced.

The report argued that:

Many of our recommendations do little more than reflect best practice, and, when taken with the simplification measures we have proposed, should add few, if any, financial burdens to a well-run and properly funded scheme. They clarify the rights and responsibilities of all parties associated with schemes, a clarity which has hitherto been lacking. As a result, both employer and scheme members should feel confident that the pension promise is more secure and that at the same time the employer's future commitments can be limited to what is considered affordable. . . . The legal regime we have proposed is designed to satisfy four essential criteria: fairness to all parties, security for scheme members, practicality, and the simplification of the law regulating occupational pension schemes and their administration. (pp. 7–8).

The most important recommendations of the Goode Committee were subsequently contained in the 1995 Pensions Act, which established from 1997 the Occupational Pensions Regulatory Authority (OPRA), a compensation scheme financed by a levy on all occupational pensions schemes, and the right of scheme members to elect up to one-third of the trustees. A pension scheme's auditor and actuary have a statutory duty to report to OPRA any irregularities that they discover. The trustees have a new duty to prepare and enforce a schedule of contributions that will satisfy a minimum funding requirement (MFR). The schedule of contributions must ensure that if the funding level is below 90% of liabilities, the sponsor has to make good the shortfall up to 90% within one year; and that if the funding level is between 90% and 100%, the sponsor has to make good the shortfall up to 100% within 5 years. The MFR must be sufficient to continue providing pensions already in payment. It should also provide active scheme members with a fair transfer value of their accrued rights, such that, when this is subsequently invested, it can be expected to deliver a pension that is at least as high as the scheme itself would have provided in respect of the same accrued rights. For younger active members, the transfer value will be based on a discount rate that depends on the return on U.K. equities; for older active members the discount rate will depend on the return on U.K. government bonds (gilts); and for active members within 10 years of normal retirement the discount rate will depend on the return on both U.K. equities and gilts with weights that switch gradually away from the former towards the latter over time. The value of the pension scheme's total liabilities will be determined in a similar fashion, taking into account the age distribution of the scheme's membership. The MFR requires the explicit use of asset–liability management techniques with the implication that, as pension schemes mature, their asset holdings will systematically switch from equities to bonds.

3.2   Current government policy[29]

The Conservative government in power since 1979 has made some radical changes to the U.K. pensions scene. The government's objectives have been to extend choice and flexibility in pensions provision; to encourage more

[29] This section draws on Blake (1992, chap. 4).

private sector pensions provision; to limit the cost to the state, whether through direct public expenditure or tax reliefs. There have been four main factors motivating these objectives.

First, the government has sought to make the pensions system consistent with its overriding policy of promoting the *enterprise economy*. The enterprise economy among other things requires increased labor mobility and offers people greater choice in planning for their retirement. Both these factors meant that the ties that employees had to their employers' occupational pension schemes needed to be weakened. This has been achieved through a series of measures that have, among other things, made occupational pension scheme membership voluntary, given additional rights to early leavers, required schemes to provide adequate information to members, and introduced personal pension schemes as an alternative to occupational schemes. In addition, greater flexibility and choice in pensions provision has been made possible by the introduction of additional voluntary contribution and top-up schemes.

Second, demographic projections indicated that the pensioner population was going to continue to expand relative to the working population. In 1989 there were more than 10 million pensioners and 2.3 workers for every pensioner. By 2025, it is projected that there will be more than 13 million pensioners and only 1.6 workers for every pensioner.

Third, as a consequence of these demographic projections, public expenditure on pensions (both on the basic state pension and the SERPS pension) was in danger of getting out of control. Public expenditure on pensions in 1993 was £27 billion, about 34% of the total cost of social security. Without the changes to SERPS, it was estimated by the Government Actuary that by 2054, public expenditure on pensions would have risen to £53 billion in 1989 prices (from £20 billion in 1989).

These factors have led the government to attempt to reduce the level of public expenditure devoted to pensions provision, both in the form of direct expenditure and in the form of tax relief. The government has twice now reduced the benefits paid by SERPS after 1999, provided incentives to leave SERPS and placed limits on the amount of tax relief available on contributions and the benefits that can accrue in pension schemes.

Fourth, the real living standard of pensioners has been steadily increasing over the past 20 years and is expected to continue increasing. Between 1979 and 1986, pensioners' real net incomes grew by 23%, while between 1970 and 1986, they grew by 45%. This increase was larger than for the population as a whole. It is estimated that about half this increase came as a result of higher state pensions (including increased pensions from SERPS), while half came from higher private incomes in the form of savings and occupational pensions. Between 1979 and 1989, expenditure on state benefits paid to pensioners rose by 27% in real terms, reflecting both increased payouts under SERPS and an increase of 10% in the number of people receiving a state pension. In 1986, 50% of all pensioners and 70% of newly retired pensioners had an occupational pension in addition to the basic state pension; in addition, 70% of all pensioners and 85% of newly retired pensioners were receiving some investment income.

So while there are still large numbers of pensioners who are very poor, the fact remains that the average pensioner has never been so well-off. This fact has provided a further justification in the government's view for reducing the level of provision financed by the state.

However, the removal of compulsory membership of occupational pension schemes in 1988 may have the unintended consequence of increasing the cost to the state of pension provision. Recent evidence indicates that 19% of new employees do not bother to join their employer's scheme immediately, although some may do so eventually. During this period they will accumulate SERPS entitlements that would not have arisen prior to 1988. This represents an additional cost to the state. So the extension of "choice" may well end up increasing rather than reducing the burden on the state.

The government's attempts to increase pension choice and flexibility, to reduce some of the inequities faced by early leavers, and to transfer more of the liability for pension provision to the private sector has brought it into conflict with these private-sector providers, even though there is substantial cooperation, and private occupational pension schemes still enjoy substantial tax breaks.

For example, occupational schemes were opposed to the establishment of personal pension schemes. Employers effectively boycotted them by refusing to make employers' contributions toward the personal pension schemes taken out by their employees, even though they would have been willing to put the same contributions on behalf of those same employees into their own schemes. The main reason for this is simple. With occupational schemes, the employer is committed to fund pensions based on final salary. Any surplus in the fund above this liability "belongs to" the employer. So there is no danger to the employer of making excessive current contributions (i.e., of overfunding the pension scheme), because any surplus employers' contributions can be withdrawn at a later stage. However, this is not the case with personal pension schemes. If an employer made a contribution to an employee's personal pension scheme which turned out to be "excessive," there is nothing that the employer can do about it subsequently: This contribution together with the investment returns now "belong to" the employee.[30] So

---

[30] Note that there is an asymmetry from the employer's position in the case of "underfunding." With an occupational scheme based on final salary, it is in effect not possible to underfund since any deficit that emerges as a result of insufficient contributions or investment returns must ultimately be made good through deficiency payments from the employer. However,

even though employers' contributions are determined to be actuarially fair in the sense that they are set at a level that should not systematically generate a surplus or a deficit, nevertheless employers have refused to put the same contributions into personal pension schemes. As a result, personal pension schemes are at a severe disadvantage in terms of funding compared with occupational schemes, even though personal schemes offer much greater flexibility to individuals than occupational schemes. There are other possible reasons for employers refusing to make contributions toward personal schemes. For instance, it would limit the huge investing power currently held by occupational schemes,[31] and it would limit the ability of the company to use the pension scheme to attract highly skilled staff or to reward long service.[32]

Many occupational schemes were also opposed to extending the rights of early leavers by giving them greater inflation protection for their deferred pensions, on the grounds that this would reduce the ability of the scheme to deliver pensions to loyal long-term employees. Some employers have threatened to wind up their schemes if the government imposes any more restrictions on their actions (occupational pension schemes in the United Kingdom are voluntary, not compulsory). This is not considered to be a serious threat so far, and it is always possible for the government to issue a counterthreat to reduce the occupational schemes' tax breaks even further if they fail to cooperate in achieving greater flexibility in pension provision in the future.

The success of personal pensions has surprised the government. In 1988, the government estimated that at most 1.75 million people would leave SERPS and take out personal pensions. By 1995, about 5 million people had taken out personal pensions.[33] The government had hoped that the introduction of personal pensions would reduce the cost to the state of providing

there is no penalty to the employer if it makes "insufficient" contributions toward an employee's personal scheme. In the case of the small number of occupational schemes based on defined contributions (i.e., COMPSs), most of these are based only on the minimum contributions necessary to contract out of SERPS, and employers' contributions at least to this level are mandatory, so that there is no real distinction from the employer's position between COMPSs and personal schemes, since the contracted-out rebate has to be paid in both cases.

[31] The value of U.K. pension funds assets is currently estimated at £400 billion, equal to two-thirds of U.K. GDP. They own one-third of all U.K. shares and 20% of all U.K. government bonds. The largest pension fund, that of British Coal, has assets of £12 billion. The top 10 pension funds have assets in excess of £50 billion, and there are more than 40 pension funds with assets in excess of £1 billion each.

[32] It is not possible (in general) for someone to belong simultaneously to an occupational scheme and to a personal scheme. Therefore it is not possible to reward long service (with tax relief) by contributing to an individual's personal scheme while simultaneously matching his or her contributions to the occupational scheme.

[33] However the majority of these are rebate-only schemes established to contract out of SERPS, rather than schemes to "contract out" of employers' occupational schemes, thereby forgoing the employer's contributions.

pensions, but a National Audit Office (NAO) report in November 1990 showed that the opposite was true.

The NAO report estimated that for the period of the rebates and special bonuses between July 1988 and April 1993, the gross cost of personal pension schemes to the National Insurance Fund would be £9.3 billion (in April 1988 prices). The savings to the National Insurance Fund in terms of fewer SERPS pensions was estimated to be only £3.4 billion. This meant that the net cost of personal pensions was £5.9 billion. These calculations assume that all those who have contracted out of SERPS will, as they are entitled to do, reenter SERPS when they reach the age at which they or their financial advisers assess that it is financially advantageous to do so.

So far from saving the state money, personal pensions have turned out to be extremely expensive.[34] The government's main fear is that most personal pension scheme members will recontract back into SERPS but keep both their personal pensions and the subsidy (special bonus) that was used to get them to leave SERPS initially. So great was the government's fear that in the 1993 Social Security Act it offered an additional 1% age-related NI rebate for everyone over the age of 30 who remained in a personal pension scheme and did not recontract back into SERPS. This additional rebate operated between April 1993 (when the 2% bonus available to all those taking out personal pensions ended) and April 1996. The government estimated that those over 30 would be most likely to recontract back into SERPS unless they had an additional inducement not to do so.

The 1995 Pensions Act introduced further incentives to contract out of SERPS. For example, the act simplified the arrangements for contracting out of SERPS by abolishing the requirement for occupational schemes to provide guaranteed minimum pensions. Instead, from 1997 COFSSs will have to demonstrate only that they offer requisite benefits that are broadly equal to those obtainable under SERPS. The act also introduced greater flexibility in converting personal pension scheme assets into pension annuities. Personal pension scheme members were obliged to take annuities immediately when they retire, even when annuity yields are low. The act permits members to delay taking out annuities until they reach the age of 75 and in the interim to draw down part of their pension fund as income (this is called *income withdrawal* or *income drawdown*).

The 1995 act has further reduced the cost to the state of pension provision,

---

[34] This increase in costs should not have caused such surprise to the government because it arises whenever a funded pension scheme is introduced to replace a pay-as-you-go scheme. People stop contributing now to a pay-as-you-go scheme such as SERPS and in return receive lower pension benefits when they retire in 20 or 30 years' time. But since current pension payouts (for currently retired employees) are unchanged, a so-called transition deficit is created. The state has to raise taxes or issue bonds to cover the transition deficit.

both public and private. We have already mentioned the reduction in the cost of SERPS from 2000 that follows from the reduction in the size of the earnings band over which the SERPS pension is calculated. In addition, the rise in the state pension age of women from 60 to 65 is expected to reduce the cost of state pensions by about £3 billion per annum. On top of this, the state has ended its commitment to pay for part of the indexing of occupational pensions. At present, employers have to index the guaranteed minimum pension up to an inflation level of 3% and any additional pension above the GMP up to an inflation level of 5%. The state increases an individual's basic pension to compensate him or her for the inflation on the GMP above 3%. But the 1995 act abolishes the GMP altogether and merely requires employers to index the whole of the pensions that they pay up to a maximum inflation rate of 5%; so there will no longer be any state contribution to private-sector inflation indexing.

4   Conclusion

Every civilized society must make arrangements to provide for its retired members. It should do so in a way that is equitable between different generations, between employers and employees, between early leavers and long stayers, between pension scheme providers and pension scheme members, between taxpayers and subsidy receivers. In the United Kingdom, the state has been willing to provide a minimal mandatory pension for the poorest members of society. But it has expected more affluent members of society to make their own voluntary and adequately funded arrangements for providing a higher standard of living in retirement because of its concern for the public purse. It is also becoming increasingly clear that the estate's role in pension provision is going to dwindle further over time and no political party is going to be able to find the tax revenue to reverse this trend.

However, there are many important issues still to resolve, as recent U.K. experience has indicated. We have immediate and urgent problems concerning the safe custody of pension assets, the appropriateness of the advice given by pension advisers and the high-pressure sales tactics of sales agents for personal schemes, although the establishment of a pensions regulator and a compensation fund should help here.

Over the medium term, we have to confront the current uncertain track record of personal pension schemes. We have yet to see whether long-term investment returns are adequate to generate decent pensions from such schemes. Matters are not helped however by high operating costs and commissions or by the unwillingness of employers to put the same money into one of their employee's personal pension schemes as they are to put money into another of their employee's occupational schemes. At the same time, something will have to be done about transfer values between occupational schemes. Unless fair-valued transfers are introduced, early leavers will continue to subsidize long stayers. This is bad for labor mobility and, in turn, for the prospects of growth in the real economy.

Over the long term, there is an intergenerational crisis brewing in pensions provision in all industrialized countries. The aging of the population is placing a growing strain on the ability of the relatively declining work force to produce the output to feed not only itself but also the rapidly increasing retired population; this is true whether pension systems are predominantly funded or pay as you go. Governments in the rest of Europe have found it extremely difficult to reduce the cost of their state pension schemes: there were riots in Rome in November 1994 and strikes throughout France in November 1995 when the Italian and French governments attempted to do so.

Individuals joining the labor force in the United Kingdom for the first time have quite a difficult range of choices to make in terms of their pensions. The state pension provides an increasingly inadequate standard of living in retirement. And although there are very generous tax incentives to join a private sector scheme, there are still problems to face. Individuals who intend to be mobile in their careers will find that they will get poor transfer values or deferred pensions if they join a series of occupational schemes. Individuals who take out a personal scheme will be confronted with uncertain investment returns and high costs and commissions.

Overall then, the U.K. pensions system, which has developed gradually over many centuries but has altered very rapidly over the past decade or so, provides many important lessons for other countries planning to introduce funded pension systems and/or greater private sector provision, both in terms of the structures that work and the features that do not work and need to be improved upon.

APPENDIX A: DERIVATION OF THE IMPLIED REAL RATES OF RETURN ON CONTRIBUTIONS INTO SERPS AND OCCUPATIONAL PENSION SCHEMES

Define:

r_1 = real rate of return in SERPS (to be determined)

r_2 = real rate of return in a final salary occupational scheme (to be determined)

T_1 = 20 = years in SERPS (the maximum SERPS pension can be achieved with just 20 years' membership)

T_2 = 40 = years in an occupational scheme (the maximum occupational pension takes 40 years' membership to achieve)

$\gamma_1 = 0.0598 =$ average contribution rate into SERPS over 20-year period (average of the following combined contracted-out rebates on NICs: 7% per year between 1978 and 1981, 6.25% per year between 1982 and 1987, 5.8% per year between 1988 and 1993, and 4.8% per year between 1994 and 1997).

$\gamma_2 = 0.1525 =$ average contribution rate into an occupational scheme

$\theta_1 = 0.25 =$ income replacement ratio from SERPS (proportion of average revalued earnings)

$\theta_2 = 0.67 =$ income replacement ratio from an occupational scheme (proportion of final salary)

$w_0 =$ pensionable real wage when joining scheme

$g = 0.02 =$ real growth rate in earnings

$S = 15 =$ years of retirement

The real rate of return is found by solving the following equation as of retirement age:

Future value of contributions at retirement date $=$ Present value of pension benefits at retirement date (1)

For SERPS (assuming a constant real pension and payments made at the end of each year) we have:

Future value of contributions at retirement date

$$
\begin{aligned}
&= \gamma_1 w_0 \sum_{t=1}^{T_1} (1+g)^t (1+r_1)^{T_1-t} \\
&= \gamma_1 w_0 (1+g)^{T_1} \left[\frac{((1+r_1)/(1+g))^{T_1} - 1}{(r_1 - g)/(1+g)} \right]
\end{aligned}
\tag{2}
$$

and

Present value of pension benefits at retirement date

$$
\begin{aligned}
&= \theta_1 \left[\frac{w_0}{T_1} \sum_{t=1}^{T_1} (1+g)^{T_1-t} \right] \left[\sum_{t=1}^{S} (1+r_1)^{-t} \right] \\
&= \theta_1 \left[\frac{w_0 (1+g)^{T_1} - 1}{T_1 g} \right] \left[\frac{1 - (1+r_1)^{-S}}{r_1} \right]
\end{aligned}
\tag{3}
$$

For an occupational scheme (again assuming a constant real pension and payments made at the end of each year) we have:

Future value of contributions at retirement date

$$
= \gamma_2 w_0 (1+g)^{T_2} \left[\frac{((1+r_2)/(1+g))^{T_2} - 1}{(r_2 - g)/(1+g)} \right]
\tag{4}
$$

and

Present value of pension benefits at retirement date

$$= \theta_2 w_0 (1+g)^{T_2} \left[\frac{1-(1+r_2)^{-S}}{r_2} \right] \tag{5}$$

Note that w_0 drops out of the calculation when equations (2) and (3) are set equal to each other; similarly for equations (4) and (5). The values of r_1 and r_2 that solve these equalities are the real rates of return on SERPS and occupational schemes respectively. Using these data, we get $r^1 = 6.7\%$ and $r_2 = 3.3\%$.

Following the 1986 Social Security Act, the government has reduced the value of SERPS benefits after 1999 in three ways. First, it requires contributions to be made throughout the career. Second, it bases the pension on average career earnings rather than earnings over the best 20 years. These changes have the effect of raising T_1 in (2) and (3) from 20 to 40. Third, it reduces the maximum income replacement ratio from 25% to 20% so that θ_1 in (2) and (3) falls from 0.25 to 0.20. The overall effect is to reduce the real return from SERPS membership after 1999 from 6.7% per annum to 1.7%, which is about half that from a typical occupational scheme. Following the 1995 Pensions Act, the government has reduced the value of SERPS benefits after 2000 by reducing the value of band earnings over which the pension is calculated. This will reduce the real return from SERPS membership after 2000 from 1.7% per annum to about 1.2%.

So within a quarter of a century of being introduced, the SERPS pension has been reduced from one that offered a real rate of return of twice that available from an occupational scheme to one offering a real return of only one-third. The government has managed to achieve these remarkable changes largely without protest, because it has always delayed the introduction of the changes by about 15 or 20 years. The British government's two greatest weapons have been the myopia and short memories of the British electorate!

APPENDIX B: CHARGES BY PERSONAL PENSION SCHEMES

When they were introduced, personal pension schemes were intended to be both portable and simple. But we show in this appendix that personal pension schemes, far from being completely portable, are subject to substantial transfer penalties and low surrender values; and far from being simple, they are subject to an amazing complexity of charges.

Commission charges

All personal pension schemes involve commission and annual management charges and these can be quite high. An initial transfer into a personal scheme might involve costs as high as 25% of the transfer value with annual commissions of up to 2.5% of the annual premium. This works out, according to a recent Institute of Actuaries report, to commissions varying between 10% and 20% of annual premiums; in contrast, the equivalent costs of running an occupational pension scheme work out at between 5% and 7% of annual premiums. Commissions on a single premium scheme might only be 4% of the premium, however.

Commissions paid by insurance companies to independent financial intermediaries have increased since the abolition of LAUTRO's maximum commission agreement in December 1989. LAUTRO was the self-regulatory organization for the life assurance and unit trust industries established by the 1986 Financial Services Act (although it has now been replaced by the Personal Investment Authority). LAUTRO has estimated that the commission paid on a 25-year personal pension scheme with monthly premiums of £50 was £366 in 1990, compared with £300 in 1989.

Sometimes the management charges are disguised. This is particularly the case with unit-linked pension schemes. The common practice among insurance companies offering unit-linked schemes is to have two classes of units: accumulation (or ordinary) units and capital (or initial) units. The capital units carry a much larger share of the costs of managing a pension scheme. This is because there is an annual charge on the capital units (sometimes called a capital levy) through the life of the scheme (although with some schemes, capital units can be converted to accumulation units at the scheme member's nominated retirement age, at which time the annual charge ceases). In contrast, there is only an initial charge on the accumulation units.

Typically, the first two years' premiums in a scheme (as well as the first two years of any increase in premiums) are allocated to capital units, although transfer values and single premium contributions are usually allocated to accumulation units. The annual charge on capital units is generally between 3% and 3.5% of the current value of the units. If only one year's contributions are allocated to capital units, then the annual charge might be as high as 6%. In addition, there is an annual management (or administration) charge of between 0.75% and 1% of the value of the fund, and a bid–offer spread on units of around 5%. These charges are extracted by canceling capital units. The contributions are invested in these units at the offer price and, at the nominated retirement date (also known as the vesting date), the units are cashed in at the bid price ruling at that time.

Table 10.B1
The effect of management charges
on unit-linked pension schemes

Value of Units after	Capital Units (£)	Accumulation Units (£)
10 years	3,233	4,327
20 years	5,654	10,244
30 years	9,890	24,252

Assumptions: £1,000 is allocated to both capital and accumulation units at the start of each of the first two years; investment growth rate of 10% p.a.; bid-offer spread of 5%; initial charges are 5% for accumulation units and 0.75% for capital units; annual capital levy of 3.5% for capital units.

Source: Equitable Life Assurance Society, *Daily Telegraph*, October 18, 1986.

The different effects of accumulation and capital units are shown in the example in Table 10.B1. The table shows that the effects of the charges on the capital units can have a striking effect on the overall value of the units after 30 years; £9,890 for capital units and £24,252 for accumulation units. In essence, this is the difference between a 10% investment growth rate and an effective growth rate of 6.5%.

The main alternatives to capital units are reduced allocation units and recurring single premium contracts. With reduced allocation units, individuals receive a smaller allocation of units in the early years of a scheme. A typical scheme might have a 70% allocation in the first 2 years, so that of every £100 of monthly contributions, only £70 will be invested. Some schemes are even more costly than this with zero allocation in year 1 and only a 25% allocation in each of years 2 and 3. Recurring single premium contracts have the lowest charges of all. This is because they are simply a series of single premium pension schemes and hence carry no extra initial charge other than a 5% bid–offer spread. To illustrate the differences, a £200 per month, 25-year scheme taken out by a 35-year-old male when there was a 10% annual return on investments and a 5% bid–offer spread would generate a fund value of £236,000 at age 60 with recurring single premiums, £223,000 with reduced allocation units, and only £12,000 with capital units.

Table 10.B2 shows the true overall cost of charges in two different 25-year unit-linked pension schemes, one based on monthly premiums of £200 per month and the other based on a single premium of £10,000. These charges comprise initial commission and annual management charges. With

Table 10.B2
True cost of charges in unit-linked
pension schemes

Monthly Premiums (£200 per month)

	Fund Value after 25 Years (£)	Total Cost of Charges	
		After 25 Years (£)	As % of No Charges Fund Value
No Charges	248,632	0	0.0
Best Scheme			
(lowest charges)	228,819	19,813	8.0
Average Scheme	193,583	55,049	22.1
Worst Scheme			
(highest charges)	167,309	81,323	32.7
LAUTRO Rules	213,205	35,427	14.2

Single Premium (£10,000)

	Fund Value after 25 Years (£)	Total Cost of Charges	
		After 25 Years (£)	As % of No Charges Fund Value
No Charges	108,347	0	0.0
Best Scheme			
(lowest charges)	94,265	14,082	13.0
Average Scheme	83,141	25,206	23.3
Worst Scheme			
(highest charges)	66,148	42,199	38.9
LAUTRO Rules	94,316	14,031	13.0

Source: *Money Management*, October 1993.

the monthly premium scheme, the average scheme generated costs of 22% of the fund's terminal value, while the worst scheme (the one imposing the highest charges) generated costs of 33%. The best scheme (that with the lowest charges) had costs of 8%. Costs calculated using LAUTRO rules are 14%. These are the costs that all schemes use in their marketing literature even though they may bear no relationship to their own actual costs; they are closer to the costs of the best scheme than the average scheme, let alone the worst scheme. However, since the beginning of 1995, schemes have to report there actual costs, not those calculated using LAUTRO rules. With the single premium scheme, the average scheme generated costs of 23% of the fund's terminal value, while the worst scheme generated costs of nearly 40%. The best scheme had costs of 13% which is the same as that calculated using LAUTRO rules.

Surrender values

When someone takes out a personal pension scheme, they normally have to nominate a particular retirement date. The difference between the nominated retirement date and the current date fixes the term of the scheme. The scheme provider's investment strategy is designed to deliver a maturity value for the fund on the nominated retirement date and not before. The nominated retirement date becomes the maturity date of the scheme. Scheme members have to make the planned contributions in due time in order for the scheme's provider to achieve the investment objectives. If scheme members cease making contributions before the maturity date and request a return on their investment, they are likely to find that their scheme has a very low surrender value (or equivalently they have to pay a high exit charge).

This is particularly the case for with-profits endowment schemes. Even if the scheme is surrendered only 1 year before maturity, the surrender value can be substantially below the maturity value. This is because the terminal bonus, which is only awarded if the scheme is maintained until the maturity date, can be very high. Table 10.B3 shows the relationship between surrender values and maturity values on with-profits endowment schemes provided by a range of insurance companies. The average terminal bonus is 52.7% of the maturity value, while the average surrender value after 24 years of contributing to the scheme is 26.9% less than the maturity value, a value that could be achieved by making contributions for just 1 more year. There is quite some range of variation. The LAS surrender value is only 36.5% of the maturity value while the NPI surrender value is only 8.2% below the maturity value.

Surrender values are particularly low if a personal pension scheme is terminated after only a short period of operation. For example, if a scheme is terminated after only 1 year, the individual might lose 90% of his or her contributions, because the commissions paid to sales agents are front-end loaded. The individual would lose 40% of his or her contributions if the scheme was terminated within 2 years. For example, with the Prudential, premiums of £50 per month would produce a surrender value after two years of £800, compared with total contributions of £1,200. It would not be until the fifth year that the surrender value (£3,300) exceeded contributions (£3,000). However, with rebate-only personal pension schemes, the surrender value exceeds contributions from the first year on.

The widespread dissatisfaction with the commissions charged on personal pension schemes led the government to introduce statutory regulations from July 1, 1990, requiring providers of personal pension schemes to publish

Table 10.B3
Surrender values on 25-year with-profits
endowment schemes

	Maturity Value £	Terminal bonus as % of Maturity Value (%)	Surrender Value after 24 Years £	Surrender Value as % of Maturity Value (%)
Clerical Medical	41,046	55.6	35,007	85.3
Commercial Union	41,308	29.8	25,862	62.6
Crusader	31,676	48.0	25,812	81.5
Eagle Star	42,067	42.0	35,468	84.3
Equitable Life	33,621	52.4	30,517	90.8
Equity & Law	42,429	63.0	36,029	84.9
Friends' Provident	42,668	57.3	16,447	38.5
General Accident	42,154	52.2	34,867	82.7
GRE	30,928	51.1	26,051	84.2
LAS	35,176	60.9	12,850	36.5
Legal & General	40,421	46.1	32,580	80.6
London Life	37,875	54.0	15,848	41.8
National Mutual	34,207	57.1	13,592	39.7
NPI	31,489	58.2	28,916	91.8
Norwich Union	42,165	45.8	36,867	87.4
Pearl	38,068	63.3	15,556	40.9
Provident Mutual	31,517	53.1	27,471	87.2
Prudential	40,805	56.2	35,768	87.7
Royal Life	32,738	40.6	17,524	53.5
Royal London	42,418	49.6	30,942	72.9
Scottish Amicable	42,158	61.1	34,602	82.1
Scottish Equitable	30,399	50.4	13,345	43.9
Scottish Life	40,109	58.7	34,840	86.9
Scottish Mutual	33,674	50.0	27,318	81.1
Scot Provident	37,726	51.0	27,874	73.9
Scottish Widows	40,137	52.8	36,222	90.2
Standard Life	43,914	63.0	38,550	87.8
Sun Alliance	35,932	49.6	24,897	69.3
Sun Life	30,830	54.8	24,472	79.4
Average	37,574	52.7	27,452	73.1

Assumptions: Male, aged 29, £20 per month gross premium.

Source: Money Marketing, *Daily Telegraph*, June 1, 1991.

information on surrender values and the commissions earned by sales agents. All new schemes must indicate the proportion of contributions paid as commission to agents and the surrender values in each of the first 5 years. However, there was still concern about the high front-end loading of commissions and in July 1993 the Treasury ordered the Securities and Investments Board to prepare a new set of disclosure rules. The Treasury explained: "The

Table 10.B4
Transfer value of a single lump sum contribution

Total Contribution including Tax Credit	Transfer Value at End of				
	1st Year	2nd Year	3rd Year	4th Year	5th Year
£ 500	520.04	569.36	623.35	682.46	747.18
£ 1,000	1,040.08	1,138.72	1,246.70	1,364.92	1,494.36
£ 1,500	1,560.12	1,708.08	1,870.05	2,047.38	2,241.54
£ 2,000	2,080.16	2,277.44	2,493.40	2,729.84	2,988.72

Assumptions: an investment return of 10.75% per annum; an initial management charge of 5% of contributions and a monthly management charge equivalent to 1% per annum + value added tax (VAT); regular contributions are monthly in advance; a bid-offer spread of 5%; the basic rate tax credit is invested at the same time as the contributions; in practice, however, there will be a delay.

Source: Rothschild Asset Management, 1987.

required changes are new rules which will provide a clear and quantified account of the effect of life offices' practices on the value of the policy if cashed in early. New rules will require illustrations of projected returns on life policies using life offices' own recent changes – not industry standard assumptions. Adaptation of the best advice regime [is needed] to allow . . . proposals for the automatic disclosure of commission in cash terms at an early stage by all distribution channels."

The new disclosure rule came into force at the beginning of 1995. The main effect of the new rules will be to eliminate the front-end loading of commissions; otherwise, potential scheme members will simply be put off taking out personal schemes at all. This suggests that there will now be level commissions throughout the term of the policy. The level commissions will either be based on the size of the premiums or on the value of the fund's assets. This will have the effect of raising early surrender values although it is likely to lower maturity values. It will also have the effect of changing the form of the remuneration of sales staff from front-end commissions to salaries with bonuses.

Transfer penalties

Any transfer value into a personal pension scheme or between schemes will be invested in a single lump sum (known as a single premium) in one of the three types of scheme: endowment, unit-linked, or deposit administration.

Despite the supposed portability of personal pensions schemes, transfer

Table 10.B5
Transfer value of monthly contributions

Total Contribution including Tax Credit	Transfer Value at End of				
	1st Year	2nd Year	3rd Year	4th Year	5th Year
£ 50	598.87	1,254.54	1,972.38	2,758.30	3,618.74
£ 100	1,197.74	2,509.08	3,944.76	5,516.60	7,237.48
£ 150	1,796.61	3,763.62	5,917.14	8,274.90	10,856.22
£ 200	2,395.48	5,018.16	7,889.52	11,033.20	14,474.96

Assumptions: as for Table 10.B4.

Source: Rothschild Asset Management, 1987.

between schemes can be very expensive even for transfers between schemes offered by the same provider. The cost of the transfer can be as much as one-third of the transfer value. For example, Standard Life and Sun Life charge one-third of the transfer value for transfers between their group personal pension schemes and their individual personal pension schemes.

A few schemes, however, have no penalties on transfer to the schemes of other providers. An example is Rothschild Asset Management. Its prospective transfer values for single lump sum contributions and for monthly contributions are shown in Tables 10.B4 and 10.B5. These transfer values, which were calculated according to LAUTRO rules, must be paid into another pension scheme and cannot be paid directly to the pension scheme member. Any transfers will not count for the purpose of Inland Revenue limits on contributions.

Annuities

When a personal pension scheme matures on the nominated retirement date, a sum of money must be transferred to an insurance company to provide the pension annuity for the scheme member. Schemes provided by insurance companies will naturally want their members to take their pension annuities from them. But all personal pension scheme members are entitled to exercise an open-market option and choose an annuity provider of their choice. Table 10.B6 shows the annuities offered by the best five and worst five insurance companies in two cases. The first case is a level annuity for a 65-year-old male without guarantee, that is, the annuity does not have a guaranteed

Table 10.B6
Gross annual annuities for purchase price of £10,000

Level annuity without guarantee, male, 65 years

Best Five Schemes	Annuity (£ per year)	% Below Best
RNPF Nurses	1,158.36	0.0
Sun Life	1,103.84	4.7
Standard Life	1,101.60	4.9
Scottish Amicable	1,097.52	5.3
Co-op Insurance	1,081.56	6.6

Worst Five Schemes	Annuity (£ per year)	% Below Best
London & Manchester	977.76	15.6
Scottish Life	964.20	16.8
Providence Capitol	960.12	17.1
Scottish Equitable	950.04	18.0
GRE	888.40	23.3

Escalating annuity (5% p.a. compound) without guarantee, male, 65 years

Best Five Schemes	Annuity (£ first year)	% Below Best
RNPF Nurses	792.32	0.0
Standard Life	765.60	3.4
Sun Life	740.12	6.6
Britannic Assurance	734.04	7.4
Canada Life	732.72	7.5

Worst Five Schemes	Annuity (£ first year)	% Below Best
Providence Capitol	623.88	21.3
London & Manchester	613.56	22.6
Friends Provident	613.20	22.6
Eagle Star	577.08	27.2
GRE	530.70	33.0

Source: *Money Management*, April 1994.

minimum period of payment and stops on the death of the annuitant. The worst annuity is 23% below that of the best annuity. The second case is an escalating annuity which grows at 5% per annum compound, again for a 65-year-old male without guarantee. In this case, the worst annuity is one-third lower than that available from the best annuity.

References

Blake, D. 1992. *Issues in Pension Funding.* Routledge, London.
   1995. *Pension Schemes and Pension Funds in the United Kingdom.* Oxford University Press, Oxford.
Goode, R. 1993. *Pension Law Reform: Report of the Pension Law Review Committee* (CM 2342). Her Majesty's Stationery Office, London.
Halsbury's Statutes of England. 1970. 3d ed. and current statutes service. Butterworths, London.
Hannah, L. 1986. *Inventing Retirement: The Development of Occupational Pension Schemes in Britain.* Cambridge University Press, Cambridge.
Tolley's Pensions Handbook. 1995. Tolley Publishing Company, Croydon.
Tolley's Personal Pensions and Occupational Schemes: An Employer's Guide. 1988. Tolley Publishing Company, Croydon.
Tolley's Social Security and State Benefits 1994–95. 1994. Tolley Publishing Company, Croydon.

CHAPTER 11

Mandatory retirement saving:
Australia and Malaysia compared

Hazel Bateman and John Piggott

1   Introduction

In recent years, the idea that retirement provision become the mandated responsibility of firms or individuals, rather than part of the tax transfer arrangements of national governments, has attracted much attention. Mandatory retirement saving schemes can operate using a variety of institutional structures, and these will have implications for their economic and social impact. In this chapter we examine two such schemes, those of Australia and Malaysia. The most important institutional difference is that the Malaysian scheme is centralized, whereas in Australia a decentralized structure is employed.

A central feature of decentralized mandatory retirement saving schemes is that private-sector financial institutions play a crucial role in investing accumulations and in administering payouts. An appealing aspect of this kind of policy is that the direct link between government finances and retirement provision is much weaker than the tax-transfer model. While in principle it would be possible to modify government policy to neutralize the overall economic impact of these schemes, political constraints of other kinds (e.g., an electorally acceptable government deficit) would probably preclude such action. In sharp contrast to the pay-as-you-go social security policies that have been widely adopted in North America, Latin America, and Europe, in these schemes full funding[1] largely prevails. There is therefore an expectation

We would like to thank conference participants, and especially Salvador Valdés-Prieto, for comments and discussion, and Gina Wu for her fine research assistance. Geoffrey Kingston offered valuable advice on earlier versions of the chapter. Financial support under Australian Research Council Grants A79030246 and A79331125 is gratefully acknowledged.
[1] By full funding we mean that monies are set aside now for the purpose of providing retirement benefits when they become payable. However, Valdés-Prieto (1993b) points out, that unless contributions are used to increase the stock of national savings (i.e., invested in physical capital or claims on foreigners), only apparent rather than true funding is achieved.

318

that the introduction of or transition to mandated retirement provision will enhance aggregate saving performance.

Very few countries have actually adopted this kind of mandatory scheme, however. The most famous example is Chile. Australia, perhaps more directly comparable to other OECD countries, has introduced a similar system, the so-called Superannuation Guarantee, and Switzerland has a mandatory plan as part of its overall retirement provision armory. Other nations, such as Sweden, the Netherlands, and France, have widespread private retirement provision, usually based in the union movement, which approaches mandatory status.[2]

The centralized model of mandatory retirement provision, exemplified by the Malaysian Employees Provident Fund, is typical of the national provident funds that were set up in many British possessions over the past half century. The best known is that of Singapore, but about 20 countries currently operate such schemes. In general, provident funds were introduced into developing economies lacking developed financial markets and sophisticated tax transfer structures. They are of interest in the present context because they can be thought of as the centralized analogue of mandated private pension schemes. Individuals are compelled to make contributions to a central financial agency, which holds an account in their name. At retirement, the individual receives his accumulation, usually in lump sum form. Like private mandating, individuals are compelled to take responsibility for their retirement accumulations, and bear the investment risk.

The critical difference is that provident fund accumulations are held in a central fund, and are usually subject to a good deal of direct or indirect government control. While, nominally, these funds are separated from general government finance, in practice the separation is far from clean. This distinction is considered by Diamond in Chapter 2, who emphasizes the degree of "political insulation" of alternative retirement income policy structures.

There is now a substantial literature on economic aspects of retirement income policy, but it largely relates to a policy context in which pay-as-you-go social security schemes are predominant. By contrast, relatively little has been written on either mandatory pension policy or provident funds. In this chapter we discuss the implementation, operation, and impact of one example of each of these latter two policies – those of Australia and Malaysia.

To fix ideas, it is convenient to summarize the typical characteristics of the two types of scheme at the outset. As Table 11.1 reveals, the major differences flow directly or indirectly from whether the schemes are centralized. Centralized provident funds are associated with direct control of asset allocation and rates of return. The decentralized mandatory schemes enjoy

---

[2] These latter schemes may not be fully funded.

Table 11.1
Typical characteristics of private and public mandated retirement saving policies

	Privately managed mandated retirement saving	Centrally managed mandated retirement saving
Administration	Many private funds	Centralized: a single publicly administered fund.
Financing	Fully funded for private employees; partially funded for public-sector employees	Fully funded
Asset allocation controls	Very limited	Direct control often requiring very heavy purchases of national government bonds.
Fund performance	In line with market performance of financial assets	Return on investment regulated: may approximate the long-term bond rate.
Administrative costs	High	Low
Determination of benefit	Defined contribution; individual accounts	Defined contribution; individual accounts
Nature of benefit	Various	Lump sum
Availability of accumulation for nonretirement purposes	Very limited	Fairly liberal
Taxation	Various	None
Regulation	Prudential supervision by government	Centralized control
Coverage	Almost all employees	Almost all employees
Additional social security programs for the aged	Australia: Age pension, health insurance, etc.	Malaysia: None

much less restricted investment opportunities, with rates of return depending on market performance. However, the administration costs of the many – private – funds model are likely to exceed those of a centralized fund of the same aggregate size.

We begin in section 2 with a summary of the two economies, emphasizing conditions prevalent when their retirement saving policies were introduced. A more detailed account of retirement income policy in the two countries is offered in sections 3 and 4. Section 5 provides a comparative assessment of the two forms of mandated retirement income saving, while section 6 concludes with lessons for developing countries.

2 Australia and Malaysia: An overview

At first glance Australia and Malaysia appear quite similar. Both are ex-British colonies with relatively small populations located in the Southeast Pacific. They have similar constitutional arrangements and systems of government, and operate mandated retirement income schemes. In fact, however, the two economies are quite different: Australia is rich and developed, whereas Malaysia is still classified as a developing economy.

Table 11.2 reports a range of economic and demographic features. Australia has experienced almost continuous economic and political stability since Federation in 1901. It is a member of the OECD and designated a high-income industrial country by the World Bank; in 1991 GNP per capita stood at U.S. $17,050. Notwithstanding the recent recession, which saw real GDP fall by 1.6% in 1990–1991 and remain flat in 1991–1992, Australia's average annual growth of real GDP over the period 1980–1992 at around 3% was one of the highest of the OECD economies. In 1991 GDP totaled U.S. $300 billion, the ninth highest of the 22 high-income economies and around 6.5 times greater than Malaysia.

Malaysia was established in 1963 as a Federation of the States of the former Malaya (which had gained independence from the United Kingdom in 1957), the Bornean territories of Sabah and Sarawak, and Singapore. Prior to independence and federation, Malaya had experienced occupation by the Japanese from 1941 to 1945 and a significant period of internal political unrest. Despite these setbacks, Malaysia has consistently been one of the fastest growing economies in the world; over the period 1980–1991 real GDP grew at an average annual rate of 5.9%. Malaysia is currently designated by the World Bank as a middle-income developing country with GDP per capita in 1991 of U.S. $2,520.

The blueprint for the economic development of Malaysia has been a series of Malaysia Plans. The Sixth Malaysia Plan covering the period 1991–2000 is now being implemented. An overall objective is to become a developed country by the year 2020.

Current economic policy concerns in Australia include the related issues of persistent current account deficits, the growing size of foreign debt to GDP, and the falling national saving rate. Between 1970 and 1991 the gross

Table 11.2
Salient features of the Australian and Malaysian economies[a]

	Australia	Malaysia
Population (1992)	17.5 million	18.6 million
Population Growth (1980-1991)	1.5% pa	2.6% pa
Geographical Area	7,662,300 sq km	330,434 sq km
GDP per Capita ($US, 1991)	17,050	2,520
PPC[b] Estimate of GDP per Capita (US=100, 1991)	75.4	33.4
GDP ($US million, 1991)	299,800	46,980
GDP Growth (1980-1991)	3.1% p.a.	5.7% p.a.
Average Annual Inflation, GDP Deflator (1980-1991)	7.0%	1.7%
Gross Savings as % GDP:		
- 1970	27%	27%
- 1991	19%	30%
Life Expectancy at Birth (1991)		
- male	73	68
- female	80	73
% Population over 65 (1991)	10.9%	2.9%
% Population under 15 (1991)	22.1%	38.6%

Notes:
a   The amounts reported in this table are expressed in U.S. dollars. In 1993 the rates of exchange were A$ 1.47 to the US dollar and RM 2.6 to the U.S. dollar.
b   PPC = purchasing power of currencies

Sources: International Monetary Fund, *International Financial Statistics Year Book*, 1962, 1992; *World Bank Development Report 1993*, The World Bank, Washington D.C.; *Year Book Australia 1994*, Australian Bureau of Statistics, Canberra, Australia. The figures are based on World Bank estimates - see World Bank (1993), p. 255. They are used in preference to domestic estimates to facilitate comparison with Malaysia.

national saving rate fell from 27% of GDP to 19% of GDP.[3] (Similar falls have been experienced by many OECD countries.) By comparison, gross saving as a percentage of GDP has increased over this period in Malaysia from 27% in 1970 to 30% in 1991 – although the rate is falling after peaking at around 33% in the late 1980s. Similar increases have been experienced

---

[3] The figures are based on World Bank estimates – see World Bank, 1993, p. 255. They are used to facilitate comparison with Malaysia.

by other developing Asian economies.[4] However, there are concerns in Malaysia about the downward trend, particularly in private saving (see Fry, 1992).

In common with many developed countries, Australia's population is aging. The aged dependency ratio is estimated to nearly double over the next 40 years to around 30%. Malaysia, however, is a much younger country with 38.6% of the population under 15 (compared with 22.1% in Australia) and only 2.9% over the age of 65. While this difference can be explained to some extent by the higher life expectancies in Australia – of 73 for males and 80 for females (from birth), compared with 68 and 73 for Malaysia – Malaysia is experiencing, and is actively encouraging, much higher population growth.

The Superannuation Guarantee in Australia is a recent event, and a profile of Australia's current economic circumstances provides a good guide to the economic environment prevailing at the time of its introduction. It must be remembered, however, that Malaysia today is a quite different economy from that into which the Employees Provident Fund (EPF) was introduced in the early 1950s. It is therefore helpful to gain some sense of the relevant characteristics of Malaysia (then Malaya), 40 years past.

At that time, Malaya was still a British colony. The economy was recovering from the Japanese occupation during World War II and the country was experiencing significant internal political and racial problems as evidenced by the long-standing guerrilla warfare with Chinese-dominated Communists.

Nevertheless, Malaya had one of the highest standards of living in Southeast Asia and was one of the fastest growing economies in the region. This was largely due to an abundance of natural resources, which made it a world leader in the production and export of tin and rubber. Furthermore, a legacy of the British involvement in tin mining and rubber plantations since the late 1800s was a well-developed (but aging) system of public infrastructure – particularly roads and rail and port facilities.

Despite its prominence in Southeast Asia, Malaya in the 1950s was very much a developing country by world standards. Production and employment were concentrated in the agricultural sector and exports, and a relatively high proportion of GDP was accounted for by just a few primary products. In 1953, 61.3% of employees worked in agriculture, compared with only 7.1% in mining and 7.8% in manufacturing. Most of the population lived in rural areas and literacy and life expectancy were low.

In its 1953 survey of Malaya, the International Bank for Reconstruction and Development suggested that the availability of medium- and long-term finance presented the most significant problem for Malayan economic devel-

---

[4] The term "developing Asian economies" is due to FitzGerald (1993, p. 5). It includes China, Hong Kong, Republic of Korea, Malaysia, Singapore, Taiwan, and Thailand.

opment.[5] The survey noted that while Malaya was well served with banking facilities, these had traditionally concentrated on trade-related short-term finance. Long-term private investment was largely financed by reinvestment or by noninstitutional means (such as the family). Moreover, due to the political unrest in Malaya and the political uncertainties in Southeast Asia, Malaya could not count on a large inflow of foreign capital.

Unlike most of Western Europe and the Americas, but in common with countries in its region, Malaya entered the second half of the 20th century without a public social welfare system. The EPF, when established in 1951, was Malaya's first form of social security – and even that provided only retirement benefits on a defined contribution, individual account, and lump sum basis. Therefore, even in the 1950s, the Malayan bureaucracy had no experience with the establishment and administration of large-scale public assistance programs.

A provident fund was therefore particularly suitable as a means of retirement provision in the Malaya of 1951. The EPF secured retirement saving that was comprehensive in coverage, yet simple to administer and provided the pool of savings that were essential to the economic development of Malaya.[6]

3   Australia: The Superannuation Guarantee

Australia is virtually unique among OECD countries in reaching the 1990s with no national employment-related retirement income scheme. In July 1992, however, legislation was passed that established such a scheme. This section describes the development and operation of this scheme, the "Superannuation Guarantee."[7]

3.1   Development and nature of the Superannuation Guarantee

Traditionally, Australia has relied on a targeted universal flat-rate age pension for retirement. Entitlement to this transfer is based on age (currently 65 for men and 60 for women), residency status, income, and assets, but not on employment history. Although tax and other concessions existed for occupational superannuation,[8] participation was voluntary. There was no government

---

[5] See International Bank for Reconstruction and Development, 1955, particularly pp. 26–28.

[6] In its 1987 report on Malaysia, the World Bank notes that the EPF has been very successful as a means of mobilizing funds for public investment. However, it is currently failing as a source of funds for private sector investment (World Bank, 1989).

[7] This section draws on Bateman and Piggott, 1993, which presents and analyzes the Australian policy in greater detail.

[8] "Superannuation" is the Australian term for employment-based retirement provision. It corresponds roughly to the term "private pension."

policy to compel participation in an employment or earnings-related retirement income scheme, as is typical in other OECD countries.

Australia's status as odd man out seems to have been more a matter of historical and political accident than of any consistent policy stance. It was always recognized that the public age pension alone was not sufficient. Between 1913 and 1938, three unsuccessful attempts were made to introduce earnings-related retirement income arrangements similar to those which were proving popular in Western Europe and the Americas. In 1938 Australia even got as far as passing the enabling legislation (but subsequently deferred implementation indefinitely). However, on each occasion the government of the day succumbed to widespread opposition: from elements of the financial sector already providing such support, from the state governments because such arrangements would extend the Commonwealth government's powers, and finally from employers who were concerned about adding to the costs of production.

In the early 1970s, the Whitlam Labor government commissioned a report on retirement income. The resulting Hancock Report also recommended a scheme along the lines of U.S.- and European-style arrangements. The report, however, was not completed until after the change of government in 1975, and its recommendations were never acted upon.[9]

History and development of the Superannuation Guarantee
In the period following the election of the Fraser Coalition government in 1975, no new initiatives on retirement income policy were canvassed. Support for an Australian national earnings-related retirement income scheme was carried in this period by the trade-union movement. Prominent union leaders argued that superannuation should be a central feature of negotiated industrial conditions.

When the Hawke Labor government was elected in March 1983, a major plank in its economic strategy was a continuing contract with the union movement, the "Accord," which survives to the present. The Accord, along with Australia's then centralized wage determination system, was the crucible for establishing the broad superannuation arrangements that constituted Australia's first working version of a national earnings-related retirement income scheme. This was known as productivity award superannuation (PAS).

The idea of building an employer superannuation contribution into a

---

[9] The new Conservative government favored voluntary occupational superannuation rather than compulsory national arrangements. When announcing its rejection of the Hancock Report in 1979, the Conservative government established a task force to examine the role of occupational superannuation and the possible involvement of the union movement. The task force reported in 1983 with recommendations for a regulatory framework for the superannuation industry, proposals for vesting and preservation requirements, and proposals to attract annuity purchase.

national centralized wage decision was discussed between government and unions in 1985. The idea became reality in 1986, when the Accord Mark II was agreed and endorsed by the Conciliation and Arbitration Commission. The crucial element in that agreement was that while compensation to employees should be a 6% wage rise, to both keep pace with inflation and distribute productivity increases, half of the increase would accrue in the form of a 3% employer superannuation contribution. PAS was born.

In its early years, PAS won surprisingly general support. The Labor Party embraced PAS because it helped to solve two problems. First, the Australian economy was booming, and it was becoming necessary to contain aggregate demand. A full 6% wage increase, consistent with real wage maintenance, was seen as likely to magnify this upswing of the business cycle. Second, PAS helped to mollify sections of the Australian Labor Party, which had been advocating a conventional pay-as-you-go social security scheme for some time. The aging of the population was making their calls more urgent. Further, compulsory saving in the form of superannuation could be seen to address the problem of deficient national saving.

The union movement saw PAS as a method of securing retirement rights additional to the age pension for its membership. It was also able to claim that it had achieved full compensation for inflation. Finally, unions saw in PAS the long-term prospect of gaining some degree of control over substantial capital funds.

Financial firms strongly supported these arrangements as they ensured their long-term involvement in retirement income provision. Employers were generally opposed. First, they did not accept that productivity increases were available for redistribution and, more important, they resented union involvement in areas that had traditionally been their domain. However, in accordance with Australia's centralized industrial relations framework, the employers abided by the decision of the Conciliation and Arbitration Commission.

It is important to recognize that the policy received broad support because it was perceived as addressing a major gap in social policy – one that many think would become more critical with demographic transition. Plans were mooted for two more such decisions that might carry the total PAS commitment to 9% of earnings. Combined with a proposed compulsory 3% employee contribution, this was expected to generate adequate income replacement in retirement.

Experience proved, however, that the PAS suffered from administrative difficulties, particularly relating to compliance. Because, under the Australian constitution, the national government has no power over superannuation policy, tax powers were used to enforce compliance. This changed the basis of the scheme from reliance on industrial awards to reliance on national legislation. Legislation was introduced requiring all employers to make super-annuation contributions to a complying fund on behalf of their employees.[10] If the contribution was not made, a charge would be levied on the employer to enable the government to make the contribution. This mechanism – the Superannuation Guarantee Charge – is the legislative linchpin of the new Australian mandated retirement income policy.[11]

Operation and policy context

The Superannuation Guarantee may be thought of as the Australian counter-part to national earnings-related retirement income schemes operating over-seas, such as the U.S. Social Security system, or the U.K. State Earnings-Related Pension Scheme. As in the Australian case, these schemes coexist with social welfare safety nets, and with supplementary occupational superan-nuation. Table 11.3 summarizes the main features of the Superannuation Guarantee.

As a result, Australian retirement income policy now approximates the three-pillar approach common throughout the developed world. The first pillar is the universal (but targeted) public age pension financed from general revenues;[12] the second pillar is the mandatory private provision under the Superannuation Guarantee; the third (and now less important) pillar is volun-tary (but tax-preferred) occupational or personal superannuation. The public age pension provided under the first pillar is withdrawn when retirement income and assets provided under pillars two and three exceed statutory thresholds.

The Superannuation Guarantee encourages employers to make superannu-ation contributions on behalf of their employees to complying superannuation funds. These contributions are then invested on behalf of the employees, in a fund chosen by the employer. In current practice, the chosen funds are frequently industry-based, with relatively conservative asset allocations. However, these allocations are becoming more balanced as the funds mature.

Employees may access the accrued benefits in the form of a lump sum or an income stream upon reaching the preservation age of 55 (currently being increased to 60). The arrangements apply to all employers and to almost all

---

[10] As well as enforcing compliance the Superannuation Guarantee also improved coverage. The previous PAS arrangements only applied to employees covered by industrial awards while the Superannuation Guarantee applies to all employees.

[11] The charge is equal to the shortfall in the minimum level of superannuation support plus an interest component and an administrative component. It is not a tax-deductible expense for employers. These provisions mean that it is cheaper to meet the mandated superannuation requirements than to incur the charge.

[12] The Australian public age pension is universal to the extent that all residents of qualifying age are eligible, but targeted to the extent that it is subject to income and assets means tests.

Table 11.3
Features of the Australian Superannuation Guarantee

Established	1992
Contributions (by 2002)	9% employer + (proposed) 3% employee[a]
Funding	Fully funded Individual accounts Many private funds No investment restrictions[b]
Benefits	Defined contribution based Fully vested, portable and preserved to aged 55 (being increased to 60) No early withdrawals Choice of lump sum, pension, annuity - tax incentives to encourage income streams
Statutory Coverage	All employees aged 18-65 with earnings > A$ 450 month Self employed not covered
Taxation	Employer contributions tax deductible Fund income (contributions and earnings) and benefits taxed at concessionary rates
Administration and Costs	Perceived to be complex and apparently costly for workers contributing small amounts. (However, there are many funds and choice of both investment strategies and retirement benefit products)
Safety Net	Public age pension provided to all elderly residents, subject to income and assets means tests

[a]   The 9% employer contribution is being phased in over the period 1992-2002. The government is committed to an additional 3% contribution.
[b]   Except a 5% maximum on in-house assets.

employees.[13] Employees earning less than A$450 per month were specifically excluded on the grounds of high relative administrative costs for small contributions.[14]

The minimum level of superannuation support is being phased in, gradually increasing over the next 8 years. The timetable for implementation has

[13] Not included are employees who earn less than A$450/month, part-time employees under 18, employees over 65, members of the Defence Reserve Forces, and certain nonresident employees and employees of nonresident employers.

[14] This threshold was the subject of considerable political debate. In the original proposal the threshold had been set at A$250. It was increased to ensure passage through the Senate controlled by the opposition parties.

been legislated, with the target of a 9% employer and a proposed 3% employee contribution to be reached by 2002. The phasing in of employer contributions was a product of both political convenience and macroeconomic necessity. An election was due in 1992 (the year of implementation) and the economy was in the midst of a recession. It was considered that over the following 8–10 years there would be sufficient labor productivity growth to more than offset the Superannuation Guarantee impost.

Employer superannuation support under the Superannuation Guarantee must be fully vested (i.e., the member is fully entitled to all accrued benefits), fully preserved (i.e., accrued benefits must remain in a fund until the statutory preservation age for access to benefits is reached),[15] fully funded, and be made into a "complying" superannuation fund.[16] The earnings base is generally that required under the relevant industrial award. This is subject to a cap of A\$80,000[17] (indexed annually to average weekly ordinary time earnings). The Superannuation Guarantee thus applies only to the first A\$80,000 of earnings.

In summary, the retirement income provided under the Superannuation Guarantee has the following features:

- privately provided,
- broad coverage,
- generally fully funded,
- benefits generally determined by defined contributions, with individual accounts, and
- choice of lump sum or income stream at retirement.

Taxation
It is possible to tax retirement accumulations at three points – contributions, earnings, and benefits. Australia is unique in applying taxes at all these points. Given Australia's heavy reliance on direct taxes and high marginal rates of personal income tax, the rates of tax on retirement accumulations are highly concessionary. Nevertheless, the implicit cascading of tax liabilities probably leads in some cases to effective tax rates that are high when compared with retirement saving taxes prevailing in other developed countries. Table 11.4 presents a simple schema of Australian superannuation taxation.

---

[15] The statutory preservation age in Australia is currently 55. It is progressively being increased to 60 over the next 20 years.

[16] The term "complying fund" is explained in the discussion on regulatory aspects. For public-sector employers, a government guarantee can substitute for full funding.

[17] A\$80,000 is equivalent to around two times average earnings. It was felt unnecessary to compel the entire statutory contribution above this ceiling. High income earners are more likely to be covered by preexisting arrangements or be capable of voluntarily providing for their retirement.

Table 11.4
Taxation of Superannuation in Australia
(All dollar amounts are for 1993-1994)

Contributions	Fund Income[b]	Benefits
Employer: Tax deductible up to contribution limits	Contributions: Employer contributions generally taxed (at 15%), employee contributions generally untaxed[c]	Lump sum: <Threshold[d], no taxation Threshold - A$ 400,000, taxed at 15% >A$ 400,000 taxed as ordinary income
Employee: Limited tax deductibility for self-employed and employees without employer support. Otherwise not tax deductible[a]	Earnings: Taxed at 15%	Pension/annuity: - Pension/annuity taxed as ordinary income less 15% rebate No rebate if commuted value > A$ 800,000

Notes:

a. Income tested 10% rebate for up to A$ 1000 p.a. of personal contributions available in some circumstances.

b. For Australian taxation purposes fund income comprises, taxable contributions and fund earnings. This allows imputation credits on dividend income to offset taxation on both earnings and taxable contributions.

c. Taxation of contributions determined by tax preference of contributions in the hands of the contributor.

d. Threshold in 1993-1994 is A$ 77,796.

Employer contributions to complying funds are tax deductible up to age-determined contribution limits,[18] but are taxed in the hands of the fund at a rate of 15%. Employee contributions are generally made out of net of tax income although a limited income-tested rebate is available and capped deductibility exists for the self-employed and uncovered employees. Employee contributions that have not received tax concessions are not taxed in the hands of the fund.

For tax purposes, fund income comprises taxable contributions and fund earnings. The statutory tax rate is 15%, but this is reduced to the extent that income accrues in the form of dividends or capital gains. Full corporate tax imputation credits are available on dividend income (which may be set off against tax on any income including capital gains and taxable contributions). The capital gains tax is indexed to inflation, but applies to all assets disposed of after June 30, 1988.

Superannuation benefits are taxed as well. As can be seen in Table 11.4, the taxation of benefits depends on the type of benefit (i.e., whether it is taken as a lump sum or an income stream) and its size.[19]

Taking an income stream (i.e., an annuity or pension) with a superannuation benefit is not compulsory but is encouraged by various tax incentives. There is no benefits tax as there is with lump sums, the limit for tax preferred benefits is higher, and a 15% tax rebate on personal taxation of retirement income is available. However, these concessions interact with broader tax and age pension policy in complex ways, which for many retirees negate the apparent tax advantages of taking an income stream. Bateman, Kingston, and Piggott (1993) analyze this issue in detail.

In summary, the taxation of superannuation has the following two features: taxation of contributions, fund earnings, and benefits; and tax incentives (but no compulsion) to take superannuation benefits as an income stream.

Regulatory aspects

We now turn to the regulatory framework within which the Superannuation Guarantee operates. Since the national government does not have direct constitutional power to regulate superannuation, it must enforce the superannuation industry's regulatory framework using alternative powers. In this

---

[18] The following age-based annual contribution limits will apply from 1 July 1994: under 35, A$9,000; 35 to 49, A$25,000; and 50 and over, A$60,000.

These limits are designed to be high enough to allow older workers who have not benefited from the Superannuation Guarantee during their early working years to make (or have made on their behalf) "fast-track" contributions, but low enough to prevent excessive tax minimization by wealthy persons close to retirement channeling large sums of money through tax-preferred superannuation funds.

[19] Benefits that exceed certain limits – known as reasonable benefit limits or RBLs – are taxed at the top marginal personal income tax rate.

instance it uses a combination of its corporations power, old-age pensions power, and taxation power. The central concept of the legislation is the "complying fund" – that is, one that complies with the requirements set out in the legislation.[20] Under the Superannuation Guarantee, contributions must be made to complying funds, and superannuation tax concessions apply only to complying funds, whether the contributions fall under the Superannuation Guarantee or not. Its trustees and investment managers are bound by various legislated duties and responsibilities and are subject to civil or criminal penalties for serious breaches. The requirements which must be satisfied by a complying fund include prudential standards, reporting standards, minimum benefit standards. A noncomplying fund is subject to tax at the top marginal personal tax rate on fund income.

Trustees are responsible for the investment strategy of the fund. (For funds with five or more members, trust boards must comprise equal representation of members and employers.) The only portfolio restrictions are:

- a prohibition on borrowing other than for short-term cash flow purposes;
- a requirement that investments be on commercial terms;
- a restriction on loans to, or investments in, an employer sponsor (or an associate of the employer sponsor)[21] to 5% of total assets (this is progressively being reduced from 10 per cent); and
- a prohibition on lending to, financially assisting, or acquiring assets from members.

These portfolio restrictions leave the maximum possible discretion to fund managers to allocate investment funds as they see fit and this is widely seen as compatible with the interests of fund members. Managers may, however, be subject to additional restrictions imposed by the trust deed (the legal document asserting the fund's existence).

In summary, in terms of the regulatory framework, superannuation provided under the Superannuation Guarantee arrangements must have the following two features: contributions must be made to complying funds; and all benefits must be fully vested, preserved, and portable.

Implementation and administrative issues

A number of implementation and administrative issues have arisen with the introduction of the Superannuation Guarantee. These include the treatment of existing employer superannuation support, the application of the arrange-

---

[20] The relevant legislation is the Superannuation Industry (Supervision) Act 1993 and the Superannuation Industry (Supervision) Regulations 1994.

[21] Associate is defined widely to include any persons or entities (in Australia or overseas) who are in any way related to the employer.

ments to transient workers and multiple job holders, the members' choice of fund and remedies for fraud.

Treatment of previous employer superannuation support. Superannuation Guarantee requirements can be met by preexisting employer superannuation support.

Transient workers and multiple job holders. The Superannuation Guarantee is well suited to the situation in which a single employer makes contributions into the same superannuation fund for an employee's entire working life – but this is unlikely to be the case. Many persons change jobs frequently or are multiple-job holders.

The requirement under the Superannuation Guarantee that benefits be fully vested, fully preserved, and portable should reduce any adverse effects for mobile workers, providing the administrative fees charged for moving accrued benefits between funds are not great. However, it appears that these fees can be substantial. Further, multiple-job holders may find that contributions are being made on their behalf into several funds. This suggests a number of potential problems in terms of administration costs as well as keeping track of the accrued benefits. In particular, multiple-job holders could face relatively high costs and charges under the Superannuation Guarantee arrangements as the norm for award/industry funds is for flat-rate charges.

A related issue is the high proportion of administrative charges that small accumulations attract. For example, industry funds charge a flat rate of between A$1 and A$2 per week to administer members accounts. Proposals currently being canvassed include the use of the Australian Taxation Office as a holding fund until contributions reach a suitable size for transfer to a superannuation fund.[22]

Choice of fund. Under the Superannuation Guarantee, employees are not necessarily given a choice of superannuation fund. Employers are only required to ensure that the contributions are made into complying funds.

Fraud. The Superannuation Guarantee means that much greater emphasis is placed on private provision for retirement. As a result, the retirement benefit itself is dependent on an appropriate investment policy and is exposed to misappropriation and fraud. Recent policy amendments have addressed these con-

---

[22] This proposal is being supported by the trade-union movement and superannuation and life industry lobby groups. The joint industry proposal recommends that small payments of up to A$125 per quarter be directed to the tax office and that, once the member balance exceeds A$900, the individual would be contacted and advised to transfer the monies into a superannuation fund.

cerns by legislating the duties and responsibilities of trustees and investment managers and introducing a superannuation industry levy to assist members who have suffered loss as a result of fraud or theft.

4   The Malaysian Employees Provident Fund[23]

Malaysia was one of the first of around 20 developing countries to institute the provident fund method of financing retirement benefits.[24] Malaysia's primary provident fund was established in 1951 and is called the Employees Provident Fund (EPF).[25]

4.1   Introduction

Under the enabling EPF Act, employers and employees must contribute a predetermined statutory percentage of the employee's salary to the EPF on a monthly basis. The contributions are credited to each member's account and interest (known as dividends in Malaysia) is calculated on the minimum monthly balance of the member's account. Full withdrawal is available at age 55, with earlier partial withdrawals at age 50 or for housing purchase.

The EPF is the only scheme in Malaysia to provide retirement benefits for employees on a general basis. Retirement benefits for some government employees and the armed forces (and other occupations such as teachers) are covered under separate legislation[26] and, although social insurance and assistance exist for invalidity, sickness, and workers compensation, there is no "safety net" public pension.

Since its inception in 1951 the EPF has experienced strong growth, due to

---

[23] This section draws on Bank Negara Malaysia (1962–1993), Bank Negara Malaysia (1962–1991), CCH Tax Editors (1990a, 1990b), Dasuki (1992), Economist Intelligence Unit (1989), Employees Provident Fund (1989, 1991), Kharas (1989).

[24] Other countries include Fiji (1966), Gambia (1981), Ghana (1965), India (1952), Indonesia (1951), Kenya (1965), Kiribati (1976), Nepal (1964), Nigeria (1961). Papua New Guinea (1980), Singapore (1953), Solomon Islands (1973), Sri Lanka (1958), Swaziland (1974), Vanuatu (1987), Western Samoa (1962), Yemen (1987), and Zambia (1965); see Dixon (1982), United States Department of Health and Human Services (1991).

[25] The Employees Provident Fund (EPF) was established by the Employees Provident Fund Ordinance in 1951 and contributions were first received on July 1, 1952. This ordinance has since been replaced by the Employees Provident Fund (Amendment) Act 1958 and more recently the Employees Provident Fund Act 1991.

Malaysia did not come into existence until 1963 when the Federation of Malaya merged with the Bornean territories of Sarawak and Sabah, and Singapore. Therefore, the reference to the establishment of the EPF refers to the Malayan EPF. Singapore's provident fund was established separately, and the Bornean territories were not parties to the EPF until 1967.

[26] However, these arrangements are being phased out.

Table 11.5
Features of the Employees Provident Fund

Established	1951
Contributions (1994)	15% employer, 12% employee
Funding	Fully funded Individual accounts Single publicly governed fund At least 70% total and 50% annual additional assets in Malaysian government securities
Benefits	Defined contribution based Fully vested Full retirement benefits at age 55 Partial retirement benefits at age 50 and early withdrawals for home purchase Lump sum benefits only
Statutory Coverage	All employees over 15 Voluntary for self-employed
Taxation	Contributions tax deductible Fund earnings and benefits untaxed
Administration and Costs	Easy to administer and low costs (but no choice of fund and no provision of retirement income streams)
Safety Net	No public age pension

widening coverage and, in recent years, high employment rates. Between 1952 and 1992 membership has grown from 0.5 million persons to 6.5 million, covered employers from 11,918 to nearly 200,000, annual contributions from RM27 million[27] to RM5.56 billion and annual investments from RM516 million to RM60.9 billion.

In addition to its role as Malaysia's primary social security institution, the EPF has been instrumental in the economic development of Malaysia over the past 40 years as the major provider of public investment finance and more recently as a source of finance for housing. By 1991, assets of the EPF totaled 40.8% of GDP (up from 17.2% in 1978), making it the biggest financial and saving institution in the country. Its main features are summarized in Table 11.5.

---

[27] RM denotes the Malaysian currency, ringgit. The value of the ringgit in terms of U.S. dollars has been quite stable: In 1963 the rate of exchange was RM3 to the U.S. dollar compared with the current rate of exchange of around RM2.6 to the U.S. dollar.

4.2   Operation of the Employees Provident Fund

Coverage

Initially the EPF covered only low-wage employees (earning RM400[28] per month or less) working in companies with at least 10 employees. Coverage has increased significantly: In 1963 it was extended to employees earning up to RM500 per month in companies with at least 3 employees; in 1964 all companies were included and since 1970 EPF membership has been extended to all wage earners.

Currently, all employees over the age of 15 and under a contract of service or apprenticeship are required to be members of the EPF and therefore to make regular contributions. The self-employed may contribute on a voluntary basis, although expatriates, domestic servants paid from private accounts, and partners in a partnership are specifically excluded from the EPF.

In 1991 around 86% of the labor force were members of the EPF. However, only around 50% of these were active members – that is, they had contributed to the EPF for at least 1 month in the previous year. This finding is consistent with an economy undergoing rapid development, in which work patterns and mores are changing quickly. It does mean, however, that the aggregate and average EPF statistics reported in this section must be interpreted with caution. Of the 14% of the labor force who were not members, around two-thirds were members of other provident funds (such as the Armed Forces Fund or the Teachers Provident Fund) and around one-third were either exempt or unemployed (Fry, 1992, p. 24).

Contributions

The statutory contribution rates applicable to employers and employees have increased almost threefold since the establishment of the EPF in 1951. Table 11.6 summarizes these changes. The contribution rates effective in 1994 are 15% of earnings for employers and 12% for employees. The base income to which the contribution rates apply includes all remuneration except service charges, overtime, and retirement benefits. There is no income ceiling.

Investments by the EPF

Asset allocation.   The asset allocation of the EPF reflects its central role as a purchaser of government debt. (We will develop this point further.) In 1991, Malaysian Government Securities comprised some 73.6% of total assets. Until 1991 it had been a requirement of the EPF Act that it hold at least 70% of its total investments and allocate 70% of additional annual investments in Malaysian government securities. Of the remainder, equities accounted for

[28] In current (1993) ringgit.

Table 11.6
Contribution rates under the EPF

Year	Employer Rate (%)	Employee Rate (%)	Total %
1952	5	5	10
1975	7	6	13
1980	11	9	20
1993	12	10	22
1994	15	12	27

Sources: Employees Provident Fund, *Annual Report 1991*, Fry (1992).

only 1.6%, with fixed interest securities of various kinds making up the balance.

In the 1991 revisions to the act, the 70% annual investment rule was amended to 50%, but the 70% aggregate was retained. The proportion of total assets held in the form of government securities has always been high and until recently, accounted for over 90% of total assets. It has been falling in recent years and is now approaching its statutory floor.

The downward trend in the EPF's holding of government securities is a direct result of the reduced demands of the government for debt finance – due to lower budget deficits and an ongoing privatization program. The EPF is now broadening its investments, in line with recent amendments to the act, which allow more scope to invest in other securities, joint ventures, real property, and foreign securities.

Dividends (interest). Subject to a statutory minimum nominal annual dividend of 2.5%, the EPF is free to set the dividends.[29] Dividends have generally been significantly higher than the statutory minimum and in only 3 years (1973, 1974, and 1981) has the declared dividend been less than the increase in the CPI. Declared dividend rates for the years 1952 to 1991 are set out in Table 11.7.

While the dividend rates reported in Table 11.7 indicate a reasonable investment performance, they do not indicate that the EPF could not have done better with a more diversified asset base. Fry (1992) goes some way toward investigating this in a comparison of the EPF dividend rates with those available from voluntary saving. His results are summarized in Table 11.8.

Fry concludes that "EPF contributions have not been subject to any implicit

---

[29] If the fund fails to generate a 2.5% dividend rate, the Malaysian government will finance the dividend through an advance (subject to repayment).

Table 11.7
Dividends credited to EPF accounts

Year	Nominal Dividend Rate %	Inflation Rate %
1952-1959	2.5	not available
1960-1962	4.0	0.1 (1962)
1963	5.0	3.1
1964	5.25	-0.4
1965-1967	5.5	1.8
1968-1970	5.75	0.4
1971	5.8	1.7
1972-1973	5.85	7.1
1974-1975	6.6	11.2
1976-1978	7.0	4.2
1979	7.25	3.7
1980-1982	8.0	7.9
1983-1987	8.5	1.9
1988-1991	8.0	3.4

Source: Employees Provident Fund, *Annual Report 1991*.

Table 11.8
Yields on domestic assets in Malaysia, 1971 - 1991

	EPF Dividends	Bank Deposits	Government Bonds	Equities	Gold	Housing
			Compound Yields (percent)			
1971-1981	95.12	103.77	102.80	445.07	1024.03	204.34
1981-1991	120.94	102.40	103.31	37.07	-21.24	12.85

Source: Fry (1992), pp. 28 and 29.

tax in the form of lower yields than comparable alternative domestic assets with market-determined rates of return" (Fry 1992, p. 27). Nevertheless, comparison of compound yields over the 1970s strongly suggests that the dividend rate was set below the average rate earned by the assets held over this period.

Benefits and withdrawals

Forms of withdrawals and benefits.   The EPF provides retirement benefits, benefits for contingencies such as death and disability, and preretirement partial withdrawals for housing purchase. Withdrawals and benefits are paid

Table 11.9
Withdrawals from the EPF in 1991

	Value of Withdrawals as Percentage of Total Withdrawals	Average Withdrawal (Ringgit)
Retirement Benefit at age 55	33.6	12,022
Partial Retirement Benefit at Age 50	14.4	7,922
Withdrawal for Housing Purchase		
- low-cost housing	13.9	8,002
- non-low-cost housing	26.8	8,324
- housing mortgage	0.1	10,602
Death and Invalidity Benefits	7.2	6,761
Annual Dividend	0.2	4,727
Leaving Country	3.7	32,732

Source: Employees Provident Fund, *Annual Report 1991*, pp. 49 and 53.

as lump sums only. Withdrawals from the EPF in 1991 are summarized in Table 11.9.

Retirement benefits.   At age 55, a member has three options: withdraw the entire amount from the EPF account, leave the amount in the account and withdraw the annual dividend only, or leave the entire amount in the EPF to accumulate further. The second and third options may continue for an indefinite period. Most members take the first option. In 1991 there were 55,014 full withdrawals at age 55 compared with 942 annual dividends withdrawals.

The average amount of the full withdrawal was RM12,022, which is about the same as the annual salary for a typical employee. In addition, a partial retirement withdrawal (of one-third of the accumulated benefit) is available at age 50. These accounted for 14.4% of the total amount withdrawn in 1991 and averaged RM7,922. All of these benefits are taken as lump sums. There are no arrangements to take phased withdrawals, pensions, or annuities from the EPF.

Withdrawals for housing purchase.   The EPF housing withdrawals are the only form of assistance given for home purchase in Malaysia. Accumulated benefits in the EPF have been available for housing purchase since the mid 1970s. There are currently three housing schemes under the EPF, all of which allow withdrawals (which do not have to be paid back) up to a maximum of RM20,000. Withdrawals for housing purchase are quite common and in 1991 accounted for 40.8% of the total amount withdrawn.

Other withdrawals. A member can also withdraw the entire amount from his EPF account if the member is physically or mentally incapacitated from further employment or leaves Malaysia on a permanent basis.[30] If a member dies, the full amount of the EPF account is available to the beneficiaries.

Adequacy of retirement benefits. A standard analysis of the EPF, based on contribution and earnings rates, reveals that current policy parameters are capable of yielding adequate income replacement in retirement. Simulations carried out by the EPF and reported in Fry (1992, pp. 35–36), show, for example, that under the assumptions of continuous employment for 37 years, with a contribution rate of 20%, no withdrawals for housing purchase or at age 50, and a life expectancy of 75, the accumulated benefits in the EPF account for a clerical worker retiring at age 55 would yield an annuity equivalent of 84% of final income. Current benefit levels, however, do not support this analysis. With average benefits at age 55 in 1991 of just RM12,022 (around a single year's earnings for a typical Malaysian worker), it appears that even if the benefit were used to purchase a lifetime, indexed income stream, the replacement of preretirement income would be far from adequate.

We have not been able to account satisfactorily for this inconsistency. But at least three factors that constitute a partial explanation can be identified. First, withdrawals for housing purchase tend to dissipate accumulations, and if this occurs early in the working life cycle, the earnings base is severely eroded. Second, and probably more important, relatively few workers in Malaysia entering the work force in the 1950s pursued continuous market employment to the present. It is possible that the average benefit to retirees aged 55 is substantially reduced by large numbers of very small payouts. This view is supported by the observation that only about half of the 86% of the labor force who belong to the EPF currently contribute. Finally, current retirees did not enjoy contribution rates at anything like their current levels through the earlier part of their working lives. As Table 11.6 shows, until 1975 the combined contribution rate stood at 10%, and was then raised to only 13% for the succeeding 5 years. The current statistical picture is that the EPF seems to deliver less than adequate performance with respect to some combination of coverage and replacement.

Furthermore, because the EPF provides lump sum benefits only, Malaysian retirees are not assured of secure income in retirement, even if the accumulated benefits are adequate. In the absence of compulsory life annuity purchase, retirees are vulnerable to inflation and longevity risk. In the absence of compulsory pension or annuity purchase, it is unclear how current retirees use their lump sum benefits. Anecdotal evidence suggests that many use it to pay off their house.

---

[30] Except to reside in Singapore.

Taxation

Saving via the EPF is effectively tax exempt. Employer contributions are tax deductible up to a maximum of 15% of earnings (the statutory employer contribution rate for 1994), while fund members are allowed a total tax deduction of RM3,500 per annum to cover employee contributions to the EPF and life insurance premiums. With typical earnings in Malaysia of around RM1000 per month, just about all employee contributions would be tax deductible. Furthermore, all income of the EPF and all member withdrawals are tax exempt. In a broad tax environment where half of total tax revenues derive from direct taxation, these concessions are very significant.

Regulation and administration

The EPF is a trust fund and its trustee is the EPF board. The board was established by an act of Parliament and has the status of a statutory body. It is under the control of the minister of finance. The board has 20 members who are appointed for 3-year terms by the minister and comprises a chairman, a deputy chairman, and 18 members representing the government, employers, employees, and the finance profession. The 1991 amendments to the EPF Act established an investment panel (of 7 members) to be responsible for the investments of the EPF. However, it cannot act independently and is subject to the direction of the EPF Board and the approval of the minister.

The board is required to submit annual accounts to the government auditor and an annual report to the minister to be tabled before Parliament. In addition annual statements are required to be sent out to active members twice a year and to nonactive members on request.

Costs

The Malaysian EPF is not costly to operate. The EPF 1991 annual report shows that operating costs in 1991 were about 1.7% of annual contributions. To put this figure in context, Valdés-Prieto (1993a, p. 52), estimates that the cost of administration of the EPF per active member is 12% of the cost of the Chilean scheme (and 19% of the cost excluding retirement income stream provision) and two-thirds of the cost of the U.S. social security system. The lower costs in Malaysia can be largely attributed to the existence of a single fund.

4.3 The role of the EPF in national development

Over the past 40 years, the EPF has been the largest institutional source of long-term finance in the Malaysian capital market. This role has been reinforced over time with the increase in the coverage of the EPF in the 1960s and the regular increases in contribution rates (from a total of 10% of earnings in 1951 to 27% in 1994).

Table 11.10
Contribution of EPF to national saving

Year	GNS/GDP	(EPF Contributions + Fund Interest)/GNS	(ΔEPF Balances + Housing Withdrawals)/GNS
1984	30.7	17.22	na
1985	27.5	22.18	na
1986	27.4	26.76	22.91
1987	33.6	21.64	18.90
1988	33.0	20.17	17.62
1989	30.0	22.65	19.36
1990	30.0	22.55	19.49
1991	27.8	25.32	na

Source: Asher (1992) , Table 6, page 27.

The EPF played a vital role in the economic development of Malaya/ Malaysia in the years following independence, providing around 30% to 40% of the public financing for the early Malaya/Malaysian Plans. It provided 39% of the finance for the First Malayan 5-Year Plan (1956–1960), 25% of the finance for the Second Malayan 5-Year Plan (1961–1965), 20% of the finance for the First Malaysian Plan (1966–1970), and over 40% of the government's total borrowings for the Second Malaysian Plan (1971–1975). The trend has continued to the present day with the EPF consistently providing close to 50% of government debt. In 1992, 52% of government debt was held by the EPF.

Moreover, the EPF has made a significant contribution to national saving. Asher (1992) has calculated that since the mid 1980s, the EPF saving has accounted for between 20% and 25% of national saving – however, these estimates do not take account of any saving substitution as a result of compulsory EPF saving. Asher's estimates are detailed in Table 11.10. The first column reports an estimate of the ratio of gross national saving (GNS) to GDP while columns 2 and 3 report two different measures of EPF saving as a ratio of gross national saving.

5   A comparative assessment

We have described the development and operation of privately managed mandatory retirement saving in Australia and its centrally managed analogue in Malaysia. In this section we provide a comparative assessment of those two forms of mandatory retirement saving and identify lessons for other countries considering implementing such policies.

The perspective from which we approach this exercise is that of orthodox economics. We assume that retirement income policies are prevalent because of pervasive market failures and price distortions affecting retirement provision. These limit the extent to which individuals provide for their own retirement, especially the amount of voluntary saving undertaken, and the kinds of possibilities offered by private markets to a retiree wishing to insure against various kinds of risks.

The criteria we use emphasize the extent to which policies address these market failures and price distortions.

5.1 Criteria for assessing retirement income policy

Criteria for assessing retirement income policy can be divided into two groups – those directly relevant to the retiring individual, and those addressing the allocation and distribution of resources in the economy as a whole.

From the point of view of the individual, a national retirement income scheme can be thought of as insurance. As Bodie (1990) has pointed out, there are many sources of income uncertainty that a risk-averse individual confronting retirement would like to insure against. In the spirit of Bodie, we list the most important in the context of mandatory retirement saving:

- *Coverage risk* is the statistical risk of a labor force participant falling outside the coverage of mandatory retirement saving.
- *Replacement rate risk* is the possibility that the retiree will not have enough income to maintain his standard of living after retiring comparable with that enjoyed during his preretirement years.
- *Investment risk* is the possibility that the amount saved for retirement will be inadequate because the assets in which money is invested performs poorly.
- *Longevity risk* is the risk that the retiree will live longer than expected, and thus exhaust the amount saved for retirement before he dies.
- *Inflation risk* is the risk of price increases, which erode the purchasing power of the lifetime savings.

The conventional criteria in an economy-wide context are efficiency and equity, both of which can be interpreted in the context of mandatory retirement saving.

With regard to efficiency and saving, policies should be designed to offset the tendency for families to provide too little of their own resources for retirement. There are a number of reasons why this tendency prevails: Myopia is perhaps the most prevalent. In the Australian case, this is compounded by price-distorting income taxation and social welfare safety net payments; in Malaysia, at least in the past, underdeveloped capital markets contributed to low saving rates. In addition, action should be taken to correct market failure related to lifetime annuities. Mandating their purchase is the most effective response.

A further complication arises when demographic transition is considered. This may well lead to a decline in the saving rate, as retirees sell off their assets to finance retirement consumption, and the savings undertaken by the future working population declines because of its low numbers.

With respect to equity, Policy should be designed to prevent superannuation arrangements from being used as a tax shelter for high-income earners. In addition, intergenerational equity considerations suggest that over a period of demographic transition, policies to ensure that the baby boomers do not place an undue burden on subsequent generations when they retire should be introduced.

5.2   Assessment

In Table 11.11 we attempt a comparison of the Australian and Malaysian mandatory pension schemes. This is not straightforward, since the economic and social structures of the two countries are very different – a fact that helps to explain some of the differences in scheme structure. We will return to this point.

One institutional distinction that needs to be borne in mind throughout this discussion is that Australia has a universal (i.e., not employment-related) but targeted (i.e., means-tested) age pension, which is seen as playing a continuous safety net role even after the Superannuation Guarantee is fully mature.

We have previously (Bateman and Piggott, 1993) undertaken a detailed assessment of the Superannuation Guarantee, and we draw on this work here. Research into the impacts of the EPF is less systematic, but we make use of those sources we have managed to locate.

In our earlier work, we educe evidence to support the view that coverage of the employed labor force and income replacement under a mature Superannuation Guarantee will be adequate. In addition, investment risk is partially insured against by the interaction of public age pension entitlements with other sources of income. To a considerable degree, and especially at low income levels, the central authorities absorb investment risk through increased age pension payouts associated with low retirement income resulting from poor investment performance.

However, the Superannuation Guarantee performs poorly in providing insurance against longevity and inflation risk, because Australian policy does

Table 11.11
Comparative assessment of Australian and Malaysian retirement income schemes

	Australia	Malaysia
Coverage Risk	• Adequate	• Concern over large number of inactive accounts
Replacement Rate Risk	• Adequate for continuous contributions	• Could be compromised by preretirement withdrawals
Investment Risk	• Borne by retiree, but addressed through asset diversification	• Limited by direct control of asset allocation; government sponsorship
Longevity Risk	• Not covered - no mandatory purchase of life annuities, ineffective incentives	• Not covered - no mandatory purchase of, or incentives for, life annuities
Inflation Risk	• Not covered - ineffective incentives for indexed annuity purchase	• Not covered
Efficiency and Saving	• Addresses myopia by compelling saving but not failure of the annuities market	• Addresses myopia by compelling saving but not failure of the annuities market
	• Enhances private saving	• Enhances private saving and public investment
Equity	• Intergenerational neutrality is adequate	• Intergenerational neutrality is adequate
	• Low-income earners forced to change intertemporal consumption stream	• Low-income earners forced to change intertemporal consumption stream

not require retirees to spread their retirement consumption financed from their superannuation payout.

By contrast, the Malaysian scheme, although already fully mature, appears deficient in both coverage and replacement. While the number of EPF accounts as a proportion of the Malaysian labor force is large, nearly half are inactive. This suggests that effective coverage is below 50%. Further, the average value of retirement payouts is about the same as a typical worker's annual salary, suggesting that income replacement in retirement is not effectively delivered by the EPF. This problem partly results from preretirement withdrawal provisions.

In addition, the EPF shares with the Superannuation Guarantee a lack of attention to insurance against longevity and inflation risk. It may be argued that village and family support for the elderly render such insurance unnecessary, but these actions are likely to break down as the economy develops and interregional migration increases. In this context, the lack of any comprehensive aged safety net program is important.

Finally, investment risk is borne by the retiree under both regimes. The EPF does offer a low (2.5%) guaranteed return, just as the public pension acts as a buffer in the Australian model. But effectively, investment risk remains largely uncovered. The Australian model is able to address this risk more effectively because of much greater possibilities for asset diversification.

We now turn to the more conventional public finance criteria of efficiency and equity. Both systems score well in generating saving, which, in the absence of government action, might be expected to be inadequate in both countries. In the Australian case, this expectation is generated by observed myopia, along with price distortions from the income tax and age pension. In Malaysia, at least until recently, the lack of a well-developed capital market meant that the government would have had difficulty raising funds for public investment, in the absence of the effectively guaranteed bond purchase by the EPF.

On equity, both schemes perform satisfactorily with respect to intergenerational equity. Within a generational cohort, both schemes seem largely neutral, although some authors emphasize that the Australian scheme gives large tax concessions to the relatively well-off; this feature stems from the progressive Australian income tax rate schedule.

6   Concluding Comments: Lessons for developing countries

This chapter has attempted a comparison of two mandatory retirement saving schemes operating in two very different economies. It contrasts the centralized and decentralized approaches to mandated saving and gives an account of each scheme.

A number of themes emerge, each with relevance for developing economics where governments are contemplating retirement income policy design. First, economists tend to see insulation from political intervention as desirable in a retirement pension scheme. The Malaysia EFP shows that such insulation is less a consequence of mandating, than a result of exposing retirement saving to a (more or less) deregulated market environment. The Malaysian centralized model, with its heavy emphasis on the (compulsory) purchase of government debt, remains exposed to a high degree of political intervention. It would even be possible to characterize the Malaysian scheme as a special case of a tax transfer model. The Australian model is free from political intervention where competitive forces have taken hold. For example, investment performance is intensely competitive. In other respects, however, exposure to political intervention remains: For example, policy changes to the public pension can have direct and important implications for retirement benefit provision.

Second, the current advocacy of insulation may not be in the best interests of all developing countries. We were struck by the extent to which the policies instituted in these two countries were suited to prevailing national characteristics. At the time the provident fund was introduced, Malaysia's economic system was characterized by a relatively unsophisticated administrative and financial structure. The provident fund proved to be an excellent instrument for channeling much needed funds to the government for infrastructure and economic development. It is unclear, in the absence of a developed tax structure and capital market, where these funds would otherwise have come from. Political insulation, however, may be an important consideration in those developing countries which have committed themselves to large-scale pay-as-you-go aged social security policies.

Australia, on the other hand, can be thought of as a developed economy with an underdeveloped retirement income system. At the beginning of the 1980s, it was virtually unique among OECD countries in having no earnings-related national retirement income scheme. Coupled with this was an increasing concern with private saving performance – a concern that, it was widely believed, would not be addressed by the introduction of a pay-as-you-go scheme. These conditions combined with political considerations, to make a private mandated scheme an obvious policy option.

Third, mandated retirement saving in these two economies yield relatively poor retirement income insurance. The requirements on the structure of benefits leave retirees exposed to longevity and inflation risk, even when accumulations are sufficient to purchase adequate insurance against them. Malaysia shares this characteristic with other developing countries with provident funds. In the Australian case, the lack of compulsory annuity purchase is associated with a strong sense of property rights over the plans held in the predominantly defined contribution superannuation accumulations, combined with a history of lump sum voluntary superannuation payouts. This lack of insurance from the private mandated scheme is, of course, offset by the public pension, which provides both longevity and inflation insurance, albeit at the safety net level.

As we see it, the lesson here for developing countries is a very general one. If it is anticipated that economic and social conditions will change rapidly, then policy institutions must be similarly flexible. The EFP is very responsive in some respects, for example, portfolio allocation. But as traditional customs of support for the elderly become less effective, flexibility will be required in correcting market failure in insurance against retirement income risk. Especially in a policy environment where long-term expectations and contracts, implicit or explicit, are pervasive, flexibility is difficult to retain, as Australian experience with retirement income streams demonstrates. But it is an important part of a retirement income policy designed to perform well under changing economic and social conditions.

References

Asher, M. (1992). "Income Security for the Old Age: The Case of Malaysia." National University of Singapore. Unpublished manuscript.

Australian Bureau of Statistics (1994). *Year Book Australia, 1994.* Canberra, Australia.

Bank Negara Malaysia (1962–1993). *Monthly Statistical Bulletins.* Kuala Lumpur. (1962–1991). *Annual Reports.* Kuala Lumpur.

Bateman, H., and J. Piggott (1993). "Australia's Mandated Private Retirement Income Scheme: An Economic Perspective." In *Retirement Income Perspectives,* pp. 1–45. Economic Planning Advisory Council Background Paper No. 30. AGPS, Canberra.

Bateman, H., G. Kingston, and J. Piggott (1993). "Taxes, Retirement Transfers and Annuities." *Economic Record,* 69, pp. 274–294.

Bodie, Z. (1990). "Pensions as Retirement Income Insurance." *Journal of Economic Literature,* 28, pp. 28–49.

CCH Tax Editors (1990a). *Malaysian Master Tax Guide.* Singapore, CCH Asia. (1990b). *Malaysian Employment Legislation,* Singapore, CCH, Asia.

Dasuki, Z. (1992). "Adapting the Legal and Administrative Structures of Provident Funds to Achieve Optimum Efficiency: The National Experience of Malaysia." Paper presented to the International Social Security Association, 24th General Assembly, Acapulco, Mexico.

Dixon, J. (1982). "Provident Funds in the Third World: A Cross-National Review." *Public Administration and Development,* 2, pp. 325–344.

Economist Intelligence Unit (1989). *The ASEAN Countries: Economic Structure and Analysis.* Economist Intelligence Unit, London.

Employees Provident Fund (1989, 1991). *Annual Reports.* Kuala Lumpur.

FitzGerald, V. (1993). *National Saving: A Report to the Treasurer.* AGPS, Canberra.

Fry, M. (1992). "Factors Affecting the Saving Ratio in Malaysia." Asian Development Bank, Operational and Policy Study Series, Manila.

International Bank for Reconstruction and Development (1955). *The Economic Development of Malaya.* Johns Hopkins Press, Baltimore.

International Monetary Fund (1962, 1992). *International Financial Statistics Year Book.* IMF, Washington, D.C.

Kharas, H. (1989). "Malaysian Saving in the 1990s: Problems and Prospects." Paper presented at the Tenth Economic Convention, Persatuan, Ekonomi Malaysia, Kuala Lumpur, August 7–9.

United States, Department of Health and Human Services (1991). "Social Security Programs throughout the World." Washington, D.C.

Valdés-Prieto, S. (1994a). "Administrative Charges in Pensions in Chile, Malaysia, Zambia and the United States." PR Working Paper No. 1372, October. World Bank, Washington, D.C.

(1994b). "Earnings-Related Mandatory Pensions: Concepts for Design." PR Working Paper No. 1296, April. World Bank, Washington, D.C.

World Bank (1989). "Malaysia: Matching Risks and Rewards in a Mixed Economy." World Bank, Washington, D.C.

(1993). *World Bank Development Report 1993*. World Bank, Washington, D.C.

CHAPTER 12

Public pension plans in international perspective: Problems, reforms, and research issues

Estelle James

During the next 35 years, the proportion of the world's population that is over age 60 will nearly double, from 9% to 16%. Populations are aging much faster in developing countries than they did in industrial countries. As young working-age people near retirement around the year 2030, 80% of the world's old people will live in what today are developing countries. More than half will live in Asia and more than a quarter in China alone (World Bank, 1994; see Figures 12.1 and 12.2).

Yet, even as the number of old people has been growing, systems of financial support for the old are in trouble worldwide. Extended families and village support networks, on which two-thirds of the world's old people depend exclusively, tend to break down under pressures of urbanization, industrialization, and increased mobility. When that has happened in the past, governments have stepped in. Public spending on pensions (and to a lesser extent on health) has increased rapidly as incomes have grown and populations have aged, and now exceeds 15% of GDP in some industrialized and transitional economies (Figure 12.3).

How these funds are generated and spent affects the welfare of the old and also affects the entire economy by influencing productivity and the size of the GNP pie. Therefore, countries should use two overarching criteria to evaluate their programs: They should protect the old and they should promote (or at least not hinder) economic growth. Existing programs in many countries fail both tests – yet countries that are starting new systems are on the verge of making the same mistakes.

Income security programs provide three main functions for the old: saving,

This chapter is based on *Averting the Old Age Crisis: Policies to Protect the Old and Promote Growth*. World Bank and Oxford University Press, 1994, of which Estelle James was principal author, and draws heavily on parts of that report.

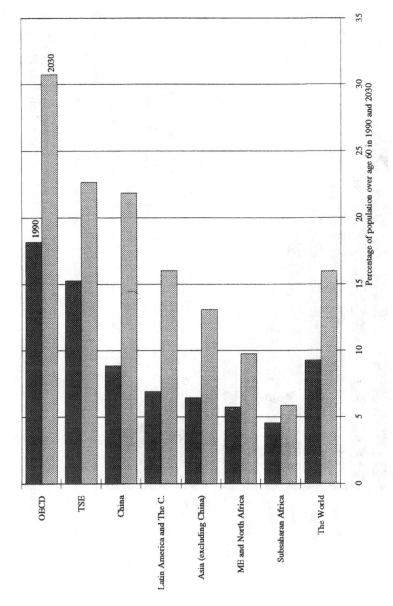

Figure 12.1. Percentage of the population over 60 years old, by region, 1990 and 2030. (Reproduced with permission from the World Bank and Oxford University Press.)

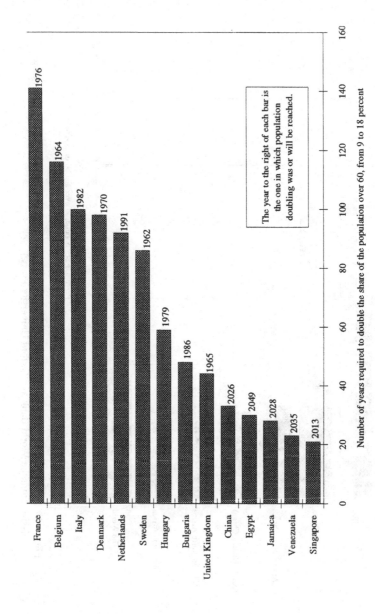

Figure 12.2. Number of years required to double the share of the population over 60 from 9% to 18%, in selected countries. (Reproduced with permission from the World Bank and Oxford University Press.)

Public spending as a percentage of GDP

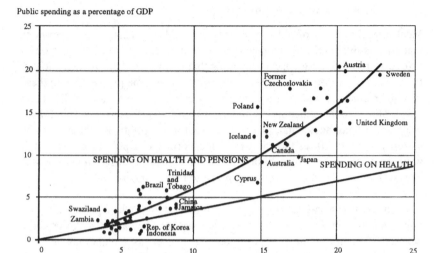

Figure 12.3. Public health and pension spending compared with population aging. (Reproduced with permission from the World Bank and Oxford University Press.)
Note: Because of space limitations, not all data points are identified. Data points show health plus pension spending data only. For health spending, $R^2 = 0.76$ $H/GDP = 0.069915 + 0.298553 \times POP60$; for health and pension spending, $R^2 = 0.92$; $(H + P)/GDP = 0.25449 + 0.369237 \times POP60 - 0.022744 \times POP60^2$, where H is public health spending and P is public pension spending. Sample covers 66 countries for various years between 1983 and 1992.

insurance, and redistribution to alleviate long-term poverty. This chapter argues that the old and the economy as a whole would be better off if governments used multiple instruments or "pillars" to provide these functions. A publicly managed tax-financed pillar would have the primary goal of reducing poverty among the old; a second mandatory but privately managed funded pillar would have the primary responsibility for handling saving; and voluntary saving annuity plans (possibly tax-advantaged) would exist for people who want more protection for their old age. Insurance would be provided by all three pillars. This chapter describes the most common problems found with dominant systems today, presents a recommended framework for a reformed system, analyzes how to get from here to there, especially in middle- and high-income countries, and suggests important issues for future research.

1   Problems with current systems

Most formal systems of old age security are publicly managed, pay pensions that are positively related to the worker's earnings, and are financed by payroll taxes on a pay-as-you-go basis – meaning that today's workers are taxed to pay the pensions of those who have already retired. The same problems with these systems recur over and over again in many countries, both industrialized and developing (see the appendix on myths and realities). This suggests that these problems are not accidental, they are inherent in the political economy of the systems, particularly in the short-run time horizons of politicians, and their willingness to promise present benefits at the expense of large future costs. A new system is needed that is more immune to these dangers.

High payroll tax rates.   In pay-as-you-go systems, when populations are young small contributions from the large number of workers make possible generous benefits to the few pensioners. However, as populations age and systems mature, these systems must charge high taxes to pay the same benefits to the growing number of retirees. Payroll taxes for pensions are already over 25% in Egypt, Hungary, Russia, Kyrgyzstan, Brazil, and Italy. As populations age over the next 30 years, contribution rates in almost all regions will have to rise dramatically if pay-as-you-go systems are retained. High payroll taxes mean lower take-home pay or more unemployment, without corresponding benefits if pension plans are not well structured.

Evasion.   High payroll tax rates that are not linked to benefits lead to evasion. This is especially the case in developing countries that have limited enforcement capacities. In many Latin American countries over 40% of the labor force works in the informal sector, partly in order to avoid payroll taxes, and the informal sector is growing rapidly in eastern Europe. In Argentina prior to recent reforms, more than 50% of workers evaded their contributions to the pension system. Evasion undermines the system's ability to pay pensions, makes it necessary to raise payroll taxes still further, and hurts the economy, since people who work in the informal sector are often less productive than they would be in the formal sector.

Early retirement.   In Hungary, more than a quarter of the population is composed of pensioners, the average retirement age is 54, and the payroll tax is 31%. In Turkey many people retire with a generous pension below the age of 50 or even 40. Public-sector employees in many countries can retire at the age of 55 or earlier. The labor force participation rate of males over the age of 55 has fallen in every OECD country during the past two decades. Early retirees stop making contributions and they begin drawing benefits that are not reduced by the actuarially fair amount, thus doubly hurting the scheme financially. Early retirees also deprive the economy of their experience. Their productivity may be higher than the value of their actuarially fair pension, but the plan gives them an incentive to stop working.

Misallocation of public resources. In 1990, Austria, Italy, and Uruguay spent more than one-third of their public budgets on pensions. The burden spilled over to the general treasury, often in an unplanned way, as taxes earmarked for old-age systems failed to cover the growing system expenditures. High public pension spending can hurt the economy if it squeezes out government spending on growth-promoting public investments such as infrastructure, education, and health services.

Lost opportunity to increase savings. Many countries believe that they have inadequate national saving and this hampers growth. But they have not used their old-age systems as a way to induce people to save more, and some economists believe existing systems have induced people to save less (Kotlikoff, 1989; Feldstein, 1995).

Perverse redistributions to upper-income groups. Publicly managed tax-financed systems are sometimes justified on grounds that they help the poor. But, despite seemingly progressive benefit formulas, studies of public plans in the Netherlands, Sweden, the United Kingdom, and the United States have found little if any redistribution from lifetime rich to lifetime poor. In fact, in the early years of the plan, high-income groups have benefited the most. (High-income people enter the labor force later and so contribute for fewer years, they live longer and so receive benefits for more years, and they have steeper age-earnings profiles so they end up with a high pension relative to their lifetime contributions (see Aaron, 1977; Hurd and Shoven, 1985; Steurle and Bakija, 1994; Nelissen, 1987; Creedy, Disney, and Whitehouse, 1992; Stahlberg, 1990; Valdés-Prieto, 1994).

Positive lifetime transfers to early cohorts, and losses to their children. Generally covered workers who retire in the first 20 to 30 years of a scheme get back much more than they contributed, but their children and grandchildren get back less than they paid in and lower rates of return than they could have earned elsewhere. In addition, because of the labor market distortions, the misallocation of public resources, and the failure to increase savings, the total size of the future GNP pie is likely to be less than it would have been otherwise. Parents may have adopted these policies without full information about their negative long-term effects – and, of course, the children and grandchildren were not around to vote when the choices were made (Boskin,

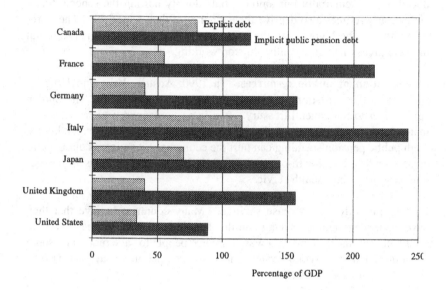

Figure 12.4. Implicit public pension debt, 1990. (Reproduced with permission from the World Bank and Oxford University Press.)

Kotlikoff, Puffert, and Shever, 1987; Moffit, 1984; Steuerle and Bakija, 1994; Nelissen, 1987; Stahlberg, 1989; Auerbach and Kotlikoff, 1987).

Old age systems in serious financial trouble.   The situation has been most acute in Latin America and eastern Europe, whose systems have been close to bankruptcy. But problems also loom for the OECD countries, whose implicit public pension debt (the present value of amounts promised to current retirees and workers) far exceeds the explicit conventional debt and sometimes exceeds 200% of GNP (Figure 12.4). Current payroll tax rates are much less than needed to keep constant the ratio of this debt to GNP and most countries will have a hard time raising them enough to close the gap. Pension benefits or other public goods will have to be reduced in the future. The implicit public pension debt is also a measure of how much capital would have been accumulated if the system were fully funded instead of pay-as-you-go. Reforms are necessary to avoid further growth of the debt–GNP ratio, but the already large debt in many countries makes reform difficult.

Inflation without indexation.   In fact, many countries have already reneged on their promises, by allowing inflation to take place without indexing benefits. In Venezuela the real value of public pensions fell 60% during the 1980s

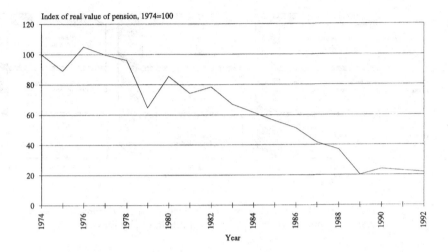

Figure 12.5. Real pension levels in Venezuela, 1974–1992. (Reproduced with permission from the World Bank and Oxford University Press.)

due to inflation (Figure 12.5). Inflation without indexation has also reduced real benefits in other Latin American and eastern European countries. This is devastating to all old people who depended on these pensions and did not expect inflation to erode their value. Indexation may seem to be a simple solution, but this would have required explicit decisions about cuts in benefit levels that had become fiscally unaffordable. OECD countries will have to make such decisions in the years ahead.

Limited coverage, funding, and portability in private pension plans. In most countries privately managed plans are voluntary, they cover a minority of workers, mainly from high-income groups, they are only partially funded, their benefits are not fully portable or indexed, and the tax expenditures involved are large.

Thus public pension plans have not always protected the old, they especially have not protected the old who are poor or people who will be old in the future, and they have also hindered economic growth. In addition, the systems are not sustainable in their present form. Most existing private pension systems are voluntary, limited in scope, and their real value is often less than workers realize, especially when they are unregulated. Although the degree and details vary from country to country, depending on their institutional structures and capacities, the broad patterns are surprisingly similar around the world, stemming from their common political economy roots.

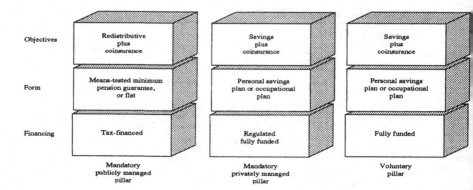

Figure 12.6. The pillars of old-age income security. (Reproduced with permission from the World Bank and Oxford University Press.)

2   A framework for reform

A good starting point for the analysis of reform options is the three functions that income security systems should provide for the old – saving, insurance, and redistribution for alleviating long-term poverty. Existing public pay-as-you-go systems have tried to perform all three functions in one system and as a result have not done any of them well. Better results may be obtained by establishing a *multipillar* system with separate administrative and financing mechanisms, or pillars, for redistribution and saving (Figure 12.6):

1. a publicly managed tax-financed public pillar for redistribution that keeps old people out of poverty;
2. a mandatory privately managed fully funded pillar that links benefits closely to contributions, for the saving function; and
3. a voluntary pillar for people who want more.

Let me start by describing the second mandatory pillar, which would differ dramatically from most existing systems. It would be fully funded, would link benefits actuarially to costs, and would be privately and competitively managed through personal saving plans or occupational pension plans.

Why mandatory?   Because it will require people to save for old age, which everyone should do but some are too shortsighted to do.

Why link benefits to contributions?   To discourage evasion and labor market distortions.

Why fully funded? To make costs clear, so countries won't make promises now that they will be unable to keep later; to prevent large unplanned intergenerational transfers, especially important in rapidly aging countries; to help build national saving; and to enable higher pensions – or lower contributions – by financing them partially with investment returns.

Why privately managed? To produce the best allocation of capital and the best return on savings. Data from many countries show that most publicly managed pension reserves earned less than privately managed reserves and in many cases lost money throughout the 1980s, because they were required to be invested in government securities or loans to failing state enterprises at low nominal interest rates that became negative during inflationary periods (Figure 12.7). In addition, publicly managed funds run the risk of encouraging deficit finance and wasteful spending by the government because they constitute a hidden and exclusive source of funds whose use is not subject to a test of market productivity or political accountability. Their investment policies are likely to be constrained by politically motivated restrictions, including prohibitions against investments abroad (see Mitchell and Hsin, Chapter 4, and Bateman and Piggott, Chapter 11, this volume). Competitively managed funded pension plans, in contrast, should spur financial market development and are better positioned to press for international diversification of investments (Valdés-Prieto, Chapter 7, this volume), thereby reducing country-specific risk and enhancing economic growth.

But three caveats are essential here. Countries must have at least rudimentary capital markets (such as a government bill market and a bank deposit market); considerable government regulation is essential to avoid investments that are overly risky and managers who are fraudulent. Some minimum reliability is required from the civil service for regulation to be effective; and a public pillar is needed to provide a social safety net for people whose lifetime earnings are low or whose investments fail.

Now I describe the public pillar. This would resemble existing public pension plans in that it would be publicly managed and tax-financed. However, unlike most current systems, the reformed public pillar would be much smaller and would focus on redistribution – providing a social safety net for the old, particularly the old whose lifetime income was low. To accomplish this, the benefit formula could be flat and means-tested or could provide a minimum pension guarantee – but it should not be positively related to earnings, as most public pensions are today.

Why is this important? Because a formula that is positively related to earnings inevitably redistributes to high-wage earners, especially in the first 20 to

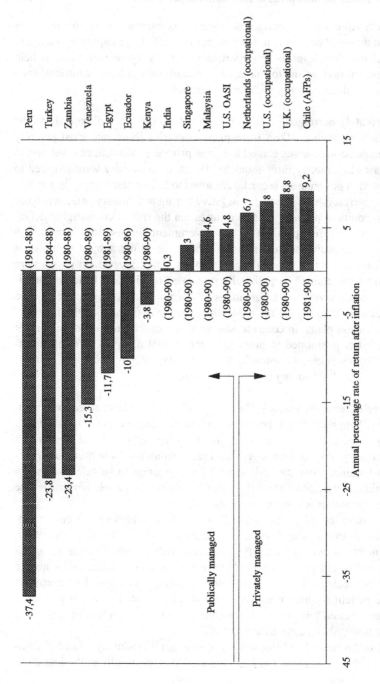

Figure 12.7. Gross average annual investment returns for selected pension funds, 1980s. (Reproduced with permission from the World Bank and Oxford University Press.)

30 years of a pension program. And, to give high benefits to high-wage earners while also keeping low-wage earners out of poverty, requires a high payroll tax rate, introducing all the efficiency problems just discussed. Tax payers will get more for their money by having an unambiguous and limited objective for the public pillar, while allowing high earners to get their higher benefits through saving in the privately managed second pillar.

Finally, a third pillar would offer additional protection, through voluntary occupational pension or personal saving plans, for people who want more in their old age. An important public policy question is whether voluntary plans should be tax-favored or otherwise subsidized (as they are in most countries). The answer to this question depends on a country's overall policy toward income versus consumption taxation (Auerbach and Kotlikoff, 1987), the degree to which it wants to rely on mandatory versus voluntary saving, and how effective and equitable tax advantages are as an instrument for increasing saving. The "right" policy on this issue will probably vary among countries (see also Cifuentes and Valdés-Prieto, Chapter 6, this volume).

Insurance against specific risks such as disability, early death, and extended longevity would be provided within each pillar. But most important for very long term planning is insurance against unpredictable events, such as economic or political upheavals, breakdowns of the government or the market, or changes in relative prices of labor and capital, which would be provided jointly by all three pillars – since broad diversification is the best way to insure in a very uncertain world. Countries should remember the old adage that modern finance has rediscovered – don't put all your eggs in one basket – especially when the eggs have to last for 60 or more years.

This is not an ivory-tower proposal. Real world examples include Chile, Argentina, and Peru, which use mandatory saving plans in their second pillar; Australia and Switzerland, which use mandatory occupational plans; the Netherlands and Denmark, in which collective bargaining has made occupational plans quasi-mandatory; and the United Kingdom, where workers can choose an employer-sponsored pension plan or a personal saving annuity plan in place of the earnings-related part of the public pension plan.

3 How to get there

Although the ultimate goal is the same for all, regions vary widely in the speed at which they are aging, in problems faced by existing systems, and in the capacity of the government and the private financial sector to undertake reform. This section presents an overview of the reform strategies appropriate for each region, and outlines options for a radical and gradual transition in middle- and high-income countries, using Latin American and OECD countries as cases in point.

Reform strategies in different regions

Problems are most pressing in the southern part of *Latin America and the former socialist economies,* where contribution rates, deficits, and evasion are high and growing. Argentina, Peru, Colombia, Mexico, and possibly Bolivia are now in the process of implementing sweeping changes similar to those of Chile, which restructured its system in 1981. And eastern Europe is weighing the pros and cons of radical change versus more moderate reforms – but has not yet decided which way to go. *Western Europe and other OECD countries,* too, will have to reform their systems; a gradual reform is feasible there only if the process begins soon. The challenge for all these countries is to find a politically viable transition path to a better system. However, it is difficult to move away from a pay-as-you-go system once it has matured because of the large pension debt: Old people are unwilling to give up the pension promises that were made to them years ago, while young people are unwilling to pay the taxes needed to keep the systems going. Borrowing is one way to finance the transition and avoid this dilemma, but this transforms a hidden implicit debt into a more obvious explicit debt. In eastern Europe so far this conflict has produced political paralysis and economic deterioration. The next two sections describe the radical transition that is already underway in Latin America and the gradual transition that has begun in some OECD countries.

East Asia is the most rapidly aging and most rapidly growing region. It will have to act quickly to meet the double challenge of aging populations and erosion of the extended family. Some of these countries are, at this very moment, evaluating alternative directions for their new and expanding systems. For them, a system that has a large funded component will be more immune to rapid demographic change than a pay-as-you-go system. These countries have or could quickly develop the financial and regulatory capacity to institute a competitively managed mandatory saving scheme. But policy makers may be tempted to retain public control of these funds. Their challenge is to avoid the problems that confront Latin America and Europe – better to start down a different path because it is so difficult to reverse later on – and to allow the market to play an important role in allocating the huge amount of capital that will accumulate in a funded system.

In *Sub-Saharan Africa and South Asia* informal systems are still strong and formal systems are limited in coverage and scope. The big danger is that they will expand their formal systems in ways that are not desirable or sustainable. Their challenge is to hold back – not to drive out informal systems, not to rush ahead with complex formal systems that they lack the capacity to administer, and not to make overly generous pension promises that they will be unable to keep. They should offer modest public plans, while developing the human capital, infrastructure, financial markets, and regulatory capacities that will allow them to establish a private pillar later on. This strategy is good for the pension system and good for development more broadly.

Radical transition in middle-income countries: The case of Latin America

Latin America offers an instructive example of how to bring off a radical pension reform when the country already has accumulated a large implicit social security debt. Chile, in 1981, was one of the first countries to adopt a mandatory saving plan, Argentina, Peru, and Colombia have recently followed suit, and Bolivia is on the verge of doing so. In all cases the reform involved setting up a mandatory saving plan as a second pillar, continuing to pay the pensions of retirees and of workers who do not switch, and agreeing to issue bonds recognizing the accrued entitlements of workers who do switch. But their plans differ in important ways that may affect the viability of the reform.

All reforming countries have given current workers a choice between the old pay-as-you-go system and the new multipillar system. If choice is given (as it probably must be for political acceptability), the terms of the choice are crucial to the success of the reform. In Chile, switching was encouraged by requiring a lower contribution rate in the new system (because of the expectation of a higher rate of return), by raising the retirement age in the old system, and by warning workers that the old system was financially unsound. New labor force entrants were required to join the new system, thereby bringing the old system to a definite end. In contrast, in Peru the contribution rate and retirement age are higher under the new system, workers in the new system must pay a "solidarity tax" to the old system, and employer payments (including payments by the government as employer) to the new system are not enforced. In Colombia and Argentina the old system continues to offer a replacement rate that is probably not fiscally sustainable – but appears attractive to workers who expect to receive it. Also in Argentina, Colombia, and Peru, new labor force entrants are permitted to enter the old system, and in some cases switching back and forth is permitted. Thus the old system may continue indefinitely, promising unrealistic benefits and incurring the additional fixed costs of administering two systems side by side.

Chile issued bonds to recognize the prior service workers had accumulated under the old system and paid a generous rate of interest to workers who switched. The other reforming countries have not yet come up with a formula for calculating recognition bonds or for implementation plans that handle problems of missing records and past inflation. Workers may be reluctant to switch if recognition bonds are unclear or not sufficiently generous. But if too generous, the cost to the government may be prohibitive, since it may involve giving explicit recognition to implicit obligations that never should have been made in the first place.

Financing the transition is particularly difficult for countries that are running fiscal deficits, in contrast to Chile, which built first a fiscal surplus. Of course, the new pension funds could be used to purchase bonds that finance the transition. In one sense, changing an implicit obligation to an explicit one does not change anything real, it simply changes peoples' perceptions of the debt. But in another sense, making an implicit obligation explicit grants it legal status and real value that it might not have had previously (see Valdés-Prieto, Chapter 7, this volume). And financing the transition by the issuance of bonds that must be absorbed by the voluntary market may have an impact on the political ability of the government to finance other functions. One option under consideration in some countries is to use the proceeds from privatized state enterprises to pay off the pension debt, thereby reducing assets and liabilities at the same time.

Chile and Colombia include a modest minimum pension guarantee in the new reformed public pillar, Argentina includes both a flat pension and a minimum pension guarantee (which costs much more), and the new Peruvian system has no public pillar at all. If there is no public pillar, the cost to the government is less but the risk to workers is greater, who may therefore decide not to switch.

The reforming countries must also deal with other implementation problems. Do their governments have the necessary regulatory capacity? Can their stock and bond markets become sufficiently well developed to provide safe investments for new pension funds? Is the country too small and poor to allow efficient operation of multiple pension funds? What is the optimum degree of international diversification? There is a likelihood that regional pension funds, run by Chilean AFPs, will develop and may help to resolve some of the outstanding issues concerning economies of scale, excessive regulation, and international diversification.

The gradual transition in high-income OECD countries

Many OECD countries adopted their current systems before World War II, at a time when private financial markets were undeveloped or in disrepute. These systems were expanded sharply in the 1950s and 1960s, at a time when real wages and population were both growing rapidly. Under these conditions, it was natural for policy makers to rely heavily on a publicly managed payroll-tax-financed pay-as-you-go system. Seemingly, everyone would come out ahead under this system.

Of course, it was never true that everyone could come out ahead, and this has been underscored by changes in the world economy over the past 50 years. Real wage growth has slowed and population growth has come to a halt in OECD countries, so that tax rates will have to go up sharply if the current system remains unchanged. It has become increasingly important to minimize work disincentives and to increase labor productivity through capital accumulation, which the public pillar is not well suited to do. Financial markets are better developed than they were before and are global in nature, allowing funded plans to seek out the highest returns in a capital-scarce world and to benefit from international diversification. Under these changed conditions, shifting increased responsibility to privately managed funded plans that tie benefits to contributions is likely to enhance economic growth and provide higher pensions than continued reliance on a payroll-tax-financed pay-as-you-go system.

An additional concern is that old-age poverty may reappear in the future, unless the public pillar is redesigned. In the past, poverty among the old was reduced without much lifetime redistribution from rich to poor, largely because the entire retired generation benefited from a positive income transfer through the old-age security system. But that positive transfer has now come to an end and is about to turn negative. At the same time, we observe a growing polarization of wages among workers in many OECD countries. Unless the public pillar (and the method of financing it) becomes more targeted toward low-income groups, we may well see a reinforcement of poverty among the young (because of the high payroll tax) and a resurgence of poverty among the old who were at the low end of the earnings distribution and did not get a positive transfer upon retirement. If middle- and high-income workers receive a large part of their pension income through the mandatory funded pillar, this will allow the public pillar to focus more sharply on basic income needs that will keep these low-wage earners out of poverty when they grow old, without an excessively high tax rate. And all income groups will benefit from diversification – getting their retirement income from more than one source, since one source can always fail.

Thus, rather than relying on a public pillar to do it all, the time is ripe for OECD countries to make the transition to a mandatory multipillar system – and they can make the transition gradually, provided they start soon. How can they do so, given the large implicit public pension debt that they have accumulated?

The first step is to reform the public pillar by raising the retirement age (continuously, as longevity increases), eliminating rewards for early retirement and penalties for late retirement, reducing the benefit rate relative to wages (by holding the average real pension constant as real wages increase), flattening out the benefit structure (to emphasize the poverty reduction function), making the tax base broader and more progressive, until a cut in the tax rate is achieved.

The second step is to launch a mandatory second pillar by setting up the appropriate regulatory structure and allocating the savings from the downsized contribution to the public pillar, together with the fruits of future productivity gains, to the second pillar.

In most cases, given the aging demography, the sum of contribution rates will have to increase or a higher ceiling on taxable income will be needed – but hopefully this will be smaller, less distortionary, and more politically acceptable than under an unreformed system (for further ideas on financing the transition, see Valdés-Prieto, Chapter 7, this volume). Ten to twenty years may elapse before the second pillar is fully established, but the process could be gradual providing these countries begin the transition now – as Australia, Switzerland, the United Kingdom, and, to some extent, the Netherlands and Denmark have already done.

4   Issues for future research

Several critical assumptions underlay the policy recommendations made here. Many of these assumptions involve the collective choices of citizens, the behavior of governments, and their interactions with markets. For example, we have made a value judgment that it is important to alleviate old-age poverty, and that this may require redistribution toward low-wage earners whose lifetime incomes are not high enough to keep them above the poverty line when old as well as when young.

We have assumed that the willingness of high-income groups to redistribute to low-income groups will not be decreased, and may even be increased, if a smaller, more transparent, and better-targeted public pillar is adopted. This is why we favor the use of a flat or means-tested benefit structure or a minimum pension guarantee in the public pillar (while the savings function is carried out separately through the private pillar). In contrast, proponents of large earnings-related public pillars argue that these will get greater support from the middle classes, and so will redistribute more effectively to the poor (Stearns, 1981). This is an empirical issue concerning the psychology of behavior. Will high-income groups be more willing to redistribute X to lower-income groups if they simply give X (a transparent targeted scheme) or if they give X + Y and get Y back themselves (a conventional redistributive scheme)? This question might be investigated using cross-national data and experimental gaming methods.

We have also assumed, based on empirical evidence from a number of countries, that if governments have exclusive access to pension fund reserves they will use these reserves as an easy nontransparent way to pursue political objectives and increase deficit finance. This is an important part of the explanation offered for the low rate of return on publicly managed pension reserves, when they exist. This topic could be investigated econometrically, using international data on the amount and allocation of government spending and deficit finance through time in countries with differing and changing amounts of pension reserves.

A third question is whether private capital markets will react differently to explicit and implicit public pension debt. This could be investigated empirically in countries that have reformed. Does the implicit social security debt affect government or financial market behavior? Does the explicit acknowledgment of this debt and the issuance of recognition bonds change this behavior? Would this effect be different if recognition bonds became tradable? While in some countries courts have upheld implicit public pension promises as a legally enforceable property right, in other countries they have not done so. Citizens and investors may not have been fully aware of the size of the implicit debt or may have been discounting the chances that it would be paid off in full. If the debt is acknowledged, on more favorable terms than expected, its real value changes and this in turn could affect capital markets as well as government behavior.

A fourth important question: Which produces higher investment returns and lower administrative costs in the second pillar – occupational plans or personal saving plans? Occupational plans may save on marketing costs, but they also introduce the possibility of financial abuse (witness the Maxwell scandal) and more general principal–agent problems (see Mitchell and Hsin, Chapter 4, this volume). In defined contribution occupational plans employers choose the investment manager but workers bear the investment risk. In defined benefit occupational plans the employer can reduce pension obligations by giving relatively low wage increases and high layoff probabilities to older workers, without newly hired workers noticing. Comparisons of the experience of Latin American and OECD countries that took into account that inefficient regulations may be partly responsible for observed outcomes might be useful here. It might also be useful to investigate empirically other methods of decentralizing control over mandatory pension funds, such as contracting out their management to multiple private investment companies; this method has been used by some plans that cover state and local government employees.

A final research topic involves the "optimum" amount of international diversification of pension fund investments for countries of different sizes and levels of development – taking into account the desire to increase yield, reduce investment risk, and constrain real exchange rate risk (given that investment income must eventually be reconverted into national currency), as well as the problem of imperfect and costly information about foreign markets.

5   Conclusion

Although the kind of reform that is needed will vary across countries, all countries should have a vision of where they are going in the long run. This vision should include separate mechanisms for redistribution and saving, and shared responsibility between the public and private sectors.

The right share of responsibility for each pillar will not be the same for all times and places. It depends on a country's objectives, history, and current circumstances, particularly the relative strength of its redistributive and saving goals, its financial market development, and its taxing and regulatory capability. The pace at which a mandatory multipillar system should be introduced will also vary – from quick in middle- and high-income countries whose systems are in serious trouble to very slow in low-income countries, which should avoid these same mistakes.

Tackling pension reform will not be easy and talk of reform elicits strong emotions, especially in countries where expectations of generous pensions have built up through the years. Nonetheless, change in current systems is inevitable and the longer reform is delayed, the more urgent and difficult it becomes. Countries *can* avert the old-age crisis. To do so, they should begin planning and educating the public now.

APPENDIX TO CHAPTER 12: MYTHS AND REALITIES
ABOUT OLD-AGE SECURITY

Myths abound in discussions of old-age security. Consider some of the most common:

Myth 1:   Old people are poor, so government programs to alleviate poverty should be directed to the old.

Fact: In most industrialized countries poverty rates are higher among the young than among the old, and families with small children are the poorest of all. The old are even better-off when comparisons are based on lifetime income rather than current income. Why? Because people with higher incomes are more likely to live long enough to become old, whereas people with low incomes are more likely to have many children and die young. Targeting young families with children is a better measure for alleviating poverty than targeting the old.

Myth 2:   Public social security programs are progressive, redistributing income to the old who are poor.

Fact: Even if benefit formulas look progressive, four factors neutralize most of the progressive effect. The first people to be covered when new plans are started are invariably middle- and upper-income groups, and they typically receive large transfers. The longer life expectancy of the rich and their steeper age-earnings profiles severely reduce or eliminate the progressivity of social security programs, when redistribution is calculated according to lifetime benefits minus contributions. Ceilings on taxable earnings keep the lid on tax differences between rich and poor. And when benefit formulas are earnings-related, or subject to strategic manipulation, as in many countries, upper-income groups benefit even more, so the net redistributional effect can be regressive.

Myth 3: Social security programs insure pensioners against risk by defining benefits in advance.

Fact: Benefit formulas are redefined frequently, so substantial political risk remains. In addition, defined benefit formulas, whether in public or employer-sponsored schemes, typically depend heavily on earnings during the last few working years, and so subject workers to the risk that their wages will unexpectedly fall at the end of their career (e.g., due to illness or layoffs), thereby pulling down their pensions as well.

Myth 4: Only governments can insure pensioners against group risks such as inflation, and most do so.

Fact: Most developing countries do not index pension benefits for inflation in their publicly managed old-age programs. And most OECD countries have skipped some cost-of-living adjustments during the past decade. Failing to index for inflation is the most common method governments use to reduce real benefit levels and escape from unsustainable benefit promises. In countries prone to inflation, the best insurance against it would be international diversification of pension fund investments – which is more likely when investment decisions are made by private managers rather than government.

Myth 5: Individuals are myopic but governments take the long view.

Fact: Governments have repeatedly made decisions about old-age programs based on short-run exigencies rather than long-run benefits. One example is the use of early retirement programs as a solution to unemployment, even though in the long run this costs the economy more in lost labor and public treasury. Another is pay-as-you-go financing instead of full funding, allowing generous pensions initially but discouraging saving and growth and lowering pensions in the long run.

Myth 6:   Government action is needed to protect the interests of generations yet unborn.

Fact: Most public pay-as-you-go pension schemes provide the largest net benefits to workers who are 30 to 50 years old when the schemes are introduced. The unborn children and grandchildren of these workers are likely to receive negative transfers as the system matures and the demographic transition proceeds.

References

Aaron, H. (1977). *Demographic Effects on the Equity of Social Security Benefits.* Brookings Institution, Washington, D.C.

Auerbach, A., and L. Kotlikoff (1987). *Dynamic Fiscal Policy.* Cambridge University Press, Cambridge.

Boskin, M., L. Kotlikoff, D. Duffer, and J. Shoven (1987). "Social Security: A Financial Appraisal across and within Generations." *National Tax Journal* 40(1): 19–34.

Creedy, J., R. Disney, and E. Whitehouse (1992). "The Earnings-Related State Pension, Indexation and Life-Time Redistribution in the UK." Institute for Fiscal Studies, Working Paper 92/1, London.

Feldstein, M. (1995). "Social Security and Saving: New Time Series Evidence." Working Paper no. 5054. NBER, Cambridge, Mass., March.

Hurd, M., and J. Shoven (1985). "The Distributional Impact of Social Security." In D. Wise, ed., *Pensions, Labor and Individual Choice.* University of Chicago, Chicago.

Kotlikoff, L. (1980). *What Determines Savings?* MIT Press, Cambridge, Mass.

Moffit, R. (1984). "Trends in Social Security Wealth by Cohort." In M. Moon, ed., *Economic Transfers in the United States.* National Bureau of Economic Research and University of Chicago Press, Chicago.

Nelissen, J. (1987). "The Redistributive Impact of the General Old Age Pensions Act on Lifetime Income in the Netherlands." *European Economic Review* 31 (7): 1419–41.

Stahlberg, A.-C. (1989). "Redistributive Effects of Social Policy in a Lifetime Analytic Framework." In B. Gustaffsen, and M. Klevmarken, eds., *The Political Economy of Social Security.* Elsevier Science, New York.

Stearns, P. (1981). "Political Perspectives on Social Security Financing." In F. Skidmore, editor, *Social Security Financing,* chapter 5. MIT Press, Cambridge, Mass.

Steuerle, C., and J. Bakija (1994). *Retooling Social Security for the 21st Century.* Urban Institute Press, Washington, D.C.

Valdés-Prieto, S. (1994). "Earnings-Related Mandatory Pensions." Policy Research Working Paper no. 1296. World Bank, Washington, D.C., April.

World Bank (1994). *Averting the Old Age Crisis: Policies to Protect the Old and Promote Growth.* Policy Research Report by E. James et al. World Bank, Washington, D.C. and Oxford University Press, Oxford.

Index

Aaron, H., 355
AFPs (pension fund management companies),
    see Chile, privatized pension system
Africa, 235, 351, 362–63
aging of population, 28, 63, 118, 139, 350,
    354, 366
    in Australia, 323, 326
    and fiscal impact of transition, 136
    and rising cash deficits, 130, 301, 356
Ahmad, E., 2
Allende, Salvador, 63
Andrews, E. S., 98
annuities, 6, 11, 51, 304, 315–6, 340, 346–7
AP funds (Sweden), 29
Argentina, 10, 20, 25, 160, 170, 234, 253,
    255, 262, 361, 362, 363, 364
Arrau, P., 127, 128, 131, 133, 135–6, 161,
    162, 164, 166, 169, 172, 198
Artis, M. J., 4
Asia, 233, 234, 235, 323, 350, 351
Assael, P., 67
Auerbach, A., 128, 133, 161, 164, 166, 169,
    179, 356, 361
Australia, 3, 20, 22–4, 25, 26, 28, 173, 231,
    234, 238, 240, 318–34, 342–48, 361, 366
Austria, 238, 355

Bakija, J., 355, 356
Bank of England, 242, 243
Bateman, H., 24, 344
Belgium, 240, 352
Bernatzi, Schlomo, 109
Beveridge, William, 60
Blanchard, O., 137, 139, 156, 191
Blau, D., 164
Bleakney, Thomas P., 100
Boadway, R., 11
Bodie, Z., 47, 343

Bolivia, 362, 363
Boskin, Michael J., 51, 355
Brazil, 253, 354
Breyer, F., 197–98
Breyer, Stephen, 49
Buiter, W., 27, 28
Bulgaria, 352

Canada, 231, 238, 240
capital controls (over internationally mobile
    capital)
    arguments for, 258–61
    in Chile, 17, 245, 251, 256–8, 263–4
    and fine tuning of macroeconomic policy,
        245
    in general, 18, 228, 257–8, 265–6
    removal in United Kingdom, 17, 241–4
    special controls for pension plans, 18–9,
        244, 246, 247–9, 269–71
    temporary controls on abnormal flows, 18,
        248–9, 265–9, 270
Cheyre, Hernán, 61, 74
Cifuentes, R., 128, 133, 135–6, 148, 161, 167,
    183, 191
Colombia, 20, 25, 362, 363, 364
competition, in pension management
    avoidance of monopoly power in public
        debt market, 15, 210
    choice and flexibility, 300
    insulation from political risk, 26, 210,
        346
Coote, Robin, 234–36
Corbo, Vittorio, 149, 150, 231
Corsetti, G., 138
cost of living adjustments, to pensions, 34,
    51, 60, 62, 66, 76–81, 356–7
Costa Rica, 10

costs and charges, in private pensions
  Australian and Chilean costs compared, 24
  and costs of occupational plans in the
    United Kingdom, 24, 285–93, 367
  monopoly provision to reduce costs, 23, 26,
    341
  personal pension plans in the United King-
    dom, 21, 289–90, 309–12, 314–5
  for small Australian employers, 24, 333
Cozzini, Angela, 237
credit constraints, 11, 14, 163
  effect of debt policy, 183–5
  and feasibility of pension reform, 174–8
  impact on output effects of pension reform,
    136–7
  meaning of, 165–6, 167
  and tax incidence, 182
Creedy, J., 355
Czech Republic, 3
Chile, 3, 20, 25, 160, 164–5, 234, 319
  government-managed (old) pension system,
    7, 60–5
  privatized (new) pension system, 6, 17, 33–
    5, 68, 82–7, 117, 144–53; capital con-
    trols for pension funds, 18, 19, 245, 251,
    361, 362; charges in, 24, 27, 341; financ-
    ing of transition to, 129, 170, 173, 205–
    6, 363, 364; political risk in, 46, 50, 52,
    54, 75–6; reduction of labor market dis-
    tortion, 127, 144–5
China, 1, 2, 323, 350, 351, 352

Davanzo, Lawrence, 231
Davis, E. P., 3, 17, 231, 236, 244
defined benefit pensions, 6, 10, 93
  and investment strategy, 234, 236
  protected by property rights, 44–5
  reliance on legislative correction, 35, 39
defined contribution pensions, 5, 50, 116–18
  Australian mandate to offer, 23, 327–9
  Latin American mandate to buy, 25
  unmet expectations, 34
democracy and pensions, 6–7, 49, 58, 72
  and capitalism, 68, 301
  legitimacy and transparency, 65–8, 206; *see
    also* political risk and visibility
  and political development, 59
  see also interest groups; patronage
demographic transition, *see* aging of population

Denmark, 72, 238, 240, 352, 361, 366
Diamond, P., 5, 6, 10, 20, 34, 59, 130, 137,
  191, 197, 205, 319
Disney, R., 355
Drake, Paul, 68
Dreze, J., 2
Duffer, D., 356

early retirement, 354–5
Easterly, W., 150
Ecuador, 360
Egypt, 352, 354, 360
El Salvador, 10
Employee Benefit Research Institute (EBRI),
  97, 117
Enders, W., 192, 208
Entwisle, B., 2
EPF (Employee's Provident Fund of Malaysia), 334–42, 345–8
  administrative costs, 23, 319, 341, 346
  implicit charges, 26, 340, 341
  investment performance, 319–20, 336–8,
    340, 346–7
  political influence, 319, 346
Epple, Dennis, 110, 116
equality in pensions, 6–7, 59, 62, 64, 65–6
Europe, 191, 235, 244, 306, 318, 323, 324,
  357, 362
exchange rate policy
  constrained by pension portfolio decisions,
    16, 229–30
  and large capital inflows, 257–8
  and level of real exchange rate, 18, 243
  to reduce exchange rate volatility, 18, 261–
    2, 263, 267–9
  and sterilized interventions, 264–5, 266

Felderer, B., 127
Feldstein, M., 13, 335
financial market development, 3, 25, 247,
  269
  exclusion of financial firms in Australia,
    326
  as externality of reform, 25, 247, 252–3
  in high-income countries, 28
  as precondition for funding, 364
  see also financial markets, reliability of
financial markets, reliability of, 28, 62, 64,
  69, 237, 347
Fischer, Bernhard, 241

Fischer, S., 191
France, 240, 306, 319, 352
Fry, M., 336, 337, 338, 340
full funding, 10, 55
   arguments in favor of, 25, 359
   as a benchmark, 141
   and excess supply of funds to the capital
     market, 172
   and short-term macroeconomic policy,
     253–6
   state-controlled fully-funded monopoly, 29,
     324
   union control of pension funds, 326
funding, 193–4
   apparent, 193, 217–9
   as backing for benefit promises, 93, 100
   determinants of degree of, 8, 99–104, 109–
     13
   and political risk, 47, 104
   as response to high labor mobility, 116
   see also full funding

Gavin, Michael, 231
Germany, 17, 236, 238, 239
Godoy, O., 6, 7
Goldstein, Michael, 235
Goode Committee, 21, 299–300
Gooptu, Sudarsham, 237
Gordon, Roger, 192, 208
Government Accounting Standards Board,
   102
Green, Jerry, 192, 208
Greenough, W., 4
Greenwood, John G., 240
Greenwood, Luci, 237
growth, economic, 350
   models of factor accumulation, 13, 14,
     129–37
   models with externalities, 13, 137, 139–40
   and the private pension system in Chile,
     152–3
Gusen, Peter, 239

Hernández, Leonardo, 231
Hills, J., 2
Hoffman, Arnold, 93
Howell, Michael, 237
Hubbard, G., 161, 164
Hungary, 354
Hurd, M., 2, 355

income distribution
   acceptability to middle class, 366
   as an aim of pension policy, 7, 25, 63,
     359
   among generations, 28, 132, 210–11, 355–6
   incentive effects of, 12; *see also* tax distor-
     tions
   and Minimum Pension Guarantee, 364
   perverse redistribution to high-income
     groups, 130, 355, 359
   poverty among the old, 28, 42, 301–2, 365
   by progressive taxation of mandatory sav-
     ings plans, 34, 54
   and transitions, 363
India, 360
inflation and pensions, *see* cost of living adjustments
Inman, Robert P., 100
insurance, 361; *see also* risk diversification;
   risk sharing
interest groups, 61, 69
international investment of pension funds, 231
   compensating inflows from foreign pension
     funds, 19, 246–7, 248
   to escape local political risk, 19
   and fiscal risk, 211–12
   vs. high domestic returns, 19
   as a source of finance for developing coun-
     tries, 237, 245, 248
Ireland, 240
Italy, 138, 306, 352, 354, 355

Jamaica, 352
James, Estelle, 100, 117
Japan, 17, 44, 238, 240, 244, 321
Jones, L., 139
Judd, K., 161, 164

Kautz, Leslie B., 231
Kenen, Peter, 241
Kenya, 360
Kotlikoff, L., 5, 51, 128, 133, 161, 164, 166,
   169, 179, 200, 355, 356, 361
Kyrgzstan, 354

Labán, Raúl, 241
labor markets
   evasion and coverage, 12, 13, 25, 326–7,
     336, 354, 357
   externalities in formal sector, 13, 137–8

labor markets *(cont.)*
informality as a result of social security
taxes, 141, 143
and labor mobility, *see* transfer values
see also taxes on labor earnings
Lakonishok, Josef, 8, 98, 109
Lapan, H. E., 192, 208
Larraín, Felipe, 67, 241
Latin America, 25, 117, 138, 199, 233, 253,
256, 260, 261, 318, 351, 354, 361–4,
367
Lazear, E., 4
liquidity constraints, *see* credit constraints
London, 297

Malaysia, 3, 20, 22–3, 25, 26, 318–24, 334–
48, 360
mandate to contribute (to second pillar)
compliance problems in Australia, 326–7
evasion in Malaysia, 334
implementation in Australia, 327–9
justification, 25, 72, 318
in Latin America, 361
and the role of the state, 71–3
Manuelli, R., 139
Mariger, R., 161
Marshall, J., 150
maturity of pension plans, 9, 10
cash flow effects of, 63, 130
immaturity as an initial condition, 10
Melbinger, Michael S., 114, 115
Merck, Carolyn, L., 102
Merton, Robert C., 43, 47
Mesa-Lago, Carmelo, 117, 119
Mexico, 253, 362
Mitchell, Olivia S., 27, 98, 100, 101, 104,
106, 112, 115, 116
Moffit, R., 356
Mondejar, John, 71
monetary policy
arbitrage between equity markets, 17, 228–
31; *see also* stock market integration
constrained by pension portfolio decisions,
16
loss of sovereignty, 17, 228, 244, 262
Mullin, John, 233, 237
Mundell, Robert A., 228
Munnel, Alicia H., 100, 115
Mussa, Michael, 235
myopia, 28, 136, 137, 283, 287n, 346, 358

Neisner, Jennifer, 102
Nelissen, J., 207
Netherlands, 231, 234, 238, 240, 319, 352,
355, 360, 361, 366
Noetzlin, Bernard, 233
non-OECD countries, 233–4, 237
North America, 235, 318
Norway, 238, 240

occupational pensions, 2–3
Australian mandate to offer, 23–4, 327–9
as a competitor of personal plans, 24, 285–
90, 367
contracted-out of SERPS in the United
Kingdom, 279, 281–3
employer aversion to personal plans, 21,
302–3
employer point of view, 4
limited funding of, 357
manipulation of actuarial assumptions, 22
risk of fraud, 21, 298–300
trust law in the United Kingdom, 21, 296–8
in the United States public sector, 93
OECD countries, 1, 17, 25, 28, 227, 233–4,
237, 239, 242, 245, 246, 248, 319, 321,
322, 324, 347, 351, 354, 356, 357, 361–
2, 364–6, 367, 369
Orloff, A. S., 5

Patronage, 6–7, 49, 59–60, 66
pay-as-you-go financing, 129
balanced mature case, 12, 13, 199
as hidden public debt, 195–6, 356
as an initial condition, 28, 363
rate of return of 8, 28, 130
sunk intergenerational transfers, 28, 364–5
Peled, D., 207
pension policy
approaches to study of, 3–4, 5
financial aspects of, 9, 130; *see also* transitions
functions of, 350
and income distribution, *see* income distribution
preconditions for three pillars, 25, 359
three-pillar proposal, 25, 327, 358
in the United Kingdom, 300–5
pension reform
benefit reduction to sustainable levels, 28,
356, 365–6

choice for current members, 363
gradual phase-in, 173
IMF role, 269
political constraints, 4–5, 7
reform strategies, 362–3
personal pension plans in the United Kingdom, 20–1, 280–1, 303–4
as a competitor of occupational plans, 24, 285–90, 367
contracted back into SERPS, 304
contracted-out of SERPS in the United Kingdom, 283–5
employer-based groups (COMPS), 290–1
group personal schemes and industry-wide portable schemes, 20, 291–3
Peru, 20, 25, 160, 173, 255, 360, 362, 363, 364
Phillipines, 199, 207
Piggott, J., 24, 344
Piñera, José, 6
political risk, in pensions, 5, 27, 29, 33
caused by electoral cycle, 67, 104
caused by fiscal risk, 42, 211, 215
commitment devices to reduce, 36; automatic adjustment rules, 46, 50, 51; constitutional constraints, 5, 38, 44–5; property rights, 6, 44, 69–70, 198–9, 347; unification of social security plans, 48
experience with Sweden's AP funds, 29
insulation against, 5, 7, 33, 201, 366–7
omission of beneficial acts, 6, 34, 347
privatization to reduce: and individual accounts, 52, 53, 70–1; independence from political interests, 27, 29, 60, 82–7, 199
visibility, 6, 48–50, 52, see also democracy and pensions, legitimacy and transparency
see also patronage
portfolio management of pension funds
investment guidelines and regulations, 17, 94–5, 98, 99, 234–6, 237–40, 332
long duration of liabilities, 102, 234
and non-tradeable government debt, 211
performance of public sector plans, 95–6, 106–9, 114–5, see also AP funds; EPF
political influence on, 62–3, 81–2, 96–7, 99, 336–7
prudent man rules, 17, 99, 240
relative performance evaluation, 16, 98, 236, 270n

Portugal, 238
Prat Commission (in Chile), 62
Prat, Jurge, 62–3
privately-managed pension plans
arguments for, 25, 210, 359
and risk of fraud, 21, 298–300, 333–4; ability of civil service, 27, 364; consumer protection, 21, 24, 288–9, 296–300; pensions regulator, 21, 300; regulation of, 20, 22, 74
and union involvement, 326
provident funds, 22, 23, 319, 347
in Malaysia 324; see also EPF
public debt, 6
equivalence to pay as you go, 10, 367
to finance transition to funding, 9, 14, 131, 135, 171–2, 183–5
nontradable, 209–10, 367
risks for future taxpayers, 212

rate of return, 8, 130, 172
funded vs. pay-as-you-go plans, 13, 28, 130, 143, 196–7
impact on pension level, 8, 71
publicly vs. privately managed plans, 23, 93, 337–8, 346
Rebelo, S., 139
Reid, G., 27
Reisen, Helmut, 241
Rey, G. M., 138
Richter, W. F., 192, 208
risk diversification, in pensions, 15
demographic, see aging of population
international, 25, 28, 211, 222, 367–8; see also international investment
well-chosen repeated legislation, 33
see also risk sharing
risk sharing
complete markets, 35, 37
among generations, 33, 208
incomplete markets, 37–8, 206–8
and neutral pension reforms, 206–8
and random legislation, 39–40, 215–16
and repeated legislation, 35, 38
and tradability of pension debt, 211–13
Rivlin, A., 2
Rodríguez, C. A., 150
Romer, P., 139, 154
Russia, 354

Saint-Paul, G., 140, 155
savings, national, 19, 132, 335, 341–2, 355
savings, private, 10–11, 12, 14, 210, 211
    Chilean evidence on, 145–52
    substitution by forced saving, 182–3, 326
Schattsneider, E. E., 49
Schipper, K., 100, 116
Schleifer, A., 8
Schmidt-Hebbel, K., 127, 128, 131, 133, 135–6, 149, 150
Schmitt, Ray, 102
Sen, A., 2
SERPS (State Earnings Related Pension System), 20, 278–9, 281n
    implied real rate of return, 20, 306–8
    reforms to, 304–5
Sheshinki, E., 139, 154
Shoven, E., 51, 355, 356
Singapore, 45, 319, 321, 352, 360
Smith, R. S., 100, 101, 104, 106, 112, 116
solidarity, *see* equality in pensions
Solnik, B., 233
Solow, R., 50
Stahlberg, A. C., 355, 356
Steurle, C., 355, 356
stock market integration, 233–4, 242–3, 244
Straub, M., 197–98
Sweden, 29, 240, 319, 352, 355
Switzerland, 17, 23, 25, 231, 234, 238, 240, 319, 361, 366

tax distortions
    with different tax combinations, 166–7, 172–3, 179–83, 355
    in initial situation, 15, 197–8
    in a transition, 132–3
tax on contributions, marginal, 11, 12
    impact on the young, 13, 15
tax treatment of pension funds, 361
    in Australia, 329–31
    fiscal impact of exemptions, 136, 137, 185–8
    forced holding of nontradable government debt, 210
    in Malaysia, 341
    as a source of revenue, 26
    in the United Kingdom, 20, 293–6, 301
taxes on labor earnings
    high level of taxes, 354, 365
    irrelevance in high-income countries, 28

and labor mobility, *see* transfer values
    due to mandate to contribute, 12, 141
    due to pay-as-you-go financing, 27, 68, 116, 131, 141, 210, 354
    due to taxes on pension assets, 26
    neutral wage tax, *see* transitions, neutral
    due to weak links between contributions and benefits, 130, 138, 142, 358
    see also labor markets; tax on contributions, marginal
Taylor, Mark, 242, 243, 244
Thaler, Richard, 109
Tiglao, Rigoberto, 199, 207
Tirole, J., 13, 196
Tokman, V., 138
Tonks, Ian, 244
transfer values, 20, 22
    and labor mobility, 22, 301
    in occupational plans, 21, 296, 303, 357
    in personal plans, and transfer penalties, 314–15
    in SERPS, 288n
transitions in financing method, 14
    cash-flow impact on government, 28, 174, 199, 304n
    equivalence with public debt policy, 9, 131
    steady state output and welfare effect, 135, 137
    intergenerational transfers, 28, 132, 135, 200
    reduction in contribution rate, 14, 201–2
    toward apparent funding, 15, 198–201
    toward tradability of pension debt, 15, 208–11
    neutral transition using wage tax, 15, 200, 202–5, 220–1
    tax-financed, 132, 135, 185
    recognition of past contributions, 169–71, 363
    capital controls to help finance, 269
    IMF role, 269
    impact on voluntary saving: see saving, private
    see also public debt
trustees of pension plans, 8
    employee representation, 23, 298
    in Malaysian EPF, 23, 341; *see also* EPF
    in public sector plans in the United States, 97, 101

in the United Kingdom, 296–7, 298
Turkey, 354, 360
Turnham, D., 138

United Kingdom, 3, 20–2, 24, 25, 28, 227,
  231, 234, 236, 238, 240, 241–4, 321,
  323, 324, 352, 355, 360, 361, 366
United States, 2, 4, 8, 10, 12, 13, 17, 24, 27,
  49, 50, 53, 92–118, 128, 133, 135, 164,
  199, 231, 236, 237, 238, 240, 244, 277–
  316, 297, 324, 341, 355, 360
Uruguay, 355

Valdés-Prieto, S., 6, 20, 23, 24, 34, 59, 73,
  128, 133, 134–6, 148, 161, 167, 183,
  191, 205, 341, 355
Varian, Hal R., 192, 208

Venezuela, 352, 356–7, 360
Vishny, Robert, 8
Vittas, Dimitri, 247

Warshawsky, M., 2
Weil, P., 139
welfare state, 6, 59, 64
Whitehouse, E., 355
Wiener, J., 2
Wildasin, D., 11
Williamson, John, 245
Winegarden, C. R., 2
World Bank, 9, 23, 26, 127, 131

Yaari, M. E., 139, 156

Zambia, 360
Zorn, Paul, 96, 98, 104

Printed in the United States
By Bookmasters